CW01267489

Brighton [courtesy of Adam Le Roy and Loz Lewin]

THE INFLUENTIAL FACTOR

A HISTORY OF MOD

THIS BOOK IS DEDICATED TO RUBEN AND KENYA.
YOU ARE THE REASON I STRUGGLED THROUGH THE DARK DAYS
AND THE REASON FOR EVERYTHING I HAVE DONE SINCE
AND WILL DO IN THE FUTURE.
A FATHER'S LOVE NEVER DIES.

TO THOSE WHO ARE NO LONGER WITH US.
SOME OF YOU LIVE ON IN THE PAGES OF THIS BOOK.
FAMILY AND FRIENDS WILL LIVE ON
IN OUR HEARTS AND MINDS FOREVER.
RIP.

PREFACE

The first edition of Influential Factor was published in 2002. It was all my own work from the research, writing, design and layout to the publication and marketing.
There were mistakes and a lot of harsh criticism from some quarters. 16 years on, I can see why. At the time though, it was hard to take.

Like anyone in a creative process, you really do put your heart, soul, time, money and effort into something you believe in. You hope people will like it and appreciate it.
Social media did not exist back then and people we now refer to as 'trolls' had limited

options to vent their spleen. When the book became available on Amazon, the comments section was one of the few places they could attack me and my work and do it anonymously. Why did they do it? Who knows? Those people did not know me. It was obvious they had not read the book, but they certainly wanted to destroy any chance it had of being a relative success. I learnt a lot from that experience.

There were only 2,000 copies of the first edition and they were all sold within 12 months. My marketing boiled down to 5,000 postcards distributed around the country; three months advertising in Scootering Magazine plus a feature article with Mark Sargent (Sarge); and great support from modculture.com among others.

With regard to the question of how to measure success, I think that depends on your own expectations. After being rejected by a number of book publishers, when I decided to self-finance and self-publish, my expectations were simple enough: sell every copy and break even financially. That is exactly what happened, so I was relieved and content that I achieved that much. In my mind, it was a success.

One of the enduring positives off the back the whole experience was meeting and becoming friends with a great many new people, not just in the UK, but around the world. Most of them are still friends to this day.

The other aspect that I still find extraordinary, is how the book took on a life of its own. It threw surprises at me, like a phone call one day from a producer of the Robert Elms radio show on BBC Radio London, asking for an interview on the show. I never knew how they found out about the book or where they got my phone number from.

As it turned out, Robert was on holiday and Jason Soloman (who has gone on to a highly successful career as a film critic) hosted the show. A few months later, BBC Radio Kent got in touch and asked for an interview. This time it was on the Dave Cash Sunday Sixties Show. Dave was one of my favorites, as I used to listen to him regularly in the 70s on Capitol Radio in London.

It was only supposed to be a ten minute chat, but Dave was enjoying himself so much, because it brought back so many memories for him, he decided on the day to do the whole two hours with me. In recent years, Dave, along with Jeffrey Kruger and Long John Baldry, have passed away and I miss them all. Roger Eagle had sadly left us just before the book originally came out, so, on the basis that their contributions in this book are the last major interviews they did, I guess it now becomes something of an 'historical' document. Their testimonies can never be repeated and I am honoured to be lucky enough to have documented their words.

It has always been a source of amusement, delight and astonishment that this book has never been out of my life. Again it was all about expectations. Once it was published, I thought no more of it, but time and again, circumstances have brought it back. In the 'Noughties', a chap by the name of Gary O'Day told me the book was being used as key source material at Wolverhampton University.

Then many years later, John Lambert asked me to donate a copy as an auction item for a fundraising event he was organising, to help a poor young boy who needed to go to America for treatment of his illness. I had kept a few copies, mainly to give to my kids one day, but I could spare one for this particular cause. The winning bid was £120. I was delighted to have helped raise quite so much.

Then there are times like the occasion I was outside the Komedia Club in Brighton one August Bank Holiday weekend, when a fellow from Germany approached and asked if I was Graham Lentz. When I said I was, he bear-hugged me so hard I thought my ribs would crack. He was so happy to meet me in person has he had bought the book years before and was very complimentary about it. Apparently, I had 'made' his weekend!

It was the same thing when I went to compere the Detour Records Anniversary event. A chap named Bernard Duffy came over, checked I was who he thought I was and produced a copy of the book (which he had bought at some expense secondhand) and asked me to sign it. I did of course, and posed for a photo with him. The absolute joy on Bernard's face that night will live with me forever, (although I still fail to comprehend why), but it is all because of this book and those memories simply cannot be bought.

By 2012, with the advent of the digital age, social media and other innovations like eBay, I have become more aware of the relevant importance some people place on the book.

Secondhand values (on the rare occasions a copy is for sale) are nothing short of mind-boggling.

This was one of the reasons I decided to update, revise and publish a second edition. I have lost count of the amount of times people have complained that they can never find a copy, or, if they do, it is so expensive they can't afford it and have begged me to 'do something about it'. I did see a copy on Amazon's secondhand market valued at $400 US and that was when I knew I had to get to work.

2013 was a horrible year, personally. A nasty and messy divorce left me living alone and with time on my hands. With the help and support of Rob Bailey (who I had been writing reviews for on the New Untouchables online magazine NutsMag for a couple of years), I got heavily involved in the mod scene; more than I ever had before.

I am not unusual in the respect that, like so many others, I drifted away from mod as life, marriage, being a parent and other things took precedent, but it has never left me. It is part of who I am and since 2013, and for the first time in my life, I have been in the right place at the right time on a number of occasions.

I have made even more friends than ever before, I became a compere for the March Of The Mods charity, New Untouchables events and the Detour Records 25th Anniversary show. I briefly joined the 'We Are The Mods' podcast as a guest host, then presented the Nutscast Sessions podcast for New Untouchables. I've become a session musician with a number of bands and all of it has been by accident, not design.

Mod has taken me to Paris, Belfast, Dublin and many other places. I've met and become friends with people whose careers I have followed intently over the decades and have great respect and admiration for them.

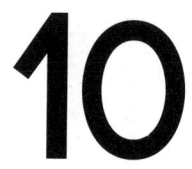

But it is the people within the scene I have greatest respect for. To the outside world, they may be regarded as unexceptional, but I have witnessed first-hand their ability to push themselves to do things they never thought they could do. For me, that is the beauty of this thing called mod. It inspires great things from 'ordinary' people. It is like a family. You get the squabbles, and disagreements, laughter, fun, the good times and the bad. Some people you only get to meet once a year if you are lucky, but they greet you warmly and behave as if you only saw them last week. Some members of the 'family' don't get on with each other, but you walk the fine line between them and hope that one day they will resolve their differences. But when you see a crowd singing along to a band; when you see them dig deep into their limited resources to give to charity to help those less fortunate; when you witness a packed dancefloor really 'going for it' to 'Pow Wow' by Manny Corchado; that is when it really hits you just how special these people and this thing called mod really is.

Am I over-exaggerating? Being too 'misty-eyed' about it? Possibly, but you have to truly understand it first; what it means to people. If 'you know' then you 'know' and by the end of this book, I hope you do - for that is the intention.

I honestly believe this edition is far better and represents the book I had intended originally. Some of the information, people and places have been well documented in other books, but it is important to remember that in the context of mod and that this is a 'history' ignoring the likes of Ready Steady Go, Pete Meaden, The Jam, Paul Weller or Quadrophenia would be plain daft.

GRAHAM LENTZ
2018

London [courtesy of Clive Tagg]

INTRODUCTION

This book is strap lined 'A History of Mod' because a definitive account of a subculture, with over 60 years of stories and reminiscences, is impossible to document in one volume.

There are thousands of people from all walks of life who have been involved in mod in that time. Some have put their stories into print. Others have told of mod history from their own point of view. Each version has its merits, because it all adds to the wealth of research into the subject.

Who is this book aimed at? It is for anyone who has an interest in mod or subculture in general. The purpose is to educate (where possible) and give some perspective and context to mod culture and its influence on people.

While some names and places will be familiar, most of the interviewees will not be known outside of the mod world. Mod is not about 'celebrity status'.

This is not a gushing tome of 'hero-worship' of Paul Weller, Steve Marriott, The Who or Oasis. Much like an over-accessorised scooter, a parka and fighting on Brighton beach, these things and people are part of mod history, but by no means the defining elements. Mod is so much more than that, as you will discover.

So this is my version. It would not stand as a body of work without the contribution of the people I interviewed and the people who helped me along the way and those people are acknowledged at the end of this book.

To most people, mention the word 'mod' and they will conjure up the stereotypical image of a parka-wearing, scooter-riding yob reminiscent of the Jimmy character in the film Quadrophenia.

But what about those who regard themselves as mods? How do they define what mod is? I asked this question of the interviewees for this book.

We begin with **JOHN SIMONS**, one of the truly unsung influencers of modernism since 1952 and the man who inspired the title of this book:

I like to deal in facts. I've lived it every day. I've got 40 years to call on, not 18 months. A lot of people just touched on it. The taxing and difficult thing for me, which perhaps I achieved to some infinitesimal point, is through every decade I've remained part of the influential factor. Even when it was difficult. It was a cultural revolution, but it would be wrong of me not to say that there are flaws in it. Modernism can be to some degree dictatorial. It is unfortunately both utopian and dictatorial, but not unbearably so. And on the basis that nothing is perfect, that's perfect enough for me.

PAULINE WATERS from Newcastle:
Walking into the Club-A-Go-Go for the first time or sitting on the back of a scooter with a top Newcastle mod.

JOHN WATERS from London:
The Flamingo, when Solomon Burke was on, and Dusty Springfield joined him on stage. I'd never seen it as packed as that. It was full of mods.
It's that or walking down to the beach at Brighton and seeing thousands of mods there.

ROB BAILEY from The New Untouchables organisation:
Mod has meant different things to me down the years. In your teens, it's the gang culture, then later on you take the individual route, but I have made a lot of good friends and had a lot of good times and I think there comes a point when you've been into it for so long, that you don't even think about it, it's something you do everyday, in the same way that other people have passions in their lives.
It means different things to different people, but I don't think you can really define it. The thing about the mod scene, is that it has run itself from within and no one has managed to grab a hold of it and turn it into some kind of commercial venture from the outside. It's self-contained. I think it has and will continue to reinvent itself.
There are people who go with the authentic style and stick to it to the letter, then there are people who want to incorporate modern styles or draw inspiration from other things and incorporate it into mod. The main thing is, it's done with style.
There will always be conflicts because people are so passionate about it, but that's not a bad thing.

ANTHONY MEYNELL, lead singer of the band Squire:
I have a photograph of us on a promotional tour. We are in a record shop doing our songs and literally a few feet away from us are all these young mods having a fantastic time. That was taken around 1982 or '83.

FREDRIK EKANDER, DJ from Sweden:
It's the passion. If you want to fully understand what mod is about, 100% dedication is needed. And when you have focused so hard and devoted so much attention to one certain culture for a few years - even if it encompasses certain elements of pop culture (music, fashion, design etc) - this passion will spill over to all aspects of your life, which will make your life richer and more intense in all senses and the whole concept of always living life to the full will be something that you'll apply to everything. I feel truly blessed to have experienced mod culture to the full, and I know my life would be extremely dull if I hadn't been caught up in this passionate and curious way of life.

FRANCESCO LISI, DJ from Italy:
The Italian style was the new style of the moment, and the mods got it. In the early 60s it was something that was exclusive for the young. It broke the rules with the conservative English way of dressing. I personally think mod is not basically British, it's just British society that allows modernism and other youth cultures to continue without too many problems. Mod is a lifestyle, with a feeling for the 60s, so everybody who wants to really 'live' can be a mod. It is without country borders.

MARY BOOGALOO, a DJ and Italian national, resident in Britain since 1980:
Mod has an eternal appeal. Modernism was an English phenomenon which looked to the United States for musical innovations and Italy and France for style. Being an extremely obscure and enigmatic movement, strongly based on utter individuality, trends inside the movement were ephemeral and as soon as something caught the attention of external groups, modernists would quickly move onto something else. Obviously nowadays we cannot be true modernists, it would be a contradiction in itself, as we are looking at the past for inspiration. But don't call me a revivalist either!

HARRY VOGEL, DJ from Germany:
I think mod today gives you a chance to follow a very individualistic, stylish lifestyle that is so different from contemporary mainstream and alternative culture that

sometimes I feel I'm on another planet or in another dimension (without taking any drugs!). I also feel that I do not rely on and cannot be cheated by big business that much! I have my clothes tailored for rather little money in little shops, I buy records from other collectors etc. Another thing is that the scene is so very international. Mods had long anticipated the European Union. I have friends all over Europe, even all over this planet. I wouldn't be the same person if I hadn't become a mod.

DAISUKE USUI, band member of Japanese band, The Absolude:
Being a mod has opened a lot of doors and expanded my social circle as I've made lots of international friends by being a mod. Even though I once believed it, I don't think being a mod attracts girls. I'm often teased or laughed at behind my back by schoolgirls. Nevertheless, I love being a mod and I won't change to suit current fashion trends. Mod style is classic, elegant and, in my opinion, timeless. I like the style. It still attracts me a lot. I don't care much about the philosophical side of mod culture but I dig the gear and I think the clothes are really cool.

MANABU KURODA, widely credited with starting mod interest in Japan:
I'm into its style and its attitude that never compromises on anything. It was 1984 when I first visited England. My impression about English mods was that they were very cool and smart. Most of all, it's an attitude. It's my attitude.

TAKU YAMADA from Japan:
Mod is a specific concept. It has strong policies and preferences that I like. I'm more or less just nostalgic. Everything including dances, bespoke suits or expensive scooters are pieces of my collection. What it meant to be a mod was far different in the 60s than it is now. Back then a real mod would never stick to such old stuff like I do. It's only a hobby for me but I shall have this hobby for the rest of my life.

NICK ROSSI, musician from San Francisco, USA:
The Brian Auger Trinity's 1965 cover version of Jimmy McGriff's 'Kiko'. For some

reason that record evokes a feeling in me that I cannot really explain, but that probably comes closest to my 'mod moment'.

PAUL WELSBY, joint founder of The Hideaway Club in Manchester.
Paul Weller's look at the time of The Style Council's "A Paris" phase. French cropped hair, Italian knitwear over an US buttondown, tailored trousers finishing just short of a well polished Bass Weejun. All topped off with a three-quarter length single-breasted Macintosh. Smart but casual. Cool but functional. But in the main, timeless. It would have looked cool in 1962. It did look cool in 1982. And it still looks cool in 2018.

ALAN FLETCHER, author and consultant on the film 'Quadrophenia'.
Walking down the stairs into the Dungeon Club in Nottingham for the first time and hearing Marvin Gaye singing 'Can I Get A Witness'. That is my mod moment.

BRIAN BETTERIDGE, lead singer with Back To Zero.
March Of The Mods Tour at The Lyceum. It was over the August Bank Holiday. It was the Sunday and the Monday was a 'do' at Canvey Island, so a lot of people had come in from Southend. Now The Lyceum had extra bands on. They had Madness, The Modettes and Selecter, as well as the three March Of The Mods bands. The way it had been advertised, it looked like the three March Of The Mods bands would be kept together with the others. Madness had just released 'The Prince' and it was going up the charts, and Madness had a hard-core following, the original Nutty Boys, who were pretty nutty. Well they thought, 'Why are these other bands on with Madness?' There was an atmosphere in there, a lot of skinheads and a nasty atmosphere. The skinheads started 'sieg heiling' and for general and personal reasons, I was hardly tap-dancing about the fact we were going on.
A few days before my dad had a heart attack and was in hospital and it was like everything was happening at once, and unlike some people who did speed all the time, I did a bit, but that weekend I did do a lot. People who saw me at the gig said I was running from one side of the stage to the other because the mods were either

side and the skinheads in the middle and I was dodging glasses and bottles being thrown by the skinheads and it wasn't a nice experience on stage at all. I got back into the dressing room and refused to go back on for an encore. I could hear the mods singing 'We Are The Mods' and the skinheads 'sieg-heiling' and I just locked myself in a toilet, but Kim from Maximum Speed kicked the door in and said 'Get back out there'. We did an encore and it seemed to calm down, and Goffa Gladding said afterwards that it may have kicked off seriously if we hadn't have gone back out, but it was cold comfort for me.

That night after the gig, I had to wind down, so I went to a party in Deptford held by a friend of The Chords and once I got there amongst friendly people I felt better.

I even had a decent conversation with Chris Pope, who was known for being difficult to talk to, but anyway, I remember in the morning someone put the 'Quadrophenia' soundtrack on, and you know the overture? It came on about 7 O'clock in the morning, and I was looking out the window as people started drifting off to Southend and seeing this line of mods going up the road with the 'Quadrophenia' overture playing in the background. I just thought; 'Yeah, this is what it's all about'. It's silly, but it's not just the fact I saw that, but the previous few days had been pretty rough.

EDDIE PILLER, music entrepreneur and owner of Acid Jazz Records:
Clean living in difficult circumstances. Pete Meaden is very special and it's a shame he's dead, because I never met him. I met Steve Marriott a few times when I was a kid, and then, when I realised my mum's roots, I went to search him out and I went to gigs with him. Steve Marriott was one of the funniest and most full-of-life people I've ever met. People like that define the mod scene, and the ironic thing about Marriott is that through the last ten years or so of his life, no-one gave a shit about him, and yet, the minute he died, everyone claimed him as their hero.

If he was alive today, you could forget about Rod Stewart and all those others. He might have been a bald headed midgit with a moustache, but he is the best singer and guitarist this country has ever produced for my money, and I don't care what anyone says. Now he's dead and there's plenty of talentless idiots out there doing Marriott, when he should be doing it. So it's tragic. Meaden and Marriott, that's what sums up mod for me. It is to be expected that there are some surprising and widely varied points of view and opinions.

As you read through the following chapters, it will become clear just how vital clubs have been to modernists. Some mod clubs have become legendary like the Flamingo in London, and the Twisted Wheel in Manchester, which began the eternal mod and northern love affair with black music.

The demand for obscure black soul music, led to clubs such as the Wigan Casino, ensuring that soul fans, who were not necessarily mods, were catered for, but then, in its own way, the Casino became the influential factor for others through the 80s and into the 90s, and so coming full circle with a renewed interest in mod and mod culture in the 21st century.

Then we have the people who are responsible for post war modernism's diversity and longevity. To a greater or lesser degree, and a greater or lesser celebrity, people such as John Simons, Jeffrey Kruger, Paul Weller, Eddie Piller, Rob Bailey, the late Roger Eagle, Don Hosie, Alan Fletcher, Paul Welsby, Dizzy and Tania Holmes, and the thousands of musicians, deejays, clothiers, publishers, scooterists, skinheads, mods and northern soul fans who have never let go of their identity or their love of music and their desire for something different that they can legitimately call their own, because no one owns culture. As Andrew Lindsay states "Mods are great 'do-ers' and there is plenty of evidence to support that assertion. Again, it becomes clear that a great entrepreneurial spirit surrounds mod culture. There are hundreds of people with small businesses connected to mod. There are people who have become highly successful promoters and event organisers;: writers, filmmakers, manufacturers, designers, artists of every type, poets, journalists and charity fundraisers. They come from varied backgrounds and from around the world.

The current and continuing growth of scooter clubs and attendances at mod, scooterist, ska and northern soul events, must say something about the current state of pop culture in the UK. Everyone from teenagers upwards gets involved in it and it should come as no surprise. After all, not everyone is taken in by the cynical manipulation of pop culture by the likes of Simon Cowell and ITV, the BBC, News International, the EMAP radio empire and the like. But it does show how powerful the media really is. In the mainstream world, marketing is everything and talent is nothing. As long as you have the right look, who cares if you can sing or write music? Those are qualities that can be bought or put through computer software to correct.

Yet, there are plenty of people who still want something different from what is available in the mainstream. There is a saying that 'to move forward, you have to look back' and this is why mod has managed to influence people over the last 60 plus years.

Sixties mod **KEITH RYLATT** from Leeds, made this observation:

If I go out now, I'd probably wear a pair of cream Levis, just a jacket and a pair of loafers. Its almost like a Marks and Spencer look if you're not careful. I think that a lot of the fashions that my mother used to dislike, like desert boots and the light wool polo shirts and ski jackets, ended up in British Home Stores as crap 'middle of the road' wear,. its all been absorbed.

John Robb's observations in his book on The Charlatans (pub 1998), shows why mod is more a subtle influence than an 'in-your-face' phenomena. In his opinion mod is at the heart of all British pop culture.

Regardless of your level of interest in the subject, I hope you find 'The Influential Factor' as interesting to read as it was fascinating for me to research and write.

GRAHAM LENTZ
JANUARY 2018

> The taxing and difficult thing for me, which perhaps I achieved to some infinitesimal point, is through every decade I've remained part of the influential factor.
>
> JOHN SIMONS

CHAPTER 1

In 1949, music arranger Gil Evans gathered a group together that included Miles Davis, Gerry Mulligan, John Lewis and Lee Konitz and produced an album called 'Birth of the Cool', the result of a years worth of experimenting with jazz in Evans's apartment on West 55th Street in New York. The members of this group separated and individually explored their own paths off the 'free jazz' road. The collective term for the music they produced became known as Modern Jazz.

'Cool' or modern jazz was a reaction to bebop, so modernists, who followed the music, reacted against the hipsters who followed bebop. The music and the visual style fell into place. A concept developed; less is more and everything became slimmer, simplified and sharper.

Also in 1949, Lou and Caterina Polledri from Piacenza, Italy, had already opened their first café in Long Acre, Covent Garden, London after emigrating. They then had the opportunity to open a second café on Frith Street, Soho. At the time, Soho was home to one of the biggest Italian communities in the country, so it was a perfect place to start a new venture. Bar Italia became an immediate success as a hub for London-based Italians and, over the next 68 years, it would survive many cultural and political changes; recessions and economic booms. It has become one of the treasured reminders of a long-lost Soho culture, and while still maintaining a large core Italian customer base, it became an important gathering place for another community; one which had its beginnings in London, but has since spread the world over.

It was not a community in the early fifties though; just pockets of like-minded young people who loved the new fashion styles emerging from America and Europe.

One young Englishman who adopted this new style was **JOHN SIMONS**. John was in his teen years in the early 1950s. He was "seriously" into clothes at that early age and took his influences from Hollywood stars like Jack Lemmon, but more importantly, from John's uncles who travelled to America and brought back clothes for their young nephew:

The main influence outside of the movies was my families exposure to clothing and style, which was second to none. The men in my family were very smart. I just fused that smartness with my exposure to film. I didn't know anyone else who was as advanced as I was at the time. I have a photograph from 1953 where I've gone from a Windsor knot to a single knot, which was a big move. I only knew one other bloke who wore a single knot. That was Jeff Cooper, who was a mate of mine in the early days. Jeff became a partner in Sterling Cooper, a famous clothing firm in the sixties and seventies. He was a very smart bloke. He used to wear a white shirt with a pin through and a red knitted tie at the age of 14 or 15.

The early modernists of John's generation also looked to the east, at Europe, just as much as to the west and America. It was openness to the new and the modern, plus the unique physical positioning of Britain that created the conditions for a true British youth culture, as **JOHN SIMONS** explains:

The first period of modernists was 1948-58 and this is important because it was an evolutionary period. It evolved directly through from the thirties and forties cultures, but it didn't evolve by harking back to those days. It evolved in a natural way, as the music evolved. The big bands went into the small groups. It wasn't mannered or self-conscious. I would say that in a way, it did then blur into what later became mod. The first post war boom of young people evolved from the way their dads dressed. They moved forward a bit. Smart, tailored, slightly slicker, American influenced. That took them into the fifties. It was quite a long time after then, that people started looking back a decade and became inspired to go forward for good or bad. I have to make that comment.

John Simons was not the only one being inspired by the new. Some 125 miles to the north of London, **GILL TAYLOR** began her life-long fascination and love of fashion and style:

My mum was a designer dressmaker and, in about 1949, I was five and she was creating Dior's new look for her clients. She used to give me the off-cuts of material and I would make little replicas of what she was making. Now my family owned sewing machine shops, so I had a little sewing machine and I was really interested in fashion and I could draw, even at that early age.

We had three cinemas in our area, one right opposite where we lived and two others, so we would go to the cinema three times a week when I was about nine years-old and I would watch the film, but I became fascinated by the clothes they were wearing and I used to draw them when I got home. I loved people like Gene Kelly and Audrey Hepburn and there was a kind of 'French Look' with the hooped tops and black tights. I was really into that.

I used to recreate those outfits at home, like the clothes from 'Roman Holiday', but no-one else was wearing that kind of thing.

My mum thought I should go to art college and I was lucky enough to get a scholarship when I was 12 and started at Moseley Art School when I was 13. We did fashion designing and I was always doing the French and Italian styles that I remembered from all those films. I would make them and wear them and people thought I was a bit strange wearing those clothes, but I loved it.

I left Art School at 16 and was wearing this style which I called 'The Continental Look', but it was unusual in the Birmngham area where I grew up. My mum hated that style and people used to talk to her about it.

It was around that time that I met Del Evans and he was very much into that sort of thing too, so we started designing them together. He would come round to the flat we lived in with my parents and he would come up with ideas, I would sketch them and we would make them. This would have been in 1960 and we hadn't heard the term 'mod' at that time. Prior to that, I used to go to jazz clubs and adopted a bit of that beatnik look, and I know there is the link, especially in London with Modern Jazz, but in Birmingham, that wasn't the case. It meant being a 'modern person', a modernist in modern clothing. Del and I used to go out and people would ask us about our clothes and style and I would say it was the 'Continental Look' and we were 'Continentalists'. That was my idea.

By 1955, young Brits were drawing on influences from modern jazz. The piano-less Gerry Mulligan Quartet typified the early sound and style. The suits were sharp and the attitude was serious. Mulligan's trumpet player, Chet Baker, like Mulligan himself, had the 'Hollywood' good looks and unbelievable talent that wooed the US collegiate as much as the UK youth looking for something different.

John Lewis teamed up with Milt Jackson to form The Modern Jazz Quartet. Their variation was jazz without a brass instrument, in its place was the smoother, more rounded sound of the vibraphone.

Miles Davis recruited John Coltrane, Julian 'Cannonball' Adderly, Paul Chambers, James Cobb, Bill Evans and Wynton Kelly and in 1959 released 'Kind Of Blue' which has since been hailed as the greatest jazz album in history.

Dave Brubeck with Paul Desmond, Joe Morello and Eugene Wright were only a few years away from achieving the extraordinary feat of having the biggest selling Jazz single in history and reaching number six in the UK Chart with 'Take Five'.

British modernists adopted the stance of their heroes, understanding the musical complexity and the spirit of modern jazz. The choice was to reject mainstream culture and forge their own style.

Nowhere was this more evident than at The Flamingo Club in London. A venue that witnessed the rise and fall of mod during the fifties and sixties. One man's vision, dream, determination and hard work brought the club to life. That man was **JEFFREY KRUGER**.

Jeffrey Kruger was working in sales for Columbia Pictures and playing in a jazz band in his spare time at the start of the fifties. He visited jazz clubs when he was not playing and found the atmosphere not exactly to his liking:

I remember the Feldman Club. From the minute I walked down the stairs it smelt musty. The music was great though. Studio 51 just smelt like a beer parlour and I thought to myself; 'wouldn't it be nice to have a place where one listened to jazz, and not necessarily have the smell of beer all over the show, (not that I was against it) and where people who dressed up nicely could meet each other and listen to jazz'.

I tried to persuade some of the people who owned the clubs to do this when my band was playing there. Nobody was interested, so I decided to do it myself.

I had a meal one night at the Mapleton Hotel Restaurant, which was on the corner of Wardour Street and Piccadilly. I went down to the men's room and down there was this nice room that was empty. So I chatted with the manager, a guy called Tony Harris, and I told him my ideas. He said the room was always empty on the weekends, but was full during the week. He said "I'll sell cokes and take the cloakroom, you can have the room for free and bring this jazz of yours in". That's how The Flamingo started.

It soon became apparent to **JEFFREY KRUGER** that his idea of what a jazz club should be was one shared by many jazz fans. The concept of the club had grown larger than he expected, even before The Flamingo had opened, so Jeffrey called in some help:

I asked my parents if they would come. My mother to take the cash and my father to greet people. I would take care of the music. We were partners from day one and they supported me, but my father was not the founder. If anything he was opposed to me going into such a precarious business, but he condoned it on the understanding that I kept my job.

Jeffrey Kruger's father, **SAMUEL**, was a gentleman's hairdresser by trade and he believed you had to have a profession in order to succeed in life. As the friendly, greeting face at The Flamingo, Sam Kruger's natural charm and way with people certainly made an impression:

He became the front man and he became brilliant at it. They loved him; he could control people much better than I could at 21 years of age. I was, I suppose, as flash a mod without being one as most of the kids were in those days. We were ambitious, we had no money. We were doing it from hand to fist. My father couldn't contribute financially at the club; I did it out of my savings from the film company, so that's how it started. Lets put that one to rest, not that I begrudge him having the credit. He did as much to sustain it as I did, but he didn't know what jazz was. We transferred to Wardour Street within the year. It was 1951 in the Mapleton and 1952 at Wardour Street when we opened The Flamingo.

We charged much higher prices than anywhere else, double anywhere else, and the men had to wear a jacket and the girls dressed up and it became the 'in' place. It was packed before it opened. It was every Sunday evening and then every Saturday and Sunday, then it went Thursday, Saturday, Sunday, and then I had to find my own place 100 yards up the road. The customers became regulars. The first 200 or 300 that we could pack in were nearly always the same guys and the same girls and there were marriages and so forth.

But the common bond was the music, no question of that. It was clear that it would be run properly, and it became a home from home. The customers were exceedingly well behaved, they could wear whatever they wanted in the terms of mod dress, and they did, but it was always smart and expensive, and there was a membership so we could keep out undesirables, and we did. I'm not saying we didn't have any villains down there. The Krays were there all the time, but they weren't gangsters as such then. They loved jazz, but they also helped keep control of things, because everybody was flexing their muscles. We never had any trouble, but we had a mixture from the East End to Hampstead and they mixed. The common bond was music, modern jazz, let me make that clear. I was very friendly with Tony Hall who at that time was working for Decca Records or Tempo as the jazz label was. He was writing for one of the music magazines, which became the Record Mirror. I put the idea to him to compere because he was the compere at Studio 51, and he loved the idea and said "If ever you do it I'll come and work for you".

Les Perrin, the great publicist, also agreed to join the venture because he liked jazz, and he said he would help us pre-promote it. I think it was Tony's suggestion that we used Kenny Graham and The Afrocubists as one of the groups that opened the club, because they'd been reformed and they'd make front page of the Melody Maker. Their theme song was 'Flamingo'. Our idols at the time were Norman Grant's Jazz At The Phil, so we called it 'Jazz at The Flamingo at The Mapleton', so that's how it started, nobody's ever asked that before so that's a first.

Anybody that admired the music that we were trying to exploit, they were good club members. As far as I'm concerned, as long as they came and behaved themselves, that was ok, and as I said both my father (who passed away in 1964) and I knew most of them by their first names and what job they did. We knew which were villains, but if anybody tried any trouble and usually it was jealousy over a girl, Curly King or the Krays would stop it right away. In fact, we had a spate once of handbags going missing while the girls were dancing.

The boys cleared it up, they broke the fingers of these couple of guys who were very smartly dressed, but they were just 'tealeaves' (thieves), and we never had that trouble again. They were delivered with accidentally broken fingers to Saville Row Police station. I don't know how they got there, but that is a true story.

Of course we spread the sessions, we opened up the Florida Club in Leicester Square to keep people off the street. Now they could join there and then, but they only got in if they were dressed smartly. That's all we asked, we didn't care if the jacket cost £1 or £10, which in those days was a lot of money, but they had to be dressed and we felt it was the only way to keep up the standards. I only have the fondest recollections of the mods that came down. I never had any reason not to like them.

According to *Jazz Journal* dated February 1953, the opening night of The Flamingo saw 1,500 people queuing to get in and police on hand for 'crowd control'. As Mr Kruger mentioned, Tony Hall became the compere at the club. Tony Hall has been one of those people who quietly played a major role in the music scene over several years and yet is very modest about his achievements and has not received the recognition he deserves. However, Record Collector magazine did pay tribute to Tony Hall in their April 2013 edition where he was interviewed by Charles Waring.

TONY HALL became the compere at The Feldman Club around 1949. The Feldman Club was the place to go in the very early 1950s and it was situated on the site where the world-renowned 100 Club now stands. Of his time at The Flamingo, Mr Hall told Charles Waring: Jeff got me to go and work with him. I became his adviser on talent for The Flamingo and helped with the bookings for many years. I think Jeff did a lot for British jazz. Some of the musicians used to feel they were being robbed, but he kept that club going for years and years. He and I never fell out over bookings at all. He just trusted my judgement and I gave him the best advice I could. And neither of us has ever regretted working together.

The patrons of The Flamingo were modernists and drew their influences from the Ivy League collegiate fashion in the United States. **JOHN SIMONS** left school and went to work for Smart Brothers menswear in Dalston, North London. In the shop next door was Warren Gold who was destined to become a major retailer during the Carnaby Street phenomena:

The manager's name at Smart Brothers was George Hines, he was a real smart guy, and he looked like a film star. While I was at Smarts I began looking at shirts and collar styles. Every single moment I was supplementing what I already knew. Then I went to work with Jack Cress who was a really good window dresser and he was working for a firm called Martin's Menswear. I became his assistant and through this I met a man

Brighton [courtesy of Amy Very]

called Henry Waltag who was one of the managers. He was an amazing character, he was a friend of all the film stars of the period and he knew everybody. Henry used to make suits for very well known people. I used to make coffee for John Gregson and his family, Harry Fowler who was quite a modish looking character, and I got to know Dandy Kim who was a really important guy in the fifties. Dandy Kim came from a working class background but somehow built up a reputation as an aristocrat playboy. It was an incredible learning experience for me. From there, through a family member, I got offered a job at Cecil Gee when I was 16.

Indeed, it is testament to Dandy Kim's reputation that people like John Simons remember him fifty years later. His real name is Kim Waterfield and there are numerous versions of his background, but Dandy Kim was celebrated for his clothes. He drove big cars, had beautiful girls on his arm and was dressed immaculately at all times. Certainly John Simon was finding himself among some of the biggest names in men's fashion when he joined Cecil Gee.

Cecil Gee tends to be synonymous with introducing the 'Italian Look' to Britain. However, prior to the Italian Look, Cecil Gee was a leading light in a small group of retailers that opened in the East End of London in the late thirties. Other shops included Albert's and Davis Brothers. The overriding influence though was American clothing.

As **JOHN SIMONS** states:

The main store selling US imported clothing was David's in Charing Cross Road. It was diagonally across from Cecil Gee's and had a totally American 1930's marble shop front look. David's sold Lyon and Troy shirts with buff-edged collars with a little loop - not button downs. They also sold Hickock belts where you could pick your initials from a panel of letters and fix them to your belt. The other person selling US import clothing was Austin's of Shaftesbury Avenue. They sold Don Richards suits, Arrow shirts, Enro shirts and American knitwear. In those days, the retailer did not play the role of designer, but more a supplier of wish fulfilment. The big shirt style of the day was the Mr B roll - named after singer Billy Eckstine. He had quite a big roll on his shirt. He was very influential. There was also Jaytex, an English shirt makers who did a flex-roll, it was like a separate collar, but it was attached and it was small, round and fused really hard into a kind of roll. If you wore it with a Windsor knot, it looked kind of flash.

1955 became a defining moment in men's fashion history in Britain. Cecil Gee launched the Italian Look. In his book, 'Street Style', Ted Polhemus made the assumption that Italian fashion and styling had been influenced by American GIs stationed in the country, and, as modern jazz was very popular, that people like Chet Baker, who performed there, also had an impact.
The fact is Italian men have always taken great pride in their appearance. It is just as feasible that people like Chet Baker were equally influenced by Italian fashion.
Cecil Gee's introduction of the Italian Look was revolutionary to Britain because it was so different to what was available to most men. Some individuals made it their business to be different. Men like Dandy Kim, Henry Waltag and Austin of Shaftesbury Avenue. Austin was a saxophone player on the Queen Mary Ocean liner, and lived at the Savoy Hotel in London.

JOHN SIMONS remembers Austin wearing shirts three sizes too big because he could not bear anything on his neck:
That was another thing about the bosses (in the clothing business) back then. It was not egalitarian. They drove American cars, they changed their shirts three times a day, they might say hello to you, but they ruled the roost. You quaked when they walked by.

However, by 1955 Italy's reputation as a focal point for style and fashion was ready to take off with the 'Italian Look'. Although Gee claimed that a holiday trip to Italy was the inspiration for the new look, Nic Cohn offered a different version of events. Cohn pointed out that the San Remo Festivals, and the work of designers like Brioni, had already made Italian styles known in Britain. Cecil Gee was the first to really promote it in Britain.

Brioni of Rome was the leading Italian stylist at the time and Gee's look was a variation of his basic shape: a short box-like jacket, with narrow trousers, in a lightweight fabric like mohair.

JOHN SIMONS, now working for Cecil Gee, remembers exactly how Gee discovered and took advantage of the 'Italian Look':

Cecil Gee, accompanied by his assistant Ivan Topper - who I worked for as a window dresser - visited Italy on a business trip. They both returned wearing wonderful ready-made Italian summer suits ala Brioni. I remember being there on the Saturday morning when they both came back wearing these cotton suits. I thought it was tremendous. It was a complete shock. I didn't know these things existed, but what is more important was they returned with Giorgio - an Italian tailor who they met and seduced to come to England. He subsequently settled here, but I immediately went to Giorgio for my first authentic Italian suit. Three-buttoned with very rounded shoulders. The Italian style became popular with modernists, but the American style stood very easily along side. They are both similar, three-buttoned and round shouldered, although the Italian look was more sensual. Manufacturers then began to use the Italian style more than the American style.

This was a style that was worn by working class and middle-class young men alike. The 'Look' was remarkably durable. It lasted in similar styles, for eight years. The Italian Look was followed by the Cardin round-collared suit and finally the, now classic, mod suit.

It was a time of capitalising on the emerging teenage market and men's fashion was not the only area of radical advancement. In November 1955 'Bazaar' opened in the Kings Road, Chelsea. Archie McNair owned it and Alexander Plunkett Green was in charge of sales promotion. The lack of suitable attire for teenage girls meant that Mary Quant designed the clothes. What Quant was providing was the female equivalent of the male fashion industry; radical, youth orientated, stylish and, to a certain extent, modernist clothing. Quant, like John Simons and others would become the influential factors in fashion for most of the 1960s, fuelled by the influence of the pre-war modernist age and of Italy. But clothing was not the only export from Italy at that time. With the consumer boom, and the advent of the teenager, coffee bars with their American jukeboxes, became favourite haunts in London serving Italian cappuccino and espresso. Teenagers were excluded from pubs by the legal age limit, and coffee bars filled that void.

Perhaps the most famous coffee bar was the 2I's where many of Britain's top singing entertainers were discovered. But, as **JOHN SIMONS** observed, even the Soho coffee bar scene had been influenced by modernists:

There was a very important culture going on in Soho where you had coffee bars, but coffee bars like Sam Widges where it was mostly jazz on the juke box, and then there was The French, where people used to hang around. The popularity of places like the 2Is came about because, for a lot of people, the modern jazz culture was too cerebral, so a lot of people, especially girls, wanted a more fun-loving lifestyle. We were leading what was a pretty cerebral lifestyle and there was a big modernist culture in that early period.

So, it wasn't all Cliff Richard, teddy boys and rock and roll Americana in Soho in the latter half of the fifties. As for the Italians, they used their now defunct war manufacturing industry to better and more profitable use. The coffee bars that suddenly appeared in city centres would usually be serviced by a Gaggia coffee machine that were designed by Gio Ponti. The Innocenti and Paggio factories produced low-cost, easy-maintenance transport in the form of scooters. The Lambretta and Vespa models, although constantly being modified, were highly popular with young people who could not afford a car and detested the greasy, heavy and high maintenance motorcycle.

Apart from anything else, the scooter design was pure modernist aesthetic. It was clean, uncomplicated, sleek but stylish. It was not required to get you from A to B as fast as possible, but just to get you there. It became so popular that a National Scooter Association was set up, organising rallies and time-trial events around Britain. Most of all, it contributed to the overall ethos of early modernists, which was to find something different to the other emerging, and highly Americanised youth culture, Rock and Roll.

While modernists were looking to Europe for their inspiration, the rest of British working-class youth looked to America and a form of music that came out of the same origins as modern jazz.

Jazz in the 1940s had embraced the blues. A hybrid of influences began to emerge in the black community, where the forces of hot jazz, blues and gospel fused into a hip, hepcat sound that swung like jazz, had a beat to it and sounded exciting. One of the first exponents of this new sound was Big Joe Turner. Turner had a hit with 'Shake, Rattle and Roll' in the USA years before Bill Haley turned it into a white rock and roll standard.

When disc jockey Alan Freed coined the phrase 'Rock and Roll', teenagers succumbed to the first great marketing exercise of the post-war era.

Rock and Roll was blamed for the degeneration and corruption of youth. The youth rebelled and in Britain, teddy boys, so named because they revived an Edwardian style of dress, took to gathering in gangs and fighting often with rival gangs.

Before too long, they began taking to the road, inspired by Marlon Brando in the film 'The Wild Ones', tearing around on motorbikes and terrorising all in their path. **JOHN SIMONS** recalls the teddy boys of north London:

They were older than me for a start. They were quite rough in the very early days; they were looking for trouble. Later on they weren't, but I'm talking about the ones in light blue suits hanging around amusement arcades in Dalston Junction in 1952. You wouldn't get too close to those them. They looked ominous and threatening. There was also another type of teddy boy at that time which was a kind of cross, a flash English bloke, like a Terry-Thomas character, suede shoes, narrow trouser bottoms.

The lumpen behaviour of teds and ton-up boys, as they became known was anathema to modernists as it was to society as a whole.

Indeed, teds and ton-up boys were the first youth scapegoats of the great English middle-class morality. Modernists were by comparison, well behaved, sensible, almost 'acceptable' to middle- England. At least they did not look scruffy, behave badly, fight, or, in the case of the beatniks, experiment with illegal substances. The media loved teds, ton-ups and beatniks. They provided great, sensational copy that sells newspapers. Alternatively modernists were an unknown entity. They sought a different kind of existence and believed violence was just not cool. Left alone to pursue their own interests, modernists remained obscure and unmolested. However, they were usually at the forefront of new styles in clothing. **JOHN SIMONS** had been wearing Burberry raincoats and sporting a modernist look in 1956 and it was the nightclubs that provided the meeting place for other modernists:

In London, the first place that people hung out was the Lyceum. I first started going in 1954. Even then, if you were a modernist you went in one little corner of the Lyceum. Then there were other clubs, The Florida, The Mapleton, The Flamingo and The Marquee in Oxford Street. You went to these clubs and danced to modern jazz.

There was a whole way of dancing to modern jazz; it was a prevailing influencing factor. At one time we (my mates from school) would go up Stamford Hill, to the youth clubs. There were other like-minded people in terms of modernism, but it was short lived. In hindsight, I've stuck with it while others let it go after a while. We were all completely devoted to it at the time though; we all bought records and listened at each other's houses. We did not know we were modernists even though the word modernist had been coined. It was an evolutionary process and we weren't echoing something that had happened before. I can remember guys had scooters who went to the Lyceum and that was 1955. They used to wear jackets with half-belt bands. There were a lot of really smart blokes in London, usually from the poorer areas. I nearly got beaten up quite a few times because I loved clothes and I used to stare at these smart blokes. We would go out every week. We might go to the Ritz Ballroom in Kingsbury. They had a tremendous orchestra based on the Shelley Mann Band and that was just a local dance hall, small and intimate. That would be around 1956 or '57. I would reckon your probably talking about somewhere between 200 to 4000 like-minded people in the whole of England. When I started going to the Marquee Club, it would be packed with really smart people.

Indeed, **JEFFREY KRUGER**, whose customers were the same smartly dressed people, had a proposition put to him by an unlikely source. The result of which, has now become the stuff of legend for The Flamingo Club:

The early sessions, the jazz sessions from 7.30pm until 11.30pm was 95 per cent white, the mods, who stayed loyal for 10 or more years, with a sprinkling of American GI s and a few Jamaicans that we would let in. Not because we were prejudiced, but because they were well dressed and they would bring in, from time to time, records in between setting up.

The GIs used to talk to me because they knew I had family in America, and they'd seen me on the base at Ruislip where a cousin and brother-in-law were stationed. I was always in the PX grabbing cigars, steaks, the lot and they used to say to me: "Look, when you shut the doors here, we've got nowhere to go. We have to go to some shady places in Bayswater, why don't you do some late night sessions? I'll guarantee you there'll be no trouble, I'm in the military police," this guy said "and we'll get you 200-300 GIs". He said all they want to do is meet the girls and behave. I said "No, it'll lead to drugs and that" and he said "No it won't, we'll keep it out". And they did, heavily.

I can honestly say there was no traffic in drugs that the police were aware of, as I had an arrangement with them. The all-nighter sessions were predominantly black, but they were black GIs and the Jamaican's playing bluebeat music as it was before reggae. But the early sessions were the mods, and the mods did not come to the all-nighter sessions. The all-nighter sessions were predominantly the GIs, which is what it was set up for and they paid through the nose. I think they paid £2 to get in, which today would be the equivalent of £50, and they'd have paid double because it kept them off the street and the music was great. We changed, you know, we didn't do a jazz policy, we went into the widest concepts of music. We had DJs down there like Count Suckle. We had the top Jamaican record systems down there. So we used to bill them after a while and they drew 300 people on their own just to play records. Then we'd do afternoon sessions with them just to play records, but it got too much trying to get everybody out by 6pm and make it clean for 7pm. It really got too much, but a lot of music was created there. The early sessions were predominantly white, and when they came out of the club at 11-11.30pm there would be 300 black guys hanging around. You wouldn't see a policeman, because they knew if they weren't well behaved their own MPs would make sure they didn't get back to camp in a good order. They wouldn't get in if they misbehaved, so they stood in line quietly, which stretched down the street and they knew the routine. We had one doorman; a big guy and he controlled them with just a look and a finger, because if they didn't get past him, they didn't get in no matter what they said. We never had that kind of trouble, but I want to make it quite clear that the early sessions were the mods, and the late sessions were predominantly blacks. I'd like that distinction drawn up.

When an American group was in town, which was rare, because there was still a union ban, they came in to play for the GIs, and the jazz boys would stay. There would be jam sessions which the GIs enjoyed just as much as their own music. So there were some great sessions there.

The best star and the most memorable performance was Billie Holliday, and I have a photograph of us in her dressing room. She had something in her eye in the little dressing room at The Flamingo, I took it out, it was an eyelash.

She signed it; 'To Jeff stay as sweet as you are love Billie', and we were friends right up until the night before she died. She called me, she was out of her head, but she called me. She was a wonderful woman, but I think that was the most memorable evening at the club.

As far as clothing was concerned, modernists were establishing their own style and image, but things were changing rapidly.

Cecil Gee's initial 'look' was refined by John Michael Ingram. He opened his first shop in 1957 and pioneered casual wear for the youth market. By 1960, Ingram opened Sportique on the corner of Old Compton Street and was the first modern shop to sell Gant authentic American shirts. Casual-wear's potential was recognised by the High Street stores, and business began to exploit the trend by producing men's clothes that could make good returns on very little capital. In short, business sanitised the teenage dream. They created their version of a teenager. In the States it was Pat Boone, Tab Hunter and Paul Anka. In the UK, acts like Cliff Richard and Tommy Steele were rounded out to represent the British 'boy next door' after serving their short apprenticeships at the renowned 2Is Coffee Bar in Soho. Just when business thought it could cash in and they were supplying what people wanted, the small band of like-minded individuals who were first to take on the Italian Look, shifted the goalposts and went in an totally unpredictable direction.

Two men were in a position to make the most of the fairly rapid change in taste, mainly because they were young men themselves. One was John Simons; the other was John Stephen. Both men saw that teenagers were dictating the changes. Adults accepted tradition, but teenagers wanted something more, something different. Stephen was ready to take full advantage when he opened His Clothes.

His first proper shop in Beak Street did not take off immediately, and an unguarded electric fire put paid to his entire stock. Within a few months he reopened on the corner of Carnaby Street.

Soon pop stars were visiting the store bringing their fans with them. His Clothes had bright kaleidoscopic window displays, loud music, vivid, bright clothes that
sometimes spilled out on the street. Stephen had countless ploys, gimmicks and publicity stunts, all of which made shopping at His Clothes a joy rather than a chore.

By the end of 1961, John Stephen had four shops dotted around Carnaby Street and Regent Street. While John Stephen was busy building his empire, **JOHN SIMONS** was getting ready to leave Cecil Gee after five years service:

I went on to be a window dresser at Hope Brothers in Regent Street, which was also Burberrys and Scotch House. I stayed with Hope Brothers from 1960 to 1964. I remember just before leaving, Cecil Gee got their first real American clothes by Stanley Blacker. He was the only manufacturer/designer of the early sixties. This was a firm of suit manufacturers who used the name to sell their suits.

John Simons spent most of his time touring the country in a company Austin Mini dressing windows. This kept him busy, but he was also finding time to pursue his own interests in clothes design and retail, but this is not the end of the John Simons or John Stephen story. Their influence will be examined in a later chapter.

Although fifties modernists were anonymous to the wider society, a forty-something author was busily writing a trilogy of novels set in London.

This cousin of former Prime Minister Stanley Baldwin and famed writer Rudyard Kipling, was burrowing into the world of crooks, policemen, black immigrants, prostitutes, ponces and teenagers.

The teenagers he chose to write about were not the teds, ton-ups or beats so beloved of the media. He had observed a new and different strain of teen culture. George Melly described Colin MacInnes as the first adult to recognise the significance of pop and write about it from a distance in terms of culture and age.

A review of the book 'Absolute Beginners' in the Daily Telegraph dated 4 September 1959 clearly indicates the 'establishments' uninformed, jaundiced attitude towards teenagers in their different groupings:

The wildlife in 'Absolute Beginners' by Colin MacInnes is homebred. The cubs are teenagers in London - not of the "Ted" class exactly, but not models of decorum from a "square's" point of view. This spokesman... might be more successful in retaining the interest of the readers he initially attracts if he did not depend upon their being "cool cats" who are "hep" enough to "dig" him all through. This novel... offers every now and then a true picture of superannuated juvenile existential expressionists as we are likely to get. If only we could be sure that we shall get no more!

'Absolute Beginners' went on to gain cult status, but The Daily Telegraph review highlights the general concern about youth, especially on the back of the more prominent teddy boy antics. One wonders whether MacInnes, who died of cancer in 1976, was trying to undermine the 'establishments' confidence in itself or simply trying to warn them. Either way they missed the point.

1959 was interesting for another reason. An eleven-year-old Mark Feld got his first glimpse of a real modernist. It left an indelible impression that imposed itself a few years later.

Modernists were nothing if not eclectic. Instead of sticking to one readily recognisable style, they sought continually to adapt and evolve their dress. According to Mark Paytress, modernist's obsessive one-upmanship was in the new spirit of competitive individualism that had supplanted the austerity years. In its purest form, modernist culture marked a sharp break from the insular, herd-like outlook of teds. Modernist culture had one vital characteristic, the attention to detail that ensured every aspect of their presentation was absolutely perfect in every way.

Mark Feld now aged 15, with fellow modernists Peter Sugar and Michael Simmonds gave an interview to Town Magazine in 1962 and emphasised this never-ending quest for perfection. Titled 'Faces Without Shadows', journalist Peter Barnsley questioned the point of the modernist's life style. They were impeccably clean and dressed. They went for days without sleep. They lived for the present.

To Barnsley, the modernist's lack of concern for the future was unfathomable, although he did detect an arrogance about them, particularly towards girls.

The modernist obsession with clothes was self-evident. Michael Simmonds pointed out how hard it was to be different, even by 1962's standards, and Feld recounted how a kid at his school teased him about the length of his jacket, only to be dismissed with a flippant "I was wearing that style two years ago".

But their insistence on finding the right place to get exactly what they wanted was a feature of the interview.

JOHN WATERS, who lived in Archway, North London, was very much a mod contemporary of Mark Feld and friends:

I actually started off as a rocker when I was 14, and even then, before the Merseybeat thing, I always liked something raunchier and different. Then I got into the mod thing and I was very slow to come out of it. As far as clothes are concerned, there were certain shops you knew about to get things. There wasn't a shortage of stuff, but a lot of what we wore was hand made anyway. It was no good off the peg. We used to go to a tailor in Highbury Corner. They said Chris Farlowe went there, and the Krays, but I don't know how true that is. He was a brilliant tailor though, and when I think back on what it cost, it was like four weeks wages. You'd have three or four fittings before it was finished. All hand stitched and everyone was slightly different because you couldn't be the same as everyone else. I never bothered with Carnaby Street though. There were some good shops there, but you didn't have to go there to get things.

Harry Fenton's was good for shirts. You'd go 'Up West' for shoes. The local shops had cheap stuff. I often wondered where the hell it all came from, because things changed so quickly. I remember at one stage, everyone had lumberjack work shirts with woollen rollnecks underneath, and I thought 'Well who started that off?' Then Marks and Spencers started selling a rollneck, just the neck part; it wasn't a jumper at all. You'd just pop this thing over your head and chuck the shirt over the top. They were only about 12s 6d. When I think back though, the groups definitely had a lot to do with it. The Swinging Blue Jeans came on once with tartan tab collars and denim waistcoats. The next week everyone had one. It only lasted a couple of months, but that was the first time anyone had seen that. The Dave Clark shirts with the plain collar and the buttons on the side were another one. It all got a bit mad at one time though, but very innovative. Personally, I wasn't too keen on scooters. I mean, we wouldn't be seen dead in a parka. I can see the reason for wearing them, keeping your clothes clean and keeping warm, but they weren't for us. We never went anywhere by scooter, we always got a taxi or a bus.

The overall impression is that to be a modernist was about good taste. Of course good taste is subjective. Like music or films for example, good taste is determined by individual preference. But modernists developed their own loose code of good taste and detail.
It was what you were drinking, how your suit was cut, the length of the side vents, how many buttons and what type of buttons, the size and shape of the collar, the colour and fabric used, the length of the trousers, the width of the trouser bottoms, were the shoes hand-made, were they Italian, with or without buckles, the type of shirt you had, with or without cuff links? If you had cuff links, were they the right cuff links? How wide was your tie? Did it have a pointed end or a straight cut-off? Did you smoke, what brand did you smoke, did you have a cigarette case, with or without a matching lighter? It was all these things and more that mattered to a modernist. If it was not exactly right it was not worth doing or using or being seen in. And that was another driving force at the heart of modernists. They spent all their time, money and effort on looking good simply to be looked at and admired. There were no homosexual overtones, nothing effeminate about

> I was standing at the train station at Twickenham. It was a very cold, foggy night and I could hear the sound of a harmonica being played down on the platform. So I went to investigate. It was the riff from 'Smokestack Lightning' which was a big tune at the time. And it was Rod Stewart playing.
> LONG JOHN BALDRY

it, although teds and ton-up boys would constantly taunt them. It was narcissism in its most complete form.

The concept of a preening dandy was not entirely new to Britain though. In the early 19th century, Beau Brummel led a mainly London-based fashion for men who were obsessed with their appearance and detail. This trend for extravagance and exhibitionism disappeared after Brummell's death in 1840 and the onset of the Victorian era, although the aristocracy and wealthy individuals developed the concept of the 'gentleman' during England's empire building years.

When thinking of the classic 'gentleman', one might suggest a fictional character like Raffles or James Bond. For men of John Simon's generation, it would be film stars like Cary Grant, David Niven, James Mason or Robert Taylor. Arguably, a 'gentleman' is regarded as being a man of impeccable good taste, good manners, a fastidious nature and wealth. The latter, being the means by which one can gain the material possessions to present the image of a 'gentleman'. A 'gentleman' dresses according to the company he keeps, the time of day or the activity he pursues. Everything is exact in every detail from his hair to his shoes.

The basic premise of a 'gentleman' is that personal presentation can say more about you than any amount of words. Perhaps for this reason, modernists were perplexing, confusing and subversive. They presented themselves as moneyed sophisticates by the way they dressed, even though it disguised a working class background.

JOHN SIMONS saw the connection between the English 'gentleman' concept and modernists:

The idea comes from the turn of the century. I think mod grew out of that and from the American gentleman's look and the Italian. It has come from the gentleman's look from all over the world really. Our generation were influenced by what our dads wore, what our friends wore, what we saw in films.

Arguably the mod who has become something of a legend was Pete Meaden. In his book, 'Pretend You're In A War - The Who & The Sixties' author Mark Blake arguably unearthed more about Meaden's life than anyone prior to 2014. Pete Meaden was born in Edmonton, north London in 1942 and by the late 1950s, he was among those early modernists frequenting clubs like The Feldman and Flamingo. He was just under 6ft tall, auburn-haired with blue eyes. He left grammar school with five 'O' levels and two 'A' levels. He spent about a year at art school before leaving both school and parental home for a flat in Hampstead and a job with John Michael Ingram as a graphic designer. Then he teamed up with Andrew Loog Oldham to form their own PR company for a short time. Loog Oldham became the Rolling Stones manager and the pair parted company due to Meaden's drug problems. He had been prescribed Drinamyl for an anxiety. His one-per-day habit escalated to the point where he was not only taking but dealing as well. By 1963, he was an addict.

As DJ Jeff Dexter told Mark Blake; 'Pete Meaden was a proper Soho boy. He had mad energy, but he was a bit fly, and he made most of his dough from flogging pills'.

By 1964, Meaden knew every club manager, pop critic, DJ and drug dealer in London. He did some publicity for Georgie Fame, the Crystals, Gene Pitney and the Stones, but he is of course more famous for being the original mastermind behind the transformation of a local London band called The Detours. The band's original managers, Bob Druce and Helmut Gordon gave him £50 as a promotional budget. Meaden renamed them The High Numbers and turned them into mods.

According to Roger Daltry, The Who first became aware of mods in 1963 via his sister Gillian. As he explained to Mark Blake; 'Her first boyfriend had a scooter. He and his mates came from Lewisham and they were the first mods I'd ever seen'.

In an interview with Jon Savage for Mojo magazine, Pete Townshend recalled a gig at the Florida Ballroom in Brighton where they were supporting the Mark Leeman Five where the entire audience was mod. After the gig, Townshend and an art school girlfriend stayed in Brighton until 5am observing the mods under Brighton Pier. Townshend was fascinated. He realised these were the people he was meant to be writing songs for and much of Townshend's output over the coming decade and more was as a direct result and influence of mods and the mod scene he had observed. This was just prior to Pete Meaden's association with the band.

He wrote the lyrics for a couple of songs and got their first record contract, a one-off single with Decca. 'I'm The Face' (which was a reworking of 'Got Love If You Want It' by Slim Harpo) backed with 'Zoot Suit' (again a reworking of The Showmen's song 'Country Fool') and set them up as a mod band.

An injection of R & B and a change of image completed the transformation. Meaden got them gigs at clubs like The Scene and eventually was bought out by Kit Lambert and Chris Stamp (brother of Terrance) for £500.

Reading an interview by Steve Turner for NME and republished in Paolo Hewitt's 'The Sharper Word', it is easy to see Meaden was right in the thick of the London mod scene. However, Meaden's view of mod is virtually the blueprint for the stereotyped 'mods' of the film 'Quadrophenia', but the emergence of Meaden's brand of mod would not make themselves known for a few years yet. He had an undoubted innate ability for PR and promotion. There were those who accepted Meaden's assertion that he was an 'ace face' on the mod scene, but this has since been contradicted by Jeff Dexter who told Mark Blake that Meaden would not have been spotted as a 'tasty geezer' and that Meaden would only buy the odd shirt when he had sold enough pills to fund them.

JOHN HELLIER concurs with Jeff Dexter's assessment:

Pete Meadon was an acquaintance of mine from the Scene days till around 1969. He wasn't particularly a mate in fact he was somebody that I used to spend most of my life avoiding. He was always speeded up and waffling on about some new venture or whatever. He died young and became a Mod legend. He certainly wasn't regarded as such at the time. I remember in the late sixties that he had a total fixation about a great little band called Grapefruit. They had Beatle/Apple connections and were managed by Doris Day's son Terry Melcher. He knew that I knew them and hassled me big time about him getting the chance to manage them. It never happened.

On 28 July 1978, Pete Meaden died of a barbiturate overdose. Meaden's involvement in the music business came at another time of great change in that industry. Modernists were still into modern jazz, but they were increasingly becoming interested in blues and R&B.

Bluesmen like Muddy Waters, John Lee Hooker and Lightning Hopkins with the emerging talents of Ray Charles and James Brown, were the influencing factor for modernists and many soon-to-be-famous British bands. For modernists, this was music that you could dance fairly easily to, although the records themselves were hard to come by.

Although not a mod himself, one man who became fascinated with R&B and soul music, would eventually become one of Britain's foremost authorities on the subject.

In 1953, Dave Godin heard Ruth Brown's 'Mama He Treats Your Daughter Mean' on a jukebox in an ice cream parlour in Bexleyheath, South London. It was the start of an epic journey through black music that Godin would promote and champion all his life.

Dave Godin attended the Dartford Grammar School and introduced fellow pupil Mick Jagger to black artists such as Arthur Alexander, Little Walter, Howlin' Wolf and Muddy Waters. They used to play jam sessions at the house of another friend, Bobby Beckwith. Godin played harmonica. Godin and Jagger did not remain friends for long, as The Rolling Stones began to cover many of the songs Godin had introduced them too.

In fact, years later, Dave Godin refused to introduce Mick Jagger to Marvin Gaye when they were on the set of Ready, Steady Go!

Godin became involved with Tamla Motown at label owner Berry Gordy's personal request. While in Detroit, he was asked his opinion on forthcoming releases on Tamla and the subsidiary labels bound for the UK. His production of a fanzine led him to become a leading writer for Blues and Soul Magazine.

It is fair to say that, without Dave Godin's enthusiasm and determination, many of the now revered R'n'B classics, and particularly the Motown releases, may not have had the impact they did in Britain had he not been such an enthusiast, although high-profile acts like Dusty Springfield deserve recognition for not just covering the songs, but doing her best to promote the label's output.

Another man to stand up and be counted (musically) was Tony Hall, the compere and booker for The Flamingo Club. He secured a job with Decca working on their Tempo label and given free reign, he signed Tubby Hayes, The Jazz Couriers with Hayes, Ronnie Scott, Jimmy Deuchar, Don Rendell and Victor Feldman in the line-up and a Jamaican trumpet player by the name of Dizzy Reece.

By 1961, the Tempo label folded and **TONY HALL** became Head of Promotion for Decca and had a huge following for his DJ show on Radio Luxembourg. It was due to Tony Hall that Atlantic Records got a toe-hold in the British charts. Decca had the distribution deal with Atlantic. As Mr Hall explained:

I became very close buddies with Jerry Wexler. I was his man in England. I broke Otis Redding here for him. Jerry was putting out all these deep soul records which weren't selling here. I used to have long conversations with him from a red telephone box on Brighton Pier, reversing the charges, and that's how we planned Otis's career in England.

Tony Hall suggested 'My Girl' from the 'Otis Blue' album to be released as a single. Jerry Wexler gave him five weeks, by which time the song was at No 7. Hall and his team did the same with Wilson Pickett and 'In The Midnight Hour'. He was also responsible for breaking Ike and Tina Turner's 'River Deep, Mountain High' and The Righteous Brothers' 'You've Lost That Lovin' Feelin' among others.

Tony Hall left Decca after the company made yet another monumental business mistake. Having already rejected The Beatles, (part of music folk-lore now), the top brass at Decca had the opportunity to sign a distribution deal with Tamla Motown, all thanks to Tony Hall's hard work. They turned it down and Hall resigned.

Setting up the first independent promotion company in the UK in 1967, Tony Hall had major parts to play in the careers of Joe Cocker, Black Sabbath, The Real Thing and Loose Ends to name but a few. He is another truly unsung hero of British pop music and it all started at The Feldman and The Flamingo.

The impact of soul and R&B that Dave Godin and Tony Hall championed in their own ways would be felt throughout mod history, but its origins were in America. The USA had avenues and outlets for new music that Britain could never compete with. A deregulated radio industry meant that R&B and soul would find popularity in certain areas of the country. Black music-based radio had a ready-made audience in the cities across the country. Very often a song by a local group or singer would be number one on the local station chart before being picked up by the larger national record companies. When that happened, the local audience switched to a new song. DJs like Rufus Thomas would play songs that only the black population of New York, Detroit, Chicago or Washington would be familiar with.

Of utmost importance was the fact that America's cities with high black populations supported singers and groups from their own neighbourhood and whose records were played on local black radio. From this fertile ground came acts that British mods regard as heroes and heroines, but their true recognition in the UK started with two men from opposite ends of the country.

Guy Stevens was playing R&B at the Scene Club in London, while in Manchester a young man by the name of **ROGER EAGLE** was embarking on a residency at the new Twisted Wheel Club in Brazennose Street. As Roger explained:

The only other club anywhere that was playing anything like the R&B that I played at The Wheel was The Scene Club in London. I used to get on well with Guy Stevens and we used to exchange records. I was getting hold of some records before their release even in the States, things like 'You Don't Know Like I Know' by Sam and Dave. I was the first person to play that record in Britain.

For Roger Eagle, Ray Charles' 'In Person' and 'Live at Newport' LPs were landmarks in the development of R&B. Others include Gary US Bonds, Fats Domino, Arthur Alexander, Lavern Baker and Chuck Willis.

As with London, coffee bars were numerous in Manchester. Places like the Cona Coffee Bar in Tib Lane were happy for their customers to bring their own records and play them.

Roger Eagle was using his ever-growing record collection to supply music at parties, and with the assistance of Mike Bocock and Roger Fairhurst, he learnt how to import records from the USA. A chance meeting at The Left Wing Coffee Bar with the Abadi brothers led to Roger's residency at The Twisted Wheel:

In the very early days, when the club first started, we relied very much on word-of-mouth. We had people coming from Bolton and Liverpool, all over the place. The Abadi's didn't really have an appreciation for the type of music that was popular. Once they insisted I play a pop record. I argued against it, but to prove a point I played it and emptied the dance floor. I didn't have the ambition or the patter to be a high profile DJ, I was happy playing the music that I loved. I would play six or seven hours solid single-handedly - with just an hour break for the band.

The long stints that Roger played were not without minor problems, and Roger's solution threw up some surprising results:
Seven hours of record playing is a long time and there weren't that many Soul and R&B records available at that time, so I had to mix in Rock and Roll tracks to fill out the time. In fact Carl Perkins was a particular favourite amongst The Wheel crowd. He even played live at the club.

As The Twisted Wheel and Roger Eagle grew in stature, so the influence of the music policy began to impose itself on people with musical aspirations:
Eric Clapton was a good friend at the time. One Sunday morning after he had played at the club, he brought a good looking young mod girl round to my place and she got completely pissed off because all he wanted to do was listen to Freddie King records. I used to be friendly with Steve Winwood. He would come round to my place and listen to records when The Spencer Davis Group played the club. Georgie Fame did some good things - very King Pleasure influenced. The important thing is to take the influence and then add a twist and take it on further.
One of the great stories, that are the stuff of legend, also involved Roger Eagle and a popular band from London, The Rolling Stones. The Stones had played a gig in Manchester and arrived at The Twisted Wheel for a cup of coffee and to wind down. What they did not expect, was to find the DJ in a mischievous mood:
The kids were just standing around them-just looking at them, not talking to them-just looking. So I played all of the original tracks off their first album, which had just come out;' I'm A King Bee' by Slim Harpo, 'Walkin' The Dog' by Rufus Thomas, Arthur Alexander; They knew exactly what I was doing, I played them in exactly the same order as the LP. It was just me saying there's a North-South thing. I actually got on OK with The Stones and although I'm one of the DJs that publicised the music, The

Stones went to the States and got Howlin' Wolf on prime time national television and that's the thing to do. I admire them for that.

As for the Twisted Wheel's pre-eminence as the mod club of the north, it was not a conscious decision, but a gradual process:
It just grew and happened. You knew what was going on. The punters were generally sharp, but some were way ahead. I couldn't keep up with them. The music came first and was paramount above everything else to me. Of course I dressed in the styles of the day. I was smart, but I wasn't at the sharp end style-wise. My money went on vinyl and importing new records. I left the clothes obsession to the kids coming into the club.

In Birmingham, **GILL TAYLOR** was taking on board the musical influences of the day while maintaining her obsession with fashion and she would witness first-hand the start of an illustrious music career:
My dad was very keen on the Platters and early black music, so I heard that and later on Tamla Motown. I saw Ray Charles when he came to Birmingham Odeon because I remembered his records being played by my dad, so black music has always been in my background. I always liked Eddie Cochran and saw his last performance in Birmingham because he had that fatal accident on the way back to the airport shortly after. The jazz clubs played some Modern Jazz, but you couldn't really dance to it, so we liked the Trad-New Orleans jazz because you could dance to that. You could jive. But one jazz club I did go to at the Old Stone Cross in Dale End in Birmingham. It used to have Muff Winwood and Spencer Davis playing there. Steve Winwood was only 15 at that time and he used to sing a few songs while the band had a break and Spencer would play piano.
Well, we all loved Steve Winwood and after a while the jazz scene faded and those lads would play on a Saturday lunchtime in the city centre, then on a Monday night they would be the Spencer Davis Group at the Golden Eagle on Hill Street and by this time the mod scene was well under way, so it was really popular to go and see them and they were our connection to the whole thing, that would have been 1963.

Meanwhile Adam Faith, Billy Fury and Marty Wilde were dominating the British charts and appearing on TV shows like Six Five Special, Oh Boy and Cool For Cats, two men on the fringes of the skiffle craze were growing tired of it. In 1957 they opened the London Blues and Barrelhouse Club in Soho and ran it very successfully over three years. In that time they presented many US blues performers, but got ejected from the pub venue because they decided to use some modest amplification.

They joined Chris Barber's Jazz Band as a blues unit within the main band, but by 1962 decided to start their own rhythm and blues band.

They called themselves Blues Incorporated and from that moment, they influenced a new generation of musicians who in turn would read like a who's who of British pop music. Those men were Alexis Korner and Cyril Davis.

The only way to really explain just how important Korner, Davis and the Blues Inc Band were is to list the people who came into contact with them. More over, they had a quality that has been sadly missing from the mainstream music industry for decades. These were not men looking to make a fortune at the expense of others. They encouraged musicians to play, to learn their craft and then go and do it for themselves, and it is rare to find two men who appear never to have claimed one ounce of credit for helping some of the best bands of the British Beat era get their start.

The occasional musicians who appeared in the Blues Inc line-up or featured at one time or another in separate bands run by Korner and Davis or bands that were given their first break included; Art Wood (The Artwoods) and his brother Ron Wood (Birds, Faces & Rolling Stones), Charlie Watts (Rolling Stones), Jack Bruce (Manfred Mann & Cream), Brian Jones (Rolling Stones), Paul Jones (Manfred Mann), Ginger Baker (Cream), Graham Bond (Graham Bond Organisation), Dick Taylor (Pretty Things), Mick Avory (Kinks), Madeline Bell, Rod Stewart, Hughie Flint and Tom McGuiness (Manfred Mann & McGuiness Flint), Eric Clapton and The Yardbirds. It was blues and R&B that inspired musicians. Davis and Korner were the catalyst for many, while others were tapping into the same source. Georgie Fame, Spencer Davis Group, The Groundhogs, The Animals, The Bo Street Runners, The Kinks, The Who (after Pete Meaden's insistence that they include it in their set), The Creation, The Mojos, The Paramounts, Cliff Bennett and The Small Faces.

They all took blues and R&B as their base material and honed it to their own individual sound. One man who became a mod favourite and worked with Davis and Korner was **LONG JOHN BALDRY:**

I started off back in the fifties, just me and an acoustic guitar. Mods used to come along when I sang in a band called The Ken Simms Vintage Jazz Band. Then of course I teamed up with Alex and Cyril doing acoustic stuff. It wasn't until March 1962 that we actually formed Blues Incorporated. It sort of developed under it's own steam from the nights we used to do at The Roundhouse pub on the corner of Wardour Street and Brewer Street. We had the Thursday night Blues and Barrelhouse sessions there. Alex and Cyril had been running that since 1956 I think. I first met them in 1957 and became a regular fixture and we sort of became a trio of sorts, taking turns to do things. Most of the people who attended those sessions were musical wannabes.

Blues Incorporated actually made its debut at a club we started. The Ealing R&B Club it was called, beneath the ABC Tea Rooms on Ealing Broadway. Harold Pendleton, who was Chris Barber's partner in the National Jazz Federation, came down to see what all the fuss was about and then offered us a Thursday night residency at the original Marquee, when it was beneath The Academy Cinema on Oxford Circus. That's when the snowball started rolling. I went off to Germany in the mid-summer of that year and when I came back Alex and Cyril had split because of musical differences - Cyril hated saxophones. So Cyril was continuing the residency at The Marquee and Alex had by then moved on to The Flamingo. So I literally tossed a half-a-crown piece to see which band I would join and it came down on Cyril's side. I would have been happy in either band.

I think the audience was fairly interchangeable between The Marquee and The Flamingo at that time. People went to both venues, although Alex's and Cyril's approaches were very different, I think the audience was the same. That's when the blossoming of the whole mod movement took place. You noticed it with the winkle picker shoes, Italian suits, Lambrettas and parkas.

Blues and R&B was much easier to adapt for British groups. Soul on the other hand was not. George Melly made a valid assumption that Soul and R&B was a natural phenomenon of Black America. White British bands could not quite pull it off, although arguably Georgie Fame was closest. So, together these bands were the sound track to most of the early to mid 1960s and defined an era.

Jeffrey Kruger and The Flamingo Club were now running two sessions every night. An early session for mods and jazz fans, and a late session for a mainly black R&B clientele. By this time, Jeffrey Kruger, with his fledgling Ember Record label and successful music publishing business, had employed Rik Gunnell to run the all-nighter sessions. Rik also got his brother John in on the late sessions at The Flamingo. The Gunnell brothers were German-born and had become managers for Georgie Fame. According to Bob Solly in his article about The Flamingo for Record Collector, Georgie Fame not only altered the course of events at the club, but also mod culture. Originally from Leigh, Lancashire, Clive Powell changed his name to Georgie Fame at the suggestion of Larry Parnes. Parnes had the Blue Flames as the backing band for Billy Fury who felt they were too jazzy for his style in 1962. As the pianist, Georgie Fame took over vocals for the band and they soon secured the residency at The Flamingo. Fame's smooth style and obsession with jazz and blues was perfect for the late-night audience at The Flamingo. DJ Count Suckle inspired Fame to switch to the electric piano after playing 'Green Onions' by Booker T & The MGs for the first time in the club. His debut LP 'Rhythm And Blues At The Flamingo' has been hailed as one of the great PR successes in the history of the club. In an interview with Duncan Heining for Record Collector, **GEORGIE FAME** explained how he was introduced to the Flamingo Club.

It was Mike O'Neill who took me down the Flamingo and introduced me to Rik Gunnell. We were in the right place at the right time because the resident band was going off to do a TV show on a Sunday afternoon. So we took the Sunday afternoon session and I reformed the Blue Flames. Rik Gunnell had to rent an upright piano for our sets at the Flamingo. Jeff Kruger wouldn't let me play the club piano because it was reserved for jazz musicians.

By the end of 1962, Georgie Fame had converted from piano to Hammond organ. One of his first sessions on Hammond was with Prince Buster on 'Soul Of Africa' and included Rico Rodriguez, a musician of immense talent who would find a new lease of life almost 20 years later. As **GEORGIE FAME** stated:

I knew Rico because I was very involved with the West Indian community at the time because half the punters down the Flamingo were West Indian and Count Suckle had his own club in Carnaby Street called the Roaring Twenties, which was a real West Indian club. Until the mods came in, the Flamingo was really a black club. It was full of West Indians, pimps and prostitutes - Christine Keeler and those - and black American servicemen. It was their base in London for the weekend.

It was Rik Gunnell who funded the album 'Rhythm and Blues At The Flamingo' recorded on a mobile rig. According to engineer, Glyn Johns in his autobiography 'Sound Man', the only independent remote recording unit in England was owned by IBC (who Johns worked for). It was a three-track Ampex machine, a console and three large speakers all crammed into a rat-infested broom cupboard next to the stage.

Georgie Fame recalls having to do the entire set twice as one of the tracks malfunctioned the first time around.

Indeed it was during a break at the Flamingo that Georgie Fame dashed over to Ham Yard to catch The Animals playing a set at The Scene Club. That was where he first met Alan Price who was playing a Vox Continental at that time. It was a meeting that became a friendship that has lasted over 50 years and continues to this day.

As for Rik Gunnell, he was known to be a hard, tough man with various jobs as a boxer, club bouncer, Army drill sergeant and worker at Smithfield market before turning his hand to running night clubs. He met Tony Harris at The Mapleton where he ran Club Americana in 1955. With Jeff Kruger now located at the Wardour Street premises, Gunnel opened additional nights as Club M at The Mapleton.

Due to allegations of drug dealers and prostitutes plying their trades in the club, Gunnell had to leave. Gunnell had fallen out with Jeff Kruger at some point prior to this (some say Gunnell forced Kruger out of The Mapleton, but this is unsubstanciated).

JEFFREY KRUGER explained what happened next:
Let's set the record straight. Rik Gunnell was brought aboard to compere the late night sessions by Tony Harris, who was my associate on the all night sessions when they started and that was Rik's function. It did develop that he used to book the all-nighter sessions, the live groups, and that he was the manager or agent for Georgie Fame and Long John Baldry and those people, and he did build a successful agency. He offered me a partnership in it, but I had my own things, so Rik pretty much ran the all-nighters. He had no ownership. The ownership never left me, or if you want to be accurate, whatever the company was or The Kruger Organisation as it became. Certainly he became more than a compere and an employee, and he did share in the profits on the all-nighters. The boss was Tony Harris, but Tony couldn't work all day down the road at the Mapleton and then come up and manage the all-nighter and not get some sleep. John Gunnell as I recall, was the younger brother, he hung around and humped the crates and did whatever he could and developed into a pseudo compere and a big head and liked to show off. They had no ownership ever. That's as categoric as I can get.

It has often been said that modernists were not bothered about alcohol. If they drank at all, it would be a scotch and coke or some kind of short with a mixer. Unbeknown to **JEFFREY KRUGER**, The Flamingo was trading hard drinks even though it did not have an alcohol license:
That is correct and that's when I fired Rik, when I found out about it. One night I came back from a business trip to America and I had a funny feeling, so I went down to the club and it shook them, they went white when they saw me, as I had never been in after midnight. It was hard work, working from 4pm to 11.30pm getting it ready for the all-nighters, plus a heavy weeks work, and when I saw what was happening I fired him on the spot. The following Monday or Tuesday he let me cool down because I had a temper. He came up to see me and, in fairness, he said "You get your share, we're not doing any harm, these all-nighter sessions are a strain, do you want to stay up all night?". So we reached a compromise, providing it was selective, it was never open, it was never advertised, I truthfully turned a blind eye to it.

Alcohol was not the only awkward issue to manifest itself at The Flamingo. As Bob Solly mentions, a very few people have gone on record (Georgie Fame being one of them) to say The Flamingo could be a dangerous place in the early 60s. Allegedly, the drug dealers, prostitutes and gangsters followed the Gunnells to Wardour Street, however, both were physically equipped to deal with any problems. Due to the implementation of the 1959 Street Offences Act, hookers could no longer ply their trade on street corners and so resorted to bars and clubs instead. One of those being Christine Keeler who was a regular at The Flamingo. It was in The Flamingo in October 1962 that Keeler's lover 'Lucky' Gordon got into a fight with another of her lovers, Johnny Edgecombe. Gordon ended up in hospital with a knife wound to his face and this incident was the beginning of the most celebrated political scandal in modern British politics: The Profumo Affair. Meanwhile the Gunnell brothers had their own booking agency and now represented Rod Stewart, Chris Farlowe, Geno Washington, John Mayall, PJ Proby and Zoot Money. All of whom spent many nights playing at The Flamingo. Indeed, it is said that the attitude among musicians at the time was that if you had not played The Flamingo, you could not consider yourself 'established'. The club and its mod clientele influenced so many people, popular culture and style. In 1961, a fourteen year-old from the east-end of London, was already on the 'books' as a junior player for West Ham United. It was purely by chance he happened to be walking along Wardour Street when he heard 'incredible music' coming from the basement below. He and his friend joined the queue and got in. That night he saw Georgie Fame and Rufus Thomas on stage. 'After watching these great performers, I had no doubt in my mind I wanted to be a musician. I thought, if I played drums I could hide behind the cymbals if I was no good. My dad bought me a drum kit and I joined a small jazz trio that usually played in Conservative clubs and at weddings. I was only with them for a short while, then I toured for a few years with a band called 'Mood Indigo'.

By the 1970s, this man was a household name and chart topping star. All because of a life-changing moment at The Flamingo Club, and David Essex has never looked back since.

Modernism began to spread beyond the small pockets of north and west London. The print media began to expand its horizons. February 1962 saw the first issue of The

Sunday Times Colour Supplement and included features on young fashions (Mary Quant clothes), modelling (Jean Shrimpton), photography (David Bailey) and a James Bond story. By 1964, what we now know as 'lifestyle' features appeared in the Telegraph Colour Supplement and the Observer magazine.

The 'lifestyle' of young London dandies became a focal point and 'Ready Steady Go' hit the TV screens in 1963, the R&B influenced bands became important to the wider modernist community. 1963 also saw the launch of an enduring, iconic brand that remains to this day.

Arthur Benjamin Sugarman was born in Brighton in 1925. Just after World War II, Arthur moved to America, became an American citizen and married the daughter of a clothes manufacturer in California.

Returning to Brighton some years later, Arthur established his first shirt factory at 21 Bedford Square, Brighton. Knowing the demand was for Oxford-cloth button-down collar designs, as sold by Ivy League purists like Brooks Brothers and Arrow, Arthur developed his own brand. He called it 'Ben Sherman'.

Meanwhile, the fifties modernists, with roots in Jazz, would soon be overtaken by a new form of modernism and a new generation. ·◊·

> Pete Meadon was an acquaintance of mine from the Scene days till around 1969. He wasn't particularly a mate in fact he was somebody that I used to spend most of my life avoiding. He was always speeded up and waffling on about some new venture or whatever. He died young and became a Mod legend. He certainly wasn't regarded as such at the time.
>
> JOHN HELLIER

CHAPTER 2

The emergence of mod from north and west London to the wider world was not because any one person decided to launch it in a mass of packaged media hype.

Modernists knew what they liked. No one told them what to wear, what to listen to or how to behave. The mod culture that was slowly developing came from people who wanted to set their own standards. It stemmed from open-mindedness, the acceptance of ideas that came from people who were not beholden to capitalism and bourgeois notions of class distinction. The modernist aim was to look your best at all times, to strive for perfection and have fun.

Initially, mods did not wear clothes for aggression. It was the notion of dressing out of self-love rather than rebellion. By 1962, jazz influenced modernists were becoming fewer as more people opened themselves up to R&B, soul, blues and ska. The numbers of the new breed were growing and mod headed down the road to mass participation.

However, some outside of London were setting their own standards of style. In Birmingham, **GILL TAYLOR** was starting out in the world of work creating her own style while keeping in touch with what was going on in the mod scene:

Things were very different to what they are now of course and you would really only listen to Radio Luxembourg because that was the only one you could get. Del Evans used to have a little transistor radio we could get it on and then things got better when Radio Caroline came along, but you found out about things by word-of-mouth or reading New Musical Express. If you wanted to hear a record, you went to the record shop with the booths on the wall and you'd listen to them there.

When I left art school, I decided I needed to learn everything about fashion and retail. The first job I had was at a Theatrical Costumers called Emile Littler, then I did some work as a window dresser and finally went to work at what was then the new Rackhams Store on Corporation Street in late '63. My friend and I worked in the fashion department and at lunchtimes we would go down to the record department in the store and get this guy called Brian Heinz to spin some records for us. Well Brian Heinz became Denny Laine. He had his own band called Denny Laine and the Diplomats and around that time they changed their name to the Moody Blues. He was always very smart. There was another guy who worked in the advertising department who asked my friend for an introduction to me. She told him I had a boyfriend, but he described me as 'that mod girl' which was the first time anyone had called me that. In my mind, I was still a 'Contintentalist'.

A lot of us went to the Old Stone Cross pub for the jazz club there. I met a guy called Tony who designed jewellery and we were going out with each other for a while. He designed and made me a ring which I still wear to this day. Well one night Del Evans saw me across the room at the Old Stone Cross and asked someone for an introduction. We met and Del always said I gave him the cold-shoulder and wandered off. At a later date we met again and Del showed me a drawing he had done of a house design which I thought was really good and quite clever. So we started going out and although he didn't go to art school, he had that kind of look which I liked. He could draw architectural stuff, but he couldn't draw clothes and he had some wonderful ideas that I drew for him. Sometimes, I'd make things for him like leather waistcoats or ties, but for the tailoring, he would take my drawings to Hepworths and they used to make them for him. Our passion for clothes ruled our lives.

However, before Gill and Del cemented their relationship, Gill had an encounter with two young lads who would go on to make their name in music:
I met Charlie Watts and Keith Richards in 1962 in Brighton. My friend and I decided to visit a couple of girls we knew from Birmingham who had moved to Brighton in early '62. They had gone there to be part of what was known as the 'Pebble Scene' in Brighton. Anyway, we wandered around Brighton for a while and found our way to a pub called the Basket Makers Arms (on Gloucester Road) and there was a back room where you could play records and that's where we met these two guys called Charlie and Keith. They were always trying to get us to go back to this barge where they lived in Shoreham. We never did though. Much later, my dad had a newspaper with an early photo of the Rolling Stones in it and I recognised Charlie and Keith and told him I knew them. He said 'They look unsavoury characters to me !' Back in those days, you met so many people you knew who might play guitar in a band or something and they might go on to bigger things, but they really were people you knew. Nowadays, popstars seem to be all celebrities and you don't get to meet them in the same way.

As 'Continentalists', Gill and Del were not alone in their love of European styling and the post-war consensus of rebuilding international relationships filtered into popular culture. **SERGE HOFFMANN**, a native of Paris who was to become a mod in the 70s gives this assessment of the link between France and Britain on a mod-culture level:
The original mods of the early 60s were inspired in part by French films such as 'A

Bout De Souffle' and singers such as Jacque Dutronc and Francoise Hardy. There have been people into the music and style that could be considered mod since the mid-60's in France, but not much of a group scene until the mod revival in the late 70's. The question of French/English cross-cultural influences is actually pretty interesting, there's a paradox where lots of French are fascinated by the UK and vice versa. For example there were French groups that appeared in the mid 60s such as Les Boots, The Five Gentlemen, etc. as well as singers Ronnie Bird and Noel Deschamps, who really looked for their influences across the channel without realising that their English idols were themselves strongly marked by the French and continental style.

Those have lots of great sounds, but the ones that really managed to transcend, to have a particularly French angle to go along with the fascination with the UK (much more "swinging London" in general than strictly modernist), created their own type of distinctively French music. They differentiated themselves not only by the French language but with a strong use of irony and humour combined with social criticism even when singing about politics and romance. The most notable would be Serge Gainsbourg, Jacques Dutronc, Nino Ferrer and Michel Polnareff.

Although those were mostly sharp dressers in the French dandy tradition, there was only one that really adopted the modernist aesthetic in particular in the sixties, a popular singer called Claude François. A great dancer with excellent rhythm, and as obsessive as any mod could be regarding clothing and style, he deserves respect for his adaptations of Motown, Joe Tex and more.

Back in Britian, modernists had mainly originated in north London, the new coarser mod heralded from west London. Instead of creating their own look, they became more physical, more herd-like and not as obsessed with perfectionism as their predecessors. Indeed it is at the start of the sixties, that the role of the modernist movement (for want of a better term) gets confused with wider cultural and political changes and has since been apparently inexorably linked with something known as 'the swinging sixties', a catch-all term that is constantly used to describe the entire decade.

As mentioned in the previous chapter, the print media were obsessed with youth lifestyles. 'The Swinging Sixties' was the invention of American-owned Time Magazine. In 1966 it proclaimed that London was 'the most exciting city in the world. In a decade dominated by youth, London had burst into bloom. It swings: it is the scene'.

The truth is that the 'swinging sixties' relates to a very short period of the decade, 1966 to early 1967. It relates to only a small, elitist group of people. They moved in the right social circles and they were arguably the first generation of British mass media 'celebrities' more famous for being famous than being noted for their achievements.

America had scandals involving Hollywood stars for decades, but not so in Britain. Not until the sixties that is. The 'Profumo Affair' changed everything. For the first time the British public began to understand the total hypocrisy of the English upper classes, but the media loved it. The new 'swinging sixties' and the 'Chelsea set', as they became known, were really only important to themselves, the media and their social circle. They were not mod. They typified what commentators and academics like to refer to as the 'pop age'.

Indeed, the 'swinging sixties' took over from 'It's a mod mod world'. But how did this mod world grow from a relatively small band of dedicated jazz fans with a sense of style into the scourge sub-culture of the mid-sixties? By closely examining the course of events in Britain it becomes easier to unravel the myth, disinformation and confusion.

As we have seen in the previous chapter, modernism already had its roots in diverse areas of culture and it existed a decade earlier than the sixties. The sixties however, produced a significant amount of influencing factors that superseded each other as the decade progressed.

JOHN HELLIER is another who has been a mod is whole life. While John was not influential during the 60s, his role would develop in latter decades as we shall see, but if we accept modernists like John Simon as the first generation, then John Hellier is definitely part of the second generation:

I lived in the Hornchurch/Romford area which was Essex back then, it's now the London Borough of Havering. We bordered onto the East End of London, I suppose, so even before I started venturing up West there was never a shortage of really good live music events to attend. In my own manor we had some marvellous local venues and some of those became Mod Mecca's by the mid 1960s. Places such as the Wykeham Hall, Nimbus, Willow Rooms and Ilford Palais would attract scooter guys over a very large radius and some of those places played host to a lot of future stars. The High Numbers (pre- The Who) played regularly here in 1964 as did Steve Marriott's Moments and The Birds featuring a future Rolling Stone.

Music has been prominent in my life from the very earliest memories. At the age of seven (in 1956) I can distinctly remember Skiffle music (Don't You Rock Me Daddy O), Teddy Boys and early Elvis records amongst other Rock and Roll music. The drum break in Hound Dog astounded me as a nipper (and still does). I was drawn to drums even back then and also remember being mesmerised by that great snare/cymbals sound of Little Richard's 'Keep A Knocking'.

My parents bought and played a lot of music on our Bush record player on which you could load 10 singles at a time. That was my birthing into the world of music, but by the time I was buying records myself, with my own pocket money, I was into almost anything American.

The first 45 I bought was 'He's A Rebel' by The Crystals and everything else the Phil Spector Wall Of Sound produced still sounds as good today (to me) as it did half a century ago.

My very first album was 'Hey Bo Diddley' on the red and yellow Pye International label. I think that was in 1963 and I still own it today and it's still in mint condition. It was always the American original songs I loved, even the early Beatles and Stones albums were peppered with US covers and I'd listen to them and then check the originals out which wasn't as easy back then as it is now. Google has made life so easy! While everybody was digging the Beatles 'Twist And Shout' and 'Money' I'd be listening to the Isley Brothers and Barrett Strong and so on.

Back in '63, while I was still at school, you never made a conscious decision to become a mod. It was just fashionable at the time and one just tended to drift into it. If I'd been born ten years earlier I'd have probably been a teddy boy!

In those formative years you didn't even think of particular clothes or music as being mod, it was just of the day. The mainstream mods and rockers rivalry thing started with the tabloids and the fighting on the beaches stories in 1964. Myself and my mates were very proud to be called mods by then but we would disassociate ourselves with the street level guys on scooters that were just out for a punch up. We saw ourselves as a bit above that. Yeah, we were snobs! We were peacocks that wouldn't contemplate messing our clothes up or indeed the hair by even kicking a tin can in the street let alone fighting on the beaches of wherever. I wouldn't even sit down in an empty railway carriage for fear of messing the crease in my trousers. Clothes wise, early on it was all about being suited and booted, tonic mohair being preferable, but by '66 it was largely smart casual with Fred Perry (type) shirts being popular. It wasn't all about names though as it seems to be nowadays. You'd be pretty happy to buy a Fred Perry type shirt from your local High Street it wasn't considered essential to have the label. As Steve Marriott famously told Nicky Horne in a 1985 interview when asked "How did success change you?", and he replied " Well, I stopped going to Woolworths and went to British Home Stores instead!". By 1967 attire was a lot more flamboyant with silk neckerchiefs and satin shirts the choice of the day.

My favourite clubs from around 1965 were The Marquee, The Scene and the Lotus Rooms. The Marquee in Wardour Street in particular. Did you know that they never even had a backstage loo at the time, so quite often punters would find themselves peeing next door to somebody famous! A little bit later than that I'd add both the Uppercut and Tiles to the list. I never went to the Flamingo probably because I never used to do the all night thing and that place didn't open 'til about midnight. A lot of the guys would go straight there from the Marquee or wherever, but I always seemed to be chasing my last train back to Romford!

I didn't know Guy Stevens personally, but remember him quite well from The Scene club which was owned by the same guy that ran Radio Caroline. I remember Guy playing lots of fairly obscure American records and remember jotting titles down and then trying to buy them myself at Imhofs in New Oxford Street.

A couple of titles that stick in my mind are 'Pills' by Bo Diddley (quite apt) and a track by Big Dee Irwin called 'Happy Being Fat', which I've only just become re-acquainted with 50 years on through the wonder of YouTube.

John Hellier was destined to encounter a band of young mods who were also musicians and a fan's love affair began that would shape John's life for many years to come.
In music, traditional jazz in Britain gave birth, via Lonnie Donnegan, to skiffle. Skiffle became very popular because it was a music that was simple to play and the instruments to play it (with the exception of a guitar) were either inexpensive or could be homemade. Many singers and musicians started their careers in skiffle bands. The most celebrated were The Beatles. They were a skiffle band known as The Quarrymen prior to conquering the world.

The Quarrymen were not the only skiffle band to produce sixties legends. **JOHN HENRY DEIGHTON** had a band called John Henry's Skiffle Group made up of friends from school: We formed when I was about 12 or 13 years old after we'd heard these skiffle records by the likes of The Vipers. We started going to the West End to the 2Is Coffee Bar after school and sit in and watch the likes of Tommy Steele and Cliff Richard. Anyway, we entered and won the All England Skiffle Championships at the Tottenham Royal. Skiffle only really lasted about 18 months and the skiffle band kind of broke up. Then came rock 'n' roll. I found a great guitarist called Bobby Taylor, who really influenced Jimmy Page. Now my favourite car at the time was the '54 Ford Thunderbird, so it was an obvious choice for my next groups name. We started playing gigs everywhere. We'd get in our little van and do places like The Club-A Go- Go in Newcastle or The Twisted Wheel in Manchester. We used to travel everywhere just to get known. There were so many clubs in those days, you could work everywhere. On top of that we had the all-nighters and the afternoon sessions at The Flamingo Club. We were doing about 13 gigs per week. To give you an example, on a Saturday we'd do Reading University at 9 o'clock, get off stage by 10, get the van packed up (including a Hammond C3 organ!) and drive all the way to the West End. We'd unload it, take all the equipment downstairs into The Flamingo and do the all-nighter. Then we'd do the Sunday afternoon and Sunday evening as well. Come Monday we'd be in Newcastle. It was nuts!

And so Chris Farlowe and The Thunderbirds emerged from a humble all-conquering skiffle band. The success of The Beatles and manager Brian Epstien's entrepreneurial spirit opened the door for the Mersey Beat sound. Intense media interest in Mersey Beat began a search all over the country for new 'sounds'. There was Brum Beat, the sounds of Sheffield, Manchester, Tottenham and the West Country. But the bands that were being pigeonholed had already been around for a while and were known locally.

At this point it is important to remember that in the late fifties and early sixties, the myriad leisure distractions and mass media of the 21st Century did not exist. Kids wanted and needed a place of their own. Very often these places were youth clubs run by local churches.

In metropolitan areas of course, night time venues like coffee bars, amusement arcades and clubs were more prevalent, but outside of London, Manchester, Birmingham and Liverpool, the church youth club was the only place to go and they became important conduits of style, taste and trends.

As a classic example, take a designated 'new town' like Crawley in West Sussex. From 1963 to October 1964, Crawley had three venues for local youths too young to get into pubs. Eric Corrie ran the 'U2' club at the Civic Hall, Marie Grainger organised 'Beat and Blues' at St Margaret's Church hall but most significantly, Mick Rogers hosted the 'Mojo Club' at the Northgate Youth Centre.

Among the bands to grace the stage at the Mojo Club were; John Lee's Groundhogs, Alex Harvey Soul Band, The Soul Agents, Graham Bond Organisation, The Animals, Pretty Things and Zoot Money.

In one memorable night on 4 September 1964 Crawley played host to John Mayall's Bluesbreakers at the Mojo and Graham Bond Organisation at U2.

Another band who appeared at the Crawley Mojo Club was Long John Baldry and The Hootchie Coochie Men. Baldry had been playing blues and R&B for a few years and he noticed the explosion of bands that used the Blues Incorporated template as the basis for their own styles and sound.

On 17 July 1964, Long John Baldry arrived at The Mojo with the band, and a young Scot

who he had met just seven months before, but who had got himself named on the bill. **LONG JOHN BALDRY**'s recollection of that first meeting was as clear as it was on that night: It was January 7, 1964, a Sunday I believe. I was on my way from Eel Pie Island and I was standing at the train station at Twickenham. It was a very cold, foggy night and I could hear the sound of a harmonica being played down on the platform. So I went to investigate. It was the riff from 'Smokestack Lightning' which was a big tune at the time. And it was Rod Stewart playing. I said "we're back at Eel Pie Island on Tuesday, do you fancy coming down and having a play?" He came down to jam and then joined the band. In fact he joined the band the same night Cyril Davis died. It was very strange. I hadn't heard him sing until he did a couple of songs, 'Bright Lights, Big City' I think was one of them, the Eddie Cleanhead Vinson song, and the crowd loved him. Although he was intensely shy back then, you wouldn't believe it now to see him. The crowd loved him. That was it. I said that we should capitalise on this, so it became Long John Baldry and The Hoochie Coochie Men with Rod 'The Mod' Stewart.
It was actually Ron and Nanda Leslie, who used to run clubs in Ipswich, Norwich and Manor House who nicknamed him Rod the Mod. You know promoters, looking for an angle. It was at one of their clubs that I first saw Inez and Charlie Foxx. It was Ron and Nanda that brought them over and they did an interval act for us. I think it was while we were still just The Hoochie Coochie Men. So they made their debut on one of my nights.

Eel Pie Island in Twickenham, Surrey was another popular club with mods. Bought in 1952 by Michael Snapper, an antiques dealer and hired out by Arthur Chisnall to be used as a club venue, the Eel Pie Island Hotel opened its doors as a jazz club with the Ken Colyer band in August 1956. Membership of the club was an Eel Pie Passport; to get across, you had to use a chain ferry until a bridge was constructed in 1957. To get in you had to pay an old woman by the name of Rose sixpence at the toll booth to get a hand-stamp and cross the bridge. Among the regulars at the Eel Pie Club was Trevor Bayliss who would invent the clockwork radio many years later.
As mentioned, the big cities had venues like Manchester's Twisted Wheel where bands could ply their trade. More importantly, those bands were listening to Roger Eagle and

Guy Stevens not only playing new R&B, but particularly in Guy Stevens' case, being given reel-to-reel tapes of tracks recorded from Guy's collection to listen to and learn how to play. Chris Farlowe still has some tapes given to him by Guy, to this day.
Another band which began their music career as The Boys, backing Sandra Barry, went through a line up and name change. They became The Action in 1965.

Drummer, **ROGER POWELL** explained how they acquired their repertoire:
We got them through Mike Evan's mum who worked for EMI, so she used to get us all these obscure records. We weren't really into mainstream Tamla, we were into Stax and really obscure stuff. There was also the DJ at the Twisted Wheel (Roger Eagle) in Manchester. We used to go back to his house after the club to hear them and Guy Stevens used to give us stuff. That's where we got a lot of the info. Then we'd learn them and try to put our own little spin on them.

The tracks the bands learnt and recorded often ended up on their own LPs. The curious fact about The Action, was the lack of a Top 20 chart hit. It was a combination of circumstances that prevented that all-important breakthrough as **ROGER POWELL** explains:
We knew we needed a manager as we needed publicity to get gigs. We'd built up a really good following on the circuit and could've carried on just doing that but Marquee Artists and Rikki Farr obviously wanted to make money and get the right record for us because we were on £100 a night and once you had a hit record you'd be on £500 or more and go to gigs in cars, have roadies and stay in nice hotels. But none of the records I felt were anything near a hit record or anything edgy enough that people would remember. We never felt comfortable going after a hit, even though we went along with it putting records out, but they weren't really doing anything. I think "I'll Keep Holding On" got to number 39 in the charts. It wasn't disheartening because we were there for the music; we weren't there for the hit record, although all the people around us were getting them: the Kinks, the Small Faces, the Who, Spencer Davis Group, Manfred Mann. It seemed everyone we played with at the Marquee had a hit record except for us. I think because they were doing original stuff and doing covers,

we never got an original cover. Something like "Ride Your Pony" would come out in America and someone else would do it in England. At the time we didn't consider writing our own songs as there was so many cool records to explore we just enjoyed playing them. If we'd had an original cover first we might have had a hit record.

It was not just musicians who visited places like The Twisted Wheel or The Scene for inspiration. As **ROGER EAGLE** explained:
I'd be playing tunes in the club and people like Rod Stewart and those guys would be listening. Peter Stringfellow used to come over and write down the name of every tune that I played. I didn't really know what was going on. I wasn't sharp enough business-wise to realise what I had going. I'm not bitter about it because I am absolutely committed to the music. It means so much to me.

Not long after Cyril Davies had passed away, Long John Baldry, with Rod Stewart and the rest of the band were booked to play The Twisted Wheel. It was their first date at the Brazennose Street venue and Rod's debut with the band as **LONG JOHN BALDRY** recalls:
It was his birthday too. I think he celebrated it either there at The Twisted Wheel or the following night at an all-nighter in Henley. Our experience at The Wheel was that they always booked us for the all-nighter, so we never got started until about one or two o'clock in the morning. You had to carry on until 6am. I don't know how we had the stamina to do it.

JOHN WATERS from London explains how the relationship between the bands and the mods worked:
It was definitely a London thing with the Small Faces. Then if you look at say, The Animals, in London, they were regarded as anything but a mod band. They were very popular with mods in London, but not a mod band. The Spencer Davies Group and The Kinks were also very popular early on. Their use of R&B covers got us interested in the originals, but The Rolling Stones were very influential for me, their early stuff anyway. It was The Animals, Kinks, Spencer Davies, Rod Stewart and Long John

Baldry, Steampacket, all those bands, they got you interested in music and then you'd find the originals of the songs they did. Our local band was The Equals before they hit the big time, and they would play in the corner of a local pub doing Chuck Berry covers before they did reggae stuff. John Hall used to play drums for them and he hung around with us for a while. Guitarist Patsy Calvey was also a mod. Eddie Grant was the brains behind the band though. He was also responsible for The Pyramids and their single 'Train Tour To Rainbow City' which was a big mod favourite. The trouble is, you didn't pay much attention at the time to who was on. I wish I had paid more attention now.

The Allstar Club in Liverpool Street was a good black club, but The Flamingo really started it all for me. There'll never be anywhere like The Flamingo again. The California Ballroom at Dunstable was another great venue.

There was also a place at Kettering Football ground called 'The Tin Hut' because that was what it was, a tin hut. They had the Four Tops on there. I had mates who'd go up to French's in Kettering. That was like the other side of the world to me back then.

On Friday 31 August 1962, arguably one of Britain's most celebrated nightclub owners, began his career in earnest with the teenage demand for entertainment. Peter Stringfellow introduced Dave Berry and the Cruisers at St Aiden's Church Hall in Sheffield. Within four weeks, he had renamed it the Black Cat Club. The Beatles and Screaming Lord Sutch were among the acts Peter booked. That was followed by the Blue Moon Club (another church hall) and as Peter began to establish contacts, bands like the Kinks, Long John Baldry and the Hoochie Coochie men with Rod Stewart, the Searchers and Wayne Fontana all played at the Blue Moon. Rod Stewart formed the Soul Agents and returned to the Blue Moon. It was Peter Stringfellow's recollections of Rod Stewart that highlight how much influence these bands had on young people. Rod was the first person Stringfellow had ever seen with backcombed hair.

By 1964, The Who, Small Faces and the Yardbirds had played the club, but Peter Stringfellow really put himself on the ' map' by opening The Mojo Club. The aim was to be part of the rhythm and blues scene that was already established in Manchester and

London. Whether Peter knew it or not, he was booking bands that were firmly adopted by mods. It was not just UK acts but soul and blues stars like Ike and Tina Turner, Wilson Pickett, Sonny Boy Williamson and Ben E. King, all of whom played at various times from 1964 to 1968 at the Mojo. Having realised early on that he needed music to fill the gaps between breaks for the bands and wishing to promote a band he was managing, Peter played records. This eventually landed him a DJ warm-up slot on Ready Steady Go. He co-presented one show and stayed for a year until his club interests in Sheffield took precedence. One band that appeared on that same episode was The Action, as **ROGER POWELL** explains:

I think we did it (RSG) three times. We did it with Peter Stringfellow who was brought down from the Mojo Club in Sheffield to compere and we played a couple of songs live on there. It was the first time anyone played live on Ready, Steady, Go and it gave us that appeal for the mods on the circuit and we got a really good following from that.

The man who succeeded Peter Stringfellow at Ready, Steady, Go was one Paul Gadd, later to resurface in the seventies as the now-disgraced and convicted child-sex offender Gary Glitter.

As for the bands, it was quite usual in the early sixties to find The Kinks playing places like Redhill Market Hall. All the bands would travel insane distances, very often overnight from one end of the country to the other just to play a gig. Church Halls were still important for live bands by 1965, as **JOHN WATERS** remembers well:

The Who were at Holy Joe's Hall in Archway. It was actually St. Joseph's Church Hall, but Holy Joe's was how it was known locally. Anyway, The Who had just had hits with 'Can't Explain' and 'Anyway, Anyhow, Anywhere'. It was packed to the rafters. We led a contingent of about 60 local mods down there and The Who brought the house down. They'd just released 'My Generation' and did the obligatory wrecking of the stage and equipment, then the fights broke out. I got caught with a right hook and came round under a pile of chairs, looking at a load of girls taking cover halfway under the stage. After the show, we went to 'The Cat' pub next door to the church, and The Who came in as well and held court. Needless to say Keith Moon was louder than anyone.

As **CHRIS FARLOWE** explains, the highways and by-ways of Britain were littered with bands plying their trade wherever they could:

The Blue Boar Services at Watford Gap was a meeting place for all the bands. You'd be coming home at three o'clock in the morning, pull into Watford Gap and there'd be The Who in there or The Stones or The Kinks. There'd be wrestlers like Johnny Quango and all those others on their way home from a wrestling tournament. That kind of thing.

It was at Blue Boar Services some years later, that Reg King, lead singer of The Action, was arrested for threatening behaviour with a plastic knife!?

LONG JOHN BALDRY remembers the punishing schedules of those days:

Most bands double gigged, sometimes triple gigged. I remember even quadrupling, that was a real killer. Through a weekend, doing four dates a night was a little too much. It usually culminated at The Wheel because they didn't care what time you started, so long as you had the stamina to keep going until six in the morning.

The explosion of new bands plying their musical trade meant more often than not, that the band had spent some time in the cities, particularly London. As a consequence, they took the current trends and fashions out on stage and to the uninitiated locals who had little idea what mod was or meant.

JOHN WATERS certainly recognised where it was originating:

There was much more opportunity for live bands back then. Nowadays, live music is nonexistent what with discos and the like. Back then, everywhere had live music on, all the pubs and youth clubs. I used to pass Rod Stewart two or three times a week in the street and think nothing of it. He used to live up the road from us. I'd see Eric Burden a couple of times. We had a drink with The Who after a gig one night, Keith Moon and the rest of them just having a drink with the lads. They were just breaking then. I wish I'd known Rod Stewart was going to be as big as he is, I would have made more of an effort to talk to him. A lot of them were down-to-earth though and Rod was very influential. Definitely a top, top mod. In London, I think the groups had a lot to do with it. They were very influential, but it definitely started on the street. The bands just travelled around a lot. La Discotheque was the place we used to go and that was a real dive. They used to have mattresses thrown in the corner at one time. I never saw it in the light; it was always so dark down there. I'd hate to think what it was like in light. The only thing I ever saw at La Discotheque was an old car radiator and headlights on the wall. Where that came from I don't know, but it was all very basic. They never had flashing lights or anything like that. It was the atmosphere and the music that made it.

ALAN FLETCHER, a mod from Newark explains how the influence had impact and difficulties:
We used to go to The Dungeon Club in Nottingham. It was THE mod club for me. It was in the basement of the Drury and Edwards Lace Factory in Stamford Street, Nottingham. The building was taken over many years later by the Paul Smith company. We'd see all these outrageous styles and you'd just get into the ethos of it all. I don't think there was a waking moment that I didn't think mod. Where I grew up there were only half a dozen of us. There was a lot of pressure from people who conformed to the Everly Brothers type suit and slick back hair. We were walking around with hair brushed up in an exaggerated French Mod cut. We'd get "You ponses! You puffs!" We just had to soak it all up. I used to avoid trouble like the plague. I couldn't see the sense in it. I was into it for the music, the clothes and the scooters. The other clubs were The Beachcomber in St. Mary's Gate in Nottingham's Lace Market, the Union Boat Club, the Nottingham Boat Club and the Britannia Boat Club. It was the Britannia that was patronised mainly by mods, and just down the road in West Bridgford was The Dancing Slipper that had a reputation for putting on good blues and jazz acts. There was a disco every Monday night at The Bowling Green Club in Newark, which most kids went to, although this was not exclusively mod like the other Nottingham clubs were.

LONG JOHN BALDRY certainly remembers those same Nottingham venues:
I used to like the boat clubs in Nottingham. They were always very enjoyable. Also The Dancing Slipper. The Twisted Wheel was always a treat although somewhat

exhausting to do. The Mojo in Sheffield was another. In fact, I guess it must have been '65, we were at the Mojo when Joe Cocker made his first ever appearance.
He got up with a local pick-up band during our intermission. That was the first time I met Joe. Sonny Boy Williamson was very much a mod favourite, especially when he wore those weird suits that he had made up, and the bowler hats and things. He had all the tricks, like playing the harmonica through his nose. One night at The Marquee, he got so loaded; he actually started playing guitar. None of us had any idea that he could actually play the thing. So he picked it up and started thrashing around on the floor with it, spinning it around making all kinds of incredible noises, long before Jimi Hendrix. All those guys had the ability to play guitar. Howlin' Wolf was able to play a decent guitar. We accompanied him and Hubert Sumlin, who was another great mod favourite at the time.

What is certain is that apart from The Who, whose adoption of the mod aesthetic was purely for commercial purposes, there was no such thing as a 'mod' band in the early sixties, merely mod favourites. **ALAN FLETCHER** agrees with this theory:
The true mod band is something of a myth - like the great American novel. It's out there somewhere. No one knows exactly who or where. I suppose the nearest thing to a 'true' mod band would be the Small Faces, who were actually mods before they started. The Who became mods as a result of management policy. I suppose in the end though, with bands like The Who and the Small Faces, the distinction between the audience and the performer blurred until therewas really no distinction at all - something akin to the punk ethic when it came along a decade later. The whole mod thing in terms of music and fashion is defined by the intimacy and affinity of audience and performer crammed together in the small clubs of the time.

This theory is borne out by **ROGER POWELL**, drummer with The Action:
Someone once said we were in the lap of the mods and I thought it was great. That's how it felt. They'd meet us on their scooters and we'd meet them in the pub before the gigs. We were like mates; there was no differentiation between us and the audience.

We were all regular guys; we didn't put on airs and graces. However, I don't think people had this idea; this thing called 'mod'. It was just smart blokes. We used to like mohair suits and very smart Italian clothes. We never really had a concept of what it was. I would say we were a sort of soul band.

Most, if not all the musical acts from the British Beat era were mainly inspired by American Rock and Roll or R&B. Take a look at the track listings for many of their debut albums and you will find a plethora of U.S. cover versions with a British beat sound.
In reality, certain bands were merely adopted by mods. It was the mods who decided which bands were 'in' and which were 'out'. Mods briefly flirted with The Beatles but dropped them after their first album. The same was true of the Rolling Stones. However, some bands managed to retain the fickle mod following.

For **JOHN HELLIER**, it was one band in particular:
The Small Faces had me hooked on the image from the first time I ever saw a picture of them. They sounded great, of course, but with them it was about so much more than that. I'd buy all the girlie mags of the day, Rave, Fab 208 etc, just for the photos and then I'd shoot up to Carnaby Street or wherever and try to buy a shirt like Steve or Ronnie were wearing. The image was one of Mod perfection for me and I still get a buzz nowadays if I find a picture of them that I haven't seen before (as does Mr Weller). I saw them more times than I heard them! Club gigs were fantastic, just like East Ham meets Memphis but pop package tours of the day would be different completely. They'd be in a cinema or theatre and they'd do about 20 minutes worth of hit singles. It was Beatlemania all over again... didn't hear a word!

Fran Piller started the Small Faces fan club for Don Arden until he unceremoniously sacked her. Fran Piller's young son would become one of the most celebrated mod entrepreneurs of all time. The girl to replace Fran Piller was **PAULINE CORCORAN**:
I wanted to change my job as I hated the previous one so much. I went to loads of employment agencies and told them that I wanted to work in either the theatre or the

Sydney [photo © Kirstin Sibley]

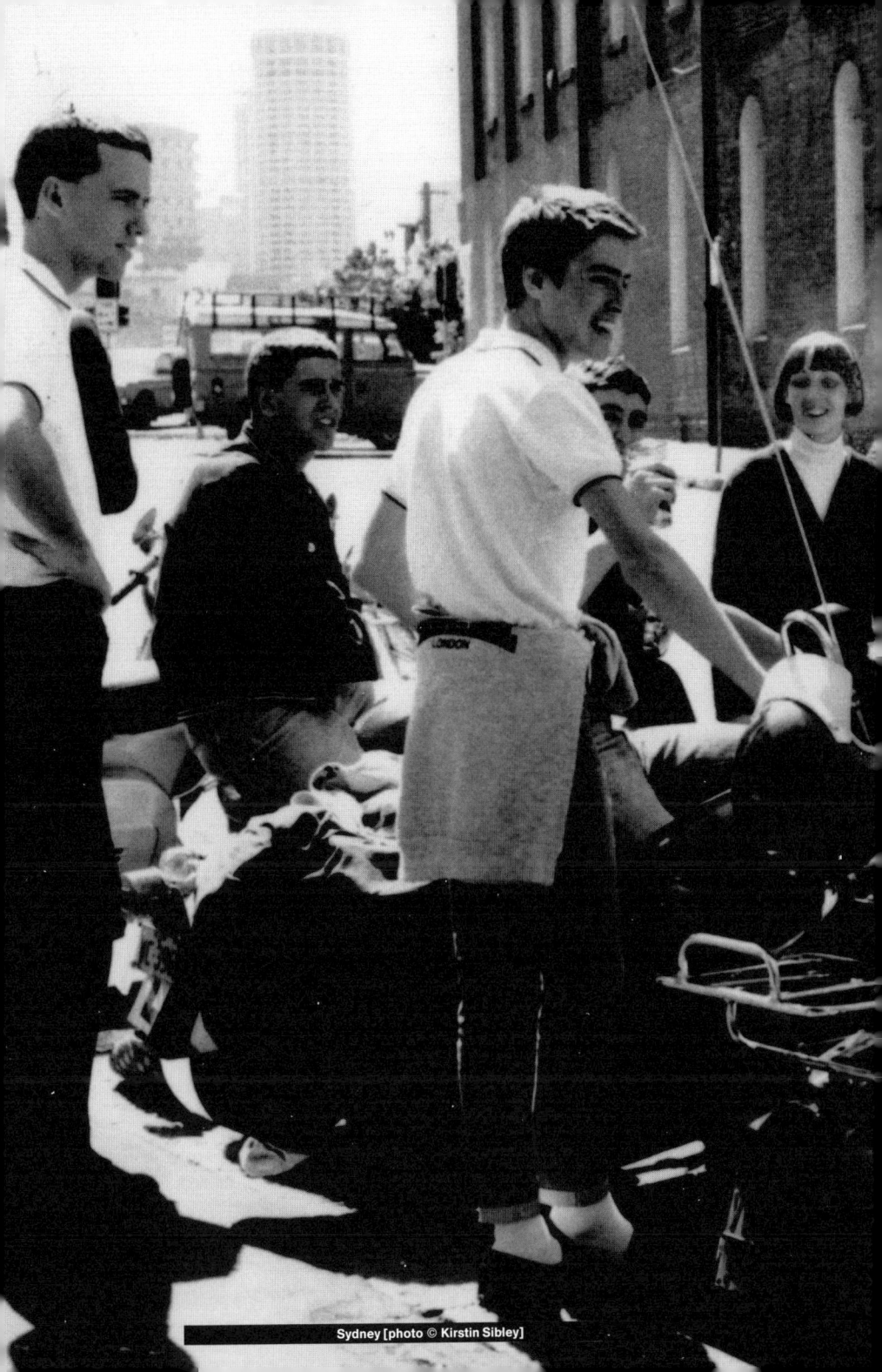

music business. They both appealed to me and sounded exciting. Anyway, one of them sent me for an interview with Don Arden in Carnaby Street. I had never heard of him before but one of my friends told me that the job vacancy was for running the Who's fan club. I loved Roger Daltrey so I was very excited about the prospect, however when I got to the interview I was told it wasn't for them at all. It was for a new group called The Small Faces. Their first single 'Whatcha Gonna Do About It' had just been released and Don, during the half hour interview, told me that they were going places. Don was very convincing and told me that he purposely wanted a non-fan for the job so as not to be in awe of the boys, just be there to do a good job. He said "Can you start on Monday?" and I did.

I met them immediately I started my new job in the office. They were a bunch of fun loving guys and always messing around. Don told me to go and see them play so I went to the Marquee in Wardour Street and was very impressed. I hadn't realised just how good they were. The place was rammed and there were screaming hysterical girls and I just felt so proud to be working with them and being part of the team. Steve and I clicked straight away and it was Steve that always led the way in the band.

Arguably, if any band could legitimately be classed as 'a mod band', it would have to be The Small Faces. In his autobiography 'All The Rage', the late **IAN MAC MCLAGAN** pointed out this very fact. Ian had seen The Small Faces on Ready, Steady, Go:
They were playing their first single 'What'Cha Gonna Do About It'. It was August 1965 and they were rocking. And they were mods, not like me, the art-student type in brown corduroy jackets and blue jeans without a pot to piss in.

But it is here that Mac highlights another fertile ground for future mod favourites; the collages and further education establishments that expanded in the late fifties and early sixties and gave school leavers with no idea of what they wanted to do with their lives a safe haven while they sorted themselves out.
Many entrants to further education took the relatively easy option of art classes. Art colleges were the perfect environment for creative people to find themselves even if

they had no interest in art as a career choice. But the lessons learnt at art college were to manifest themselves in pop culture later in the sixties.

To get an idea of how important art colleges were, here is a sample of those who, now revered as rock, pop and mod legends, started off as humble art students: John Lennon, Keith Richards, Chris Dreja, Eric Clapton, Jimmy Page, Pete Townshend, Ray Davies, Andy 'Thunderclap' Newman, Eric Burdon, John Steel, Roy Wood and Christine Perfect, to name a few.

Colleges were ideal because of the relaxed regime. The student common rooms became musical battle grounds where middle-class bohemian types with a preference for trad jazz and an emerging folk scene would fight for control of the record player with working class students with a desire for blues and R&B.

In addition, collages provided ideal practice venues for bands, but these bands needed to play live and there was no shortage of opportunity for bookings, especially with the hundreds of youth clubs and dance halls all over the country clamouring for new sounds in the wake of the Beatles success.

The real prize though was a residency at one of the top clubs in the country. The Flamingo in London was one such; where playing to a packed house every night gained valuable exposure. **JEFFREY KRUGER** remembers the host of famous names who played The Flamingo, as well as some famous customers in the audience, and a now celebrated music entrepreneur who worked in the club:

On the early sessions it was everybody from Tubby Hayes to Tony Crombie, Ronnie Scott, Ian Rendle, Tommy Whittle, who ever was there in the British Jazz scene played there, if they didn't play there they weren't anybody. It's like the time when the Moody Blues manager came to see us and said "Look, we're bringing them down from Birmingham and you are publishing the song 'Go Now'". It was their first attempt at a hit. We put them on at the club, but we couldn't on weekends, we were full, so we opened Wednesday evenings. The first night we put them on, there were 25 people there and all of them were from the record company.

We didn't even cover the electric bill. The second week it was like 100 and by the fourth or fifth week we couldn't get through the door, so the club helped records and records helped the club.

Chris Farlowe played regularly, the late Peter Bardens, though with different groups like the Chaineys, they played Jimmy Reed songs, had Mick Fleetwood on drums. Then Peter appeared with a group called Them, an Irish group with lead singer Van Morrison, and I don't have to tell you what happened to him. The next time he came back he was called Peter B's, then he returned as Shotgun Express with a new vocalist, a young Scottish guy by the name of Rod Stewart, and then of course Peter, who never hit it big, put a group together in the seventies that worked for us, they were called Camel and they were promptly successful. Who else played there regularly? The Animals, that was when Alan Price was on piano, Chas Chandler on bass, Long John Baldry, Ronnie Jones & The Q Set, Herbie Goins & The Nightimers, he had John McLauglin on guitar in those days and John Paul Jones was on bass and the blues were sung by Mr John Mayall, so they all got their start there.

Others included John Lee Hooker, Garnet Mimms, Lee Dorsey, Rufus Thomas, Otis Redding, Inez & Charlie Foxx, Little Richard, Jerry Lee Lewis. There's many more. The Yardbirds were always down there, Wilson Pickett, Deep Purple, Stevie Wonder, Status Quo, Geno Washington and The Ram Jam Band, and you know in Zoot Money's band was Andy Summers from The Police, Led Zeppelin and The Who. Spencer Davies appeared down there, Ben E King, Bo Diddley, I remember his name on the work permit was Oather Ella Speights McDonald, and I never forgot that one, Major Lance, Freddy King, the Platters. As for celebrities, you want a list? My God anybody from Hoagy Carmichael to Mel Torme, Billy Eckstien who'd finish the Palladium and come down and play trombone, Sarah Vaughan, Adelaide Hall, Ella Fitzgerald, Frankie Laine, Billy Daniels, Dizzy Gillespie came in, my friend Errol Garner, BB King, But you know we'd got the hoi-polloi in, Harold Robbins the author, Lord Spencer Churchill, a lot of Royals came in. Jimmy Witherspoon, Bill Haley, when he was over, The Supremes played there, Howlin' Wolf, Patti Labelle, Ike & Tina, they played there four or five times, there were so many of them there are too many to remember.

CHRIS FARLOWE has good reason to remember his time at The Flamingo:
That was our club. We didn't have a residency, but as our manager (Rik Gunnell) ran The Flamingo all-nighters, he got us down there whenever he could.
It was THE place. There were cinema seats down at the front and because the American GIs were still over here at the time, they'd all come down in their soul suits and they'd bring records for you.
One night, I was singing for an hour and a half and my manager came up to me after I'd finished and said "Did you see Otis Redding watching at the front there?" I said "Nah, that weren't Otis Redding, that was a GI". So I went back to the dressing room and started changing. There was a knock at the door and Otis Redding was standing there. "Hi Chris". He said. I thought, 'oh bloody hell!' He said "You're a great singer man, you're a soul brother. I want you to be on my TV show". So that's how I got the gig for the Ready Steady Go! Otis Redding Special. He invited me along with Eric Burdon. It was a spur of the moment thing on his behalf.

Chris, in an interview for Shindig magazine, expanded on his association with Otis Redding; 'We did three concerts together. He told me I was a "soul brother". One of the Barkays told me he must really like me because he doesn't call many people that. I was really knocked out. We got on a storm. During the Stax Volt tour of 1967 I went around with them watching the whole tour. We went to a night in Boston (Lincolnshire) and just as we pulled into town I saw a big poster on the wall saying "Otis Redding and His Band plus Chris Farlowe & The Thunderbirds". It was a great show. Even today when I tour people come up and say, "I was there that night".

Another story that has attained legendary status, is the night the World Boxing Heavyweight Champion decided to pay a visit to The Flamingo Club, as **JEFFREY KRUGER** recalls:
Henry Cooper's wife had a restaurant just along from where Ronnie Scott eventually had his club, which was the turning opposite. You come out my front door and it faced you. I don't know if Henry came down with Cassius Clay or told him about it, I don't remember, but I was not there. I did get a call to say he'd come down with an

entourage and was it ok? I wasn't actually there but it was in the News Chronicle, which was a daily newspaper at the time.

JEFFREY KRUGER also had a certain Andrew Loog Oldham working at The Flamingo behind the burger stand during this time:
Andrew Loog Oldham worked there. I don't think anybody, including Andrew knew him very well. I wished him luck when he started the Immediate label. I felt he mixed with the wrong people, but that's just my opinion. Then he got very esoteric, was it then that he met Marion? I don't remember, but then I didn't have much to do with him.
Indeed, Andrew Loog Oldham confirmed his time at The Flamingo in his autobiography, 'Stoned'.

When not on stage **CHRIS FARLOWE** was a regular member at the club:
I used to go down The Flamingo on Friday and Saturday nights. I'd pick up my membership paper and there'd be 'Tonight - Larry Williams and Johnny Guitar Watson'. I'd say "Should we pop down and see these two then?" (laughs). There'd be Solomon Burke one night, John Lee Hooker and Jimmy Reed another, there'd be Nina Simone, you could go down there every night and see someone. You'd also get bands like The Stones in the audience and every night it would be packed. Lots of Jamaicans. It was an amazing place.

Certainly the Beatles created a climate for a new and vibrant youth based attitude. The media could not get enough of the fab four, as their numerous appearances on radio and in both music and mainstream papers will prove. But undoubtedly, television was the key to unleashing the new mood on an unsuspecting public.
The concept of a music-based youth TV show was not however, a new idea. In the fifties programmes such as Cool for Cats, Oh Boy and Six-Five Special had limited runs. They were pale imitations of America's Bandstand. Mostly the acts featured were home grown and Cliff Richard in particular became a household name as resident singer on Oh Boy. In August 1963, the Redifussion Television Company redefined youth and music shows

in Britain. When Ready Steady Go (RSG) began broadcasting on the ITV network, it was not with a bang, but more of a solid, purposeful start. The acts on the debut show were not typical of the final show in 1966. Nor were they the kind of acts that mods would flock to see. In truth, it would take a few months of trial and error to get the format and balance right, but when they did, it was one of the most popular shows of its time. As with all programmes of its type until Top of The Pops emerged on BBC TV in 1966, its host was Keith Fordyce, a middle-aged symbol of parental control, much like the people who ran the local youth clubs.

Before too long, Fordyce became an irrelevance to the show as fresh-faced Kathy McGowan emerged as the main host.

When Ready Steady Go proclaimed "The weekend starts here", it inevitably did for thousands of young people all over the country. After the initial teething problems, the shows producers tapped into the bands that were popular in the London area, and particularly bands that had a mod following. It was not long before The Beatles and Rolling Stones were making way for Georgie Fame, Rufus Thomas, The Yardbirds, The Animals, The Who, The Kinks and many other acts from the British Beat phenomena and hitherto unknown Americans.

Ready Steady Go was the first to present special showcases such as the Tamla Motown edition 1964 and the Otis Redding Special in 1966.

RSG set the standard and the BBC followed with their own show Top of The Pops.

The presenters on TOTP were popular radio and club disc jockeys such as Tony Blackburn and Pete Murray. The format for TOTP was to feature songs from the Hit Parade performed live on occasion or mimed in the studio.

What TOTP did not have was the mod kudos of RSG. The 'Faces' or top mods would be seen in the audience at RSG, and from these mods sprang the inspiration for others to follow. The clothes and dance steps were meticulously copied. RSG's resident dancers Patrick Kerr, Sandy Sergent and Teresa Godfrey would be regular visitors to The Scene Club in Ham Yard, picking up dances and moves that they could replicate on the show.

ALAN FLETCHER was one of the regular viewers. The fact that the show's dancers got their moves from the mod clubs gives credence to Alan's assertion that RSG's influence was not all one way:

What is equally important is the impact of mod culture on Ready, Steady Go! Apparently the producers used to trawl round the Soho clubs - The Scene, The Marquee, and hand out tickets for the show to the kids down the clubs and thus they ensured the audience was as hip and cool as possible. Mods used to watch RSG, not just for the acts, but to pick up on any new fashion trends or dances being displayed or performed by the mainly mod audience.

Ready, Steady Go! was an influential programme, but the whole thing about mod is that it had its own energy, its own kinetics, its own driving force. Mods made fashion on a street level basis. There was none of this designer label or 'must have' clothes mentality. If Woolworth's or C&A were selling something which fitted in with the 'look', then you'd buy it from there and not think twice about it.

RSG would often allocate time to discussing what was 'in' or fashionable in any one week. **KEITH RYLATT** was perhaps a typical RSG viewer:

You'd see something on Ready, Steady, Go on a Friday night and you'd have to either adapt things or just hope that a little shop in Leeds would get some tabbed shirts or hipster trousers in. RSG was the main thing that you watched and you'd scrutinise every inch of the screen.

George Melly recognised the importance of RSG. He remembered seeing small mining communities in Yorkshire where fashion trends were almost five years out of date and in the borders of Scotland, the girls' dresses had hardly altered since the middle thirties. RSG changed all that.

JOHN WATERS remembered one particularly amusing offshoot from RSG:

It was at The Marquee. Someone had the bright idea of putting out a show on Radio Luxembourg called 'Ready, Steady, Radio'. It was a Sunday night and the format was similar to the TV show. Keith Fordyce was the compere and the night started with a set by Gary Farr and The T-Bones. (Gary was the son of heavyweight boxer Terry Farr.) They did a 20-minute set that was not featured on the radio. The first guest of the evening was Sandie Shaw who, after a few words with Keith Fordyce, went into her latest record. To our amusement she was miming on a radio show! What was the point of her being there? However, the main stars were the Righteous Brothers. After the obligatory interview, they did a couple of numbers.

Although their songs were being recorded for the radio, they sang live over the tracks and they could really sing.

This also highlights the other media to win mod support. Before the pirate radio stations, Caroline and London began broadcasting, the BBC was by-and-large the only radio choice. The pirate stations won the mod audience by being less formal in presentation, less restricted in content and far more experimental than the BBC would ever dare to be at that time.

They moored at sea beyond British jurisdiction and helped to promote R&B and Motown. Ronan O'Rahilly, who owned The Scene Club also owned Radio Caroline. The station began broadcasting in March 1964. Needless to say, when the BBC finally caught up and used its influence with the Government to ban the pirate stations, it also poached the best talent as well. The line-up of DJs to present BBC Radio One looked like a who's who of the pirate stations. John Peel, Tony Blackburn, Kenny Everett, Dave Cash, Johnny 'Emperor' Roscoe.

By early 1964, the media interest in mod was becoming greater, but only as a curiosity. The newspapers and current affairs programmes on TV were fascinated by this new youth culture. The media also worked wonders for some of the mods adopted singers and bands. **CHRIS FARLOWE** explains how he benefited from media exposure and mixing with mod favourites:

I used to get loads of mods in the early days because of the club work. I got involved with Stevie Marriott and the Small Faces. They even wrote a couple of songs that I recorded. At the time you knew everyone. I knew The Who and Pete Townshend.

So, when they all started getting famous, I was involved in it and I was getting famous too. I've still got press cuttings from those days. There's one, 'Stevie Winwood, Chris Farlowe and Bob Dylan spotted chatting together in The Speakeasy Club'. As a result of things like that, you got people buying your records that wouldn't normally have done. Steve Marriott and Ronnie Lane were great guys. They liked me as a singer and that's what's nice about this business. When you're regarded as a good singer, or even a great singer, by people like Eric Clapton or even Otis Redding, you know you're there. I've got a front page of a 1966 Melody Maker where they're interviewing Paul McCartney. They ask him for his views on the upcoming year and he says "Chris Farlowe will definitely make it big this year". Now when you get that, it's all you need. A kind of seal of approval.

The media investigated and marvelled at the apparent arrogance of these mods, this young and new post-war generation that had no direct relationship with the war itself. The mods were directed by their desire to acquire material goods. They wanted the best clothes, the smartest transport, and the latest records; in fact they had money and were ready and willing to spend it. The fashion trends changed weekly if not daily. Even mods themselves had trouble keeping up, particularly those who were not on a good salary or not permanently in the centre of London where most of the trends had come from initially. But the constantly shifting nature of mod fashion generated inspiration and creativity in others outside of the capital city.

ALAN FLETCHER explains the process for mods in the provinces:
You'd take aspects of it and make it your own. You'd see a guy perhaps wearing a polo neck shirt under a Fred Perry. He probably wouldn't be a mod, but it would look good, so you'd get it and do it yourself. You'd watch and then to some extent exaggerate it. Like when suits first came in, it was the length of the centre vent that defined you. It gave you street cred. It would be 15,16 or 18 inch centre vents, and you'd notice if someone had the wrong length. Also the slant of the pockets. It was the detail that made it so exciting. You were continually reinventing yourself. That's what it boils down to.

The downside to the spread of mod across the country was the almost inevitable arrival of commercialism:
The main thing about the first mods was that they were true purists in terms of jazz music and clothes. The focal point for the new generation was a hitherto unknown back street in London's Soho.
Much has been written about the growth of Carnaby Street. Its story has become the stuff of legend. While it is true that John Stephen helped to create its popularity by supplying to the new demand, it was not long before true capitalism rubbed its eager hands and moved in. Patronage by some of the most high-profile pop stars of the day just added to the sense of wonderment along Carnaby Street.

The day after **IAN MAC MCLAGAN** joined The Small Faces, the four of them went shopping along the 'Mecca for the mods':
We went from John Michael to Topper's, and then onto Lord John. It was incredible. Topper's was the place to buy wild Italian shoes. No other shoe shop came close.

The Small Faces manager, Don Arden had set up accounts at all the stores along Carnaby Street for his clients and it took some time for the band to realise what they were doing was spending their future meagre earnings. **PAULINE CORCORAN**, who was running the Small Faces Fan club also went with the band on shopping trips:
When it was my lunchtime they'd drag me out. They'd go mad, they wouldn't take one shirt off the rail they'd take handfuls in all different colours. They must have spent an absolute fortune. Shoes, leather jackets... they'd just help themselves. A lot of the clothes never even got worn; there were always loads of shirts still in wrappers around the house. Sometimes they'd say "What size is your brother? Here take these for him". He was only about 15 and I'd bring him home all these Small Faces clothes. He was over the moon, still talks about it today. Fans would just stare at them whilst shopping but they never got any hassle in the street unlike gigs. I used to travel with them quite a lot in the beginning but after a while I started travelling on my own, the hysteria was frightening. I remember one particular time in Lewisham when I

was travelling home with them. There were literally hundreds and hundreds of girls outside the venue. There were bouncers, but not enough of them to cope with those numbers. I got in the car first, but the boys literally got clawed to bits, they really did. Inside the car it was so claustrophobic with fans pressing their faces and bodies up to the window. It's amazing how the windows weren't smashed. After that I told Don that I couldn't travel with them anymore. They loved all the adulation but then it got too aggressive. You couldn't hear a note they played above the screaming girls. That did frustrate them, I know it did. One minute I'm working with a group I'd never heard of and now all this! They were always dressed very smartly in a mod casual type of way. I'd quite often go round the house unexpected at all times of the day and they'd always look immaculate. Most managers would say to their band "You've gotta look smart 24/7" Don Arden never had to do that.

For some bands, like The Action, it was the complete opposite as **ROGER POWELL** explained:
We bought our clothes ourselves. There's a picture of us outside Harry Fenton's, once we'd put the clothes on and had our photograph taken we had to put the clothes back. The strapline read; 'The Action supplied by Harry Fenton, but they never gave us anything. It was the same with drums. If I wanted to play Premier drums I had to buy them. You needed a hit record before they'd give you anything. Keith Moon got a contract with Premier.

For **LONG JOHN BALDRY**, at six feet seven inches tall, Carnaby Street clothing was not an easy option:
I always kept ahead with the fashions, but because I'm so large, very rarely could I go to Carnaby Street and pick something off the rack. I've got abnormally long arms and legs, so anything that I wore would have to be made. It was rare for me to go to John Stephen's and buy off the rack, but I do remember one time I bought a very long black coney overcoat and had them put on an extra piece along the bottom. I had that coat right through the sixties and seventies until it got stolen. 15 years I had that

coat, which John Stephen had actually done up for me as a freebie. He used to give me quite a lot of things if I would wear them in photo shoots. A lot of bands would do that. One particular instance where they did go out of their way to make up something larger, they were very bold striped suits that Rod (Stewart) and I had made up. Cotton summer suits, white with a dark blue stripe. More like pyjamas than suits! We wore those in '65. Before that in '64, we went for the whole tartan look. I remember we'd got some Royal Stewart tartan trews, and of course that was right for Rod, but I had no right to be wearing Scottish tartan! We'd got that set-up together for a trip to Scotland where we were playing Aberdeen and Inverness and the like.

In Birmingham, **GILL TAYLOR** and boyfriend **DEL EVANS** were making occasional trips to the capital:
Before Del and I started going out, he would go to Ken Colyer's club in London which became the Marquee. A lot of photos that are online were taken on the Embankment or Trafalgar Square in London. We would catch a train from New Street Station on a Saturday morning and we would go to London. I would make sure I wore a different outfit every time for the photos.
We went just before it all really got going. We came out of the tube station and asked a street sweeper where Carnaby Street was. He said 'I can tell you how to get there, but it's a real scruffy place!'. When we finally got there, there wasn't much going on. John Stephen's shop and Mod Male was open, but that was about it. The shop assistants looked great with back-combed hair and one had eyeliner which we thought was quite cool then.
That was the day we went from there to Trafalgar Square and took the photos of me in the leather two-piece with the round neck top. We used to go to London quite regularly to have a look round and Del might buy a few things, but I never bought for myself. I have never wanted to wear something other people might wear as well. By 1965 of course, it was totally different, it had become the place everyone recognises and all the other shops appeared. We only went for day trips.
By the time it got to 1965-66, we would go to places like Torquay which had quite a

> Personally, I wasn't too keen on scooters. I mean, we wouldn't be seen dead in a parka. I can see the reason for wearing them, keeping your clothes clean and keeping warm, but they weren't for us. We never went anywhere by scooter, we always got a taxi or a bus.
>
> JOHN WATERS

big mod scene and Bournemouth too for weekend trips. The club in Torquay we went to was The Scotch.

For like-minded serious mods, retaining the original modernist style meant going to shops like Clothesville 1.
By 1963 **JOHN SIMONS** was expanding his horizons. His friend Mark Russell opened a shop and John became the Display Director, while starting a new venture with another friend Jeff Kwinter:
We started doing market stalls around '63. We bought paisley shirts, polka dot shirts and that sort of thing from East End wholesalers. We were just trying to make a few bob really. Gradually I found this Greek dressmaker. We would unpick American imported shirts and jackets and she'd put them together for us and we were trying to sell them in the markets like Petticoat Lane. We wanted cheap versions of American originals that we could sell to kids in East London. This is what led to the first shop.

John and Jeff were dealing with a manufacturer whose factory was next to the Hackney Empire. The factory had a huge entrance that was not being used, so John and Jeff suggested they use the entrance as a shop. They designed and sold the clothes that were made by the manufacturer and worked on a commission. The manufacturer was Matty Marley as **JOHN SIMONS** recounts:
We'd design the clothes in the morning and Matty would have them made by the afternoon. It was incredible. Matty's wife used to call him 'Horse and Genius'. 'Horse' because he was a big tough geezer and would carry cloth up and down the stairs all day and 'Genius' because he could make a pattern of anything you told him to. He wasn't actually a creative person, but he was a really good pattern designer. He gave us the shop entrance and 'Clothesville 1' was born.

Clothesville 1 became one of the first, if not the only true mod shop. John Simons was using his influences to design clothes for mods:
I took my Burberry raincoat and did it in ten different colours of corduroy. Then we

shortened the Burberry and gave it a button-down collar and button-down pockets and that became very popular. It was a pot pourri of influences. It was Burberry, Cecil Gee and so on. It wasn't a purist Ivy League look. That didn't come until the Ivy Shop, but it was a good mixture of influences and was quite creatively interesting. Other people were doing similar things though.
Brent and Collins were doing stuff in Romford (that was Sid Brent). This was the beginning of mod, the fusing of modernist with mod.

By 1963, John Stephen had become very wealthy. He owned shops across London and was making deals to go into Europe and America. John Stephen's business was said to be worth £1 million and the Daily Mirror called him 'King Carnaby', the Observer dubbed him the 'Million Pound Mod'.
Some have argued that John Stephen was not an original or creative designer. In the same way that John Simons was using influences to produce variations on a theme, John Stephen was selling round-neck jackets (Pierre Cardin had the original concept), leather jackets, fleecy sweaters (Brioni) and hipster trousers (worn in St Tropez for years).
While John Stephen and the rest of the Carnaby traders like Warren Gold and Irvine Sellers took to commercialising the street, serious mods who kept a watchful eye on the situation moved on to pastures new. Carnaby Street became a circus invaded by tourists by the thousands. John Stephen became less influential, but he hung on in Carnaby Street into the 1970s. Fair-weather mods (those usually from the suburbs or too young to mix with the big boys) believed the media hype that Carnaby Street was the place to be. Sadly, it has never been the same since and probably never will.

But while Carnaby Street suffered from it's own success, **JOHN SIMONS** and his Clothesville 1 shop was going from strength to strength. So much so in fact, that John and partner Jeff Kwinter were asked to expand the business:
We founded Clothesville 2 in Walthamstow, which was just along from where Stanley Adams had his first shop. We were doing more of the same in both Clothesville shops. Not long after that we saw these other premises. I used to go for coffee at the

L'Auberge, which was a famous coffee bar in Richmond. (The Rolling Stones used to go there.) So we went to Matty Marley and said "Why don't you open a shop in Richmond?" He said no, so Jeff and I decided to have a go ourselves. Jeff was engaged to a girl whose father was very influential and fortunately he guaranteed the lease. We would never have got it on our own. It was £14 a week and we never had to look to him to help us with it. We paid it from day one, but he underwrote it, so The Ivy Shop was born.

We had Albany shirts, which pre-dated Ben Sherman's by quite a long way. Our first American shirt was Dickeys. They were known as Dickeys 'Tigerfoots'. They were ace shirts. We got in touch with Titon Garforth who were an English shoe manufacturers. They used to sell us their sub-standard export shoes, which were brogues and plain caps. We never had loafers at that time. We had Levi Sta-Prest and Fruit of the Loom sweatshirts, which were lovely thick cotton then.

While the serious mods distanced themselves from the new younger mods, the media's interest in the mod phenomena began to dilute it. They used the term indiscriminately. Mods once shopped at Carnaby Street, so it was mod. The Beatles were mod, David Bailey, Anthony Armstrong- Jones, Mary Quant, the Chelsea Set, Jean Shrimpton, the Austin Mini, Chelsea boots, it was all mod. By 1965, the term had lost all meaning and relevance. Because of this thousands of teenagers became mods without knowing what the real concept was. The media told them they had to have a parka, a three-buttoned suit, desert boots, a Fred Perry tennis shirt, a Who record and, of course, a scooter.

Even fashion photography was getting in on the act. People like David Bailey and Bryan Duffy were gaining recognition for their work, but as Duffy admitted to the Sunday Times Colour Supplement in 1964 they were... imparting an attitude, a look, a stance, a way of expression of a body, which one hopes... people will adopt. We'd spend an evening in the East End... watching mods and rockers... I wouldn't go down there consciously, thinking I'm going to observe them and then come back and do a fashion picture from their attitudes of standing, but one finds one does'.

So here we find another of the 'swinging set' using mod influences to make their name in the 'Pop Age'. Without being properly informed and not really bothering to find out more, a new lumpen mod faction grew. These teenagers weren't bothered about real mod values, they were hanging around in dance halls, getting into fights, and buying into everything Carnaby Street had to offer, which was not much at all, apart from being cheap and tacky. It is from this background, that two of the most enduring images connected with mod first came into the public domain. In truth, the connections to mod are somewhat spurious, while connections to 'Pop Art' are more realistic.

Two pop art images that were very popular were the Union flag and the roundel or target. From 1963 the Union Jack could be seen on mugs, trays, alarm clocks, plates, cushions, tea-caddies, tablecloths, bedspreads, carrier bags, tea towels, aprons, handkerchiefs and clothes.

The roundel motif also appeared on numerous items of merchandise. Even the title sequence of Ready Steady Go included a target. The Who had become almost the archetypal Pop Art band. Pete Townshend was photographed wearing a 'Union Jacket' and drummer Keith Moon often sported a target T-shirt. With the band's now legion mass mod following, the demand for the Union Jack and target motifs was considerable and has since become the classic insignia of mod when it really belongs to Pop Art.

This blurring of boundaries between mod and Pop Art has overshadowed modernism's true influence and sustained the myth of mod as merely a youth cult of four years in the early to mid 1960s. Mods invented the concepts of style and taste within their group from music, dance and fashion to the customising of scooters. It came from the street. Mods were not participating in pop culture; pop culture was lifting ideas from mods and profiteering from it. Nigel Whitely correctly observed that at a time when the original pre-war modernist movement was being heavily criticised in the academic world, there were more reproductions of modernist design and more demand for it than at any time previously.

Perhaps The Who are the most significant manipulators of the mod aesthetic. As previously mentioned, with Pete Meaden's help they assumed a mod mantle, but they were by no means the only ones. Mark Bolan's musical career began while he was a mod. Initially as a solo artist and with bands like John's Children, mod helped Bolan establish himself in music. But a few life-long contemporaries of Bolan's also used the mod tag as the platform to launch their careers.

David Jones was not a mod when he fronted David and the King Bees. With the commercial failure of 'Liza Jane', released in June 1964, Jones left the band and joined the Mannish Boys from Maidstone, Kent. The Mannish Boys were playing Eel Pie Island and the Flamingo Club by the time David Jones joined them. Despite some modest successes both live and recorded, which included tracks like 'I Pity The Fool' produced by Shel Talmy, The Mannish Boys began to falter and David Jones was on to his next venture. The Lower Third came from Margate and were formed in 1963. They auditioned for a new member in 1965 at La Discotheque. Steve Marriott of the Small Faces was watching and joined in a jamming session with David Jones
and the band. With Jones in place, he began to influence the band's direction.

The Lower Third began copying The Who's sound. A change of management led to The Lower Third adopting the mod 'look'. It was as a member of The Lower Third that David Jones changed his name as there were already many acts using the name David Jones. Jones became Bowie and the Lower Third used one of his songs as a track for a recording session. 'The London Boys' tells of pills, depression and the loneliness of London for an out-of-towner. It was certainly a popular tune at the band's live shows, but again failed to make the chart breakthrough.

Within a few years, David Bowie had ended his association with The Lower Third and mod, only to resurface as a solo performer by 1968.

Rod Stewart followed Long John Baldry to his next venture after the Hoochie Coochie Men folded. Steampacket were arguably the first 'supergroup', even if they did not realise it at the time, Baldry and Stewart teamed up with Brian Auger, Julie Driscoll. They never officially released any material (although demos and live recordings do exists)' but they gigged almost constantly for a couple of years before splitting. Baldry had a successful solo career. Auger and Driscoll formed Trinity. Stewart joined Shotgun Express with Peter Bardens and Beryl Marsden before finally teaming up with The Small Faces after Steve Marriott left that band.

Others like Bowie, Stewart and Bolan, who found fame and fortune a decade later included Elton John with Bluesology and The In-Betweeners who became Slade. It is not so-much about mod, but more the climate of the Sixties, that gave these eventual superstars a chance to start their careers. Some flirted with the mod image, some did not. Most dressed in the styles of the times which were mod-influenced. It did not necessarily make them mods. They might have had a mod following, but again, it did not follow that they could be labelled as such.

But the sheer impact of mod, music, radio and television of the sixties meant it was becoming a major influence on very young kids and it was being exported to other parts of the world.

In the late 50s and early 60s Australia, courted immigration from Britain to their shores with the promise of a wonderful sunshine-filled living. Many who took up the offer found themselves in Adelaide. Thanks to his fascinating book 'Top Fellas', Tadhg Taylor has identified the origins of mod down under and its eventual metamorphosis into a home-grown youth cult of its own. Although the surnames of interviewees are missing, there are important contributions that explain how mod made its way across the globe and had an impact for years to come. **RANDY** was one such migrant to Australia:
I came to Adelaide from England in 1959. I became a mod when I was in high school. Mod happened in a big way in Adelaide, there were even a lot of scooter gangs which wasn't really the case anywhere else in the country except maybe Brisbane. At school I'd say in a class of thirty, about twenty five would've been British working class, from the north and midlands. Places like Elizabeth and Adelaide Hills were full of English immigrants. To come from those harsh industrial cities to Adelaide, which was really beautiful then, was amazing for them. Every three weeks a new boatload of immigrants would arrive and the kids would tell us about the latest fashions and bands, consequently we were never that far behind what was happening in England.

Some of those British kids who landed in Adelaide began to move out into other areas, Melbourne in particular, and there the exported mod influence began to change youth

culture. Melbourne was still rocker country in 1963, but by '64 the mod style was taking hold as **DENNIS** explained:
There was a lot of emphasis on clothes because of the mod thing in England. We were working class guys dressing up, we didn't have much money, but at least we looked like we did. The point was always to look sharp. That's why people started calling us 'sharpies'. We never called ourselves that, you were just one of the 'fellas' or not one of the 'fellas'.

The emerging style was not to be foppish or dapper. It was all about being and looking sharp. There were also many Italian migrants in Australia and their style influenced the young Sharps as much as the mod scene did. The Sharps were obsessed with Italian style and it was at its strongest in the areas where there was a strong migrant population which usually meant shops that stocked the clothes and shoes would be in abundance there too. Going out to dance for a Sharpie meant wearing your finest suit, usually in dark colours, pinstripes, herringbone or tonik. The jackets were three-buttoned or double-breasted worn over a Ban-lon or Crest-knit shirt which was very similar to the tennis shirt or polo shirt which had also become popular in Britain around the same time. Also very popular were white single-breasted trench coats. The shoes were known as 'points'. Although the basic shape was the same, 'points' came in a very wide variety of styles and colours. Flat or Cuban heeled, suede or leather, chisel-toed, two-tone or alligator skin or weave patterned. 'Points' were the shoe of choice.

The Sharpie cult was not exclusively a male environment. Girls got in on the act as well, but unlike the prevailing trend in Britain, Sharpie girls opted for their own style. They avoided the Mary Quant look as **DALE** explains:
I left school at fifteen and got a job, which got me into being a sharpie girl because I could afford to buy clothes and go to dances. There were tailors in Richmond who'd make your trousers. I had a grey pinstripe pair. The first jeans I bought I had to get from the menswear department at Myers. Sharpie girls wore round-necked dresses, sort of woollen material and short-sleeved.

At the time it was all short skirts but we wore knee-length pleated Sun-Ray skirts in pale pinks and blues. We had darker colours for the winter, but we were very straight and sophisticated.

The hair was of the short Mia Farrow/Cilla black style. Twin sets were popular, worn with pearl earrings and necklaces. The girls also followed the boys in the trench coat fashion stakes. However, the Sharpies style which began with mod tendencies, was transforming into something else with influences that harked back to a by-gone age. In Melbourne, the style of the 1920s and 30s was in the ascendency with Sharpies. There was a hint of 'Larrikin' about them in terms of their general demeanour and behaviour. Larrikins were under-class, slum-dwelling gangs of the very late nineteenth century and were involved in all sorts of gang and criminal activity.

While the Sharpies of the 1960s could not be accused of the same criminality at the beginning, the gang-mentality was taking hold and a hierarchy developed. The guys who were both the most respected and most feared became known as the 'Top Fellas'.

By 1966, Melbourne was a Sharpie stronghold, but there was some confusion as to what defined a Sharpie from a mod. **PETER M** helped to explain:

In 1966/67 when I was about 15, I became a mod. Being mod was about sartorial elegance, you dressed the way you believed was super-smart and particularly noticeable. That didn't mean you went around in outlandish clothes, you just needed to look like you were paying a lot of attention, not just to your appearance but to everything that was going on. Sharp Italian suits, loafers, short hair - that was the quintessential mod look, which peaked in England around 64/65. For some reason, and I can only put it down to the tyranny of distance, that look lingered in Australia for some years and that's how the people I mixed with dressed. But at the same time the average Australian's idea of mod was long hair and outlandish clothes, while the people who dressed in the original mod style were called stylists.

Australian mods music tastes mirrored those of their British counterparts. Soul and Rhythm and Blues were much in favour, bands like the Chelsea Set and the Purple

Hearts, Billy Thorpe and The Aztecs were favourites, but by far the biggest band of all was the Easybeats.

From '62 to '63 four young migrants had found themselves at Villawood Migrant Hostel on the outskirts of Sydney, where new arrivals were housed until they were processed to move into the wider society. Harry Vanda came from Holland, Stevie Wright's family was from Leeds. The Young family (all nine of them) included George Young and came from Cranhill, Glasgow. Gordon "Snowy" Fleet arrived from Liverpool with his wife and child and started out at East Hills Migrant hostel.

Tony Cahill was the only Australian. He grew up in the suburbs of Melbourne.

It was their second single "She's So Fine" that launched them to national stardom and by the end of 1965 they were the most popular and successful pop band in Australia. Their concerts and public appearances were regularly marked by intense fan hysteria which was very similar to 'Beatlemania' and which was soon dubbed 'Easyfever'. During 1965 and early 1966, they released a string of hit singles in Australia, all co-written by George Young and Stevie Wright.

The group left Australia on 10 July 1966 to relocate to London where they were eventually paired with Shel Talmy, who had achieved great success with his production for the Who and the Kinks. One of the tracks they recorded with Talmy became their first big international hit, 'Friday on My Mind'. It sold over a million world-wide. The song also marked the end of the Wright-Young partnership. Harry Vanda replaced Wright as Young's song writing partner. They wrote and produced several major hits for other acts over the years and produced the first six albums for AC/DC which included George's younger brothers Angus and Malcolm.

While mods and sharpies co-existed relatively peacefully, the sharpie cult outlasted mods and thrived through the 70s and the early part of the 80's, but by 1984, the sharpies and top fellas had run their course. However, mod came back via yet another migrant family as we shall see later in this story.

There is much evidence to prove The Beatles and the 'British Invasion' did much to inspire young people around the world and those of a 'mod' persuasion, The Who, Small

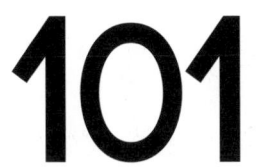

Faces, Kinks, took the image of mod to the far-flung corners. In New Zealand in 1964, Ray Columbus and The Invaders had a Number 1 hit in their home country and in Australia with 'She's A Mod'. Two years later, Columbus arrived in California looking for a support band. He found the Newcastle Five fronted by brothers **RICHARD** and **TOM FROST**. As Richard told this author in an interview for newuntouchables.com:

We just hit it off right away. We were mods one and all. As far as music is concerned I've journeyed through a lot of different genres over the decades, but the mod influence has always been there in one way or another. We were not the only ones though. I lost my High School girlfriend to a mod musician in Los Angeles. He's still a 'Dandy' to this day. I identified with Pete Townshend taking his youthful anger and frustration out on his guitar and pulled in by his cool chord changes, melodies and lyrics. I was a troubled teen myself and expelled from high school three out of four years for refusing to cut my hair. I grew disdainful of authority and The Who represented a voice for me. The band was a refuge away from society. The mod culture provided a place of belonging and gave me an identity that was different to everybody else. We never tried to mask ourselves as a British band, but there weren't many of us playing that style.

The nucleus of the Newcastle Five, who became Art Collection, would then move with the times later in the sixties and the Frost brothers would be a part of one of those great legendary stories from the music industry as we shall see later.

So while mod was making its presence felt on the other side of the world, it was still having an impact on young kids in Britain who were mere infants and juniors through the 60s, but this influence would not manifest itself until the late seventies. Many kids became hooked on music at a very early age.

ANTHONY MEYNELL is perhaps typical of the kind of kids who would have the indelible mark of mod and sixties culture heaped upon them:

My sister Kathleen is older than me, and she was a mod in 1964-65 and I was only six years old when this was happening. We lived in New Malden in Surrey and one of her first jobs was with Decca in the pressing plant and she used to bring home all the test pressings. I didn't realise the relevance at the time, but we had adjacent bedrooms and she would play these records while getting ready to go out as any 15 year-old would. My brother and I would sing along to these records, like you do when you're five or six, because we loved the music. Our house was full of music and of course The Beatles were a phenomenon and with a 15 year-old girl, who wanted to be a mod in the house, her friends would come round and they looked so glamorous, the boys and the girls. We were mesmerised by this.

Anyway, at the time the Decca plant was pressing the Decca label, Immediate, Capitol, Stateside, Tamla and we were hearing these records before they came out. So in a way, it was unavoidable that I would be into that kind of music. Although The Beatles were my favourites, I had such a soaking of soul music and I have still got all those records. A couple of years later, when my sister got married, I bought them off her for two quid or something because she didn't want them anymore. She was a mod, but she lost interest when she married and settled down, so I had them, and until my brother and I could afford to buy our own records, these test pressings were all we played.

We were total pop fans and my older brother had a guitar. He is left-handed and he couldn't get to grips with it, so I figured out how to string it right-handed, taught myself how to play and kept it. Now, I don't know how or why, but a friend of my sister left a snare and bass drum at our house for some reason, so my younger brother got into that and we would thrash along to records.

That's really how I got into mod. It was music mainly. As I got older I got into my own stuff, and then when I played in school bands it kind of stayed with me and between bands I started writing songs and that's where it came out.

In northern England, **PAUL WELSBY** was another young lad who was being exposed to the delights of black music via slightly older female family members:

I was looked after every Saturday night by three female cousins - while my mum and dad had a night out at the local labour club. Inevitably I ended up with the youngest of these sisters Lynne - who begrudgingly dragged me along to the local youth club, where I first encountered the then current sounds of Motown (My Cherie Amour, I Heard It through The Grapevine) and some of the revived-Motown sounds that were popular at that time (Put Yourself In my Place, This Old Heart Of Mine). Lynne and her gang used to meet up and knock around with boys who had scooters. I remember always being impressed by their ariels and foxes tails!

Clearly this stuck with me as I got a bit older and started to buy the Motown Chartbusters LPs and the odd single or two, which then developed into a fully fledged love affair with all kinds of black American music.

Without question, the proliferation of soul music was having a marked influence on mods. It began the lasting and varied relationship mods had with the black community and black culture.

For mods, black culture in the form of music, has always been a focal point. From acts like Miles Davis and the Modern Jazz Quartet to the entire Tamla Motown stable, mods have a great affinity with black music. It could be said that the common denominator was the working class backgrounds of both communities, but it is hard to see how young working class white boys from Britain could really have an empathy with lyrics produced by a journeyman blues player from the Mississippi delta.

However, mod's ability to feel the music without necessarily relating to the subject matter meant that black music became an important part of the mod culture. In true mod tradition, the craving for a new record or black act from the United States became as much a part of being mod as clothes and style had. Also, mods continued to move on, dropping a tune or act once they had broken into the mainstream, and transferred their attentions to lesser known singers and songs.

This demand for the rare was taken on wholeheartedly in the north of Britain and evolved into a scene that stood alone, driven by this desire for the elusive.

The mod relationship to the black community also can be seen in stark contrast to the attitudes of the teddy boys of the late fifties who were instrumental in the Notting Hill riots of 1958. The teds were overtly racist, as was much of the white population, and although mods may well have used terminology now unacceptable, the general acceptance and recognition of black cultural worth was found in mod society.

Mods found black immigrants and US GIs a rich source of information, enlightenment and more crucially a conduit for obtaining those hard-to-find records from across the Atlantic. The West Indian influx into Britain brought with it new sounds, new culture and a sense of life to the country. The black community brought calypso in the fifties, but for mods, the really exciting sounds of blue beat and ska typified modernist desires.

Blue beat and ska was popular among the rude boys of Jamaica, who also had remarkable similarities with British mods, in that they had taken on the Ivy League aesthetic from the USA and adopted it to their own requirements. It was minimalist and slick with attitude.

The music itself came about as a derivative of influences from American radio stations broadcasting out of the southern states and in particular the city of New Orleans. R&B artists like Fats Domino, Professor Longhair, Buster Brown and Roscoe Gordon were particularly popular with the young in Jamaica. Local entrepreneurs such as Sir Coxone Dodd and Duke Reid started taking sound systems around the island playing R&B.

The rivalry to obtain new sounds from America became intense, but soon a home-grown version began to appear.

By listening to the American R&B artists and comparing it to records by Owen Gray, Laurel Aitken, Derek Morgan and The Blue Beats, it is not difficult to hear where the influences came from. The home-produced music made its way across the Atlantic to the black community in Britain. By 1962, the beat became so pronounced it required its own term. Numerous people have laid claim to inventing ska, but it has become a moot point. The fact is, it was Jamaica's first real homespun music and a worthy export for the newly independent nation. Ska also became known as bluebeat, mainly because of the Blue Beat record label founded by Emile E Shalit, a Serbo-Croatian businessman, also responsible for the Melodisc label.

In Jamaica, labels such as Black Swan, Rio, Studio One, Ska Beat, Dr Bird and Island became the most successful and the most sought after in Britain.

The black community also held blues parties, where exciting sounds could be heard from the street. These sounds found their way into mod clubs. While Millie Small was storming up the UK chart with My Boy Lollipop, the mod demand was for Byron Lee and the Dragonaires, Prince Buster or the Folks Brothers 'Oh Carolina'. Indeed, Prince Buster became so popular, he even had a 'bodyguard' of mods following him around Britain while he was on tour in 1964.

JEFFREY KRUGER already had black American GIs at The Flamingo for the all-nighter sessions, but they were not the only black people to frequent the club:
We attracted the West Indian population through guys like Count Suckle who played records. The first time I heard the Maytals was down there, the first time I heard Desmond Dekker or Dennis Brown was down there.
That's how the West Indian population came, but some of them could be trouble. We wouldn't let them in, they would offer me fortunes to get a membership card, but they looked trouble and they were trouble, so we let them go to their own clubs. Those that came in were the cream of the Jamaicans and if you say we were snobby, yes we were snobby, but I wanted to protect the music first.

ALAN FLETCHER acknowledges the influence black culture had on mod, even though the black population was sparse in many parts of the country:
Most of the music that the mods turned to was black music or covers of black music. I think there is also some crossing over of the colourful fabrics brought over by black immigrants in the 1950s into mod fashion - before that it was all white shirted. Having said that, the circles I moved in were white working class. There were very few black mods in the groups I encountered or hung around with, although it was their culture that was arguably the biggest influence. This is something I've never really been able to square, nor feel totally comfortable about, but that was the way it was back then in the mid sixties.
Mod to me was the mind's eye opened. It was the acceptance of an alternative life style in the form of what you could wear and a refusal of all things negative.
I think mod in its widest sense was the template for much which happened since in fashion, in music and the breaking down of previous prejudices, in the form of racial

tolerance, the breaking down of sexual, social stereotypes, or the ritual burning of the white sports coat.

JOHN and PAULINE WATERS saw two distinct sides to the race issue, more based on region than culture. As Pauline recalls:
We didn't have any black people up in Newcastle back then. We never had (racism) where I come from, because we never had that mixed race community. But we've brought our kids up to not have those sorts of (racist) attitudes. I suppose it was different for John being in London.

Indeed, JOHN WATERS did witness the other end of the race spectrum:
I don't think they mixed too well in those days. There wasn't much trouble, but you had black clubs and white clubs. The Ram Jam in Brixton and The Roaring Twenties in Carnaby Street, they were black clubs.
It was very strange though, because where I was it was very much gangs, big gangs of mods and they could be very racist. No black members at all, but there was never any trouble. They kept to their own clubs and so did we. There was no integration. It is a very strange situation, because you'd get all these mods slagging off blacks, and yet they'd go to clubs and listen to black music all night. There are people who are still like it now after all these years. A complete anomaly.
Back then in the early to mid sixties, the blacks were mainly into ska music. The mods tended to go for soul. Later on the mods got into ska and bluebeat, but at the start they were very separate.

While researching modernism, it is interesting to find that very little has been written about the black contribution, but they are not the only ones to be ignored.
Modernism and mods have become synonymous with males. It is portrayed as a male dominated culture. This is nonsense and a fatuous omission that girls had no part to play in mod culture. It is a sad fact that women are portrayed as 'dolly birds' in the context of the swinging sixties.

For ordinary, working class girls, the mod aesthetic was not easy to assimilate into a female context. It was very hard for girls to find a way into the mod environs, especially as mod boys were preoccupied with themselves, not as homosexuals, but as stylists and purveyors of taste and fashion.

Mod boys had little time for girls. Girls were expensive, in a time when boys were still expected to pay for a night out. Mod boys knew that they would not be judged by the girl on their arm, but the cut and quality of their suit.

However, girls did manage to integrate themselves, not so much on the boy's terms, but on their own terms. The mod girls were just as inventive and creative as the boys, perhaps even more so.

After all, mod boys relied on sisters to make alterations to clothes. With the necessary skills to make their own clothes and create their own styles, girls did not look out of place in mod circles.

PAULINE WATERS was a young mod girl from Gateshead in the early sixties:
Black soul music was my thing, I loved it. It was the music to dance to and it's stayed with me the whole time. You'd hear things on Radio Caroline that you never heard before, but it's the best music to dance to. The Club-A-Go-Go was the place to be in Newcastle. That's where I started.

I went to a place before that, but that was an old-fashioned rock and roll dance hall, and the kids used to go and dance to rock and roll music. It was just up the road in Gateshead. I can't remember the name of it now. But then I went to the senior school and that's when the YMCA became the place to go really.

They'd put live groups on there and also have someone playing records. We would also go to The Key Club in Birtley or a coffee bar in Coatsworth Road. I think the YMCA was important because of the music and the fashionable people went there.

The Sect were a mod-type band and I suppose at the age of twelve or thirteen and even though they were men, their hairstyle had an influence on me. I went total crop. The short hair was the style then, although Ready Steady Go and people like Kathy McGowan and Sandie Shaw were influential, but they had long hair.

I think it was a girl that came to my school that got me into it. I went with her to the Club-A-Go-Go. You could go there on a Saturday afternoon and I remember thinking when I walked in, 'My God, I'm in heaven'. The music was fantastic.
There was a girl there who was killed in a horrible train crash at Hither Green in the late sixties, and she was a top mod in Newcastle. She probably had a major influence on me, but I can't remember her name. She was absolutely perfect in style, a fantastic dancer and I thought, 'Oh I want to be her' you know? She was brilliant. That was it though, I was hooked.
But the music as well, that was fantastic. You never knew who was singing or what it was called because the DJs never said a word in those days. Then the live bands came. I had a fight with my mother to go and see Wilson Pickett, but she made my brother come and pick us up because it was late at night.
The mods I knew were real scooter fanatics. It was a scooter culture. They used to travel to London to get suedes and leathers because you couldn't get much up in Newcastle. Just about the only place we went for clothes was Handyside Arcade next to the Go-Go on Perry Street.
The boutiques in there had some really different gear. There were a few good shops, but we had a hell of a problem getting the clothes that we wanted.
A lot of people used to make them because you couldn't get them. We'd see things and think 'where can we get that?' But there were about half a dozen lads with fantastic scooters that were well-off who used to take orders from people then go down to London to get stuff in Petticoat Lane. You just couldn't get what you wanted in Newcastle at the time. It was starting to happen, but they were behind the times. The only decent thing you could get in Newcastle was shoes. We used to wear such short skirts and the tiniest jacket on the back of a scooter and you'd absolutely freeze. We never travelled far though on scooters. It was more an image thing I think. We used to sit there talking by the scooters. We'd go to parties on them but that was about all. When I think of some the houses that got wrecked at parties, I mean, it used be round people's houses when the parents had gone on holiday. They'd go on for days. You'd go home, get changed, go to work and then go back and start again. There was always

a party at the weekend, after the Club-A-Go-Go had closed at 2.30. If you didn't have a scooter ride, you'd walk miles and miles to get to a party, at that time of night as well, and you never gave it a second thought that something bad might happen to you.
The Club-A-Go-Go had a Jazz Lounge where you could get alcohol, and the other side was the Young Set as we called it, and that was soft drinks only. But the Jazz Lounge had live bands on and they also had jazz and blues on, but you had to be eighteen to get in. We got to know the staff quite well. We went on a Friday and Saturday at first, then we went in the week as well. The bouncers used to let us in and they'd stamp your hand. It felt more like a bar, and it was always heaving. You couldn't move. Alan Price used to play in there and he was resident at The Downbeat Club.
Chris Farlowe used to play The Bowling Alley in Gateshead. They used to put special guests on. It was a big part of the mod scene in Gateshead. I played a game of bowls with Chris Farlowe, then he went upstairs and sat chatting to everybody. He was a really nice bloke. I never did get to The Twisted Wheel in Manchester. We always intended to go, but never made it. My friend, Margaret Mowbray did, because she had relatives down there. She loved it. We definitely knew about The Wheel in Newcastle though.

Mod girls were certainly influenced by the top models of the time like Twiggy and Jean Shrimpton and designers like Barbara Hulaniki of 'Biba' and Mary Quant. In 1966 Mary Quant defined the female 'Look' as a total image:
What a great many people still don't realise is that the look isn't just the garments you wear. It's the way you put your make-up on, the way you do your hair, the sort of stockings you choose, the way you walk and stand; even the way you smoke your fag. All these are part of the same feeling.
You could forgive Mary Quant for reciting word for word, the unwritten mod book of style, if only she had not tried to pass it off as her own conception. Access to the media was and still is everything.
It is too often the case that people assume mod to be purely a 'London thing'. Nothing could be further from the truth, although the mod influence radiated out from London.
KEITH RYLATT from Leeds remembers how Ready Steady Go influenced young mods

Milano [courtesy of Daniele Savaré; photo © dominichinde.com]

from the provinces. Keith was in his teens in 1963 and explains some of the problems of being a provincial mod:

If you were in a working class town such as Leeds or smaller places like the mining towns you couldn't really dress that flamboyantly because you'd get beaten up. So you would need to modify certain things plus there wasn't the stuff available. You'd see something on Ready Steady Go on a Friday night and you'd have to either adapt things or just hope that a little shop in Leeds would get some tabbed shirts or hipster trousers. The key thing about being a mod in the sixties was that the mod uniform of hipster trousers, black and white shoes was a bit impersonal and certainly up north, people seemed to do their own thing a bit more and I don't think they stuck to that regimented look as much as they did in the south.

The availability of choice for mods in the north was very limited. All too often it meant a trip to London to get what you wanted. Again, **KEITH RYLATT** was one such mod who resorted to weekend excursions to the capital:

In Leeds there was a little shoe shop at the bottom of Brigate called Character Shoes, which did have some lovely things. There was a place called Bunnies in the arcade and C&As or Lewis's where you could get one or two nice things. In Peter Brunskills leather shop you could get suede jackets and Stylo shoes were popular.

But by 1965, we used to meet up at the top of Cloves Lane in the Corn Exchange and you could get a Wallace Arnold bus down to London if Leeds United were playing in London. So we would get on a bus at midnight in Leeds which cost about £2, and then you'd be in London for about six or seven in the morning and the bus would pick you up again at midnight from Paddington Station, so you had about 18 hours down there. A lad we knew from Wakefield called Rusty had a brother who managed one of John Stephen's shops. The first time we went it was to the one in Carnaby Street, then we went to the one in Kings Road. The best shoe shop was Toppers in Carnaby Street. Back then it really was the 'business'.

The trips to London with football fans gave Keith a real insight into the massive gulf between northern and southern style:

What impressed me most was when Leeds played Fulham, half the kids getting off the bus from Leeds would be dressed in studded leather jackets and filthy jeans with teddy boy haircuts, while the crowd from Fulham would be dressed in v-necks with polo shirts underneath and maybe Hush Puppy shoes. The south was mod. The north wasn't.

There was more than just a north-south divide with clothing. Taste in music was becoming wider. Although places like the local Mecca Lorcanos would play a diet of pop music, they began putting on soul nights as a means of boosting takings on traditionally quiet weekday evenings. In Leeds, Monday night at the Mecca or the Spinning Disc in County Arcade on Fridays would be soul nights. Soul music had a profound effect that would be felt for decades afterwards in the north. It slowly grew into a scene of its own.

KEITH RYLATT remembers its impact:
You'd feel totally different from the other kids. You felt you were better than them. It sounds really awful now, but you thought the clothes you wore were the business and the crap music they listened to was totally inferior to what you were listening to. Things like 'Gimme Some Lovin' by Spencer Davies Group and the whole Tamla thing. It was a minority because the Twisted Wheel had two floors and five decent rooms, and even when Ike & Tina Turner was on, they'd be looking at 750 tops. We'd go to the Blue Gardenia in Leeds and even though it was packed there must have been no more than 60 people there.

Older people would go to Manchester and certainly the Mojo in Sheffield. Bradford had quite a few clubs like the String of Beans, the Hole in the Wall and the Ambassador. You'd go to these places and then the following week they'd be closed. It was a tiny scene back then. In the bigger cities there were enough people to make it look as if there was a lot going on, but it was a minority really.

By contrast, **JOHN WATERS** recalls a typical weekend for the north London mods who had easy access to the burgeoning nightlife in the capital:
Friday evening kicked off the weekend. Three or four of us would meet at my mate's house to watch 'Ready, Steady, Go'. It played a vital role in the culture, as it was the

only TV programme that reflected the fashion and music that was so important to mods. From there it would be down to our local pub where another half-a-dozen mates would be waiting. Friday was definitely a night for 'pulling birds' and we would be appropriately 'suited and booted'. There was always a heated discussion about where to go. Some would go to the East End and pubs like 'The Two Puddings' or 'The Green Man'. Others might want to go North to Finchley or Muswell Hill or perhaps 'over the water' to the 'Apples and Pears' down the Old Kent Road. We would invariably split into a couple of groups and grab taxis to various destinations. Most of the pubs we went to had live bands.

We would normally meet up again on Saturday afternoon in one of a couple of places. Outside the tube station sitting on the railings, DeMarco's café or the Co-op that had a record counter next to the tea bar. I usually headed to Broadmeads where the girl that ran the record counter loved soul music. (She got sacked for selling too few records due to the fact she never ordered stuff by The Beatles and those groups.) A few of us would spend an hour or two in there listening to the latest from Stax or Motown, discussing all the 'birds' we didn't pull the night before. Saturday night was the big night. Meeting in the pub, we would head 'up West'.

First call would be the 'Coffee An'. It was a basement coffee bar situated in an alleyway at the bottom of Wardour Street. The entrance was a pub-type cellar door in the pavement. It used to be a beatnik place, but the mods commandeered it.

The next stop might be 'The Eagle' or 'The Intrepid Fox' on Wardour Street. 'The Fox' was particularly popular because it was close to The Marquee and the bands that were on there would have a drink in 'The Fox' as well. From there it was on to a club. For us it was normally La Discotheque. The entrance was up a flight of stairs. It was dark and dingy and always packed. They mainly played vinyl and occasionally put on a live band. We considered 'The Disc' as our club. There was a fragile truce between the various mod gangs in the West End, but I've no doubt other gangs felt the same way about 'The Disc' as we did. We were there for the music, to dance and get stoned. We did go to other clubs though. The Flamingo was my favourite.

Early on Sunday morning, you'd see a motley assortment of dishevelled mods leaving

the clubs. We would head for the 'El Passant', a first floor coffee shop on The Strand. It was packed with bleary-eyed mods, many on a 'come down'.
We would wander around for most of the day, sometimes having a sleep in a park if the weather was good. Then we would meet at a café and head off to the local Odeon cinema for a few hours and come out just in time for the pubs to open. After a few pints, that would be the end of the weekend.

IAN HARRIS, also from north London, describes how he came to be a mod:
I left school in 1963, I became a messenger boy for Fleetway Publications, which is now IPC in Farringdon Street, and there was a guy there who to my eyes was exotic, wearing a paisley shirt with a tab collar and this amazing bouffant hair and Cuban heeled boots with trousers just cut into the boots, all very specific. He was a messenger boy as well, but about a year older than me and he said he was a mod. So I asked him where he got his clothes, and he said there was a little street called Carnaby Street at the back of Oxford Circus and that I should check it out. Well, I was running around London all day and often in that area and I popped round to this side street, and there were four shops that were absolutely incredible, like Domino Male. It was a bit 'camp' and I wasn't sure whether to go in or not, but I had to. So I went in and bought my first pair of tonic mohair hipsters and that just started it for me. Then I had a jacket made for £5 per week and I used to spend all my wages on clothes. Clothes were vital, but the music was the most important thing for me.
From then I started going to clubs. There was a fantastic place called The Fenton Club in North London. It was just a Conservative Club hall, but I dressed up in all my finery and decided to go and Georgie Fame was on, and that was the first gig I ever saw. But anyway I was in the queue to go in and I didn't know you had to be a member, and when I got to the desk, the guy looked at me and said 'You've got to be a member'. And the guy behind me passed me his membership card, so I handed it to him and the guy on the desk said, 'What's your name then?' and I said, 'I don't know'. I mean, what a stupid thing to say, but he let me in anyway.
In the hall were these two guys I went to school with and they were dressed the same,

we recognised each other as mods and we started going out to places almost every night in the week. I used to give 30 bob to my mum and the rest was mine to spend.
I saw some amazing bands, usually at The Fenton. I saw Sonny Boy Williamson with The Yardbirds, Howlin' Wolf, Cliff Bennett, John Mayall pre-Eric Clapton and after when Clapton joined the band, and there might have been only 30 people there.
We could walk right down the front and they would play jaw-dropping music, and we thought Clapton was 'God', because it was just taking you somewhere else. Then there was Graham Bond who was the most superb all-round musician I've ever seen in my life. We used to say 'If only Eric Clapton would join the Graham Bond Organisation, that would be the most perfect band there ever was'. Then of course Graham Bond didn't look the part really. He didn't look like a pop star, he was more a muso-jazz renegade, but when Clapton joined up with Ginger Baker and Jack Bruce, that to us was like the epitome of everything in 1966, but going through the mod years, we'd see Rufus Thomas, and the fights we had in these clubs, well, we would get beaten up, not badly, but it wasn't by rockers, it was by other gangs of mods. That was what it was like then.

As mentioned earlier, the media have had an influence on the ebb and flow of mod over the years. When trouble began to flare up on Bank Holidays at seaside resorts, the media reacted, as Stanley Cohn argued, to the perceived deviant behaviour of a section of society. Oddly enough, this was not a new social problem.

Brighton is regarded as one of the landmark sites of the mod /rocker battles in the sixties, (a reputation enhanced by the film Quadrophenia in the late seventies), but it was not a new phenomenon.
Author Graham Greene had documented the riots and pitched battles in Brighton one Whitsun in his book 'Brighton Rock'. In fact those pitched battles between rival razor gangs at the racecourse were common occurrences in the 1920s and 1930s.
An elderly couple that Cohn interviewed in 1965 commented that the mods and rockers had less of an air of menace than their predecessors did.

JOHN WATERS identifies where the supposed 'lumpen' mod behaviour came from and the influences in London came from a surprising source:

There were gangs where I lived. Some of the gangs had a couple of hundred members all with their own areas. The one thing people seem to forget about is just how violent it was in the sixties. I thought it was a very violent time. People think mugging and all that is new. It isn't, it went on back then in London.

I know of people who were beaten up, stabbed, shot, but there wasn't the outcry then as there is now. People go on about Moss Side in Manchester and places like that, but there were areas like that in London. The thing is though, the gangs back then just happened to be mods. It wasn't because they were mods. Everyone was tooled up. It was the same with the teddy boys before the mods.

People like the Krays and the Richardsons had an influence on the gangs. We wanted to be like them too. You'd see them all the time in the papers and they'd look really smart, go to the best places, have the big cars and the fantastic looking women on their arm. That's where you wanted to get to. That was what the gangs wanted to be, a Kray or a Richardson. But again, they weren't mods but the gangs were. So it wasn't because they were mods, it's just the type of people they were. They got into a bit of criminal activity, nothing big though. Back then London was divided up into 'manors' run by large gangs of teenage mods. I came from Archway and we were split into 'big' Archway and 'little' Archway. I was part of the 'little' Archway gang. We were aged between 15 and 18. There were about 60 of us and our 'manor' covered roughly 15 square miles. Within that we reigned supreme. We were surrounded by larger gangs, the Highbury mob, Somers Town and Mars. Other well-known gangs around London were the crews from Mile End and Elephant & Castle. Although we were enemies, there was an uneasy truce between us and the Highbury mob. There would be skirmishes and 'raids' into each other's territory and weapons were often used, but the West End of London was a no-man's land, a sort of peace zone.

Apart from that, the only other time we ever formed an 'alliance' of any kind was when rockers were involved. Alexandra Palace was our nearest rocker enclave. Once we spotted the 'Tolly Park' gang (they were aligned to the Highbury mob) looking for back up. Some of their members had a run-in with some rockers from Ally Pally. We had a quick call round the pubs and cafes, got about 60 together and headed by bus, car and scooter over to Ally Pally. The rockers were soon put to flight, with a few bumps and bruises for their trouble. Needless to say our reputation increased after that.

Two nights later though, four of us were in a local café called 'The Jiffyburger' when we noticed a lot of motorbikes and a couple of vans cruising past. We saw a van pull up over the road and leather-clad bodies emerging from the rear. We dived into the kitchen of the café and hid in the toilet. Through a crack, we could see dozens of rockers out on the street. They marched into the café, produced a shotgun and declared they were looking for the 'Archway' mob. They didn't find us or any of our members, so they decided to leave. They roared off, apart from one hapless soul who had trouble getting his bike started. We had a great laugh at his expense as he tried to escape up Holloway Road being pursued by one of our gang hitting him on the back with a chair leg.

Pride demanded we retaliate and later that week a group of about 20 paid a visit to a rocker café in Crouch End. They found a couple of rockers inside and one gave them some lip. Apparently, he disappeared under a hail of blows. Someone had used a knife and he was seriously hurt, stabbed within an inch of his heart. The fact that it made the newspapers and no one was caught added to our 'invincibility'. We believed we were untouchable. At one stage, Kentish Town police had two plain-clothes officers assigned to follow us around. We led them a merry dance. After all, we had a reputation to uphold and we were mods.

Although Brighton was to become infamous as a mod /rocker battleground, it was Clacton on Easter Weekend 1964 that set the pattern. Stanley Cohn conducted extensive research into the whole problem and his evidence destroys much of the myth surrounding the stereotyped "mods 'n' rockers" legend.

The Easter weekend of 1964 saw the worst weather in living memory for that time of year. Clacton-On Sea in Essex was just one of many seaside towns suffering because of it. It was also the chosen venue for a mod away day.

Local businesses were used to having family groups visiting the town. Their mood was not friendly when faced with a large crowd of mods who became bored very quickly. Some shopkeepers, pubs and cafes refused to serve these youngsters and they in turn, began to create their own entertainment. The local police force was equally unprepared to handle the number of mods and rockers who raced up and down the streets of Clacton. The extent of damage and violence over the two days amounted to someone firing a starting pistol, a few smashed beach huts, broken windows and minor scuffles. What happened at Clacton set the tone for virtually every bank holiday weekend from then on. If there had been anything newsworthy going on that Easter, Clacton might have been passed off with a few column inches. As it turned out, the national papers were short of good stories, and Clacton 'saved' them.

On the Easter Monday, all the national papers except The Times carried front page screaming headlines. Coverage even extended to America, Australia, South Africa and Europe. One unnamed journalist remembered a few days after Clacton that the assistant editor of the Daily Mirror admitted that the Clacton incidents had been "a little over-reported".

Stanley Cohn looked into the language and techniques used by the press to sensationalise the mod / rocker phenomenon.

Local papers in Brighton reported 'deserted beaches' and 'elderly holidaymakers' escaping 'screaming teenagers'. On closer inspection, and buried within the paper of May 18, 1964, it transpired that the 'deserted beaches' was because of torrential wind and rain. Such 'holidaymakers' as there were, had actually travelled to Brighton just to watch the mod / rocker battles. The classic example of over-reporting and use of language came from the Daily Express of 19 May 1964: 'There was dad asleep in a deck chair and mum making sandcastles with the children, when the 1964 boys took over the beaches at Margate and Brighton yesterday and smeared the traditional postcard scene with blood and violence'.

From this example, it is easy to see why mods and rockers became the 'scourge' of society. Being mod or rocker meant you were a stereotype of the image created in the mind of the public by the media.

Some of the great myths of mod from the 1960s came from these same newspaper reports. The '£75 cheque' story is one such that was given further legendary status by the film 'Quadrophenia'.

Again, it has not been difficult to reveal the truth behind a story that was at base level correct. Jimmy Brunton was one of many mods arrested during the August bank holiday of 1964. When his £75 fine was handed down, he asked if he could pay by cheque. Three days later he confessed to the London Evening Standard that he did not have a bank account and had never signed a cheque in his life. None of the other national papers bothered to report this, and as a consequence, the impression left on the public was that fines could not touch these affluent young people.

Other myths concerned a 'Mod' who fell to his death from a cliff outside Brighton on Whitsun weekend 1964 and in August the same year another 'Mod Dead In Sea' story. Neither incident was related to the disturbances and both were accidents. But it did highlight a worrying trend in the press. Anyone who fitted the image became a 'mod'. It was misleading to say the least.

For example a man was found stabbed to death in a Birmingham park on the Saturday night before the first incident at Clacton. This unfortunate person, aged between 21-25, was found wearing a 'mod jacket' (?) according to a police statement. As the news of this death spread across the country, the headlines and reporting of the facts became blurred in media mod hysteria until the Dublin Evening Press ran a headline 'Terror Comes to English Resorts. Mutilated Mod Dead In Park'.

By far the most distorted inaccuracy went to the Glasgow Daily Record who described mods as being dressed in 'short-jacketed suits with bell bottoms, high boots, bowler or top hats and carrying rolled-up umbrellas'. This description conjures images of characters from Kubrick's 'A Clockwork Orange' rather than self-obsessed mods.

The media then went looking for mods and rockers to interview, to find out what was really going on in the minds of these 'thugs'. Needless to say, there were plenty of willing volunteers who were happy to brag, lie and give the media exactly what it wanted, sensational copy.

Others in society saw their chance to make a name for themselves on the back of this 'mod thing'. Mr Thomas Holdcroft, the prosecutor at the first Clacton trial used this opportunity to denounce the accused with all sorts of colourful and descriptive language. Mr Holdcroft's verbal onslaught was encapsulated in the term 'the wild ones'. The press pounced on his speech and this upped the stakes against mods and rockers. However the worst was yet to come.

Dr George Simpson, an unremarkable and unknown magistrate at Margate in 1964, saw his opportunity for fame and grabbed it. This is the man who uttered those words of mod legend "Sawdust Caesers".

Such was the impact of his obviously preconceived 'speeches' (he and his wife visited the cells of the 44 arrested that weekend) that one journalist in the Spectator, 22 May 1964 said "... by Tuesday, papers were being influenced not by what happened, or even what their own reporters were telling them what happened, but what Dr Simpson said had happened".

What followed for Dr Simpson was media saturation. The press hailed him as some kind of heroic figure standing up for 'good, decent, ordinary people'. He was interviewed on a number of occasions to express his opinions about a range of social issues, not just about the mod/rocker situation. Within a few short weeks however, Margate and Dr Simpson were yesterday's news and he drifted off into his former state of obscurity.

But who were these mods responsible for all the chaos and lawlessness? The first incident in Clacton, proved that the hardcore of 'troublemakers' was actually very small. Out of 97 arrests, 24 of these were charged with various offences. Of those, 23 had previous convictions. Margate was allegedly one of the most violent events. Of 64 arrests, there were two recorded stabbings and a man being dropped onto a flowerbed. Hastings, August 1964, 44 found guilty, three were cases of assaulting police. Brighton, Easter 1965, 70 arrests, seven for assault.

Even the cost of damages sustained by the resorts was not as bad as the public were led to believe. Local authorities estimated that between them, Clacton, Bournemouth, Brighton and Margate had costs amounting to £1,263 of damages. Even by 1964 standards, it was not going to deplete the council's budget for the year. Indeed, an official from Margate Council conceded that the 50 broken deckchairs sustained was not much more than for a normal bank holiday weekend.

Thanks to author Stanley Cohn's research, it became apparent that there was another side to the whole sorry saga that went unreported and deliberately suppressed by the media. Police brutality and victimisation.
The National Council for Civil Liberties (NCCL) produced a report, which identified 110 arrests in Brighton during Easter 1965, the vast majority of which were as a result of indirect provocation by the police. The NCCL received letters alleging wrongful arrest. There were also another 15 cases that were successfully appealed for wrongful arrest. The documented evidence proved that the police were simply acting on two basic principles. Firstly, a high arrest rate dissuades others from getting out of line and looks good on the figures, which leads on to the second, high arrest rates justify the massive overtime paid to those on duty.
There were first-hand and independent witness accounts of mods being kicked, punched or held face down on the floor once the police van doors were shut.
Once inside the cells, they were refused water or washing facilities and in one case a boy was given only two bread and tea meals in 27 hours between arrest and removal to Lewes Prison to be remanded in custody. The NCCL claimed that Brighton police had 60 youths packed into one cell. The police refuted these allegations as one might expect.

JOHN WATERS was one of many mods who went on these bank holiday trips:
Brighton was our favoured destination. We would normally make arrangements on the Saturday night and meet up at Victoria train station on Sunday morning. The trains were packed with mods from all over London and any rivalries were put on hold for the weekend.
The carriages were the old corridor type, and for every fare-paying mod, there was one hidden in the luggage rack covered with coats or under the seats.
On arrival, we headed for the sea front where hundreds of mods would be

congregating. By late morning there would be a huge mass of mods on the beach. We would search out our mates and there was always an air of anticipation. Sooner or later the cry would go up 'Grease!' and the whole beach would rise as one and run in the direction of the rockers. The truth is, the rockers were never there in the first place. Inevitably, as the mob ran through the streets, anything that wasn't fixed down would be sent flying. Windows would be smashed with a bit of looting from time to time. The public were terrified. The police would eventually move in and the mob would disperse and regroup back on the beach until the next wave. Rockers would cruise along the sea front, but the police presence prevented too many confrontations. There were always a few arrests, some were herded out of town, and throughout the day there would be intermittent skirmishes. By night, the pubs and coffee bars would be taken over. It wasn't much fun at night because there was no where to sleep, although the beach area under the pier was the favourite. People used to go to the parks as well, but the police would continually move people on.

By Monday morning, it would be time to think about heading back to London. This was very tricky because all our money was spent and for those of us without a return train ticket there were two options. Hitch a ride or dodge the ticket inspector. I tried both on occasions. The train was risky. Trying to be clever, I scrounged enough money to buy a ticket to the next station. When I tried to get on the train, I was grabbed by two policemen and hauled along the platform to join a dozen or so sorry-looking mods who were waiting for the 'special' train to take them to the next station! I watched the London bound train out of the corner of my eye, and as it pulled away I made a run for it. My mates held a door open for me and I managed to scramble on board. It was just a case of mingling with the hundreds of other mods on the train and bulldozing our way passed the ticket collector at Victoria station. He had more sense than to try and stop us. We tried hitching once. Four of us walked through the night and halfway through the next day before we got a ride on the back of a lorry. We had to steal apples from people's gardens just to survive.

If we didn't go to the coast, the fun fairs were the other big bank holiday event. There was a large fair at Hampstead Heath twice a year and huge gangs of mods and a few gangs of rockers would be there. Fights were frequent and more often than not it was between rival mod gangs from other 'manors' than with rockers. You would also see 'faces' at the fairs too. I remember seeing Kathy McGowan, Dave Clark, Rod Stewart and Keith Moon at Hampstead Heath Fair.

With all the bad publicity surrounding mod culture, the writing was very definitely on the wall. Even the hallowed rooms of The Twisted Wheel were experiencing change. **ROGER EAGLE** departed for The Blue Note Club:
I left because the owners wouldn't pay me a decent wage. After years of hard graft for maybe £3 a night I asked for a fiver and they said they couldn't afford it. I was also getting bored with the music and there were a lot of pills going on. Kids were in trouble with the pills and all they wanted was that fast tempo soul. At The Blue Note, I was able to play the kind of music I liked. The pill freaks only wanted the same dance beat-which is what makes it so boring, and you're trying to talk to kids off their heads all night on pills. It's really hard.

Although Roger Eagle may have noticed a change in the attitude of mods, the same could not be said of **JEFFREY KRUGER** at The Flamingo Club:
The change, if there was a change, was more at the late night sessions. They got casual and we couldn't stop that after a while, smart casual or they didn't get in. But the bands then changed from being smartly dressed to even smoking on the stage and they never played there again if they did that.

Andrew Loog Oldham, along with people like John Paul Jones, who went on to become a member of Led Zeppelin, all concur that The Flamingo was a jazzier venue than The Scene or La Discotheque.
Jeffrey Kruger's strict policies worked extremely efficiently. The Scene in particular, was known for being more pop orientated than The Flamingo, and as such drew the crowds that Jeffrey Kruger did not want. French blues and purple hearts were almost a staple diet in other clubs, but not The Flamingo.

Pete Meaden claimed he discovered drynamil in 1962 and mods did not exist at that time. It could be argued that Meaden's view of being mod was the very factor that eventually caused its demise. It is particularly interesting to note that Meaden seems to have only ever gone to The Scene Club in Ham Yard for his drug purchases. It appears to be fairly accepted that The Scene was an easy, tolerant place when it came to the trading and consumption of pills. It seems almost as if mod was split in two depending on your preference. You could go to the drug-free jazz environment of The Flamingo early in the evening, or the more relaxed all-nighter session later on. But if taking pills and speeding out of your head was your preference, you went to The Scene. It may well be the case that The Scene became a victim of its own policies toward music and drugs. Certainly DJ Guy Stevens was a major attraction because he played the music that was in demand. When it became apparent that the pill trade would be over-looked, The Scene certainly came to the attention of the police and eventually closed down in 1966, coinciding with mod's fall from fashion.

ALAN FLETCHER was one mod who preferred not to get immersed in the pill-popping craze:
For many people pill popping is synonymous with mod culture, and in some respects this is true. There was a lot of amphetamine around in the form of French Blues, Purple Hearts, Bombers, and as dances started to evolve into all-nighter affairs, then many kids would pop pills to keep on from dusk till dawn. It is said that there was a strong mod contingent in Nottingham and its environs, largely because of the presence of the Boots factory. All the drugs that were leaving the factory gates were leaving legitimately or otherwise! For my own part, I wanted the experience of the mod days of the mid-sixties at first hand and not through a filter of pilled-up confusion.

ROGER POWELL explains one of the reasons why the bands might resort to drug taking:
We were all on leapers most of the time because we were doing all-nighters; otherwise you couldn't keep going. We got busted at The Birdcage for amphetamines. We were all in the dressing room, when suddenly all these policemen came in. Everyone was

dropping stuff. I think they found some amphetamines in Mike's pocket and took him away to the police station. So we had to go and try getting him bailed out so we could finish the gig.

JOHN WATERS was a mod who did not allow drug use become an unbreakable habit: It was just weekend stuff, something for Saturday night. You didn't bother with it any other time, just Saturday night. You couldn't get a drink in the clubs either. You either had to take something or have nothing at all. I was told you could get a drink at The Flamingo if you knew the barman. A drop of Rum and Coke.
I think there was a lot of that going on in the other clubs. The police just laughed at it at first, but as time went on it became more of an issue and they started raiding the clubs every Saturday night.
I don't remember any dealing or anything like that in The Flamingo. Some might have been high when they went in, but nothing went on inside as I remember. We used to go a little place called the Coffee An. We used to go down there first, it was full of mods. You'd get what you wanted down there, take it and go on to somewhere else. If anybody wanted anything while they were in the clubs, they'd get their hand stamped and go outside to get it. The police really started closing them down though. It all seemed to happen all at once.
They all got closed about the same time. It really was just Saturday nights for taking something to give you the energy to dance all night. At one stage we did some pushing when a local villain heard that he was to be raided and offloaded several thousand dexadrine to us for next to nothing. We couldn't go wrong and sold the lot in no time. Of course the 'come down' the following day was a nightmare and along with a bad trip, it was enough to make me see the light. I had bought some stuff from an unfamiliar 'face' one night and had a few dexys as well. I can still remember lying on the floor of the club looking up through a haze at faces looking down on me. I was quickly dumped out on the street. I truly felt I was dying. I was totally disorientated, felt sick, and kept hallucinating. The effects lasted several hours during which time I was staggering around the back streets of Soho in the pouring rain and freezing. It stayed

with me forever and finished any longing I had for getting high. I can remember a few weeks later seeing a 'face' I knew sitting on the pavement outside the club. He had puked up in the gutter and he was picking tablets out of the bile and swallowing them. That was the end of drugs for me. Although we almost all took amphetamines, I don't know of anyone who progressed to hard drugs.

The worst that happened was one or two arrests. One particular blow to us was when our top 'face' Alex 'Haggis' Hamilton was arrested and given a choice - borstal or go back to Scotland for good. Needless to say he went back and never returned. ·◊·

> When we learned more about mod and mod music, it got more interesting because it is such a broad church. In '79 no-one really knew much about it. It was like punk wearing Fred Perry's and targets and by 1981 it was stylists dancing to jazz and sixties soul.
>
> EDDIE PILLER

CHAPTER 3

Just as John Waters had been involved in a 'mod' gang in Archway, north London, **IAN HARRIS** witnessed similar gangs in his area:
The Harrow lot, they were a very aggressive bunch, but you had to go through almost like an initiation, so they beat you up one week, and the next week you were accepted. There weren't many black mods around at the time, but there were these two guys called 'Cherry' and 'Blossom', I mean you couldn't get away with it now, but they revelled in that and they were the faces of the crew.
Once you had passed your initiation and were on nodding terms with them, you were

fine. There was a lot of violence and a lot of drugs, and to me it was the same then as it is now. It's just youth culture. Purple hearts, black bombers. I knew people on heroin in 1964. You didn't have to get involved though. It was your personal choice. There was peer pressure, but that's always there.

By the start of 1967 the 'mod thing' was all but finished. The so-called riots on bank holidays had become a bore. The original modernists were long gone and the mods themselves went looking for new horizons. The lumpen mod movement of 1966 effectively split in three, affected by the general social climate.
American pop culture was re-establishing its dominance again after a period of prolonged British supremacy led by The Beatles. The Beatles retired from touring in 1966 to concentrate on their new album. Other acts that had come in on the Brit wave were finding longevity hard to sustain. Some like Herman's Hermits became virtual cabaret bands. For mods, The Who's sound was becoming noticeably rock orientated, especially after 'My Generation'. The Creation were now the real exponents of Pop Art, and people like David Bowie and Mark Bolan joined the swelling ranks of a new culture. Jazz had long since been kicked into touch, the once reliable Tamla Motown stable had gone commercial and Otis Redding had tragically died in an aircraft accident.

In America, Ray Columbus decided to return to his native New Zealand leaving his backing band, Art Collection to move on to Los Angeles to pursue their dream. They had 'form' having appeared with The Wailers, Eric Burden and The Animals and Music Machine on stage, but they needed a record deal. What happened next is a story worthy of the tag 'legendary'.
In mid-1967, while staying at the Sandy Koufax Motel, Richard Frost answered a knock on their door at around midnight. It was Neil Young who was still with Buffalo Springfield at the time. Young was looking for a band called The Youngbloods who happened to be in the next suite.
Richard Frost and Young struck up an immediate friendship. Young attended an Art Collection gig the next night and through Rodney Bingenheimer, an audition for the

band with Buffalo Springfield's management was set up. It was held at Gold Star Studios, but Art Collection were of no interest to Charlie Greene and Brian Stone.
However, one of Greene and Stone's other clients heard about the band and went to see them at The Galaxy Club. Another audition was arranged where Art Collection became the support/backing band for Sonny and Cher.
After their first gig on tour, Art Collection's drummer left the band. Richard and his brother Tom Frost reorganised, a new drummer was taken on and Art Collection became Powder. Their set was a mixture of original numbers and covers which included tracks like 'Have You Ever Seen Me' by Small Faces.
As Sonny and Cher's backing band, Powder failed to build a fan base, but they did record a number of tracks at the Gold Star studios. It would be another 25 years or so before Powder's recordings would be fully appreciated by an audience on the other side of the world who's roots came from the mod world.
The same could be said of another USA band from Boston, Massachusetts. Barry Tashian led The Remains who formed in 1964 at Boston University. Their popularity never managed to grow outside of New England State despite high-profile TV appearances. They moved to the West Coast and recorded their only album in 1965 and in 1966 they were signed as the opening act for three weeks on The Beatles last U.S. tour. Sadly it was in late '66 they band broke up. They were signed to Epic who released their only album after the split, but unsurprisingly, it went virtually un-noticed. Like Powder, The Remains would slowly gather cult status over the next couple of decades when they would receive their due recognition.

Back in the UK, by 1967 The Flamingo club was still going strong, and its reputation for innovation and creativity by this time, had become international. So much so that people visiting Britain would make it one of the top entertainment priorities of their stay.
There is one story that perfectly illustrates the immense pulling power and deserved reputation of this venue. **JEFFREY KRUGER** recounts a story that shows just why The Flamingo was so special:
One night I'm on the door and this gangling American came up to me and he was

carrying an acetate. It was about 10.30pm and my mother was in the box office. He said "I'd like to meet this Jeffrey Kruger". And she said "He'll be out in a minute". I came out, he said to me "I've just arrived in the country and this is the first place I've visited and I heard about you in New York from Chas Chandler. My name's Jimi Hendrix". I said "Oh yes?"; he said "I'm a great guitar player, can I sit in?". I said "Well, as you can hear Tony Crombie (or whoever was on, Johnny Dankworth, whoever), they don't like people sitting in with them".

It turned out Chas Chandler, who happened to be walking down the stairs at that moment had invited Jimi to sit in with The Animals who were doing the Allnighter. Jimi said "I've got my first record here, I'd like to play it for you". I had no way of playing it whilst there was music on. He said "I'm gonna be a big star". I said " I've heard it before and I've no doubt some of you are going to be". He said "If ever I make it because of your courtesy towards me, even if I star at the Albert Hall, which I will, on that tour I'll come back here and play for nothing". I said, "Great!". Never gave it a second thought. He did play that night and of course he knocked everyone out, and he'd pop in occasionally. By that time he'd found various women to come in with, but he was always polite and respectful calling me 'Mr Jeffrey' or 'Mr Kruger'. He wouldn't call me 'Jeff'. Then, as he grew in stature, I saw him less and less. Some time later I bumped into him somewhere, and he said: "I told you I'd become a big star". I said: "I'm thrilled". I think it was at Polydor Records, I was coming out or he was coming in, anyway he said: "do you want to come to the Albert Hall to see the show?" I said: "Jimi, I can't. It's Saturday night and I've got to be at the club". So he said: "I'm going to keep my word, I'm going to bring the group down, so you let me know which Saturday night, I can do this, this and this date".

I said: "Fine". He said: "you can bill it". I said: "I can't afford you". He said: "I told you the price, you pay the musicians scale," whatever the union scale was, he said: "You know what they're like". And sure enough Jimi Hendrix did play a session at the club. The same tour that he finished at the Albert Hall. Eventually I got hold of the record where Jimi played with Little Richard and put it out on the Ember label, only to be told by Little Richard when I went to his induction at the Rock & Roll Hall Of Fame: "Jimi was a side man, you billed him equal with me," he said "he couldn't make a living in those days, I was king then and the drummer who was also my valet on the record is that James Brown who thinks he's a star".

In 1967, the political landscape of the USA was filtering through to Britain. The opposition to the Vietnam conflict and the rise of the civil rights movement was being felt. The student body in Britain became more politically active than it ever had before. Drug culture moved in to hyper-drive and a new ideology for the human race was taking shape. Love and peace would solve the problems of the world. Finding your inner self and elevating to a higher state of consciousness would free the people, if only the people would join in. Indian mysticism was one of many ways to reach this spiritual plateau.

The softer, more flamboyant mods discarded suits for radical fashions led by the 'Swinging Set'. The fashion was for tie-dye fabrics, kaftans from the East, turn-of-the century military wear and 'roaring twenties' American gangster fashion. The catch phrase was 'turn on, tune in, drop out'.

Mod and Small Faces fan **JOHN HELLIER** recalls his own transition at that time:

The mod spirit was still there. I've read many times of how 60's mods evolved into skinheads. I never ever saw that. In the main, myself and my mates went the opposite route and by 1967/68 we were absorbed into the whole San Francisco scene and started growing our hair along with an assortment of weird moustaches and beards. Spiritually we were still mods, visually we were very different from our old selves.

With the advent of harder drugs, particularly LSD, psychedelia made itself known. When The Beatles released 'Sgt Pepper's Lonely Hearts Club Band', it became clear that more than pure inspiration, creativity and the technical genius of producer George Martin was at work on the album.

ROGER POWELL, drummer with The Action gave this assessment of the times that he witnessed first-hand:

By '67 all the underground stuff started happening in London with the UFO Club in Tottenham Court Road. A lot of the psychedelic bands were self-indulgent. I didn't like Pink Floyd or any of those bands, I couldn't get into it. At the all-nighters at the Roundhouse, people were all over the place. The drugs had changed. With the old amphetamines everyone liked a chat, wanted to be your mate, it was brilliant. When people were taking acid it was totally different. It's an important thing drugs and culture, they're a totally interlinked. Even if the mods weren't taking uppers they were very chatty, friendly people. At the Roundhouse people were isolated in their own heads, doing their own thing. It was like chalk and cheese. Mod gigs and the Roundhouse. It was an unbelievable difference. I didn't like the Roundhouse, it was also too self-indulgent. I wouldn't call it psychedelic by any means. It was more jazzy, rock-jazz, but I liked the three minute things. In the space of half an hour you could get loads of brilliant records rather than one long thing. We lost touch with the club scene after a while, at the end of the Action, I got a bit disenchanted with it. The early days of the Action were the most exciting, when we were playing the Birdcage and stuff like that. That was an incredible time in the clubs.

In Birmingham, **GILL TAYLOR** and Del Evans got married in June of 1967. It was a marriage that would last 47 years. The happy couple maintained their love of mod styling despite the changing times as Gill explains:

I've always kept that smart mod look and utilised it in different fashions. I was selling my designs to boutiques for years anyway, so Gill Evans Designs has always been there. From '67 onwards, I continued designing for the current trend of the times, so there were shorter dresses and different materials that reflected a more flower power image with psychedelic patterns and designing hot pants that we sold to a woman who had connection to the pop industry at the time. I don't know who she was selling onto, but we did quite a lot of that. I always tried to reinvent my business to keep it fresh over the years.

Independent designers like Gill Evans were few and far between. Female mods had a few icons or role models from whom they could take inspiration. Those that were around have become almost clichés in reference to the 1960s. Biba, Twiggy, Mary Quant, Jean Shrimpton, Cathy McGowan, Audrey Hepburn, Diana Rigg as Emma Peel in the TV show

'The Avengers'; pop stars like Dusty Springfield, Lulu, Marianne Faithful, Cilla Black and Sandie Shaw were conduits of female style. It does not appear to be that case that female mods had the same opportunities for individual tailoring in the same way their male counterparts had.

Rather, female mods had to invariably wait for the 'designers' to provide the invention and the shift dress was one item that was versatile enough to be creative. As journalist and author **CLAIRE MAHONEY** explains:

The functional form of the shift dress has its roots in the sack dress of the late 50s which was designed by Givenchy. The style at this time was more fitted than its 60's reincarnation. But the main elements were there.

The neck would often have a slash or boat neck. There would be no sleeves and there would be a couple of darts sewn in at the bust. Sometimes it would have a kick-pleat for more freedom of movement. Lily Pulitzer was an American socialite living the dream in Palm Beach with her husband Peter who owned a number of orange groves there. She decided to start selling juice from the fruits that they grew to then sell to the tourists. She asked her dressmaker whether she could run her up something that wouldn't show up the juice stains. The result was a series of shift dresses in bright colours and patterns that suited the relaxed sunny attitudes of Palm Beach at the time. Soon Lily was selling more dresses than juice and they became known as 'Lilly' dresses. Her designs really took off when Jackie Kennedy was photographed for 'Life' magazine featuring one of her outfits. Lilly dresses were suddenly all the rage and a fashion brand (which still exists today) was born as a result.

The early 'shift' dress wasn't as short as its later 60s counterpart. It fell somewhere on the knee. It wasn't until Mary Quant shorted the dress by 7-8 inches that it took on a new life again. Quant was influenced by earlier modifications of the dress by iconic 60s designer Andre Courreges, a designer that was heavily influenced by pre-war modernist design. Courreges, loved the streamlined look the shift lent itself to and would often use the basic outline shape as a tunic to be worn with trousers.

Towards the mid-60s, the outline of the dress started to become more 'A-line' and with a flare-out from the waist and modern fabrics enabled this outline to hold its shape. Variations on the shift dress resulted in the so-called 'tent' dress and the 'trapeze' dress which was almost triangular in shape and flared out at the sides so it would 'swing' as you moved.

Designers began to be more playful with the designs - they introduced cut-out shapes such as circles and key holes or panels with plastic or even metal details. The more space-age and utilitarian the better. As the decade progressed the shift became the subject of bright colours and patterns and 'op-art' designs. Block colour panels were also a popular feature such as those on Yves Saint Laurent's now iconic, 'Mondrian' dress which paid a homage to the bold work of the modern artist.

It's no surprise then that the shift dress has endured over the ensuing decades. Not only is it a simple dress to make - it's also simple to wear. All you need are some well-chosen accessories. But most of all it represents a period of emancipation for women who wanted to express their new found freedoms in a shape that didn't define their gender and instead allowed them to define themselves.

With the rapid cultural changes going on in the 'Western World' in 1967, Roger Hutchinson, was part of the editorial team of 'Oz' magazine. He identified the roots of psychedelia.

To Roger, mod was a tolerant and broad-based concept. The direct link with beatniks was the fact that both groups used and sold drugs unashamedly, although mods preferred speed while the beats went for weed. The advent of LSD was a revelation to some, but in London, and against this backdrop, the working class or 'hard mods' had little choice but to create their own new culture. They were distinctive for wearing their hair a lot shorter. Crew cuts had been around for sometime, but the style worn by the hard mods was even shorter than a crew. They also changed their style of clothes. The suits and smart look of 1962-63 was now being used for evening wear only. During the day and especially when riding a scooter, boots and jeans were much more practical. The Harrington Jacket was also very popular. John Simons manufactured the Harrington in the UK. There was no need for parkas.

The jacket we now know as the Harrington was first seen in 1937 and was produced by

John and Issac Miller in Manchester at their Baracuta factory. The original concept was to develop a shorter version of a Macintosh that would protect from rain, but allow more freedom of movement. The core market for this product was golfers, hence the model of the jacket became known as the G9.

Simon Fraser, 24th Lord Lovat and head of the Fraser clan in Scotland, gave permission for the Millers to line the G9 with the Fraser tartan. Needless to say, the G9 was hugely popular with golfers in Britain and it soon got exported to America where high-profile names like Bob Hope and Bing Crosby (both keen golfers) wore the jacket. When Elvis Presley wore one in his film 'King Creole' in 1958, the G9 really took off in the wider world, but in Britian, it was **JOHN SIMONS** who introduced it to High Street fashion and gave it the name that has stuck ever since:

We didn't bring in the Baracuta Harrington until 1967, exactly the same time as Payton Place was on TV. Harrington was the name they were known by over here, but they were always known as Baracutas in the United States. We noticed a character from a popular US TV show of the time called Peyton Place was wearing them and we started calling them the 'Rodney Harrington jacket' and that eventually got shortened to the Harrington. Now it's become a generic name for that style, or even any zipper style of jacket. We had The Squire Shop in Brewer Street at that time. Stuart Malloy, the manager of Jones and Quincy's, a shop in Covent Garden, started with me as well. He was a mate from Bristol I met in the West End. He helped build The Squire Shop. It was an old butcher's before we moved in. We created this kind of baronial hall with all these Ivy League clothes in there.

We sold Truval Korea Club shirts. Ben Sherman bought Korea Club shirts from us. I think that's how he started. He was an American who had a shirt factory in Brighton. We pre-dated him and what he was doing at the time. We'd get a lot of black guys coming to The Squire Shop. They were into button downs, brogues and plain caps. They called brogues and plain caps 'blockbusters' and loafers were known as 'de canoes'. There was quite a time when West Indian guys were into the Ivy look. They all queued up on Saturdays for brogues and if you didn't have their size, they'd take a different size! We kept with the Ivy League look. A Modern Jazz look. The customers were younger than us, what I would describe as Suedeheads. Wearing authentic button downs, short-ish college boy haircut, quite hard guys, but not really hard. They were very smart though. We were unique. No one had done what we had done. The look worked well. It could also be manipulated to produce something else. I think it mutated into The Skinhead look. The early skinheads were very smart. The ones who wore the cheaper end - the later Jaytex look - they weren't very smart. I've never stocked or sold a Jaytex nor a Ben Sherman in my life. We only sold the authentic item. The Squire Shop opened in '69. It closed about 1980 or some time around then. I sold my interest in the shops, but I created them and opened them.

The early customers that John Simons remembers may well have been the forerunners to skinheads; the hard mod. London's East End was home to numerous gangs of such mods. Other cities like Glasgow, Liverpool and Birmingham also boasted large numbers of hard mods.

In Newcastle, **PAULINE WATERS** and her friends still considered themselves mods: I can't remember the skinhead thing at all in Newcastle. I started going to different clubs, but it was more heavy metal that took off up there. The other thing was the live bands moved out of the clubs and into bigger venues. The Go-Go got closed down. It was on the top of a huge old building and underneath was the bus driver's canteen. It was right in the heart of Newcastle and how it stayed open I don't know. It was such a fire hazard and I think it was the fire officers that got it closed down. I saw Cream at the Go-Go and we were locked in it was that packed. There was loads more people outside, and I remember thinking I was going to suffocate in there. In the end, someone broke the door down because we had to get out. This was up four flights of stairs and they were big flights of stairs too. It was also horrendous for drugs, but that never interested me at all. It was up to you, if you did wrong or did right, you made your choice. There were plenty that went the wrong way, and one that went on to hard stuff, but she came out of it. There were gangs up there too. There was Gateshead, the Westend of Newcastle and Westerhope, but they weren't rival gangs though.

JOHN WATERS had left London for a couple of years, but when he returned, the changes that had taken place in London hit hard:

Mods were still very much in evidence, but the hippy movement was well under way. Many of the old clubs had either shut or changed music policy. We used to go to Top Rank at Watford, Dunstable, the Lorcano at Stevenage.

The funny thing was, all the clubs were closing in London, then I went up to the North-East and the place was still jumping, and to be honest, in London, we had never heard of the Twisted Wheel. It was probably better than most of the clubs in London.

In later years I heard about The Dungeon in Nottingham, but we never knew about those places at the time. We used to think we were way out in the sticks if we went to High Wycombe or Borehamwood, you know? The best club was the Flamingo without a doubt. I didn't go there often, but when I did, it was excellent.

John explains how he came to move to Newcastle and how he met wife Pauline:

This company I worked for offered four of us a lot of money to go up to Newcastle, and when I was going up there, I thought 'Oh God, all cloth caps and whippets'. When I came out of the train station, it was exactly as I'd imagined! (sic). But within a week, I realised the place was heaving with good clubs. We went out every night. We were paid a lot of money and we were being a bit flash. Nobody trusted us at first. We were flashing the cash. We weren't liked at all. The girls liked us, but the blokes hated us. I was putting a sprinkler system in at Jackson's the tailors, which was part of the Burton Group and Pauline was a typist at Jackson's as well.

It was a six-month job that lasted eighteen months. We dragged it out a bit because there were 800 girls in that place. We thought we were in seventh heaven. We were getting twice the local wages of anyone up there. I used to order a suit from Jackson's and put the manager's name on it and it would be inspected at every stage. So even then my clothes had to be perfect.

In the late sixties and early seventies up there, it was the real place to be, the nightlife was fantastic. The Bailey Organisation was one of the biggest club owners in Europe at the time, they had something like twenty clubs, and they were based in the North-

Leeds [courtesy of Jonathan Marsden]

East. They had five or six in Newcastle. The Dolce Vita, Sloppy's, The Cavendish, The Latino and The Chelsea Cat. There were other independent clubs as well like Rupert's, Bloomers, Sombrero and Sands.
I can remember seeing Chairman Of The Board, The Chants, Johnny Johnson and Tammi Lynn at Dolce Vita.
In London you had psychedelic clubs like UFO going, but in Newcastle, they were still playing all the good soul and R&B right through to about '72. So going up there for me was brilliant.
I just carried on. Then coming back to London, it was all gone. All the mods I knew were just in pubs or drinking clubs.
In Newcastle though, even right up to the early seventies there was Julie's on the quayside and Annabel's in Sunderland and a lot of what you would call ex-mods went there. We saw Chris Farlowe and Clyde McPhatter at Annabel's. The Mayfair Ballroom would put on Soul 'packages' from time to time; Junior Walker, Root and Jenny Jackson, Bob and Earl. They also had emerging funk bands on like BT Express, Brass Construction and the like.
It was the lot from the Go-Go that went to Julie's. It was sixties soul and a bit of funk that sort of thing they played there. They didn't go into disco, but by the end of the seventies they had all gone.
I could never get into skinhead. I could never understand it, you won't get anything blacker than ska music, and some of those skinheads were really racist. And yet they'd jump around to Jamaican music. It doesn't make any sense. The only good thing about it was, it did a lot for ska music. What was portrayed in the press was a stereotype, they weren't all like that, but they all got tarred with the same brush.
We got married in 1969 and looking at the wedding photos, you can still see it. I look at them now, and I think 'Christ, we were all still mods then'.
Everybody else was into the mainstream stuff. As the seventies went on, obviously we did change, but not to the extremes that other people went to. It's like the Northern Soul thing, I liked some of the music, but all those vests and big trousers and that, it wasn't for me. I think the mod thing was too deeply entrenched.

The hard mod, in keeping with mod tradition, rejected mainstream commercialism and adopted a different music as well as fashion. Bluebeat and ska had been around for a few years, promoted and produced by white Jamaican Chris Blackwell among others. TV journalist and presenter Alan Whicker ran a feature on ska for the BBC. Anyone who had even the slightest knowledge of popular music in the UK could mention one ska record. 'My Boy Lollipop' by Millie Small.

But that was just the tip of a very large and untapped iceberg. Throughout 1967 and 1968, the terms ska and bluebeat were being supplanted by a new word to identify Jamaican music.

Reggae was the catchall for the great sounds coming out of Kingston, Jamaica. Desmond Dekker's '007 (Shanty Town)', The Ethiopians' 'Last Train To Skaville', The Skatalites' 'Guns of Navarone' and Prince Buster's 'Al Capone' all made it into the UK charts.

With the music came the style. In Jamaica, the young men who were growing up through the early part of the sixties were influenced by the modernist Ivy League styles from the USA. Like the UK mods, they also adapted the look to suit their tastes. These Jamaicans became known as Rude Boys.

The style was transported to the UK and as the mod interest in the music took hold, so the rude boy look was adopted by hard mods. The trouser length was noticeably shorter, the preferred suit material was two-tone tonik worn with loafers and a 'Crombie' coat.

Hard mods also turned to football matches, the bastion of male working class entertainment, as an alternative to Bank Holiday beaches for a bit of aggro. For this reason, Harry J and The Allstars' 'Liquidator' became a virtual anthem for the hard mod supporters of Chelsea Football Club.

Boot boys, as they were then known, took the gang mod culture to the terraces. Rivalry has always been part of soccer, and violence at matches was not a new phenomenon. There is plenty of evidence that periodic fights and rioting had been going on for decades, but the Boot Boys took it a lot further. Most clubs by 1968 had their gang of Boot Boys. The style was hard mod. By 1969 however, the term Boot Boys was replaced a new word for these gangs. Skinheads were becoming a recognised entity in youth culture and at football matches. The first skinhead gangs became visible during the 1968-69 season when Leeds United were one of the most successful teams in England. Nothing did more to spread the skinhead style than travelling gangs who would start fighting before, during and after a match.

KEITH RYLATT, who had seen London mods a few years earlier on his trips with Leeds fans to the capital, noticed the new fashion and a closing of the north-south style gap:
When I first came across skinheads they were at Tottenham Hotspur when they played Leeds, and the clothes they were wearing were the same as we were wearing. But it was like an overlap because they were the younger brothers of the people that we were.

By 1969 the term skinhead was widely used. Reports in the media told of vicious and ultra violent skinhead gangs who were now carrying an assortment of weapons for use on rival football gangs. The original purpose was to 'take' the home team's end of the ground. Before long, it was being organised and orchestrated. Ambushing rivals at pubs and railway stations or en route to the ground were common tactics, as the police became more efficient at separating gangs inside the stadiums. As the police began to exert control at matches by carrying out searches and confiscating weapons and even laces from the now popular ox-blood coloured Doctor Martens boots, the skinheads went looking for aggro elsewhere.

There were plenty of targets; hippies, homosexuals, students in university towns, squadies in barrack towns. By far the most willing adversary outside of soccer grounds was the 'son of rocker' known as greasers. They styled themselves on California's Hell Angels, although roaring up and down the A1 on motorbikes was hardly living the liberated life style of their American cousins heading up the interstate highway from San Francisco to Oakland.

Perhaps the skinhead's most publicised target for violence was the Asian community. 'Paki- bashing' as it became known, was widely reported by the media.

Enoch Powell's 'Rivers of Blood' speech set a race agenda for Britain. The speech and the influx of Asian immigrants meant competition for jobs and houses for the white population, just as it had a decade earlier when the first West Indians arrived on the SS Windrush. Skinheads were just one of many groupings who supported Powell's point of view at a base economic level where resentment festered, which in turn led to pure race hatred.

Powell was certainly intelligent enough to know that fear always has and always will be the easiest way to gain mass support for a controversial point of view, and it is a technique that is a favourite of right wing politics.

It actually took almost ten years for the extreme right wing to gain control of the skinhead movement and implant fascist dogma and nazi sympathies. By that time a new generation of skins were in place with their own definition of being a skinhead.

Another fact, overlooked by many, is that the original skinheads were not all as hypocritical as they may have been portrayed. Many a skinhead gang had black members.

There were even all-black skinhead gangs. If trouble erupted, it was mainly over territory or a feud of some kind. Skinheads were not generally known for attacking the West Indian population in the late sixties. Again, it was ten years later and the new skinhead generation, fuelled by the extreme right wing that took that stance.

EDDIE PILLER did some research on skinheads for a TV programme that was shown in the UK late in 2002, and he gives this assessment of what happened to the skinhead movement:

Skinheads had invented a working class background that had been reinforced by the cultural emigration from the West Indies, which in turn had come from an Empire background which was much more of a working class identity. In Britain, we had lost our working class identity by the seventies.

The original skinheads were influenced by this West Indian understanding of working class identity and created their own identity which paralleled the Jamaican one, but didn't really exist. And it was only when the Jamaicans turned to Marcus Garvey and Rastafarianism, that the skinheads resented that fact and they were now excluded from something that had been their scene for three years, so they became negative and created a white working class mentality. It's all explainable in sociological terms because when society has a need for something, it happens.

By the start of the new decade, being a skinhead was becoming more trouble than it was worth. The authorities came down hard. The class of '66 were growing up and settling down. Although the numbers and the profile of the skins were shrinking, it never died.
By total contrast, the softer mods of '66 began to follow the 'swinging' scene. As The Who began to harden their sound, and guitar technology became more advanced, bands who were R&B or Beat influenced went in a new direction. The guitar became distorted and fuzzy sounding, the production was more experimental and The Beatle's 'Sgt Pepper' album showed what could be done.
However, the lesser-known acts began recording tracks that were somewhere between beat and this new sound. Although the name for this sound was not invented for another decade or so, the freakbeat era began. Included in this category were acts like The Birds, pre-John's Children Mark Bolan, The Small Faces and The Action.
This period of experimentation gave rise to bands like The Pink Floyd, fronted by Sid Barrett. Pink Floyd began life in 1963 when Nick Mason, Roger Waters and Richard Wright formed Sigma 6. Syd Barrett and Bob Klose joined later and the band changed its name to The Tea Set until they were booked to play a gig with another band by the same name, so they changed it again to Pink Floyd. Their earliest recordings included a version of 'I'm A King Bee' by Slim Harpo. They had been playing the London circuit for a while and had an early chart success with 'See Emily Play' in 1967. That single is arguably the link between the Freakbeat sound of Mod and the Psychedelia sound of Hippies. After 'See Emily Play', their debut album 'Piper At The Gates Of Dawn' would be regarded as a classic of its type and influence many bands that followed for decades to come.
In terms of style in London, the choices were relatively simple. You either became a skinhead, or a hippy, or you got out completely. Being mod was not an option. It was dated and out of touch with popular opinion and trends.

For some, like **IAN HARRIS**, being a mod led to a career in music:

My friends were in a school band. Barry was a bass player, Phillip was a drummer and I had inclinations to be a vocalist. They started rehearsing and I joined them and we thought, 'Mods playing to mods, that would be brilliant'.

So we formed a band and got gigs in local church halls, pubs and clubs. The first name we had was The Third Party and then we became The Conviction, but as time went on, mod was starting to fade and by 1966 it was becoming a bit psychedelic through to 1967 when Cream came along. But in Conviction, we got these jackets dyed in different colours and got arrows on them and we thought we looked good. We did quite a lot of gigs, nothing major, but we were quite a well-respected little band. That led onto everything I've been doing ever since. We had a lead guitarist who couldn't really hack it, so we advertised for a new lead guitarist in Melody Maker and this guy turned up in this bubble car, all six-foot four of him and we thought he looked a bit like Jeff Beck, but it turned out to be Alan Parsons. At the time he was working for EMI as a second engineer, recording everybody from Joe Loss to Cliff Richard in the mid sixties, and he just wanted to be in a band. Alan came from a very different social strata to us. We were ordinary working class boys from North London, and Alan went to Westminster School and had connections, but he wanted to be in a band and we were into blues then. It was the John Mayall, Peter Green influence as well as the black artists, we just wanted to play blues, and Alan was a brilliant guitarist. From then on we did better gigs.

Now, Melody Maker was the bible for bands, and we saw this advert saying, 'Club owner wants band to run club'. So we phoned up and it turned out to be Ronnie Scott's old place in Gerard Street. Now this guy, John Fordham, owned the premises and Ronnie had moved to Frith Street, but the old place was still a club and he wanted it to carry on, on a Friday and Saturday night, so we ran it as a blues club called The Coffin Club, in the basement at 37 Gerard Street We did the music and two live sets from ten until four in the morning on a Friday and Saturday.

It became quite an important little club for about a year, with write-ups in Disc Magazine, and we invited musicians along to the sessions. Through that, we were discovered and signed an album deal with Mercury Records. This was about 1968. By then we were called Earth, because we were playing earthy blues. We wrote the songs and rehearsed for about a week in Swiss Cottage, and Alan was still working at EMI, and he would come in and play us Beatle songs he'd recorded that day. This was around the time of 'Get Back', and it was fantastic. So we recorded an album in a studio off Tottenham Court Road in one day and then the bass player and the drummer left the band as soon as it was recorded. Alan didn't want to tour and the band fell apart.

The amazing thing is, the bass player, Barry Mitchell, left Earth to join Queen. He was the original bass player in Queen and he is the man who left them before they made it. By 1970, I wasn't in a band, I got married and settled down, working as an art director on magazines, but I still had music in me. It's like a fire burning within you. You can't ignore it, so I've always written songs and 'Just a Little Mod' was written in 1969. I wrote the lyrics because I wanted to write about being a mod.

In the north of England, the choice between being a skinhead or a hippy was not so stark. With their staple diet of R&B and soul music, northern mods found the hippy culture utterly irrelevant. To them it was a 'London thing', skinhead was by far the better option and unlike their southern counterparts, the northern mods had no intention of giving up their scooters. So by the time skinhead had spread across the country, the north was populated by scooter riding skinheads with their passion for soul and R&B still intact. Again, numbers were not quite what they were, but they were there all the same.

The clubs were changing music policy as well. Roger Eagle became more interested in a new black sound known as funk. Acts such as Sly and the Family Stone, James Brown and The Parliaments, led by one George Clinton, were pioneering this sound.

The African American population was finding its political voice and creating its own identity out of funk and soul. The small, local record labels and radio stations were still forging ahead with new talent and out of that came a whole new generation of labels and acts that would become known worldwide.

Back in the UK, some southern skinheads were evolving their image again. This time, their hair was being grown longer. By the end of 1969, they were known as Suedeheads. The style of the Suedeheads was mod influenced. A casually dressed suede might go for loafers, Levi's stapress, a Fred Perry shirt and a Harrington jacket. At night, on went the gleaming brogues, a suit, a Ben Sherman and the Crombie.

The suede's peak period lasted until the end of 1971. Although they had separated from the main skinhead body and were pretty much recognised as a group apart, the music was still reggae and soul-orientated. In the north, the fascination with U.S. soul and R&B continued unabated at street level. The collectors and DJs were going to extraordinary lengths to unearth a rare track. Frequent trips to America often resulted in a treasure trove of classics that had only seen the light of day in the city of its origin. Because of the British DJs and collectors, obscure labels such as Okeh, Cameo Parkway and Ric Tic were becoming known in the northern clubs.

Bigger labels like Capitol, RCA and even Tamla Motown had stocks of untapped gems. In the clubs, DJs were beginning to move away from the 'mainstream' of Stax/Atlantic and Motown sounds that were fairly medium paced and gaining airplay on radio. Instead they introduced faster dance tracks from the States that had heavy soul influences, but were different from the 'radio' soul of the time.

It was 23 September 1973 when one of the new, but now legendary all-nighter clubs opened its doors to the public. The Wigan Casino's 2am to 8am sessions were hosted by Russ Winstanley and Ian Fishwick. It had been a locally known club prior to the all-nighters, and was typical of the UK club scene through the late sixties and early seventies, mixing live acts with DJs.

RUSS WINSTANLEY came from a mod background and in an interview with Scootering Magazine, he explains how his love of music developed:

Like most people, in my early teens The Beatles hit it big. I liked that type of stuff. From what they wrote and sung, and what they talked about, I ended up hunting out Motown records. I was hooked. I got into The Small Faces and The Who as well at the time; basically the diet of mods. I remember we had Radio Caroline North at the time. They played Small Faces, stuff on the Immediate label, P P Arnold, Chris Farlowe and

Motown as well. One of the things I got really interested in was the Immediate label. I got into the whole mod image thing. It was brilliant; I had a Lambretta Li 125 when I was 16.

After a spell with a covers band called Rainbow Cottage, Russ became interested in DJing particularly after seeing Manchester DJ Tony Charles who played a lot of Motown. After Manchester, Russ would go to the Blackpool Mecca:
What a venue that was. Downstairs held 3,500; upstairs was the Highland Room. It was where I first heard Northern Soul. The DJs - Ian Levine, Keith Minshull and Tony Jebb were playing things like 'Queen of Fools' and 'Out On The Floor', and lots of other Northern Soul things. This was around '71, and at the time I was DJing at Wigan Newtown British Legion on a Thursday, and at Wigan Rugby Club on Wednesdays and Fridays. They started off as 'ordinary' discos, with a bit of current pop music as well as Motown, Stax and Atlantic. I began to play more and more Northern Soul records. I started getting records from Selectadisc in Nottingham and Record Corner in Balham, London. I really began to get into it. At Wigan Legion and the Rugby Club people who went to the Torch all-nighters started coming along, so they became mainly Northern Soul nights.

Within two years, both he and the Wigan Casino would be in direct competition with the Blackpool Mecca and The Torch in Stoke. It is pointless to argue which club had the greater following, but it led directly to interest from the media and the music business. It was left to Dave Godin, now a journalist with Blues and Soul Magazine, to give this vibrant club scene a name. He called it Northern Soul.

PAUL WELSBY, now in his mid-teens remembers going to a local venue where soul was still the staple music for clubs:
There used to be a 'teenage' disco at the Lancastrian Hall in Swinton (a Manchester suburb) every Monday night, which everyone of that same age in the town went to. As well as playing the chart fare of the time (George McCrae, KC & The Sunshine Band, "Sex Machine") the old school DJs played what would have been at the time

the commercial end of the Northern Soul scene - I recall tracks like "Backfield In Motion" or Arthur Conley's "Funky Street" (which everyone used to do a kind of line dance to) as well as all the expected Motown tracks - even Max Romeo's "Wet Dream" got regular spins (to under 16!). I started going to gigs around about aged 15, my best mate at the time, Polly, and myself went to see every black artist to visit Manchester. We saw the likes of The Miracles, Kool and The Gang, War, Toots and The Maytals and Herbie Hancock at The Free Trade Hall, Marvin Gaye, The Detroit Spinners, The Manhattans, Brass Construction, Harold Melvin & The Bluenotes, The Brothers Johnson and loads more at The Apollo. We even saw George Benson at The Palace Theatre.

I got an 'E' grade in my A level maths after falling to sleep in my Pure Maths paper having been out the night before to see James Brown at The Apollo in Ardwick. It was serious stuff.

My interest in Tamla Motown and the more commercial end of the soul spectrum got me into R&B. When you discover something as powerful as black American dance music you have an unwritten duty to explore it in more depth. If you understand this, then you'll know what I mean. If you don't you never will! As you would expect, I started picking up on Atlantic, Stax, Chess etc. And if you delve into Chess... where does it lead? To the source.

As usual, the music industry tried to manufacture the music, and as usual it did not work. There were some singles that made the charts, but the mod ethos of elitism and street-driven culture saw off the pretenders. **KEITH RYLATT** remembers how the transition evolved:

The elitism that the original mods had and the soul boys had with the clothes started to become elitism with records. That's why the clothes side started to go down. It eventually turned in an anti-fashion statement.

Indeed, fashion was changing very quickly. It was borne out of necessity rather than style. Immaculate suits and ties could not stay immaculate for very long when you were spinning and flipping head-over-heels in a nightclub. The fast and energetic music demanded fast and energetic dancing and neither was compatible with sharp dress.

The clothes were not what got you noticed; it was the way you danced that did the trick.

KEV ROBERTS, who became a Northern Soul DJ and the man behind the Goldmine / Soul Supply labels saw something of the unique mixture of influences that were taking shape in northern Britain as he told Scootering Magazine:
I grew up in Mansfield; my first venture into the world of soul was in Nottinghamshire. At the time the crowd I was hanging out with were wearing Levi sta-prest, brogues and Ben Sherman's. I never actually owned a scooter, but I rode on the back of lots of them, usually SX225s. Mansfield was a Lambretta town.
I was quite into the fashion end of things, I had a parka and a Crombie, it was a bit of a crossover between the mod and skinhead thing. There was this place in Mansfield called The Folk House - they didn't play folk music though.
There were a couple of local DJs playing a mix of ska, soul and mod. Their playlist would go something like Desmond Dekker 'It Mek', Skatalites 'Guns of Navarone', and then they'd follow with Little Hank 'Mr Bang Bang Man', Tommy Neal 'Going To A Happening' and Julian Conway 'A Little Bit Hurt'.
It was my first encounter with 'unusual' soul - I'm using the term 'unusual' as opposed to rare because the soul records they were playing weren't rare as such, but they were unusual.
Kev Robert's introduction to scooters and the remains of mod culture was one that appears to have been shared by many across the country.

A new generation of youngsters were growing up and being influenced by the skinhead/ suede look. In 1971, an 11 year-old Robin Williams, who would become better known by his nickname **YOB**, was listening to, amongst others, Dave and Ansel Collins and a former skinhead band from Wolverhampton, Slade.
Living in the Bournemouth area on the south coast, Yob had witnessed at first hand, the mods and rockers skirmishes back in the sixties. By '71 he was wearing Royal loafers, Ben Sherman's and half inch braces, the kind of attire skins and suedes around the country were developing. He noticed girls were doing something similar. Tonic suits with

short skirts, crepe soled loafers, Levi 'red tags' and a form of skinhead haircut for girls known as the 'feather cut'.

The one other factor he noticed, was that the older boys with scooters had a bit more luck with the girls. By the time he was 16, Yob already had a fascination with scooters. He'd even been 'modifying' scooters and using them as off-road scramblers for a few years. His first on-road scooter was a SX150. While just about everybody else of school-leaving age was tearing around on Yamaha FS1Es, or 'fizzys' as they were known, Yob and friend Alan Prax were certain they were the only two scooter boys in the Poole and Bournemouth area.

In 1976, Yob heard of a group of Northern Soul fans that rode scooters. He went on the 15 mile run to Swanage and duly found what he was looking for. Before long, the informal get-togethers of scooter-riders from the major towns in Dorset decided to form a scooter club known as the 'Lowriders'.

Eventually, they found a photocopied fanzine called 'Scooter and Scooterist' produced by Norrie Kerr, and discovered they were not the only ones who persevered with scooters. In 1977 the Lowriders attended the Vespa Club of Great Britain rally, even though they and south coast were dominated by Lambrettas. From this meeting, the club got to find out about the healthy northern scooter scene and the unofficial runs to places like Scarborough. After that rally, the Lowriders decided a name change was needed, and so the Modropheniacs was born as **YOB** told Scootering Magazine:

There was no stigma attached to the term mod. Many scooterists considered themselves mods, although they wore wide jeans, Doc Martens, greatcoats or parkas. There was no animosity between the North and South; it was just a feeling of belonging to a tremendous brotherhood.

The Modropheniacs would continue to grow and take part in a film shoot in Brighton a few years later.

Back in London another man who would play a part in the longevity of mod culture was beginning his career as a DJ in 1974 with his brother Rob. Tony Class played mainly sixties and Motown when they first started.

> Eric Clapton was a good friend at the time. One Sunday morning after he had played at the club, he brought a good looking young mod girl round to my place and she got completely pissed off because all he wanted to do was listen to Freddie King records.
>
> ROGER EAGLE

By 1977, Rob had bought a Lambretta Li 150, which he called 'English Rose' and it was Rob and five others who formed the Viceroys Scooter Club, meeting at the Hercules Tavern where they were doing discos. In 1979 there was a shortage of mod discos so Tony and Rob did their first one on November 9 at the Hercules. After Rob decided to quit because of the amount of fights at the discos, Tony carried on. His real influence was to be seen in the next decade.

The late sixties and early seventies were definitely a barren period for mod. It even took its toll on one of its most ardent champions and one of its most famous clubs. First, **JOHN SIMONS**:
In the seventies, I got out of the clothing trade. I went to study art and modernism, but then I got back into it in '78-'79 and it affected my business greatly because that's when I opened J. Simons. So from '72 to '79, it was a wilderness period where I used it for other agendas that I had. But there wasn't much happening because the demand was for the 'flowery' type of fashion.

JEFFREY KRUGER explains what happened to The Flamingo Club as the seventies past the midway point:
The trend for R&B and the allnighter sessions held steady right through pretty much to the end, mainly because we managed to persuade and get hold of most of the visiting Americans to come down. The kids could always see a John Lee Hooker or a Stevie Wonder in an atmosphere where they would never see them ever again, close-up, shoulder to shoulder and literally they would have to make way. There would be an inch wide gap for Stevie Wonder to be brought through, so they could touch him, see him and feel him, but the earlier sessions were definitely a cause for concern.
We decided we had to change with the times and bring in 'Flower Power', so our booking policy changed and at one point in the late sixties we called it The Pink Flamingo and redecorated inside in pink and with the groups we could get, it was like a resurgence of the old days.
For a few years we did super business, but we were all getting tired and I truly didn't

have a hands-on situation. You know, if you have a one-on-one business, if you let go, the business goes down and eventually it went down, and I started to let out odd nights to the guys who had bought the Whiskey-A-Go-Go upstairs, Elliott Cohen and Elias Alyas, and they were running Thursday night gigs, but nothing really worked.

We had to strip the place and start again, but we could never get permission from, as it was then, the LCC, London County Council, because we had trouble with emergency exits and so a decision was made sometime in 1974 to shut the place down. It had to be closer to 1977 actually, because I had a 25 year lease and that would have been up in '76 or '77 and it was about a year before the lease and that's all I can recollect about that time. We had the best of the flower power groups, power house groups, they wanted to play the club, they loved the atmosphere. I think the money was nice but it was not commensurate with what it was taking out of me personally and professionally.

Rik Gunnell had a very successful agency and there were so many rumours about what happened to him. I heard he went to Australia, but he was part of the allnighter sessions almost to the end.

If anything we went out with a whimper, but it was mobbed on the last night and there was a tremendous amount of press, but the club was looking its 25 years, and the entrance, which I hated from day one, I could do nothing about because it was a common entrance and the LCC wouldn't even let me paint it without special permission. It got to a stage where I couldn't bear it.

I had always liked promoting, viz The Flamingo and the Jazz At The Flamingo units we used to put on at the Palladium and take all round the country and into Europe, so I decided to concentrate on concert promotion from 1971 onwards.

By the mid seventies another new scene was making its presence felt. Malcolm McClaren grew up in north London, in the very same places which had seen teddy boys and then mods grow and develop.

Vivienne Westwood had married Derek Westwood in 1962. Derek was putting on club nights across north London, which included the Railway Hotel in Harrow and Wealdstone, which was also frequently host to The Who. It was at the Railway Hotel, that Malcolm and Vivienne first met. Both had one thing in common. They had spent time at Art Schools, the same environment that had inspired many of the musicians and songwriters of the sixties. It was at Art School that McClaren began to formulate a new idea and concept of sub-cultural significance.

In 1975 McClaren and Westwood opened a shop called Sex on the Kings Road, Chelsea. The scene became known as Punk and its aim was to counter the sanitised and dominant pop and rock establishment and had socio-political pretensions. From this base, a disparate group of people came together; not least of whom were Johnny Rotten, Paul Cook, Glen Matlock and Steve Jones. With McClaren as their manager, the four became The Sex Pistols.

Once they had started playing gigs, The Pistols displayed 'mod' influences, if only due to their early gigs being made up of The Who and Small Faces covers with slight changes of lyrics.

JOE FOSTER, who would be in a punk band himself in time, made this observation:
I think there was a bit of mod influence in The Buzzcocks and so were the Sex Pistols. Their choice of covers tells you that. It was always Small Faces and things like that. I think a lot of people saw themselves as mods really before punk had a name. Some of them looked like mods and some looked like weird 'Rocky Horror' types, but they all went to the same gigs and nobody thought to call it punk, except the Daily Mirror, or was it Malcolm (McClaren)?
It was just one of those things where all these different people who were strange in different ways, got together and said let's just agree not to laugh at each other and we'll get on fine.

With McClaren's penchant for publicity and The Pistols willing to go along with the plan, punk exploded onto the unsuspecting public.

The true origins of punk are hotly disputed. Some claim it was started in New York with bands like The New York Dolls, The Ramones and the pseudo-mod influenced Blondie.

Others claim it started in London. Arguably, the London scene was by far the more prominent, had greater impact and changed the face of the music industry. From the early London scene came The Clash (whom writer Jon Savage describes as a classic mod group in their early days), Siouxsie and The Banshees, Billy Idol, Adam Ant and Sid Vicious to name a few. It became a liberating force for many whom, for a variety of reasons, would have otherwise remained in obscurity. It offered the chance to do something and be somebody. Punk gained notoriety for its visual style, its anti-establishment stance and being rooted in the British working class. Punk also suffered as all youth sub-cultures do. Over exposure, confusion spun by an ignorant mainstream media and being labelled as a threat to society.

That said, from 1976 onwards, it helped to spawn a mass of new bands that were eagerly snapped up by an equally stale and ignorant music industry, greedy to get in on the new trend. Elvis Costello, The Clash, The Damned, The Stranglers, The Jam, The Police, 999, Generation X and The Buzzcocks were all signed up quickly by the industry.

The term punk was grossly misused by the mainstream media and the music industry. The term New Wave had been coined by Malcolm McClaren originally, but the media adopted it. New Wave could be applied to bands that were not punks in the true sense, but identified the new crop of bands that had the 'sound' that was similar to punk.

And it was not only in London that the punk / new wave scene took off. DJ and R&B champion of the sixties, Roger Eagle opened a club in Liverpool called Eric's, which gave new bands a venue to play live.

In Manchester, it was the Electric Circus club that brought people together, who would form bands out of punk inspiration.

One punk band who had sixties and mod influences was The TV Personalities. Lead singer **ED BALL** explains the early days of a band whose members would have a profound effect on British pop music years later:

Growing up when I did in the early to mid seventies and going to secondary school, there were five of us who used to hang out. Dan Treacy, Joe Foster, John and Gerard Bennett, who were brothers, and me. Dan was a massive Who fan, Joe was a fan of

Velvet Underground and Sid Barrett's Pink Floyd, and I was a fan of early Pink Floyd as well, but also The Beatles and The Kinks. I think we were kind of anachronisms at the time. It wasn't the case that we didn't like the bands of the time, you know Wizard, Sweet or Mud, but it seemed a bit garish to us compared to how we thought bands should look and act like. There was also a deeper resonance when bands like The Who, The Beatles and Sid's Pink Floyd wrote songs that even at 12 or 13 years old, we could understand.

As an extension of that, we would buy what records we could. Now, at the time, '73, '74, obviously there were no CDs and reissue boxed sets you get now. You had to really hunt for copies of 'Piper At The Gates Of Dawn', the Velvet Underground album, The Who's 'Sell Out' or The Kink's 'Face To Face' and it was all done on pocket money. I think Record and Tape Exchange had just opened in Notting Hill Gate and there were a couple of Beggar's Banquet shops that used to do second-hand records as well, so that's where we would buy our stuff.

So we were already anachronisms in terms of being into sixties music and added to that, Dan used to tell us stories about how his sister used to be a mod. She was five or six years older than him, and he would tell us about how she would ride on the back of her boyfriend's scooter. It was all these things going on, then Paul Weller and The Jam appeared. Now before punk happened, we were listening to The Kinks, The Who and Beatles songs and we were in a band.

Then punk came along. It was exciting and great to be part of, and we were part of it by making our own records, but the problem was so much of punk was garbage and lacked humour.

It was bands like Chelsea and Eater, although there were a lot of great bands, there was a lot of rubbish and what we were doing with things like 'Part-Time Punks', 'Where's Bill Grundy Now?' and 'We Love Malcolm' was trying to bring a sense of humour to the proceedings, which we thought was in keeping with mid-sixties comedy songs that The Beatles and The Kinks used to specialise in. But The Beatles did say that when they were writing 'Rubber Soul', they wanted to write comedy songs, something with an element of humour, like 'Drive My Car', and a lot of Ray

Davies' stuff was like that. The Small Faces, especially with 'Ogden's Nutgone Flake' is brilliant. It was that and Paul Weller being so overtly early Who, he was our unsung hero really. So, this is how I became interested in mod and in terms of going beyond our hearts in the shape of the band, that would be about '78, '79.

Prior to that, we had a band called O Level. We called it O Level because we were all doing our O level exams at the time. That was our defiance and on the first single, we put the names of all the teachers we hated. We didn't even credit ourselves and usually on your first record, you can't wait to see your name on the credits, but we just wanted to get those people back, so we did some singles as O Level and then TV Personalities. We did 'Fourteenth Floor' and 'Part-Time Punks' and then bands like The Chords, The Purple Hearts and Back To Zero (BTZ) came along and we were really good mates with BTZ and Brian Betteridge.

We had been making records for about a year and a half before them and getting played by John Peel on Radio One and getting features in NME and Sounds. We were getting what you would now call a profile. We didn't know that's what it was, we just thought we were famous and we'd had a big selling single, 'Part-Time Punks', but we met these guys and they were more our age. The punk mob were all about five years older than us, so we found a kindred spirit with a lot of those bands.

To learn how to play songs, we'd get old Who, Pink Floyd and Beatle albums and learn those things and that's how we learnt how to write, to tell a story and have a dig as well, and it was a good thing that John Peel and a few bright-spark journalists picked up on it.

I think in comparison to a lot of the mod bands, we were quite twee. I mean, we never practiced, we never tried very hard, everything we recorded was done on the first take, and it shows. But you listen to The Chords, and they sound raw now, but they do have a spunkiness about them and energy, but they were trying hard to play well. So they probably thought we were jokers.

JOE FOSTER was another member of the TV Personalities, and he explains how the band ended up bridging the gap between punk and mod of 1979:

Well it was that whole kind of Art School thing and we were very much into the pop art aspect of it. I got to know Kenny Pickett of The Creation and that kind of brought it into a reality. Years later I met the people from the Velvet Underground, but it's not quite the same thing. Kenny and Eddie (Ball) were the chaps up the road, you know? But it was that pop art thing, an affectation almost, dressing up to annoy other art students. They'd all show up with fake dreadlocks and you turn up looking like Brian Jones, it really pisses them off. We couldn't afford to do the full thing on student grants, but it was good enough. We got into the habit of dressing like that and doing our own thing and at a particular point we were recording at a studio near The Wellington in Waterloo. We popped for a pint and got to meet all those guys that were doing the '79 thing. It was very interesting meeting people who were coming at it from all different angles and they all had one thing in common. It never occurred that some guy working in a shop in Walthamstow wouldn't know what we were talking about because they invariably did, and I think it was the last gasp of like, working class people having interests and being quite clever. I was talking to Tony Barber about this and he was saying that nowadays people seem to be really thick. Years ago there would be someone you're dad knew who was a brick layer or something and he would know everything about the Roman empire or something like that. That's when people had interests.

The publicity and furore surrounding The Sex Pistols and punk inspired many young kids to have a go themselves. While The Buzzcocks flew the flag for Manchester, a band named The Killermetres were putting Huddersfield on the punk map. Formed in 1977, Mick Moore and **VIC VOMIT** (as he was known in his punk days) were typically inspired by The Pistols and The Damned. Vic had been interested in music while at school and learnt to play bass guitar. His earliest musical memory is hearing The Beatles' 'Sgt Pepper' album and being into The Kinks and Rolling Stones.
The Killermetres certainly worked hard, gigging regularly and supporting some major punk and new wave acts like The Slits, X-Ray Specs and The Rich Kids (featuring ex-Pistol Glen Matlock and future Ultravox frontman Midge Ure.) They even supported the Rock

Against Racism gigs that had risen in opposition to the increasing fascist leanings in certain quarters of the music business, most notably the Sham 69 following of hardened 'political' skinheads. As Vic states, the DIY ethos of punk was a huge inspiration:
The best bit about punk was, you could write and perform your own songs no matter how good or bad they were. You were encouraged to do it because everyone else was doing it.
Although we were doing loads of gigs, we couldn't get a record deal. We played the Pulse in Manchester and Tony Wilson was there from Fiction Records. He told us our stuff was too melodic!
Things really started to change for us when we saw The Jam at the Huddersfield Students Union Hall. They were so full of energy and I think, because our songs were a bit eclectic and sixties influenced compared to other punk bands, we kind of connected with Paul Weller's writing and what he was doing with The Jam.
It was about that time that our lead singer decided to leave and I got pushed into doing the vocals. We also had Tony and Sid Ruttle in the band and they were really into mod. I got into it from then and that would have been towards the end of 1978.

It would also mark the end of Vic Vomit and the emergence of **VIC VESPA** as frontman of The Killermetres. As Vic hinted, one of the best aspects to come out of punks manifesto was the do-it-yourself attitude. This inspired people like Mark Perry to start a fanzine called Sniffin' Glue. Although Sniffin' Glue was the original inspiration for many others that followed in punk, the fanzine tradition it started, carried an influence on for many years within subsequent sub-cultures. For those in London who got into the punk scene proper, it was losing its appeal and vitality by 1977.

GOFFA GLADDING was one of many such punk fans:
Musically I was terrifically interested in punk around 1976, 1977. As it turned out, the people I got to know subsequently had also been interested in punk, but had lost interest really by late '77, early '78. So there was an element of; 'What do we do now that the buzz has gone out of punk? What was the next direction and what was the

next area of interest?' That's where the mod thing came from. Paul Weller and The Jam are hugely influential in all this. But of course if you look at 'In The City', that was '77, and this is where some of the kids who started following The Jam, first got the idea. Some of the kids who supported West Ham United, they were big Jam fans. They were big punk fans too, but they latched on to The Jam image. They'd been through the safety pins and gelled hair thing, but they pursued the more modernist look, if you like. It just kind of kicked off from there.

I'd been a massive Who fan since I saw them in 1971 on the 6 November at the Rainbow. It's something I'll always remember, but I was a fan anyway, and that was the time of 'Who's Next', and then 'Quadrophenia' came after that.

So I had an interest in youth culture anyway, but mods always held a particular fascination for me. It was something about the clothes and the music in particular. I've always been a fan of R&B and soul, as well as what is termed mod music of the sixties, you know, The Small Faces. I'm not sure how big a part that played in the mod scene, but they've always had that mod tag as well as The Who. So it was the music for me really.

Punk music was fantastic for a period of time, then it deteriorated quite quickly for me into a lot of trash and there was nothing I was really interested in. But, when I first went to see The Chords play, I think the first time I saw them was one of their first nights at The Wellington at Waterloo on a Saturday night which was fantastic, it just seemed to bring back all that was good about punk music. It had echoes of the brilliant days of Generation X at the Marquee, 999 and people like that in '77.

All the energy and the excellent songs were there. So that was terrific for me and it was the start of something new and quite excellent, and also small, that was the thing. You can loose interest if you go to see The Clash at the Lyceum or some big venue, but to see a group close up in a pub like that, you get to feel the energy and it's that much better.

Meanwhile, Brian Kotz was going to punk gigs on a regular basis in 1978, although he always referred to himself as a mod, even at the age of 16.

Brian had been in a school band called The Unexplained and due to splitting up with his then girlfriend Sarah Betteridge, Brian adopted her surname by way of teenage retribution.

In October of '78, Brian was going to see a band called The Crooks who had a residency at a pub called The Pegasus. There along with members of local band The Scooters, he met John Wheeldon, a school friend, who was forming a band with another friend, Mal Malyon. They called themselves The Modern Boys. A week later, John, Mal and Brian were at a Chords gig at North East London Polytechnic in Walthamstow. The Who's 'Substitute' was on the jukebox and Brian sang along with it. That was his audition, and he joined The Modern Boys. In time, Sam Burnett joined as a guitarist and John Wheeldon left. Andy Moore joined, became the bands drummer and by the middle of February 1979 Sam Burnett's sister Hilary mentioned the band to her boyfriend Clive Reams. It was Clive who gave the band their new name. Back To Zero.

Clive then recruited two friends, Kim Gault and Goffa Gladding to help with managing Back To Zero, and from that, the three started a fanzine for the emerging bands and scene that had come out of the shadow of the punk explosion.

Maximum Speed became quite important for both bands and mods alike, although some of its editorial policy caused a problem here and there. As **BRIAN BETTERIDGE** explains:

I could go through issue one to nine and pick out the things that were wrong with it. But let's say they had their favourites and their 'non-favourites'.

I think The Crooks were given a really rough time as bandwagon jumpers. The thing is I'd known a couple of members of The Crooks since I was 14.

When we started, even as Back To Zero, The Crooks gave us equipment and stuff they didn't want; they gave Mal Malyon his first bass amp. They really helped us and got us our first gigs.

They were also under the management of Jaz Summers, who is a big cheese in the music industry right to this day. He said 'Well you've got a mod following, dress as mods'. I thought it was un-necessary, but a lot of people took offense.

Brighton [courtesy of Loz Lewin]

I didn't take offense, but I remember a gig in May '79 at The Pegasus, The Scooters were all there and they did nothing but stand in front of The Crooks and abuse them all night. Mal and I both went up and shook the lead singer, Deano's hand to say, 'Look this isn't us'. The sad thing is, after The March Of The Mods Tour, the first gig I went to in September '79 was a Crooks gig at the Bridgehouse. Deano totally blanked me, but Tim the guitarist said 'We're not supposed to like you'. So we talked about how they were treated and I absolutely agreed with his point of view, these were my friends, but because I was there and to him I represented Maximum Speed and because Back To Zero were managed by them, after about three or four songs, Deano said on stage "I want to say something about Maximum Speed, we think it's shit, we don't like it. They say we're old men, here's Micky our 18 year-old drummer" (they were considered old men because they were 23).

They were given a seriously rough deal and I don't care if anyone disagrees with me. I flatly refuse to criticise The Crooks and if you're going to criticise anything, it's the direction Jaz Summers made them take not the band themselves. But if they thought Jaz Summer's management was going to help them, would any band say, 'Were going to stick to our principles and play in toilets all our lives?' Of course not.

Aside from the emerging scene building in London, The Jam, after a solid start to their career in 1977, had suffered the punk tag. Their associations with bands like The Clash indicated to the mainstream that they must be punks. It was obvious though, that The Jam were not punks at all. They may have had a rough, raw sound. They may have had the attitude, but they were definitely not punks. Their inspiration came from another time. Just as The Clash had taken reggae as their influence, so The Jam took theirs from the sixties.

On the 3 November 1978, The Jam released arguably their greatest album 'All Mod Cons'. It was highly acclaimed by the music press and became a landmark in the bands history. More importantly, it marked the starting point of a renewed interest in the mod subculture for a wider audience.

With 'All Mod Cons' reaching number six in the album charts, The Jam's fan base expanding at a rate of knots and Weller's style references to mod, interest in the subculture began to grow.

It was around this time that two more individuals would meet by chance on Great Marlborough Street in London. Terry Rawlings was on his way to Carnaby Street when he saw another mod heading towards him.

As there were so few mods around at that time, meeting another mod would instantly lead to introductions and so it was that **TERRY RAWLINGS** met **GARY CROWLEY:**

My Uncle Dave and Auntie Christine were mods and I would interrogate them when they popped over to the flat. That was the initial seed of interest and then when Punk happened and I got enamoured with the Jam, it was chocks away. I was in hook, line and sinker. I'd been waiting for a band like The Jam to come along. Pre punk I had a fascination with 60's pop culture/mod and The Jam encapsulated all of that as well as putting a contemporary spin on things. I can vividly remember going to see The Jam at the Lyceum Ballroom on the Strand in the early summer of 1978 (between the releases of 'This Is The Modern World' and ' All Mod Cons ') and distinctly remembering seeing a row of scooters parked outside and thinking something is definitely happening here. I always thought of myself as a cross between a mod and a punk. I loved the clothes and music of the early to mid 60's, but I equally had one foot in the Punk camp with its contemporary cutting edge and bands like the Clash, Generation X, Buzzcocks and later The Specials. I took the best from both worlds.

At that time, **GARY** was a post room boy at Decca Records:
I wrote to all the record companies but Decca, who were probably one of the uncoolest labels going at the time (1978/79), were the only ones who answered!
But it was a fantastic company with some amazing people there who I learnt an awful lot from. Plus I got to meet my first girlfriend Niamh there. She was the younger sister of Siobhan Fahey, who was the receptionist and would go on to be a member of Bananarama. When I first met Terry Rawlings, I think we were both admiring each

other's threads on Great Marlborough Street. That's what you did back then. My lovely Auntie Olive knitted me a lovely red and black Pop Art style jumper which I absolutely adored and wore till it literally fell apart in my hands, now that jumper used to spark up a lot of conversations with people.

It turned out to be a very lucky meeting for **TERRY RAWLINGS**, as Gary explained he was leaving his job at Decca and that Terry should apply. He got the job and Gary moved on to New Musical Express:
I got the NME gig through popping up there on a regular basis as the Decca office boy, taking over from Danny Baker on reception at their offices in Carnaby Street.
At this time the weekly music paper was at the centre of the Post Punk explosion under the editorship of Neil Spencer. I would sit there on reception watching people like Julie Burchill, Tony Parsons, Nick Kent, Charles Shaar Murray and Adrian Thrills file by. It was exciting times for an 18 year old believe you me.
After being there for nearly a year, I then met at a gig a lovely fella called Clive Banks who was THE top radio/tv plugger and I subsequently got a my own radio show on Capital Radio, and at 19 became the youngest radio DJ in the UK.

Terry Rawlings stayed at Decca and he and Gary Crowley would compile the Decca maxi mod single 'London Boys' featuring tracks by David Bowie, Dobie Gray, Small Faces and The Birds released in 1979.
Terry Rawlings was also going to the Thomas A Becket on Old Kent Road where he would see Stan's Blues Band featuring Dennis Greaves and Mark Feltham who would go on to form Nine Below Zero and The Truth.
It was also at that venue where Terry first met Billy Hassett, who was looking for gigs for his band The Detours which included Martin Mason, Chris Pope and Paul Halpin.

Another band and contemporaries of The Jam in Woking, Surrey had just started to get things together as **ANTHONY MEYNELL** explains:
By the seventies my family had moved to Guildford and Squire came from Woking,

which is only five miles away, but Guildford has its own music scene and if I was in any of it, it was in school bands from Guildford. Squire formed in 1974 as a bunch of friends from school and they had played together on and off for four years until I met them in 1978. I met them because my girlfriend Carolyn, worked as a hairdresser in the same shop that Enzo worked in. He was in a band, so she mentioned that I had just left a band and had written some songs. So I went with my brother, who had been in bands with me before, but we were always playing to someone else's agenda and I wasn't very confident as a front man and lead singer, so I always joined as second guitar. I did some demos and my girlfriend played them to Enzo who liked them and he suggested that, as Squire wasn't doing anything, why don't we get together and do a rehearsal? So my brother Kevin and I went to Woking for the rehearsal.

Now they had got into a bit of a rut. They rehearsed on a Sunday, so they set up at 11 o'clock, the pubs would open and they would go to a pub, get smashed, come back and thrash about for half an hour and go home at 3 o'clock. Well, after three Sundays of this, Kevin had enough and decided to do something else and I had to leave as well because we wanted to do something together.

My songs were very 'poppy' and as a songwriter you want the confidence to know your songs are good, so I did a demo tape of ten songs, which I called 'The Numbers' because I wanted a band called The Numbers and took it to Step Forward Records which was Mark Perry's label set up with Miles Copeland, and Mark had been writing a fanzine called Sniffin' Glue, so it was very much a punk thing and I gave him these tapes and he said the songs were singles and where was the band? I said I didn't have a band, so Mark said get a band and we'll do you a deal.

Carolyn mentioned this to Enzo, whose ears shot up and he was very interested in that. Enzo was ambitious. He had played in his band, but he wanted more and that's how he and I connected really well.

They had all gone to school with Paul Weller in Sheerwater and Enzo knew Paul quite well and I think Steve Baker may have been in the same class as Paul, I'm not sure, but by this time The Jam were successful and had left the area and they weren't in touch so much. Anyway, Enzo heard the songs and wanted me back in the band and they had a gig coming up supporting The Jam at Guildford Civic Hall and they didn't want to do it as a three piece, they wanted to go as a four piece and do the songs of mine they had learnt, but they needed me in the band to do them. So I rejoined Squire, and they had Ross Dilanda, their original drummer back as well. Kevin had only stayed for the three weeks.

The Jam gig refocused Squire. They wanted to do something, and they knew my songs were 'poppy' where they had been 'punky'. I think the rest of the band were awkward about it and you can tell from the photos that there was the three of them and then me. I was in the band, but not part of it at that time really.

The Jam gig was phenomenal, 1978, 1,000 people, The Jam at the height of their career, 'All Mod Cons' was just about to come out and they were on a role. 'A Bomb In Wardour Street' was the song of the moment and we're on stage with them in our hometown. I think Enzo had auditioned for The Jam at some point, but they chose someone else. So The Jam and Squire had both started at about the same time, 1974, as school bands and The Jam went on to better things and Squire got left behind, but then The Jam were always managed by Paul's dad, John, who was so loyal to the band and focused that success was inevitable, and it was John Weller who got Squire the gig. They knew John and he was always hanging around Woking anyway looking at and watching bands and he did pick up and manage The Vapours rather than Squire. I think this was because it was a bit too 'incestuous' in that Squire were the other main Woking band and we were mod, when The Jam kept saying they weren't. But as for the gig itself, I don't remember much more than people just saying hello to Paul and he came to a party after the gig, but the didn't stay long. You could tell he had 'moved' to London by that time and his head was there.

I think the gig crystallised what Squire were about to do. They were a covers band and they had some soul numbers in the set like 'My Girl' and 'Dancing in The Street'. The reason for that was, Enzo had learnt those songs for The Jam audition. I know this because Enzo gave me a Tamla Motown songbook that Paul Weller owned at one time, and it has all the songs marked with the key that The Jam would do them in. Paul lent it to Enzo to learn and Enzo had never given it back, then I got it and I still have it today. So, for Squire it was a case of letting me write and get those songs into the set. That was the way it was going to go. The first songs we did were from the 'Numbers' demo tape. 'Living In The City' and things like that. They were quite punky, but they weren't written with a particular band in mind, and I suppose some would say they were unsuitable. A lot of them ended up on a Squire fan club album as an interesting artefact because they were the first songs I gave to Squire to learn.

We decided we were going to get a PA, get a demo tape together, do some gigs and see how far we could go. So Enzo and I quickly became friends and we did a demo, three of my songs and one of theirs. I think they wanted it to be two and two, but for whatever reason it was three and one. A friend of theirs became the manager and they sent the tape off to Rok Records who were going to put some singles out. They liked it and they wanted to put out 'Get Ready To Go' which was one of mine, and their second choice was 'Living in The City' which was also one of mine. That kind of confirmed the fact that the songs that they wanted were mine and we found ourselves with a one-off record deal.

It was quite an important step for us, because it meant we could start getting into London and in 1978, it was a strange time because it was between punk and whatever was to come next. All the excitement of punk had dissipated and anarchy had turned to apathy. The punk bands that were on a roll weren't anymore.

If you look at The Jam for instance, their second album hadn't sold well and the demo for the third album was rejected. This was the publisher telling Paul Weller "this isn't good enough". And then he goes away and writes 'All Mod Cons' which is my favourite album. I love the story of the demo being rejected because I think Paul really dug deep into himself and that album was right for the time.

The Sex Pistols had gone, The Clash were just about to put out 'London's Calling' which was rock and the second wave of punk were really a bunch of chancers from the suburbs. Some of them were good and you had bands like The Members who were okay, but they weren't the leaders of anything, they were the followers of everything and there were so many of them. So punk was over. I suppose Squire could have been in that bracket as well. After the Jam gig, we were called bantamweight punk because that's what people heard. When the single came we knew we had to get the image right and next door to the hairdressers where Enzo worked was a clothes shop and the guy who owned it had been a mod in the sixties, heard the music and said we sounded mod. He suggested we wear Harringtons and Staprest and he would supply the clothes for us to go to London, so we did.

When we went for the photo shoot for the single cover, we were a mod band totally, and we thought we were the only ones! Obviously we weren't, but somewhere in London, something had happened and we discovered the more we played in London, the bands we heard were like us.

The first we heard about it was a snippet in New Musical Express that said a band called The Chords were playing a gig in Hampstead, so we went to have a look and there were twenty kids in parkas. This was our audience, we knew they would like us and Maximum Speed were there and we spoke to them. That made a big difference to us because we were in issue two of this mod magazine.

We had a gig coming up in early 1979 at the Rock Club, which was upstairs at Ronnie Scott's. The reason behind that was because The Jam had got a lot of record company interest by getting a gig upstairs at Ronnie Scott's in 1976-'77 and they shipped two coach loads of fans up from Woking to be rent-a-crowd and invited record company people down who saw all these fans loving the gig and it worked for them.

So we decided to do the same and booked this gig and took two coach loads with us. By that time we had met The Purple Hearts and we did a deal where they would support us at Ronnie Scott's and we would support them at their next gig, so they brought their crowd and there were all these people wedged into this small place but it was fantastic. We had crossed over and that opened the door into London.

In a short space of time we had done The Jam gig, got the single, got the image right that suited the music and we were focused. It made sense to us.

Mod had already started in London, mainly because of Jam fans, who were fanatics. They would go to every gig and they became the revival in a way.

There weren't many of them, but they had that in common and they dressed in parkas and so on, and that became the audience. Nick Roeg was filming Quadrophenia at the start of 1979 and he used those people as extras, so you knew something was happening and it was good to be part of something that was fresh and very young.

We were all 17 or 18 and it was like punk, but the antithesis of punk at the same time. It wasn't razor-sharp, but people looked good even though we were all broke. It was good enough and you could be in the scene.

The Jam and Paul Weller are as crucial to the history of mod as any one or anything can be. However, it was never the intention of this book to rehash the story of The Jam and Paul Weller. That story is more than adequately documented elsewhere. Neither does this book pretend to add anything new to the material already available, but to try to ignore the contribution of The Jam and Paul Weller to mod culture and British music would be an exercise in futility. The evidence that Jam fans were just as responsible for renewed interest in mod as The Jam themselves is indisputable.

PAUL WELSBY is just one of many thousands of people who readily acknowledge The Jam's influence:

My first "formal" introduction to mod came - like many others of my age - in the late seventies via The Jam. That was when I first realised that poor fitting tonic suits, parkas and Who-sounding bands equalled mod.

This was quickly widened out to include the ska and Rude Boy sounds of The Specials et al. What took me a while to realise, was that all the stuff I had been listening to since the age of 12 - sixties Motown, Stax and Atlantic, and Trojan reggae had more to do with mod than the stuff that I then considered mod.

To analyse the musical contribution of The Jam, **ED BALL** sums up just how vital their success has meant to British music:

The importance of The Jam has still not been fully appreciated. Paul Weller as a young man, was naturally artistically gifted without the benefits of having gone to art school like some members of the other punk bands had. But it was Weller who was the first to bring pop art imagery back to pop music. He was brave, insolent, pioneering, arrogant, inspiring and I so badly wanted to be him. The charade of the Pistols theatre and The

Clash's world view politics probably made them ironically internationally famous, but Weller's songs and the sound of The Jam has never encapsulated the sound of young Britain more. Absolutely no one before or since did that without American influence.

I think it is fair to say that The Jam's musical career can be viewed in three periods: Punk '77-79, perfectly mod inspired by Beatles '66 and the Soul Movement.

The second period for me is absolute perfection. Lyrically, Weller may stand as one of Britain's finest ever poets. Also, his targets are well aimed, the band had not become too big to make the right observations about the right enemies.

I've always been pleased for Paul Weller's success since The Jam, but there is a romance to those combinations that God seems to throw together like John, Paul, George and Ringo or Steve (Cook) and Paul (Jones) and of course Bruce, Rick and Paul. ·◊·

> It means different things to different people, but I don't think you can really define it. The thing about the mod scene, is that it has run itself from within and no one has managed to grab a hold of it and turn it into some kind of commercial venture from the outside. It's self-contained.
> I think it has and will continue to reinvent itself.
> ROB BAILEY

CHAPTER 4

It seems to be widely accepted that two particular events brought together the small pockets of Jam fans that became the start of the mod revival.
The first was the Great British Music Festival at Wembley on 29 November 1978, where The Jam headlined. The second was in February 1979 when a trip to Paris to see The Jam was organised by Grant Flemming. Among them was drummer **BRETT BUDDY ASCOTT** who had just joined Chris Pope, Martin Mason and Billy Hassett as The Chords a few weeks prior to the Paris trip:
Billy Hassett was my gateway into finding out about it. The trip was extremely messy -

especially for me. Somebody told me the French police would be searching everyone on arrival, so I took all the speed I had on me - which was a lot! Everyone was off their heads on this stuff, it gave us such bravado. I think there was quite a bit of fighting at the actual concert, probably between French and British mods, and the drugs wouldn't have helped. I ended up sleeping on the floor of Jo Wallace's brother's flat (I think) trying to come down - I felt terrible! I don't remember meeting the group that night, not me... I think they were very pleased to have such a massive contingent there to support them - we all got in on the guest list, after attending the sound check. I went home the next morning.

BILLY HASSETT takes up the story:
I knew of Grant Flemming by being at gigs. I didn't know him personally, but we were on nodding terms which developed through this trip. Martin Mason and I were in our school's concert band. Both of us were then in the London Schools Concert Band, which was a mighty achievement, especially for lads from Bermondsey. Mind you a lot of the chaps in the school band progressed and many led the way. So, music was very important for us, and it very much was a part of our lives. We got our first guitars when we were around 14/15 and always had a dream to be in our own band. When punk came about, it gave us the freedom and confidence to try and we played our first gig at our schools 6th form party. In a nutshell, we both had a firm background of classical training and for us forming our own band was a development from those experiences. After the Paris gig, we split and returned to London and the other guys went south. I remember meeting French mods before the gig; Weller being so blown away that he got us backstage after the show and let us finish off the food.
There was a club we took over after the show; sleeping together on a metro platform; a couple of old French guys saluting us. Many fond memories, but there was a level of excitement, craic and good bonhomie that was maintained throughout the trip. Unforgettable! The gig itself was magnificent. We were all at the front with flags and stuff, and the French crowd were ok with us. There was a healthy vibe and we met many French mods who helped us get to the club after.

Billy Hassett's brother **MIKE** also went on the trip. Here are his recolllections:

We found out about it in the music papers that The Jam were doing a European tour and we pretty much decided we would go to see them in Paris. Apart from myself and Billy, there was also Don Begley, Tesco (Neil), Brett, Jo (she used to work in HMV) and those two lads from east London think they were called Dave and Steve. We went to Charing Cross and found out about trains and the hovercraft and decided to go. About two weeks before we went, someone turned up at a gig (it might have been The Members at the Marquee) saying they knew someone else that was going and had a phone number. The number was Hilary and they were going on the same train. We got to Charing Cross - Brett got on at Sevenoaks - about 10 mins after we got there about 20 or so ex Sham 69 following West Ham fans turned up. Some of them were known as the Benfleet mob (they got a mention on the album sleeve of All Mod Cons). Grant Flemming led them out! First thing he said was "Are you Millwall!?. We recognised Dave Lawrence... we saw him when we were standing outside a Jam gig at Brighton, the November the year before. He pulled up on a scooter in front of the stage door opened it, and he went in. We both thought lucky bastard - at that stage we never had a ticket! Anyway, we got on the train then a A4 photocopy came out titled Mods Pilgrimage. On it there was an itinerary of sorts it was then we found out they (the mob not mods) were going for two gigs Paris and Reims. Most of us never had passports. There was a system in place where you could get a permit to travel to France I think it lasted 36 or 48 hours. Most of us had these permits but on the way back those who went to Reims had expired permits!

I remember leaving Charing Cross around 6.30 getting to Paris around 2pm. The journey was horrible, I can go into more details but it's mainly about bored teenagers looking for something to do. The train between Calais and Paris was where Dave Lawrence popped the first of his pills and he was hanging out of the window waving a union jack at unimpressed French farmers.

When we got to Paris we broke up into two groups. A group went to the Eiffel Tower and were mistaken for American GIs (it was the parkas); me and Billy went with the other group to find the gig. It was in a sports hall under a block of flats on the outskirts of Paris. When we got there the Jam were doing a sound check. We all ran down the stairs and the band stopped - they did genuinely seem pleased to see us. They knew Grant and a few others. We were told don't worry about tickets - one of the few times I got into a Jam gig for free - they finished the sound check and we went to the Wimpy Bar. After that we went back to the venue, most went in, some of us including me stood outside waiting for the others to arrive. There was a desk where you bought/showed your ticket. Anyone with a green parka who spoke English could avoid paying. I think nearly everyone was in and we were about to go in when someone in a green parka turned up with a Newcastle accent. He was about to pay but we nabbed him and got him in for free as well. Don't remember his name - I do remember he worked for British airways! When we came back on the Saturday we were in Wardour Street and a French dude came up to us and in broken English he said "I met you at The Jam gig" he was over for the Five Nations rugby tournament.

JO WALLACE was already heavily influenced by mod culture and was another member of the British contingent who travelled to Paris:
I grew up in the Medway Towns - I was born in Rochester but veered towards Chatham with its lure of nightclubs, sailors and record shops. I got into the mod scene via a much older brother who, while on babysitting duties in 1964/5, used to take me to the local mod hangout 'The Parlour' coffee bar. With the rows of scooters lined up outside and a shiny Gaggia espresso machine on the counter just inside the doorway, it was heaven. The crescent shaped seating was red leather, there were neon Olympic rings and a sunburst clock on the wall, a machine that made metal luggage tags, flying saucer Pyrex coffee cups and a juke box. Not just any juke box - a juke box that had Marvin Gaye's 'Can I Get A Witness' on it - the mods would give me money and send me up to press the chunky plastic buttons to select - M3 - my little fingers just managing to complete the task. That was my introduction to Motown and the portal to all things mod. I started working at HMV's in Oxford Street in May 1978 - the flagship store - after passing the entrance exam with 99/100. There really was an entrance exam to work at HMV's and I scored the highest score on record since the exam was held - Julie

Covington from 'Rock Follies' scored 98. Anyway, I'd got to know Kevin Collins, the Ilford Mods, Grant Fleming, the Bromley/St Paul's Cray lot - most of the movers and shakers, guys that hung out at the Shakespeare's Head in Carnaby Street, Brian Kotz... all young and all passionate about music and the mod lifestyle.

A mod came into HMV's who worked at Polydor - and shame on me, I can't remember his name - and he said 'you like mod stuff, here's tickets for The Jam - in Paris!'.

As far as I can recall, the gig was that weekend and it was midweek and I didn't like The Jam - but hey, it was a trip abroad. My (mod) brother lived in Paris by this time and I headed for the basement in HMV's to misuse the phone in the Mail Order department. They had an international line and I pretended I was phoning an overseas customer - God loves a blagger. Having sorted out my accommodation for the trip, I booked a train ticket for Paris on the boat train (no Eurostar back then) - so, the journey was already taking on fairly epic proportions before I'd even started out. There were some last minute arrangements made at the pub and on the Friday, we all headed off - there was another girl called Michelle from Chislehurst who had cropped blond hair and wore tailored suits - a really great look.

I can't remember much about the trip getting there - there was probably pills and alcohol consumed by others in equal amounts to blot out the ridiculously long journey. On arriving in Paris, I took off to my brother's place and hooked up with everyone later at Porte D'Ivorie - and laughed at the French mods for having square targets on their parkas. I watched the gig through gritted teeth as the band massacred 'Heatwave'... I was only there because I'd been given free tickets! But I did go backstage - I'd been given a 45 of Dobie Gray's 'Out On The Floor' to give to Paul Weller and been told to get the money off him, all of £1.50.

There he was, sweating profusely, coming down after a monumentally athletic performance and I've gone 'Here's that tune you wanted. £1.50 please'... I'm saving the rest of the story for my memoirs...

I think the rest of my lot went off to Le Rose Bon Bon nightclub, slept in subways and got nicked by the Parisian flicks... I slept in a comfortable bed, ate croissants and met up with some very tired and wired mods and came back to London.

Although The Jam's gig in Paris is memorable for those who went from Britain, it was also memorable for the native Parisians in the audience. One of those young fans was **SERGE HOFFMANN:**

I was born in Paris, and have never lived anywhere else. My mother lived in the apartment I grew up in - in the 10th arrondisement - where my father had a tailor service upstairs. My parents were immigrants from Poland and that was a popular neighbourhood to settle in at the time.

My parents weren't really musical, but the first musical encounter that I really remember was listening to the Beatles at the age of six and loving it, my older brother had their records, along with Michel Polnareff, the Rolling Stones, Jacques Dutronc and Antoine. My mother had the radio constantly playing, and I remember one morning hearing bossa nova on the station (must have been Serge Mendes) and really liking that, I would have been about seven. Later on, around 13/14 years-old, I started to buy records myself, in the beginning really following my brother's tastes but also branching out on my own. Being a big Sergio Leone fan I loved Ennio Morricone, and also Burt Bacharach.

I started to want to play music myself when punk arrived around 1978, listening to The Clash, The Jam, The Pistols, as well as Elvis Costello and XTC. I bought my first guitar when I was 16, it didn't even have a label, an imitation Gibson SG. My first group was The Venturas, started in 1983, very much influenced by The Jam and The Undertones. It was really The Jam that got me introduced me to mod. I was a huge fan and saw them play live three times in France (1979, 1981, 1982). The first time I heard them it reminded me of The Beatles and other groups that my brother had listened to when I was little. With that I was also very interested in their influences and discovered modernism, soul music, etc.

On the French side there were mainly punks (I was still between punk and mod!). On the English side, only parkas. It was the first time I saw mods! Very young people, between 16 and 18 years old, like me, (I was 17 years old). They were at the front of the stage and looked very happy with their union jack flags .

The room was not full. In France, The Jam was less popular than groups like The Clash

or Buzzcocks. (The French punk audience was a bit primitive and uneducated). The first band was Extraballe, a rather insignificant French punk band. I remember staying on the stands with my buddy Bruce (and yes, his name is that!).
I just bought The Jam's third album 'All Mod Cons'. I listened to it all day, alternating with the two previous albums. I loved their new compositions and it was quite unique to put a track like English Rose at the end of side one. I thought this was a perfect album. There were both harmonies to the Beatles and energy was always present. Very Kinks too. 'Fly' was one of my favourite tracks.
At the stadium concert, Weller was all in black, turtleneck and filigreed costume. The sound was clean and scathing. There was something very special, a mixture of harshness and restraint. An incredible class. The sound of his Rickenbacker was unique: warm, saturated, sharp and crystalline at the same time. Between the three of them, they had a rich and coherent sound. Foxton was incredible, with his leaps that resembled the pogo. The set was almost in the order of the album. "In The Crowd" was sublime. I was fascinated. I thought of England, a place I had not yet visited and a fantasy nourished by the sonorous reminiscences of a childhood rocked by the Beatles records. We were just out of punk, and all this was influencing my mind as a teenager. The set lasted about 40 minutes. As the encore, I remember that they had played 'Away From The Numbers' and 'The Modern World'.
Since then, I did not miss one of their concerts in Paris and every release of a new single was an event!

Serge Hoffman was not the only Parisien to be influenced by mod. Here, **LAURENT GRUX** and **ALEXANDRE SAILLIDE ULYSSE** give this valuable insight to the growth of mod culture in France:
At the end of the 1970s, following the emergence of the mod revival in England and the first major concerts by The Jam in France, modernist culture asserted itself and gradually settled in our capital. Undoubtedly, Paris is one of the first cities in France (with Caen in Normandy) to see young people attracted by what was for them a new subculture coming directly from across the Channel. Before the film 'Quadrophenia'

was released in France in April 1980, the first mods appeared little by little in the city of Paris. It should be noted that from the outset, the Parisian scene would tend to develop in a way that would be quite specific to it on a national level. Indeed, unlike other cities in France, the first mods in Paris had no specific meeting point for all to gather. They gathered in small groups, in different places, and a certain number of them remained isolated.

In Lyon, the capital of the Gaules, in contrast, the mods of the city and its surroundings gathered very quickly around a specific location: the Place Bellecour. As a result, the first significant gathering point for the mods in Paris, Rue des Archives, in the 1st district, was not really established until the beginning of 1981 after initially meeting the 'Scooter' in Les Halles. In fact, the vast area of the capital, and its urbanism so specific with its districts, explain only in part this particularism of the mod scene in Paris. We should explain a fact about the whole French Modernist scene of this period. This was extremely poor in the face of the actual scenes that were present on the continent, especially in comparison with the organisation of our Italian friends, the flourishing and very diverse Spanish scene (numerous local scenes, modzines, gatherings, musical groups) and the level of excellence of the Belgians in Brussels.

To be more precise, even during its peak in terms of participation, from 1980 to 1983, the mod scene never distinguished itself in its understanding of Modernism. French mods did not really attempt to organise or progress in the same way the other European scenes had. We have people who remained mods after the initial 'Jam/ Revival' period. We also had our fair share of 'plastic' mods that joined because of the fashion at the time, but soon left the scene.

Although it was a small scene compared to others, we did have a number of Scooter Clubs and Mod Societies across Paris. It is useful to remember certain names such as the Vespa Club, the Jet Club, the Crystal Dancer's, the Smart Boys of Lutetia, the Gambetta Original Mods, the Mod Society of City Gents, and the 75 M.N.S. Thankfully, there are enough modernists from that period who have never given up and are the cornerstone of mod in Paris today. These are the people that have a deeper understanding of modernism. They have been through the difficult times when mod was not fashionable, but have always maintained a very high standard of dress, music and the lifestyle.

One focus of the new post-punk mod could be found at a pub venue called The Wellington in London's Waterloo. It could be found in The Jam fans that were featured in a small item in Record Mirror.

They were buying their 60s original clothes from jumble sales and trying to get hold of scooters. Hailing from Southend and Stratford in East London, they did not consider themselves as retrospectives or revivalists. They were simply following the band. It could also be found in a few fanzines like 'Maximum Speed'. **GOFFA GLADDING**, with Clive Reams and Kim Gault were managing mod band Back To Zero and, through Maximum Speed, supporting other mod bands:

I used to go to see West Ham United play every week. There were a group of kids who I was vaguely aware of who started dressing up in mod style and who, as I got more interested in the music side, I used to see not only at football but also at various gigs and things, which were not particularly well advertised and weren't very big. But there was something building up there and that was 1978.

So that was the genesis of it all as far as I was concerned. Then as the interest grew, the idea for the magazine just came. I think it was Clive's idea originally and we produced the first fanzine, for which there are about 20 copies, just really to give a bit of publicity to the people we knew and who got a buzz out of seeing their name in print and photographs and that sort of thing, so that's where it came from.

I think a lot of them, The Chords, The Purple Hearts, although different in their own way, were coming from a punk base, especially when you listen to their stuff now. There was nothing new musically, but then if you had said to The Chords at the time, 'You're a mod band' I think they would have reacted quite strongly against that. I think in the public's eyes, a mod band was either Secret Affair or The Merton Parkas. I think The Chords regarded themselves musically as being different and on a more sophisticated level.

It's funny and bizarre in a way because without meaning to be, we became sort of

Paris [photo © Derek D'Souza at www.blinkandyoumissit.com]

mod entrepreneurs. We were knocking out the magazine pretty infrequently, but it was just a bit of fun. It was basically a Xeroxed thing and we tried quite hard with it really. Various people helped us out with the typing and it was all a question of getting the pictures and photos cut out and sticking them on the page.

It was a fairly unprofessional level of production but it was from the heart and we loved doing it. The last edition was number nine, and that was the best in terms of production and what we were getting into. I think we still owe 400 people their advance subscriptions for number ten at 20 pence a go, but we should draw a veil over that one. We used to have it produced towards the end by Rough Trade who did a printing service for any number of fanzines really, but we used to hand collate 10,000 copies because we would save ourselves 'x' pence per copy by them not doing it automatically, so we just used to sit around in Kim and Clive's flat in Stamford Hill, north London and physically put the copies together. It was plain crazy and I can't believe we actually did that. We started off going round with a plastic bag full of them to sell at Chords gigs at Waterloo and we'd sell them out in no time at all.

We were managing Back To Zero, as much as you could call it management, and probably because they're not now Oasis is probably down to us because we didn't do a good job on them.

We also used to put on gigs as well. That was the brilliant part, it was fun, but we only did four events and they were fantastic. Because we knew the bands well, we just asked them direct if they wanted to come and play. We'd hire a hall, sell tickets by word of mouth for a quid or whatever it was in those days and typically they'd be fantastic events that even now, people come up to me and say the camaraderie plus the fact that it wasn't the Marquee or The Music Machine in Camden, meant that it was such a memorable event. I'm quite pleased about that really when I look back on it.

In fact, the four gigs laid on by Maximum Speed were: 11 April 1979, Howard Hall, Enfield; 26 April, Cambridge Hotel, Edmonton, 3 May Acklam Hall, Ladbrooke Grove and 25 May, Red Lion, Leytonstone. The Edmonton event was also an unknowing host to a mod from the sixties who had recorded a single and was selling to mods that night. **IAN HARRIS** had been out of the music business for a few years, but had a song about his experience as a mod, collecting dust for almost ten years:

By 1978, I did a demo of 'Just A Little Mod' with some friends of mine and my brother was on drums. I gave it to my friend Andy Powell who handed it onto a manager he knew, John Sherry and he liked it. Of course the mod revival was happening. So we recorded it, and it was wonderful for me. It was a reawakening of my mod credentials. So Andy and I got together and thought about a name.

Well, my brother's name is Terry and I thought, tonik mohair, then I thought, 'Well, Terry Tonik, I can live with that, I can be Terry Tonik'. It's light and humorous. So I bought the suit, and we recorded the single, funnily enough in Gooseberry Studios, Gerard Street, opposite the old Coffin Club we had run in the late sixties. We did the single and the flip side in a day with a couple of session guys that Andy got. It was a wonderful couple of hours, and Andy related to it because he was a mod in the sixties as well. I designed the cover and I had been writing about my time back in the sixties and mentioned it to John Sherry who said we should sell it as a fanzine, so he got it printed up in conjunction with the single. Then I worked as a plugger for John for a year promoting Wishbone Ash and some of John's other bands. I plugged Terry Tonik as well and got play listed on Radio Pennine, which was weird. I even had some fan mail from up there. It isn't a great single, but it was more the mod credentials really, the fact that I was an original mod from '65 and I played on that fact. I mean, I was ten years older than everyone else, but I got into punk, I loved punk, and seeing Ian Dury, who was older than me getting away with it, I thought, well why not me. It's not an age thing, it's more the feeling. There was this big mod rally in Edmonton and we took the single and magazine down there and sold quite a few for £1.50 I think it was. Then Virgin shops took it up. They had about 200, and we only had about a thousand pressed and it sold about 400. There's probably a hand full that have been made into ashtrays or trodden on, and some that I gave it away to anyone who would listen. That's why it's so rare and valued at £100 and rising. There was a fanzine called 'DRC' (Direction, Reaction, Creation) and I sent them the single and they wrote a nice little piece about me. Terry never played a gig. I was up for it, but it didn't happen. It wasn't manufactured particularly, but I cherish it because it was sincere. It wasn't a novelty piss-take. It was me. Maybe the name Terry Tonik was the worst thing and people thought it was cynical, but it's not, it was sincere. In fact, John Sherry wanted me to do 'Just A Little Mod' with a ska beat, which might have been quite good, but I didn't want to do it at the time because I thought 'Poison Ivy' by The Lambrettas was cynical. I wanted it to be vaguely Who-ish.

ED BALL had seen how '79 mod had been taking shape from the sidelines. His analysis of how and why it happened is a very good bench mark by which to understand the context of it:

When the original mod thing happened in the sixties, that came out of a period of gentleness really. Okay, there had been teds, but really, it came out of a period of gentleness, beatniks and peaceniks and general middle-class laidbackness. Britain wasn't really a scary place, if anything it was on the up, so the original mod thing could afford to be fairly aggressive in its attitude, with Margate, Clacton, Brighton and so on. When mod came back in the seventies, it was after a very cynical period of punk and the re-emergence of skinheads and going to gigs and playing gigs was a scary experience in those days. Sham 69 gigs were really scary affairs. So if a movement was going to come after punk, it was going to be fairly aggressive and adopt a lot of the musical precedents of punk. It was going to be speedy and aggressive to a point. I suppose there is an element of truth to the 'punk in parkas' theory on that basis. It couldn't have been based on sixties twee stuff, it would have bombed.

What I would say is that most of those '79 mod bands had at least one if not two great songs in them and making singles that some of us will go to our graves with. The Chords would do something and I'd think, they've really got it, they hold the key, but then The Purple Hearts would do something and you'd think, my God that's amazing. At that time I think I was really looking for a band that could bridge the gap between that mod sound and, not psychedelic as such, but be a bit more experimental, because when you think back to The Who, they had Townshend at the helm and they were very experimental. If you listen to the 'Sell Out' album, it's like a precursor to

Prog Rock in some ways. I think that's where we saw ourselves, it was somewhere between the experimental and musical. A couple of TV Personalities' songs like 'King and Country, 'Day In Heaven' or 'This Is Tomorrow' by The Times, there were a few things that verged on that kind of experimental thing. You see, in '79, mod wasn't a dirty word. The reason it became a dirty word was because most journalists, if not by birth, then by nature, are middle-class, and the mod thing was, you'd have to say, a working-class or lower-middle-class thing.

I'm sure a lot of lads who played in the mod bands came from nice homes and that, but maybe it's not middle-class, but a university thing. I have resented it at times because it's not that those university people are particularly intelligent, but they use it as a kind of mafia thing, and this is why I love Paul Weller, because he didn't go to art school, he didn't become punk, but what he did, particularly in his sort of pop art period if you like, is he kind of inferred a do-it-yourself thing and I really do believe the TVPs and The Times picked up that gauntlet with things like 'Pop Goes Art', with 20,000 spray paint sleeves and being self-taught is what I'm really trying to say, because you never really learn anything at school. You learn how to pass exams, you learn things parrot-fashion, you learn how to get that first job, but what Weller was basically saying was go out and learn for yourself on songs like 'This Is The Modern World'.

In the north of England, **PAUL WELSBY**'s love of American R&B took a momentary backseat as mod of the late seventies gathered momentum:
At the time it was really exciting. Despite always being into black American music, The Jam in particular struck a chord with me at that age. Angst and all that crap I suppose. And they always did tip their hat to soul and R&B, just look at some of their early cover versions and the inside sleeve to 'All Mod Cons'. Clearly I wasn't interested in mod when I first got into The Jam in a big way. Why should I want to look like The Who in '65? But as they developed, so did Weller's look and finally the penny dropped.
In 1979 I thought the height of cool was a black Fred Perry with Yellow embellishments, turned up straight leg Levis, Clarks dessert boots and a Parka. Then came Secret Affair and all those others, who just reinforced my ignorance.

It was particularly exciting in the north though, you didn't see many others of the same persuasion, so it was like being a member of an underground sect. There wasn't the information around as there is today. Thursday night (I think) was "Mod Night" at Pips nightclub - just behind Manchester Cathedral. I didn't know that "She's A Woman" by The Beatles wasn't a mod record, but that's what they played. The night always ended with a dancefloor scrum to 'My Generation'. Hoards of olive green parkas bouncing up and down shouting "Why don't you all... f f f fuck off" and the inevitable chants of "We are the mods". There was another club night, I think it was over a pub on Oxford Street called The Huntsman. I only remember going to one night there, so I suspect it was a one off. But it was pretty much the same fare as Pips. The important thing at the time was going to gigs. The Jam at Salford University, then at The Apollo. The March of The Mods Tour at The Apollo (with Holly and The Italians!), The first Two Tone Tour at The Apollo. The Crooks at Salford University. Dexy's at Manchester Poly (after blowing out a promised appearance at Pips a couple of days earlier because Dance Stance had sold a few copies).

Basically anyone and everyone that visited Manchester over a two year period were fair game. I suppose it was a combination of Dexy's Midnight Runners, the two Motown mod compilations and the Sue reissues via the Ensign label, that finally made me realise what I'd so far managed to ignore... second rate watered down power pop was nothing whatsoever to do with mod. And with a couple of years hindsight I could say Hallelujah. I'd finally seen the light.

For an 18 month period I liked all the '79 bands. The Jam without doubt were the masters. But I did like The Chords, presumably because they sounded much like The Jam, Back To Zero and The Killermetres. But I must say that I gave most of them space on my record shelves at the time. I still have the records but I haven't played any of them for donkeys years and I can't see any immediate need to rectify that situation (with the exception of The Jam of course).

One 15 year-old who got involved in mod and epitomises the 'DIY' attitude that began with punk and continued through bands like The Jam, and was to become one of the prime movers on the scene for many years, was **EDDIE PILLER** whose influences were very close to home:

My dad was a modernist. He never called himself a mod, but he used to drive a Lambretta and wear suits. My mum was an out and out mod as well as my auntie, in fact they were all mods. My other auntie used to hang about with The Who when they were The High Numbers. The first time I became aware of it was the day my dad bought my mum the 'Best of The Small Faces' album. I asked him what it was and he told me what The Small Faces were about and that was it. I never thought I'd ever see another mod. I knew what one was, I didn't think of myself as a mod, but then someone said to me 'I'm a mod' and I thought, well I want to be one and that was how it happened.

Eddie soon began publishing his own, now legendary fanzine and running club nights:
In issue two of Extraordinary Sensations, we had three photocopied pages from the Small Faces fan club newsletter. A biography of the band and a picture, that kind of thing. My mum's Small Faces Fan Club involvement did have an influence, but all it did was make me more curious. You could not help but be influenced by it when Kenny Jones comes round your house in a Rolls Royce. That's when I thought this music business must be alright, when Kenny's Corniche convertible is parked outside your house and all the people in the street have come out to look at it.

I first did a club called Barry's in Ilford in 1979. A very small working men's club and I did it with Ray Margetson. Then we moved to Hackney and we did lots of sixties soul clubs, but the reason I started was because I was sick of seeing old men playing mod records. I thought I could do better than that, and I did. Then I did the Alldayers. I was too young to sign the papers to hire the Alexandra Palace from the Rank Organisation who owned it then, so my dad had to sign for me. I was about 17 and we did seven of them in all, sold out everytime, 1,500 people with lots of bands playing. They were really successful and they were probably the most successful events post '79. They ran from 1980 to about 1982. Hastings Pier through '79, be it Secret Affair or The Teenbeats, those were important gigs for me. The early scooter runs to Brighton,

Hastings and Margate in 1980 and Tony Class's do's. Our do's were not any better than anybody else's, but we just happened to be doing it. We started playing black music in between the band's sets. The Purple Hearts used to complain that they would hear the same black music records every night and they were getting fed up with it. Things like 'Needle In A Haystack', 'Ghost In My House', and 'Seven Rooms Of Gloom' and that used to drive them mad, so the next logical step when the bands got bored and fell out of it, was the records took over. When we learned more about mod and mod music, it got more interesting because it is such a broad church. In '79 no-one really knew much about it. It was like punk wearing Fred Perry's and targets and by 1981 it was stylists dancing to jazz and sixties soul.

Another popular fanzine was Patriotic run by Ray Margetson. As **BRIAN BETTERIDGE** recalls, one contributor to Patriotic went to bigger and better things some twenty years later: Ray Margetson used to follow us about for a while, and he named 'Patriotic' after a song by a local band called The Variations. They never recorded but they were a good little band. They had a bit of rivalry with a band called 007 who became The Scene. Now The Variations main fan was called Kathy who used to write about them in Patriotic. That particular Kathy was Kathy Burke the actress. Russell Woodhall who was in The Variations confirmed this to me.

Out in the provinces though, people were being inspired to get involved in the mod scene that was emerging. **GARETH BROWN**, who would become an important figure in scooter culture in later years, bought his first scooter in 1978 and his first tentative steps into mod seems to have been a familiar story for many, as he told Scootering Magazine: We were very much mods, although we didn't know what mod was. We'd been too young to totally embrace punk. We had ripped t-shirts and safety pins. We were probably the laughing stock, and were too young to do the scene, but we thought we were punks. By the time 'our time' came, we just adapted to the mod thing. We didn't know it was a national scene, it was just what appealed to us. We were big fans of Paul Weller and The Jam. We bought suits from a jumble sale and started dressing the part.

I thought I was a mod from 1978, and I suppose I became a better mod as I learned more about it and time went on. The first rally I went to was a bit of a cheat. It was Great Yarmouth 1978, but I went on a coach with my mates from Chelmsford. There were 500 or 600 scooters and we couldn't believe it. To us it was all the scooters in the world in one place at one time. I'd been to Italy the summer before and saw hundreds and hundreds of scooters there, but it didn't mean the same because they were just used for commuting. The next rally I went on was the now legendary Southend 1979. It went mental and kicked off big style. I was a teenager and I'd never seen anything like that before. There were loads of skinheads and about 300-400 scooters for this official Lambretta club rally. There was a strong northern contingent and at one end of the seafront there was an altercation with some rockers. The police intervened and it all went pear-shaped. There were big lads in parkas and they turned over a police car. It was mayhem. I didn't get involved because I was too scared. I thought, 'This is fantastic, I definitely want to be in this scene'.

Across Britain, the renewed interest in mod was spreading. In Ipswich, a young teenager named **STUART CATLING** was taking his first steps in the mod world:
I was about 13-14 years old around 1978 when I got into it. I started buying NME and Melody Maker and I was listening to Ian Dury and the Blockheads, Boomtown Rats and The Clash. One day I was reading through one of the papers and there was this big article about mod and this film being made called 'Quadrophenia'. Well, I couldn't get in to see the film until I was 16, but when I did see it, I just thought 'How cool is this?' because I didn't have a clue about mod until that point. My sisters took me to a few gigs to see Ian Dury and the Boomtown Rats, but I didn't realise at the time what an influence my sisters were having on me in terms of musical taste.
My sister Lynette, who is six years older than me, she was listening to Rod Stewart and The Faces, and my other sister June, who is 12 years older were listening to the Small Faces. But they both listened to Motown, ska, reggae, 'Double Barrel', 'Isrealites' and all that kind of stuff, so it was all having an influence on me. There were two pubs, the Coach and Horses on a Saturday and Tuesday they would do a kind of 'mod' night

with a mixture of mod, punk, ska, 60s and amazingly, they'd almost drag you in off the street even though you were only 14 years old and serve you! After two and half pints, you'd be paralytic. But me and my mate Darren Kent would make sure we got the half-ten bus back so we could get home before our parents. When I was a bit older, I used to go to the Albion Mills which was another pub with a cellar and a spiral staircase. The room was tiny, it could only hold about 80 people and it was hot, sweaty and smokey. It was an Irish guy who ran the place and he'd play records, but he also had a trumpet, so he would play Secret Affair and play his trumpet along with the record. The other thing I remember was all the boys used to hang about underneath the staircase and watch the girls going up to use the toilet! By the time we were 16-17 years-old, we had scooters, so we could get around more and go to other places. There was a pub in Chelmsford on a Sunday night that used to do a soul night and I first met Tony Clayton there. Tony was a Northern Soul DJ, but he was also a Chruch Of England vicar. He had a fantastic collection of records, but I only recently found out he passed away towards the end of 2016.

There seems to have been mixed emotions and opinions about the mod revival by those who had been original modernists, as **JOHN HELLIER** explains:
Looking back on it now there were some good things to come out of the era but at the time it went right over my head. Perhaps foolishly I regarded my generation as the real thing and these were just kids playing at it.

For **GILL EVANS** it was an opportunity:
It never went away because I always thought of myself as a mod girl and I was always trying to find ways to bring it back, so when the revival happened, I thought there must be a way to reintroduce all my designs again, but it wasn't a very big scene in Birmingham during the revival. What you find is people are more interested in buying a High Street look rather than paying that bit extra for something unique.

The momentum though had started in London and from this background, a cluster of

'mod' bands began to make a name for themselves. On the 7 May 1979, a showcase of bands was being recorded live. Six bands were featured: Secret Affair, Beggar, Small Hours, The Mods, Squire and the Merton Parkas.
The resultant album, 'Mods Mayday '79' gave 'provincial' mods an insight into this new crop of bands. **GOFFA GLADDING** explains the scene, the venues and the album:
The Bridgehouse is not the sort of place where you would expect things to start. I mean it was a pretty grim venue and area. Then you've got this grizzly old pub in Waterloo that was dead as a doornail on a Saturday night. Suddenly you'd have these hundreds of kids all having a fantastic time there. Then we were putting on gigs at the Howard Hall, Ponders End, Enfield. It got into the local papers and nobody knew what the hell was going on, but it was fantastic and it was those kinds of things that set the scene apart because it was genuinely grassroots people setting out to have a good time. The Bridgehouse was in Canning Town, East London. It's probably come up in the world a bit now, but back then it was a pretty depressed area of London, and it wasn't the sort of place you wanted to be wandering about late at night. The pub was run by Terry Murphy who was terrifically supportive and the great thing about having a band on at The Bridgehouse, was the fact that Terry was the fairest guy in the world in terms of giving you a straight percentage of the door. He was quite a formidable character and had two sons who were boxers, if I remember rightly, one of who was in 'London's Burning' TV show.
Terry always gave you a terrific crack at the whip and was fantastically fair and it was a great place to play and of course they had the Mods Mayday thing that they recorded live there and you got all these great bands playing at this unusual venue.

ANTHONY MEYNELL recalls how Squire got onto the Mods Mayday album:
We started to do gigs. We took anything we could get and we did one with The Mods, who asked us what we were doing the following week. They told us about the Bridgehouse and how the gig was going to be recorded and they suggested we should go along. We said we hadn't been invited, but they said we should go anyway. Enzo and I definitely wanted to go, but the others weren't so enthusiastic, but we

> When you discover something as powerful as black American dance music, you have an unwritten duty to explore it in more depth. If you understand this, then you'll know what I mean. If you don't, you never will!
>
> PAUL WELSBY

loaded the van anyway and went up there to blag ourselves a gig. We just thought we could get in front of an audience, even if they didn't record us. When we turned up they told us to piss off, but as it turned out, a band called The Little Roosters were billed to play and didn't show. So we were first or second on and there weren't that many people there because it was the middle of the afternoon. Our entourage was making as much noise as they could and that's how we ended up on the album, by sheer fluke really. I don't think they quite knew where to place us. I mean The Purple Hearts, The Chords, The Mods, these are all quite obvious names and we weren't from London, so we didn't get the calls quite so much. Although we were getting gigs, we were building our own following rather than people asking us to play. Mod's Mayday was actually a vehicle for Secret Affair. It was paid for by Arista, distributed by Arista and although it was on the Bridgehouse label, it was really an album to whet people's appetite for Secret Affair before they were ready to launch at the end of September. The marketing was geared up to that. They had done some gigs with The Jam and Paul Weller hated them, which knocked them back a little bit, but we all had the same publisher, Bryan Morrison. The revival was almost a Bryan Morrison creation because he had The Jam, Secret Affair, Back To Zero and us. He had the lot. That's how we ended up on Arista and he heard us on the Bridgehouse album. When you listen to that album, I think we stand out. I couldn't really understand where bands like Beggar and Small Hours were coming from, but they were pulling numbers which is why they were there, but there weren't that many bands around at the time. That same weekend The Chords and The Purple Hearts were playing The Marquee and this is the reason we didn't go on the March of The Mods tour. Asgard Promotions were doing Chords, Purple Hearts and Back to Zero and Arista was very interested in Secret Affair and us. So you had two camps effectively, and this kept occurring and crossing over wasn't possible anymore because when you were doing a gig, they were doing a gig somewhere else and we didn't get to meet up as much.

There are some iconic images from the revival that define the period; none more so than the front cover of the 'Mods Mayday '79' album.

Robert Lee's introduction to mod was fairly typical for any teenager at the time; starting with the Small Faces and 60s music via punk and new wave following a band local to his area: Sham 69. Their appearance at the Reading Festival in 1978 meant they were on the same bill as the headliners for that night: The Jam.

From that point, Robert made the conversion from suedehead to mod. He found out about The Bridgehouse Monday night gigs from a friend and went to see Secret Affair for the first time. By the May Bank Holiday of 1979, Robert and his friends had travelled to Brighton during the day and got back to The Bridgehouse too late to get into the venue, so they hung around outside listening to the bands.

Robert takes up the story as told to **TONY BEESLEY**:

The following Monday evening, as I pulled up outside the pub, Terry Murphy and a photographer approached me and asked if they could take a couple of photos of me and the scooter to help promote the forthcoming album release. I agreed. Not realising at the time that one of those photos would end up being used for the sleeve.

As 1979 progressed and the mod interest grew, things happened very quickly. So quickly in fact, that it took the members of Squire by surprise and this is borne out by Squire's gig list for that year, as **ANTHONY** recalls:

I've got a gig list for 1979 and if you look at it, its like February there are four gigs, March there are ten, April there are 20, May there are 25, June there are 30 and in July there are two. This is because everyone had booked their summer holiday because they didn't know anything was going to happen. So Enzo and the rest of the band went off to Tunisia for two weeks with their girlfriends. I said they should cancel everything because of the momentum Squire had got, but they said their girlfriends would go mad, so they went and we were out of it for a month.

It was shame, but other things were happening as well. We had another single deal in the pipeline and an album offer and a new manager, whose own band wasn't doing so well, but he was trying to ride them in on our backs, but at the time we thought everyone was in it for the music and everyone was going to be honest.

We found ourselves slipping a bit and Secret Affair were looking for a band to sign to I-Spy. I think they had asked Back To Zero, but they had gone with Fiction. Secret Affair liked 'Walking Down The Kings Road' and our manager jumped at the offer and we ended up with Arista and on the Dancing In The Streets tour for that autumn.

In May though, after the Mods Mayday gig, we were doing a lot of gigs with bands like The Records. The agency we were with, Cowbell, saw us a pop band and we were doing one and two thousand seater venues in places like Portsmouth and Southampton, because Cowbell wanted us to get that kind of experience. So we were taken out of the mod pub circuit and the March Of The Mods tour was being put together at that time. We just weren't available. By all accounts the tour was a bit disorganised but great fun and it was the first time the provinces had got a taste for what was to come. Although we had done the same thing, but in a different way, you could see something was happening.

Paul Weller's writing and the superior quality of The Jam both on record and live was the standard by which all other bands would be measured.

In the main, the bands all came from London and the South-East. The Purple Hearts from Romford, The Chords from Deptford, South London, The Merton Parkas from South-West London, Back to Zero from Enfield, Squire from Woking, Secret Affair from the East End. The notable exceptions were the Lambrettas from Brighton, Beggar from Cardiff, and The Killermetres from Huddersfield. By 1979, The Killermeters had acquired Steve Dorrell as their manager. Steve had been the social secretary for the student union at Huddersfield Polytechnic. **VIC VESPA** explains why they chose Steve to manage them: We thought Steve would be really useful because being involved with the student union, he could get us gigs at other universities and colleges. He did get us loads of work, but we also played The Coach House pub in Huddersfield so much it was like a home from home, even though it was just about the roughest pub in the whole town. We supported The Undertones, Eddie and The Hot Rods, The Chords and all the other bands of the time. I remember walking into a newsagents one day and saw a copy of New Musical Express, and on the front cover was a picture of a scooter rally and suddenly mod was 'in', and here we were, The Killermetres, doing the same thing. So I wrote to NME and Sounds to tell them that it wasn't just a London 'thing' and sure enough, Gary Bushell got in touch and came up to see us play.He even stayed at my flat that night, and credit to him, the following week, we had a four page spread in Sounds including a review of our gig at The Albion.

John Reed, in an article from Record Collector posed the question; what defined a mod band? His answer was simplistic, but on reflection, quite possibly a correct one. A mod band was any outfit that dressed mod, called themselves mod and were mods. They drew from The Jam or some aspect of sixties music and ideally had a perfect blend of both the look and the sound.

It is fair to say that most of the bands had their beginnings in new wave. A typical example would be Secret Affair, as **DAVE CAIRNS** said:

In our previous new wave band, 'New Hearts', we wore second hand mohair original Mod jackets and button down Brutus shirts with drainpipe jeans and converse baseball boots (the uniform of almost every teenager right now I notice) and with my guitar leanings towards Pete Townshend and Steve Marriott and Ian with Motown and soul, where Secret Affair ended up was just a natural progression. We were a band whose musical and fashion tastes were very influenced by mod culture. It was evident that people with the same tastes would like the band, though it wasn't a prerequisite for liking the band or coming to our shows. Being part of the Mod Revival at its peak was a very exciting time, but selling out the Rainbow Theatre in Finsbury Park with Secret Affair, where only seven years earlier I saw David Bowie as Ziggy Stardust as a school kid in 1972 was amazing to me.

Both **DAVE CAIRNS** and his lifelong musical partner Ian Page were heavily influenced by their respective older brothers who had impressive record collections. Dave takes up the story:

My older brother Ian back in the 70s had a huge record collection so I listened to anything from John Mayall's Bluesbreakers with guitarists Eric Clapton and Peter Green (who inspired me to play guitar) to Jim Hendrix and Dr John and the Night Trippers to Pink Floyd and The Who. I bought all the Bowie and Lou Reed albums at the time, a bit of prog rock and lots of blues records and anything with country rock guitarist, Albert Lee, the list is endless really! Thinking about it though, one of the singles I played over and over again at the time was 'I Heard It Through The Grapevine' by Marvin Gaye, and whenever I hear that great record it sends me right back to my adolescence in an instant and maybe just maybe Ian (Page) was listening to it at the same time and perhaps there was a shared influence there that would bring us together in time. My brother also took me to a lot of gigs including Emerson, Lake and Palmer when I was 12 years-old and Pink Floyd and the Rolling Stones at Knebworth Park, so I got a taste for live shows. However, it was seeing Pete Townshend with The Who at Charlton Football Ground and Steve Marriott with Humble Pie in 1974 on the same bill that gave me the courage to play in a band as a stand-alone rhythm and lead guitarist, as at the time you either stood at the back strumming chords or you were down the front as the lead guitarist noodling away which I always hated as a band format.

The consensus of opinion tends to highlight Secret Affair as second-only to The Jam in the mod revival 'pecking order'. With successful singles and their debut album 'Glory Boys' following on from the 'Mods Mayday '79' release, the music press latched on to the band and gravitated towards Ian Page as an alternative 'mod spokesman' when Paul Weller was avoiding attempts to brand him as such. **DAVE CAIRNS**:
We were published by Bryan Morrison Music who also handled our business affairs but all creative decisions were taken by Ian and I so any direction we took was our own decision. There was no svengali manager pulling the strings.
My personal take on this 'spokesman' tag is that with Secret Affair on the front covers of Sounds, Record Mirror and NME for instance, the music press were very happy to get behind us and the mod revival to begin with, but with the emerging success of Two Tone and Ska music they effectively did a u turn and turned against us and anything marked mod, so Ian ended up in a very unenviable position where whatever he said made no difference, it had become something to sneer at.

IAN PAGE gave this abrasive assessment regarding the music press at the time:
We were a band with mod influenced music and style, not mods who happened to be in a band. I personally thought that the re-emergence of interest in those styles and sounds, and to some extent beliefs, was significant in terms of pop and youth culture and it was important to me.
Apart from the NME, which is now a very different publication from the music newspaper of that time - all those publications are dead, gone, failed. So what they branded me or called me or said about me really isn't relevant anymore. They are ghosts and I'm still here.

One band who played at the Mods Mayday '79 whose set did not appear on the original album was the Merton Parkas.
They gained mod celebrity after they were featured in a 'Sun' newspaper exclusive. The band was formed by brothers Mick and Danny Talbot, Simon Smith and the late Neil Hurrell. Their outlook on mod was a little too 'purist' for some. Harder mods did not like the clean-cut image of the Parkas; not that it bothered them.
As Mick Talbot told Record Mirror in 1979: *"For the past three years there's been so many bands saying we're tougher than you. We're not into all that. We're just enjoying ourselves and couldn't care less if the hard core London mods call us clean cut. They can think what they want, we're not gonna get involved with slagging anyone off".*
Maximum Speed were possibly among the people Mick Talbot referred to.
GOFFA GLADDING states why this might be the case:
People used to think we had a big thing against The Merton Parkas because they did look to us to be extraordinarily manufactured. I saw them once at a venue in south London and it was pretty average really. That's just my opinion. Some people really liked them, but not my cup of tea. For someone brought up on Generation X and The Lurkers, The Parkas didn't push any buttons for me. The Chords did because of their energy and their great songs.

The Chords were another highly rated band. They displayed a clear understanding of

London [courtesy of Dave Edwards]

what seventies mod really was. They were discerning enough to see the anomalies between the sixties and seventies and were painfully aware of the pitfalls that were waiting just around the corner for the movement as a whole.

Billy Hassett and Martin Mason were cousins who recruited Chris Pope and finally Brett Buddy Ascott. Within four months of their first gig at The Kings Head in March of 1979, they had been filmed by London Weekend Television for a programme about the mod revival, Paul Weller had seen them play and liked them, Jimmy Pursey signs them to his label, but becomes part of the problem when a full-scale riot and stage invasion occurs at a gig in Guildford and after a session for John Peel on Radio One, they finally sign to Polydor. Like most of the bands at the time, they too had their critics from the music press, most of it unjustified, but they had a huge following and the songs to back it up. In an interview with Record Mirror they gave insight and assessment of the movement at the time:

RM: "What do you think of the mod scene?"

Chris: "The Press thinks it's a hype and so they don't even listen to what we try to play and do. They created the hype in the first place".

Brett: "Mods today haven't got enough style, no panache at all".

Martin: "Both situations (60s & 70s mods) are obviously very different".

Chris: "That's good, 'cos they don't want to go out now and say 'We've got to do that, 'cos the mods in '64 did it'. It just isn't like that".

Billy: "If '79 mod is punk in parkas, we don't want any of it. But we don't want a revival of what it was in '64. We've got our own sound".

Their raft of singles, a debut album and two appearances on Top Of The Pops throughout 1980 should have led to bigger and better things, but by 1981, the 'mod' tag was the 'monkey on their back' that they just could not shift in the music press. By the time 'In My Street' was released a major row broke out ten minutes into a gig between Billy Hassett and a section of the crowd, which resulting in Billy leaving the stage and the band.

Indeed, at the end of an interview with The Face Magazine in June 1981, journalist Tony Fletcher sums up the problem, not just for The Chords, but all the other 'revival' bands;

I meet a friend who asks where I've been. Interviewing The Chords I say. "oh I don't like them, they're a mod band". If this is the way the British treat one of their better young bands, it stinks.

That said, The Chords made a big impression on a 13 year-old kid at the time. His name is **DAVE EDWARDS**:

I grew up in Southwark, sandwiched between Waterloo, Borough and Elephant & Castle. In 1976 aged 10 we moved to Sittingbourne in Kent but in early '79 I was spending most weekends back in Southwark.

Most of my friends in London were already into The Jam but for me it was seeing Secret Affair and The Specials on Top of The Pops. The suits, the songs and the attitude both bands portrayed swung it for me. Sittingbourne was like a commuter satellite town where most people travelled to London for work and there wasn't a lot to do there in all honesty, and although everyone in school were little mods, coming back to London at weekends probably saved me. I'd go to watch football and hang around with my mates.

The first mod around our area was Rory Weatherburn, he was about two years older than us. We tried to get into The Wellington at Waterloo one night when The Chords were playing but being 13 and looking about 10, I stood no chance, the doorman wouldn't let us in as we were so young, so there were five of us trying to peer through the windows trying to catch a glimpse of something. Other than that it was reading the music press and the odd trip to Carnaby Street.

Dave Edwards would become one of many highly respected club DJs who began their love affair with mod in the late 70's and early 80's.

Meanwhile, Bob Manton, Simon Stebbings, Jeff Shadbolt and Gary Sparks found some commercial success as The Purple Hearts. They played their first gig in May 1978, but as The Sockets they supported the Buzzcocks in June 1977.

Being labelled a post-punk outfit did not sit well with The Purple Hearts even though they admitted the punk influence.

In a Record Mirror interview, Bob Manton summed up The Hearts preferred position in the overall mod scheme: *"We have got the aggression and energy of punk but we're closer to The Byrds' 'Mr Tambourine Man' than to (The Ruts) 'London's Burning'. But then compared to the Merton Parkas we're the Angelic Upstarts".*

The Purple Hearts had reasonable success in the charts with their singles 'Millions Like Us' and 'Jimmy'. Brian Betteridge, Andy Moore, Sam Burnett and Mal Malyon, as members of Back To Zero, had been a regular band on the mod circuit with The Chords, Purple Hearts and others. It was not long before their chance to join the other bands on vinyl arrived. By mid 1979, they were faced with three contracts, as **BRIAN BETTERIDGE** recalls:

The publishing deal was for however long it was, I can't remember now. The Fiction deal was a one-off single with options. We didn't take the options, The Purple Hearts had a similar deal, they did take up the option, and they put 'Frustration' out and then the album. We didn't even have to speak to Chris Parry. We knew he wanted to go with just one of the mod bands. The Purple Hearts were that band and we weren't. We also signed up for The March Of The Mods Tour because it was the pre-promotion for our single.

Comprised of three bands, The Secret Affair, The Purple Hearts and Back To Zero, the March Of The Mods tour went nationwide in August 1979. Because Back To Zero were in, so too were their managers, Maximum Speed. **GOFFA GLADDING** explains how that tour had an impact on the magazine:

Yes, that was a hoot! We were playing at rock stars. Secret Affair took it all terrifically seriously and they had their road manager dropping their suits off at 9 o'clock in the morning to be dry-cleaned and picking them up at 11 before we moved off to the next venue and they would look sharp every night. But they were set on world domination I think. As I recall we were stuck somewhere in the north of England and they were helicoptered back to London to do Top Of The Pops, otherwise they would have missed it. I suppose it's still the same today, if you get Top Of The Pops it can change your life, so it's not the sort of thing you pass up.

Secret Affair were tied up with Bryan Morrison's management and publishing company, who were quite influential, so they were taking it very seriously indeed.

Mod was always tainted from the word go with this rather sad shallow copy of what had gone on either in punk or in the sixties, because it was neither one thing or the other. But then it wasn't as good as anything that had gone before and that's the way people used to regard it, so it wasn't ever going to be a long term thing.

For the people who were interested in it from the early days, there was often a kind of a 'football' background and there were quite a few fairly tasty characters who were involved, for whom going to football and fighting at football was of primarily interest. You would have to say they saw it in some ways, as an extension of doing that. There were 20 or 30 guys who I knew reasonably well, who attached themselves to Secret Affair, The Glory Boys, and these were fairly rough characters and it would always go off at some point. They'd have 'Glory Boys' tattooed on the inside of their bottom lip and they were almost all West Ham fans and it was almost another outlet for doing what they liked doing best. It was a very thin line between mods and skinheads, and a lot of the people who went along to these events were skinheads and they enjoyed what used to go along with it, but it got to the point where we went on the March Of The Mods Tour, and these guys had a bit of a reputation and there would always be a local firm keen to have a go, and that's often what happened. There were some gruesome incidents of people fighting in the gigs or outside. When the March Of The Mods tour got outside of London you'd meet a lot of these guys and there'd be a 'look at the state of his flares' type of attitude, but that's what they were into, stitching beer mats onto parkas and wearing big flares and very scooter based.

We used to think the music was rubbish because they were into Northern Soul, so the music never really crossed over at all and they used to think we were tossers and vice versa at the time.

You used to get some lively encounters with local scooter boys and particularly in, what was for me being a southerner, the more remote outposts if you like. Not so much in the big cities like Liverpool and Manchester, but when you find yourself in Whitby or somewhere like that you'd find a mob of scooter boys whom you'd been blissfully unaware of at the time. They had their own scene going, and I think they thought us ludicrous calling ourselves mods when a lot of us wouldn't know one end of a scooter from the other. That was their attitude, but our mod was not about that really, ours was more about the music. Maximum Speed became almost the official programme for the tour with a colour front cover, and by that time we had shops selling it, and quite a lot on mail order. It was crackers at one point. We were seriously considering trying to get it sold at W.H.Smiths. I must admit I did like 'Jamming' magazine. That just evolved and broadened and I thought that might happen to Maximum Speed, but I guess we were too lazy really and some of us were more interested than others. By the last edition, I was probably doing most of the writing, but it just got a bit boring and we all lost interest.

DAVE CAIRNS gave this response when asked about The Glory Boys:
Ian wrote the lyric to Glory Boys about a year before we started performing the song as Secret Affair and it was then adopted by a great bunch of East End lads who started coming to all our gigs. It was impossible not to notice the early East-End following who adopted our song as their anthem.

EDDIE PILLER was a member of The Glory Boys and gives this first-hand account of what they were all about:
They were mod-football nutters. I've still got some mates from back then. A guy called Spanner who is a good friend of mine. They were a mixture of mods and skinheads and they would fight skinheads. It wasn't about youth culture, it was whether you were one of them or not. I was a couple of years younger than most of them and I was tolerated. You had to have the tattoo on the inside of the lip. Most of them had it. It really hurt. Then you were accepted, but the thing that really amazed me about them was they were so tough. It was Grant Flemming and basically the West Side of West Ham in '79. Either the West Side or the South Side. I was always in the West Side and that's where I met Goffa and all that lot. The Glory Boys were very hard and they were like Ian Page's private army. He would say 'You don't wear parkas or target t-shirts, you wear tonic suits and Italian-made gear and basket weave shoes' and it worked. I went to some of the gigs, but that was 'our' thing you know? Apart from Back To Zero,

the other bands were all from our area. Secret Affair used to drink in my local pub, which is how I got to meet them. Ian Page was always quite difficult to communicate with. He is very focused, he knows exactly what he thinks and Dave Cairns is similar, so they were a spikey band to follow. I followed them for a while, but my main bands to follow were The Chords and Long Tall Shorty and The Jam. So The Affair and The Purple Hearts were our bands from our part of town, and The Mods, who were from north London and the Borehamwood lot, they had quite a hard following. The rest of them didn't really have big followings.

The Glory Boys being tough was handy though, and you've got to remember what it was like in London back then. You'd go to a gig at the Electric Ballroom and you'd come out to see 50 skinheads waiting to beat the crap out of any mod they could get hold of. So, then when we had this really hard football crew who travelled around in transit vans and on scooters, no one bothered us.

I had a few fights alongside Crank, but the thing about the Glory Boys was they were so tough that no one messed with them. They only lasted the one summer of '79 and by the spring of 1980 they were gone.

A lot of them went casual. That was an extension of mod from most people's perspective, even though mods didn't like them and they didn't like mods. But most of them were mods or aware of mod anyway. After the Glory Boys disappeared, we set up the Bow Street Runners, which was not trying to emulate the Glory Boys, but be a contemporary version of them in suits. We still had fights with people. It was part of youth culture then. It doesn't happen now.

I wouldn't swap that period of my life for the world. The feeling of camaraderie and belonging. I think, when you're a kid, you want to belong, but not to the mainstream, so when something has rules that you can belong to, but isn't the main fashion, it a good thing. Then when mod did get big, a lot of those people couldn't handle the post 'Quadrophenia' boom. Kids running round in parkas and that. After the summer of '79, the 'family' feeling was gone. You couldn't go to a gig and see the same people you saw last week in the crowd. It died with success, but it was a great period. I loved all the bands.

BRAIN BETTERIDGE saw what the Glory Boys antics were doing to the March Of The Mods tour as a whole:

The actions of the Glory Boys affected the sales of Maximum Speed in some of the places we played. For example in Birmingham, Barbarella's 16 August, not long after the beginning of the tour, the Glory Boys would threaten people for not buying Glory Boy badges. The locals would think, 'Who are these bastards from London doing this?'. So then anything from London was hard to sell, including Maximum Speed. They thought, 'Well if I don't buy a copy of that, am I going to get bashed over the head as well?'. I remember one guy who bought a copy and then tore it up and things like that were going on. I didn't see this, but evidently, people were throwing glasses at Ian Page that night and no way would I condone anyone throwing a glass at a musician, but what I will say is it was a result of the aggressive and antagonistic behaviour of a bunch of teenagers from London, and people thought, 'Well these people wouldn't be here if the band wasn't here'. I guess I turned a blind eye to it because I thought I was on this great thing that was happening and something really good might happen tomorrow.

Some of the March Of The Mods gigs were great though. In Liverpool, at Eric's, they had a policy that there was a matinee for under eighteens and the main gig. They had the support on last, so people could see the headline band and still get home, but they all stayed and treated us like the headline band and that was an amazing night.

By this time, Back To Zero were on a whirlwind couple of months that started with the recording of their one and only single 'Your Side Of Heaven':

We recorded the single at the end of July and it came out the end of September. It sold 5,000 the first day and sold 9,000 all together. The fact is two minutes forty-one seconds of my life is still appreciated, so I'm proud of 'Your Side Of Heaven' and I hope Sam and Mal are as well. Andy Moore had left by the end of the March Of The Mods Tour. We made number 96 in the trade top 200. Mal went up to Andy and said: 'You're in the chart at number 96' and Andy said: 'So what'. So he wasn't that proud of it even then.

Arguably, 'Walking Down The Kings Road' was one of Squire's best-known songs. It was written by **ANTHONY MEYNELL** and he explains the inspiration behind it:
It was simply that I had spent a lot of time on the Kings Road. It sounds corny, but it was that obvious. The Kings Road and that late sixties thing are close to my heart, because originally, I came from New Malden, it was easy to get to. I'd been to Carnaby Street and Kings Road in the sixties as a kid, so I know what it was like.
In the seventies, I still went there because the boutiques were still there and the vibe, but it was disappointing with all the punks. You wanted it to be the same although you knew it never would be, so 'Walking Down The Kings Road' was sort of a time tunnel, wishing you could turn around and it would be the sixties. The B side, 'It's A Mod, Mod World' is a snap shot of my sister's life. She went to Boxhill on a Sunday afternoon, she was a hairdresser, and all her money was for clothes.
It was just a mod, mod world. The songs were written from inspiration and they became a bit anthemic, which is a bit worrying, because you think it's a novelty song and not taken seriously, but it was pop and I love pop, so it was everything I wanted it to be; three minutes with a beginning and an end and it punched the air with enthusiasm. Then people enjoyed it, so it was a success and around the world it has become a bit of a catch phrase. I'm told that a couple of years ago when Chelsea won the FA Cup, they played it as background music and I thought, my God isn't that silly, but isn't it nice that can happen.

For **GOFFA GLADDING**, involvement with the March Of The Mods tour and Maximum Speed led to him being invited to write for the music paper 'Sounds':
They had a very cooperative attitude at the time. They would invite anybody who genuinely knew what was going on to write for them rather than dredging out their old journalists who didn't know anything. They wanted people to write about the bands. Sounds used to come out on a Wednesday lunchtime and the first people to get it used to be a newsagent at the back of Carnaby Street, so there'd always be a gang of people meeting Wednesday lunchtime to see if a particular article was in there.
I remember somebody once said that over a couple of months Sounds was like buying

a copy of Maximum Speed. Gary Bushell was quite supportive of this sort of thing and he was quite a big wheel at Sounds, and it was remarkable that comparatively minor bands were getting front-page covers and big articles. Nobody ever thought this music was going to change the world, and it irritates me slightly when people say 'These tossers were playing at it', but it was a huge amount of fun for a time.

Sounds were so enthralled with the mod scene, they even had a 'round-table' forum to discuss the whole thing. Goffa was among the invited guests:
I'd all but forgotten it until you reminded me. Even at the time, I thought 'This is ludicrous'. It was like the G7 leaders get together to discuss global warming. You know? Sitting around a table and solemnly considering mod and where it's going. It was ridiculous. I think Dave Cairns was there, Gary Bushell was definitely there, and a couple of people who just thought it was a waste of time and they were kind of the 'anti's'. But it was crazy and even now I've no idea what the point of it was, and I'm sure people reading it must have thought the same.
I'd have done better if I'd have had 14 pints of strong lager. It was dreadful. One of those cringe moments when you're reading what you had said and you think 'Christ I wish I'd never been part of that'.

From then, Goffa was among the regular contributors until he was sent on a particular assignment:
Sounds said "Would you like to do some other stuff?' and I said 'Yeah I'd like to do that', so they gave me a couple of assignments to review bands and, I think it was bands like Iron Maiden and The Fall.
Actually the key thing for me was The Lambrettas where the record company, through Sounds, basically paid for me to go to Paris for a few days to meet and review them. It was the first time I'd really become aware of how closely linked the music press was to the record companies.
I hadn't realised for example, that when you read a review or somebody interviewing somebody in Los Angeles, that person's record company had paid for that journalist to

go out there. There is quite an unhealthy relationship going on there, and I remember very clearly the piece I wrote on The Lambrettas started off with a quote that went something like 'Why do you think a record company would pay a few hundred quid to get a journalist to Paris to review a band? Answer, they think that by doing so, that journalist will give a favourable review.

Question, does this always work? Answer, 'no' and I went on to completely slag them off and the work dried up a bit because I hadn't realised the delicate relationship that exists between the press and the record companies.

The Lambrettas were a great bunch of lads really, but they blotted their copybook with 'Poison Ivy' which I thought was pretty dreadful. Although they did have a track called 'Concrete and Steel' which I thought was a cracking track, so there was obviously some talent there. After that, I became just a normal music fan, but people say to me 'Oh you must be mad, you were writing for Sounds and now you're in a normal, everyday job, but that incident in particular, that record company thing spoilt it for me and the second thing was I didn't fancy writing about music I didn't like. There isn't much fun in that. I remember going to see The Fall at the Acklam Hall and thinking 'What am I doing here?' and I took longer and longer to write the reviews up so after a while Sounds stopped asking me.

For Back To Zero, problems arose after the March Of The Mods Tour ended on 1 September 1979. **BRIAN BETTERIDGE** explains:

Andy Moore only stayed on for the March Of The Mods Tour, so we auditioned three drummers and Nigel Wolf joined. Now at the time, he was from east London, I think he knew some of the Glory Boys and we thought he suited our style more.

But looking back, musically we replaced a great drummer with a moderate drummer. He could keep a basic beat, but that was it. That's probably where things went into decline because we didn't recruit a good enough drummer after Andy left. But then when we went out of London to do gigs, we found that the DJs were playing things like 'Green Onions' and other stuff from the 'Quadrophenia' soundtrack as well as the Two Tone stuff to a venue packed with mods.

Two Tone hit a popular nerve that the mod bands were never likely to hit, but you can't knock that. I liked the Two-Tone bands, I didn't love them, but I liked them and you can't knock that kind of mass appeal. Some of the influences might have been the same, and there were people who were into both, but then there were a lot of people who were into Two Tone who weren't even aware of mod bands. It all shot up at the same time. I mean at the beginning of '79, Madness were playing just down the road in Islington. So by then at the gigs, they were dancing to that stuff and 'My Generation' and then going home or going to the bar when the band came on.

I remember seeing Long Tall Shorty in Sheffield, and I remember the place packed with 14, 15 and 16 year-old mods and kids with dyed blonde hair and loads of 'Police' badges. They were obviously thinking 'This is what Sting looked like in the film Quadrophenia, so he must be a mod and we will dress like him', so there was that sort of attitude going on. What did they know about Long Tall Shorty? They were just waiting for 'My Generation' to come on.

That happened to us. There was a certain amount of apathy outside of London and I guess we were a bit naive because we thought that what had happened up to and including the March Of The Mods Tour was some sort of a crest. It may not have been the case for us or a lot of the other bands. The Hearts and The Chords continued to sell records and rightly so, and maybe because Fiction carried on with them or because of better management or more money put into them, they did well, but for the rest of us lower down, we suffered a bit, especially outside of London. Us, Squire, Teenbeats and bands like The Fixations were already casualties before the end of '79. Meanwhile, out of town there were bands that were starting, and they did get it right because they were starting after the big surge. They had the time to get their own reputation by '80, '81, '82 even though they were inspired by '79.

They didn't have the pressure on them, and we're talking about bands like Small World, who didn't have the burden. I wouldn't say '79 was a millstone round our necks, but if Small World had started in '79 at the same time as us, they might have split by 1980, whereas they could carry on and do things in their own time.

Then you've got The Lambrettas. They did the circuit and they got on that album on the

Rocket label. Now Rocket were clever, they thought it was something they could work with, but Rocket never marketed The Lambrettas as a mod band, they marketed them as a pop band with a capital 'P' with mod trappings. By doing that, if the mod thing fell, they could go somewhere else with them. That's why 'Poison Ivy' made the top ten. It wasn't a mod band, it was a pop group making the top ten. Anyway, we were getting crowds in London, not so much outside of town, but then we got on the second Secret Affair tour, The Dancing In The Streets Tour.

Squire were supporting them on that tour, but they had some misfortune. One of them went down with chicken pox, and then a lighting rig almost fell on the drummer. I think it did graze him a bit and he just missed serious injury. Squire pulled out of the tour and we were on it.

ANTHONY MEYNELL explains exactly what happened to Squire on the Dancing In The Streets Tour:

Well, we had done a ten-date tour with Secret Affair already and we went on the 30-date tour, but by the 25th date something happened that meant we had to leave the tour. It was really unlucky.

It's a strange story, but our manager had decided two bands were too much and his loyalty was with his main band who were also university friends of his.

I think he got his band our deal and they toured with Madness, which was supposed to be ours, but we were tied to Secret Affair.

He introduced us to a road manager, who was going to look after us on the tour. This new guy was nice enough, but an odd character and strange things started to happen. We were staying in five-star hotels and Secret Affair were in three-star hotels. He was really into the band, but he would do things like buy a Rickenbacker and give it to me as a present. He would go into studios and everyone seemed to know him. Certainly all the roadies knew him, but we thought he was in the business.

We were getting limos everywhere and we couldn't figure out where the money was coming from. We just thought we had made it and this is what happened.

Then at the Leicester gig, something very weird happened. We were on stage at

> It was the time of 501s, penny loafers and Acid Jazz towards the end of the decade, which I personally became more interested in, as I began to lose interest in a strict sixties music and style direction.
>
> MARK SANDON

the university; the stage curtains closed and they hit the lighting gantry and sent them crashing down across the drum kit. They hit my guitar lead and destroyed the back line and almost my brother, who just saw the lights move. He was covered in lacerations and had to go to hospital. Needless to say the gig was pulled.

We missed a day and then got back on the tour, but my brother was so ill that within a week, he contracted chicken pox and couldn't continue. Something else happened as well. The last time we played with Secret Affair, Dave Cairns came over and told us to get rid of our manager and they didn't want to deal with us anymore.

We did a Christmas gig with the guy and he was setting up a tour of America because he thought we would go down well over there, but then we never saw him again.

Then in January 1980, the police showed up and asked us if we knew this guy. We asked why, and they said he was a conman who hadn't paid a single bill on the tour and he ripped everyone off blind. The agency, the record company, the publisher, everyone and they thought the lighting accident was part of an insurance claim scam. So we ended up with nothing. We couldn't even use the name Squire, because every time we did, a writ would turn up for an unpaid bill. The police eventually caught up with the guy and he did six years in prison.

BRIAN BETTERIDGE recounts how he found out about Back To Zero joining the Dancing In The Streets tour and what happened to the band not long after:

The first gig we did was at the Rainbow a 3,000 seater, all sold out and we didn't know about it until the night before. I was with Long Tall Shorty in Nottingham at the Sandpiper Club. One of the Maximum Speed lads phoned, but I wasn't around and Keith of Long Tall Shorty took the call for me. When I got back they were sitting in the dressing room saying, 'You're on the tour Brian, you're playing the Rainbow tomorrow night'.

It was scary, but that Rainbow gig was the biggest crowd we ever had and it was a good one. A lot of people remember that night. So we played some really big crowds, but it was all Secret Affair orientated. Some people liked us, but they had mostly come to see The Affair and they didn't really care who else was on.

Then the internal politics of the band surfaced and basically we had been living in each other's pockets too long really.

Although the band had only been going for eight or nine months, it doesn't sound too long, but as Sam has always said, it was too much too soon and we were very naive. We were not given the time to develop and we were thrust out there. It's like what I was saying about Small World or even a band trying to make it today. They'll be doing the toilet circuit for months and months before they get their first play on the Steve Lamaq Show. We also started to think Nigel Wolf wasn't the right choice as a drummer. He was pissing people off and being a bit arrogant. I remember Secret Affair arrived with a ton of food one night after a gig and he nicked a load of it and they pointed the finger at us, but it was Nigel and he just said, 'Well I don't like them anyway'. which is sort of funny now, but it reflected on us. Then Sam and I had different ideas about the bands' direction. It was always Sam's band, I always knew that, but he thought it was going to my head because I was hanging out with a completely different crowd for a start.

I was spending time with Long Tall Shorty and other mods around London and I was out almost every night. Whereas the others were like a peer group from the age of 12 onwards and I felt they were being a bit offish to people and it was going to their heads, so there was conflict going on and Nigel as well.

After the Dancing In The Streets Tour, we did one gig at the Bridgehouse and that was it. There was a band meeting on the 1 January 1980 at the Rising Sun pub in Southgate, and they told me they didn't want me in the band. At the time, the official line was I had left, but now after all this time, who cares?

Then about a week or two after that Nigel said he was leaving to join The Cockney Rejects, which he did, and two weeks later he was on Top Of The Pops doing 'I'm Forever Blowing Bubbles'.

So that was it for me, they carried on and did another four or five gigs and another demo, which is the one on the 'We Are The Mods' album. Sam is mystified as to how that got on there because even he doesn't have a copy of it.

I was asked by a drummer friend of mine to join a band called Bee's By Post which was a sort of sixties influenced garage, punk thing. We did a few gigs including supporting

Long Tall Shorty and Speedball who were another amazing band from '79. It was a bit of post-mod fallout really.

Bee's By Post folded by November 1980 due to nothing happening, and it's really ironic, because a few days later on a platform at an underground station, I ran into John Wheeldon, who was the first person I met to say 'I'm a mod' just two years earlier. It seemed like a lifetime, but it was only two years previous, and he said BTZ had split, Mal had sold his bass and that was it, but it was ironic hearing that just days after Bee's By Post had split as well, so it ended with a whimper rather than a bang.

Squire were also finding it tough going, and **ANTHONY MEYNELL** noticed a certain change in the attitude of the music business:

There was something that happened at the end of 1979 and going into the new decade. The press had never been more friendly and I think the music press were very influential, but they never really got into mod. Concurrently there was ska, which made the audience three times the size to what it would have been and they wore the same stuff and were much the same crowd, but the press much preferred that from a credibility point of view. They preferred The Specials, who had more credibility than Secret Affair, even though they had the same thing. They had their own label and other bands on it, so it was the same. But mod was seen as a revivalist thing and people in the business were original mods from the sixties and they were very jealous and didn't consider it to be a real mod thing. They still wanted to find bands that weren't mod but could ride the mod thing into something bigger. So when The Chords supported The Undertones, it was obvious they wanted The Chords to go that way.

By late 1979, some of the mod bands were openly saying they weren't mods because they could see it would be the kiss of death.

The mod revival was effectively over on 1 January 1980 and Squire broke up soon afterwards. At Arista, The Beat were bigger than Secret Affair, so they became the priority act. That had a lot to do with Dave Cairns saying they couldn't carry on with us I think. Although we had already done some demos for an album and the future had looked rosy.

Just like Back To Zero, Squire suffered from a combination of too much, too soon and internal politics. With no time to develop as a band, Squire ended their brief career as **ANTHONY MEYNELL** explains:

Basically, I had hi-jacked the band, not deliberately, but it turned out that way. I joined as second guitarist and was writing the songs. At rehearsals, I would play the other members of the band my new songs and Enzo would say "I can't learn those in time for our gig next week, you sing them". So, I wasn't centre stage but I was becoming more of a focal point because I was singing as well.

By August of 1979, the lead guitarist got fed up. We did an afternoon gig and were due to play The Wellington in the evening. After the first gig he just said "I'm not doing this anymore. It's not my band anymore". And that was that. We went to The Wellington as a three piece and blew the crowd away on pure adrenaline. Then when the Arista deal came up, Arista said they didn't like the drummer and couldn't record with him and we would have to get another drummer. Well that's impossible, except that my brother wasn't in the band and he wanted to get in. Even Enzo agreed that if it meant the difference between getting and not getting the deal, we would have to do it, so my brother was in the band. It was very hard for Enzo because the drummer was his childhood friend and suddenly his band wasn't his band anymore. Within three weeks, we had lost the lead guitarist and the drummer and went on the Secret Affair tour as a three piece and a different line-up. Suddenly I was singing all the songs and leading the band. It was good for me, but everyone else was upset about it.

When it came to Christmas and we had pulled out of the Dancing In The Streets tour and that police business had gone down, Enzo was so disillusioned. We did another single, 'My Mind Goes Round In Circles' for an independent label and a sort of tour, but the single came out after the tour and it was all a bit hopeless.

Only by looking at the worst, it was clear that mod was not flavour of the month and the new thing was New Romantic and if you were a mod band, it wasn't going to do you any favours in 1980 unless you had a lot of backing. Enzo realised this and by the middle of 1980 he left.

That's when Hi-Lo Records started because the distributor said we still had a deal and if I recorded material, they would distribute it, and slowly I built it back up to being bigger than it was before.

We had to use the name Anthony Meynell because we couldn't use the name Squire as I explained earlier. I had the demos of Arista stuff and other things we had done and that became the Anthony Meynell album.

The distributor took it on but it fizzled out and I went back to college for about six months. I couldn't let it go though and someone wrote a letter to me saying they had this record and it was Squire, so we stickered the Anthony Meynell album as a Squire album and the distributor by now had become international and was sending it to really odd places like California and loads to Ireland.

What became apparent was that mod hadn't died, it had just gone underground.

I went to see the Purple Hearts in late 1980 or 1981 just to see what was going on and it was pretty dead in London. They were playing in front of 50 people again. I couldn't get a band together to do the old stuff because no one wanted to play to 50 people, but I was still writing and I had a name and my brother was drumming, so with multi-tracking, we did another single called 'No Time Tomorrow' which was very much what I was into then, more psychedelic.

I had gone from 'Hard Days Night' to 'Revolver' and I was very into Small Faces, Kinks, Creation, The Action. So 'No Time Tomorrow' as a result was psychedelic in 1980.

It dribbled out. We did a thousand copies and they sold out, then another thousand and Hi-Lo really got going from there. It was mainly in response to the letters we were getting from people who liked it and wanted more.

It was great for me because it meant that I could write songs and release them when I wanted to instead of being tied to a label.

The thing about Squire and the whole '79 thing for me was that it was there and then it was gone. I went to gigs in 1980-81 and there was a second generation of mods in the crowd. The original lot had gone, which I thought was very mod as well, rather like the sixties. It was fun and exciting, it had its 15 minutes and then it was gone. If Squire had done an album with Arista, we may have become disillusioned and may not have carried on.

In the north, The Killermetres were suffering from a manufactured split in the mod camp as VIC VESPA recalls:
There was this north-south divide, which was basically created by the media. The main music papers talked it up. We even did an interview with Maximum Speed and they did the same thing. They went on and on about which bands disliked the other and it didn't do anyone any favours. The Purple Hearts and Secret Affair were definitely not respected in the north. It really all came to a head in Huddersfield. We did a gig with Secret Affair and there was a massive fight outside between northerners and southerners. We had a lot of northern scooter clubs turning up and Secret Affair brought a couple of coach loads of Glory Boys with them. It was a lovely summer Saturday night and the Great Hall of Huddersfield Polytechnic was lined with scooters outside. Once the trouble started, the coaches that the Secret Affair fans came in had their windows smashed. It was horrendous. We never played with Secret Affair again. We were supposed to go on tour with them when our single came out, but we got dropped.
We always had great support from the scooter clubs in the north, so anytime a southern band came up, it always seemed to end up in trouble. We were naive as well. One night, we offered half-price entry to scooterists as long as they produced their crash helmets! Looking back, I don't know what we were thinking when we did that. It was ridiculous though. The southern bands would get slaughtered when they came up here and we would get slaughtered when we went to London. The thing is, we actually liked the other bands, even Secret Affair. I wouldn't begrudge their success, they were a great band. We got on well with The Chords, they were down-to-earth, but musically a bit rockier. We kept working and gigged so much, Radio One's Newsbeat proclaimed us the hardest working band in Britain. Then we did our first single 'Why Should It Happen To Me' and fortunately, John Peel, who's wife is Huddersfield born and bred, saw us while visiting in-laws in Huddersfield and he played our single on his show.

Although the bands were on a roller coaster ride, mods had sprung up almost everywhere and director, Nick Roeg was in the latter stages of completing a film that had former

sixties mod **ALAN FLETCHER** working as a consultant. Alan had written 'Brummell's Last Riff', a television script about mods, in 1973:
It went round all the TV companies and it nearly got through at Granada Television. The script made it through all their internal processes until it got to the last stage, the Head of Drama, and then it got rejected. Anyway, it would have been phenomenally expensive to make and it was at a time when all TV drama was being produced in the studio. There was very little being made on location. A guy at Central Television told me it was too expensive to make and I should write it as a novel. It took me twenty years to do it! In the end I sent the script down to Pete Townshend just as they were planning 'Quadrophenia' as a film. Pete liked it and asked me to submit a script for 'Quadrophenia'. Chris Stamp was writing one, but he didn't come through with it or it wasn't accepted. Anyway, when you get involved with a film, everyone gets involved. The script eventually came about by committee. Everyone wants to put their two-penneth in. The Director, Pete, the Producers, the Band. In the end though, it was credited to Franc Roddam, Dave Humphries and Martin Stellman.
I put my two-penneth in with Pete when I was given the shooting script to write the novel from. I said the dialogue was too weak, then I got a revised script back which said "additional dialogue by Martin Stellman". So I felt somewhat vindicated in that respect. Then Pete asked me to write the novel.It was largely as a result of the Corgi editorial input. I went down to Eel Pie and stayed a week at Pete's Cultural Centre with a guy from Corgi and we rewrote it. It sold 90,000 copies - nothing to do with Alan Fletcher. It was obviously the film that sold it, I'm under no illusions there.

The stories surrounding the making of 'Quadrophenia' are now well-known; Sex Pistol frontman Johnny Rotten originally being considered for the lead role of 'Jimmy' for example. Phil Davis, who would eventually get the part of 'Chalky' was also in the running, but Producer and mod of the Sixties: Bill Curbishley finally settled on Phil Daniels.
An interesting side note that Phil Daniels mentioned in his biography 'A Class Actor' is his recollection of a young ambitious lad who wanted to be a pop star:
Another musical legacy that can't be pinned on me is the stylistic evolution of Gary

Kemp. The mod revival was in full flow. Gary's band at the time were called the Makers - they hadn't become Spandau Ballet - and I remember them playing on a Friday at the Old Red Lion, all dressed as mods. They obviously had a manager who knew the score (I think it was Steve Dagger, even then), and what they would do was jump on any image that came along until the right one eventually turned up.

For the actual filming of 'Quadrophenia', the production company didn't have too many problems recruiting mods and scooterists to re-enact the Brighton mods and rocker fights. Among those recruits was the Modropheniacs Scooter Club. Robin 'Yob' Williams and the rest of the club had travelled to the Lambretta Club of Great Britain (LCGB) rallies at Southend, Essex in 1978 and 1979. The very same 'legendary' events Gareth Brown referred to earlier, and they were the first occurrences of fighting with local teddy boy revivalists and hell's angels. The '79 rally was the scene of so much violence that Southend did not host the rally again. While at one of the Southend rallies, the Modropheniacs were asked to appear in 'Quadrophenia'. As **YOB** told Scootering Magazine:

We thought the whole thing was a wind-up until one of the directors turned up at the New Inn in Poole waving a cheque book. After the filming, 18 months before its release, there was so much hype that the Modropheniacs membership went into three figures.

For **GOFFA GLADDING**, the film is not now regarded with as much fondness as some might think:

It's always cited when you look back now that mod in 1979 was as a result of 'Quadrophenia', and that is nothing to do with the truth at all. It was always there and it had all come about through innovative fashion-minded people around the East End and into Essex, who were constantly looking for new trends or new interesting things and basically to set themselves apart from the crowd a bit. These are the people who started it all off and this was at least a year before 'Quadrophenia' came out.
We knew the film was in production, but the scene was absolutely nothing to do with

'Quadrophenia' at all and in the same way that mass interest in punk in '77 was the death knell for a lot of people who were quite involved in it in the early days. The launch of 'Quadrophenia' and what that turned into was the death knell for a lot of the people who were the original innovators from 1978. So I would say 'Quadrophenia' is pivotal for some people in that having seen it they copied it, but for the sort of people I'm talking about and really almost everything we're talking about, it was all happening anyway and 'Quadrophenia' had no impact on us at all.

BRIAN BETTERIDGE remembers the film well:
Quadrophenia came out in August 1979. At the time in London, the attitude was 'It's going to finish the scene, we're doomed'. I thought that was a bit 'precious' and that any fresh interest is always good and people might have got into a whole lifetimes worth of stuff just because of that film. We were all invited to see it at a special preview in Wardour Street two weeks before it came out. That was quite amusing because The Jam were sitting in front of us and Secret Affair were there.
Ian Page and Paul Weller couldn't stand each other and they were studiously trying to avoid each other around the sandwiches before the film. I know one of Secret Affairs first gigs was supporting The Jam, but what Page was about was totally different to what Weller was all about and their personalities were totally different, but it was quite amusing.
The late Philip Hall, who championed the mod bands in Record Mirror, asked me what I thought of it after the film. The thing was, we all saw the scooter going over the cliff at the end of the film and we didn't say a word as we left the cinema. I said to Philip 'None of us had anything to say, we all knew what we thought, Quadrophenia was brilliant' and he went and quoted me the next week in Record Mirror.

When asked about the so-called 'animosity' between The Jam and Secret Affair camps, both Ian Page and Dave Cairns had this to say:
IAN PAGE: Early on John Weller offered to help us and we were grateful that someone with a bit of sway, who we trusted would be able to help us extricate ourselves from a

record contract that was preventing us signing Secret Affair to a new record company and to progress. After a few months John had been unable to arrange the meetings that were needed and time was short for us, so we moved on. Let's not forget, John was managing The Jam who were hugely successful and took up all his time.

Paul Weller seemed to misunderstand what had and hadn't happened at that time, and I assume has laboured under that misapprehension ever since. Personally, I had never said more than 'Hello' and 'How are you?' to John, who I thought was a great guy with a very talented son. How anyone can nurse a grudge (incorrectly) for more than 35 years is quite beyond me.

DAVE CAIRNS: I'm rather puzzled about this because on the odd occasion I've bumped into Paul Weller over the years we have only ever had a pleasant chat so if there was any problem between us I'm sure he would have said something. Our involvement with Paul and his father really goes back to New Hearts when we supported them in 1978 on one of their UK tours and we were treated very well by them and they were very supportive. When we formed Secret Affair we were invited to support them at Reading University in '79 as one of many gigs we had planned and then we basically went our own way and lost touch.

For ordinary mods, Quadrophenia is either an inspiration or an abberation.
MIKE WARBURTON from Salford, Lancashire, who has been on the mod scene for over 30 years, made this assessment of the film:
As a story, it's quite enjoyable, but I do not consider it gives an accurate picture of the original mod scene. After all, it is only about the events leading up to Brighton 1964, which in my opinion, sounded the death knell of mod and the beginning of the scooter scene. In any case, very few London club going mods of the early sixties would be seen at something as tacky as Brighton '64.
A much better film in my opinion is 'Stepping Out', showing excerpts from the London clubs and gigs of late 1979. It captures the vibrancy and excitement of mod the second time around when it was in its infancy.

> I'm into its style and
> its attitude, that never compromises on anything.
> Most of all, it's an attitude. It's my attitude.
> MANABU KURODA

Some observers have suggested that the '79 mod was a backlash to the scruffy, anti-establishment punk movement. Others suggest that kids took to The Jam and being mod, when they would normally have become skinheads, soul boys or punks. Most commentators agree that, aside from The Jam, the film 'Quadrophenia' was just as responsible for the mass participation of mod in the late seventies. There is evidence to support this claim. The East Grinstead Courier ran a feature article in 1979 on local mods. Phillip Ford, then 19 years old, said he was influenced by Quadrophenia "*I was a mod before the film came out. But the film really started it off for me in a big way, mainly because of the way the actors dressed*".

This article really sums up all that was wrong with the mass mod revival. As the journalist states: *"The most important item in a mod's wardrobe is his green parka. Mods' parkas are splattered with Union flags and badges naming bands like The Who, Secret Affair, The Lambrettas, The Jam and Madness".*
Another interviewee was Raymond Abbott. Raymond spoke of a trip to Brighton *"We met up with about 50 younger mods on Palace Pier. Then we got attacked. About 20 rockers and a few skinheads started running at us, armed with a few bricks. The younger mods fled, leaving us, and the police broke it up".*
Later the same day Phillip and Raymond met up with mods from the north who had arrived by train. Raymond continued *"They were chanting 'we are the mods' and talking about where they came from. The Rockers were afraid because there were more of us".*
That particular day, Raymond says he was dressed casually in a parka, red socks and trainers because he could run better in them!
This is hardly the image of sartorial elegance and cool that was a central theme to being a modernist. 'Quadrophenia' certainly inspired thousands to become mods, without necessarily understanding what it was all about.
There was room for salvation though. In the same year Richard Barnes published his book 'Mods' through Eel Pie Publishing. This too had become a critical source of reference for the more serious minded mod in 1979, and has since been quoted by numerous academics in the wider field of cultural studies.

Unlike 'Quadrophenia', 'Mods' identified the components that made modernism as it traced its path from the early to mid sixties, and the demise of the scene.

Some detractors saw it as a cash-in, but irrespective of whether it is or is not, the book still served as an excellent source of research for those who wanted to find out what sixties mods were about.

Meanwhile, The Chords had acknowledged their sixties influence while citing bands like The Jam, The Clash and The Buzzcocks who were just as influential, although they quickly dismissed any comparisons between themselves and The Jam.

They did, however, make a lasting impression on a young punk-collecting devotee. **DAVID DIZZY HOLMES** had been collecting records since he was 14 years-old:
I bought punk stuff. I was always trying to be different. I bought the Buzzcocks and the Clash, but as I got older, I started buying really obscure stuff. We went to see the Undertones in 1979 at the Guildford Civic Hall. A load of people turned up in parkas and on scooters. I'd never heard of mod before then. They looked so cool on their scooters. The Chords were supporting that night, so it was seeing the Undertones and the Chords that got me started.

Dizzy's home town of Midhurst in West Sussex was 'biker' dominated at the time, as were many southern towns outside of London, but mod numbers grew until there were 35 of them. They decided to form into a club and Dizzy recalls how the club got its name:
There was this guy called Silvio Bacquades who was into everything. When punk came out, he was into it, when mods came out he was the first one in the town to have a scooter. He had all the early magazines and everything. He got the name Detour from The Who because they were known as The Detours early on.

The mod and scootering 'bug' was making an impression throughout Midhurst and particularly in the local school. **TANIA WOODMAN** was one of those who was being influenced:
The Jam really started it for me. Then the scooter club got going and there was five

or six of them at the time. We also had the upper school mods who were real cool people to be seen with. So that's how I got into it, and because they had scooters, it became even more cool to be seen with the real mods. I didn't get a scooter until about '83 - 84.

We'd have people from Chichester and Bognor Regis coming to The Grange Centre, which was our local sports centre. Friday nights they'd run a disco and that's where everybody would meet up. We had bands like The Gents down there.

We also used to ride down to Bognor, which, on a scooter, would take about three quarters of an hour, park them up all in a line, sit on a wall for three hours and all come back again. In the early eighties, everything in this town revolved around the scooter scene. Girls at school were dressing modish, hanging around at lunchtimes hoping a scooter would drive by, right up to those who were old enough to have scooters, riding up and down the High Street. It affected everybody, but no one remembers that anymore.

DIZZY HOLMES and those older scooter owners eventually began to travel further afield: At first we stayed in the south. We never really went to London at all. We went up to a Wasp do once and that was a real trek for us. We also used to go to Bournemouth, to Gossips, which was run by Yob. He used to put dos on for us. Then we went to Scarborough in '80 -'81 and it took three and a half days to get there. When we did get there, it was time to go home.

Both Dizzy and Tania would go on to make their mark on the scooter/mod scene, and particularly in music, where their future was right in front of them, even though they did not realise it at the time.

Of the many bands that had the mod mantle bestowed upon them, few managed any real longevity. The unfortunate facet of this crop of mod bands was that a few reflected the scenes instability and commercialism.

A prime example of this came from Nigel Oliver, the manager of the band The Mods, who claimed to have been a mod in the sixties and was quoted by Record Mirror as saying the new movement was exciting, but: "Anyone can be a mod, you don't have to dye your hair, you just have to put on a parka".

John Reed's assertion that defining a mod band was a simplistic one, could also be used to define the whole mod resurgence of the late seventies. Nigel Oliver's comment adds weight to this argument.

The fans deification of The Jam coupled with 'Quadrophenia', Richard Barnes' book and the release of The Who's biopic 'The Kids Are Alright' served as catalysts to a commercial and media frenzy that was always going to kill the goose before it had grown wings. Business exploited the market just as they did in the sixties, and started producing poor quality and overpriced clothes. Record companies rush-released back catalogue material like Decca's 'London Boys' EP and tatty parkas were being bought in their thousands from army surplus stores to be resold at inflated prices.

The media threw together pages of 'The Story So Far' features and slots on current affairs TV show like 'Nationwide'. The 'London Weekend Show' fronted and produced by Janet Street-Porter had managed a small degree of credibility with the youth of the day by being far more accurate when she examined the punk scene's emergence. She did the same with the new mods, focusing on the new bands and the fanzine, Maximum Speed. The rest of mainstream press were mostly misinformed and really only looking for the same thing that had increased circulation figures in the sixties. Namely, violence. It was not long before they got it.

History was repeating itself. As it was in the mid sixties, so it was in the late seventies. The more serious-minded mods learnt all they could and tried to live the mod lifestyle, but the London scene that drove the renewed media interest had run its course.

GOFFA GLADDING explains:

It was all quite compressed, and when I look back on it now, there was always something happening all the time, but it was no longer than from '78 through '79 and very early stages of 1980. The key period was the first half of '79 and the big events were things like, the biggest mod gig of the time at the Music Machine in Camden Town, which subsequently became the Camden Palace, which was I think The

Chords, The Purple Hearts, Secret Affair on 7 May and that was the pinnacle if you like. After that it must have been on the wane in terms of public interest by mid '79.

There were some really great records though. I mean The Purple Hearts brought out some great records. The Secret Affair brought out some good records, and they were terrific live, certainly in the early days. They were tight and worked really hard, but I don't think the records, particularly things like 'Time For Action' ever really did it, although I can see why they released it as the first single, but I didn't think it was a strong enough song really.

Some of the other bands though like Speedball from Southend, they brought out a single called 'No Survivor' and The Killermetres did a couple of really great singles, one of them is worth a bit of money now. Some things are quite embarrassing though like the Janet Street-Porter weekend TV show, and I have to tell you I have never watched it even though someone gave me a copy a few years ago.

The scene was quite close amongst a particular group of people, not the people you'd see in the LWT show, but they tended to be people in it from the start who kicked it all off, people like Grant Flemming, he was always over West Ham and that's where it all started. I think this is where the media have quite a difficulty, because they would brand these people as thugs, but they were actually quite innovative and forward thinking people who were setting trends and not slavishly following them.

The football connection was a key element of it as it developed. I mean, at The Wellington, there were guys there, who were Millwall fans, because The Chords came from Deptford, South East London, but they weren't on the same scale as the Glory Boys, but they were pretty fearsome.

We would always find somewhere to go after The Wellington, we'd go to parties and that sort of thing and you'd end up being chased down the road, and one of these guys used to carry an axe around with him! But I'd have to say, if you were in a spot, these were the guys you wanted close by.

By that time, mod was becoming much more widely known, so you'd get the sort of 'mod by numbers', lots and lots turning up wearing Fred Perry's and that kind of thing, a parka with a union jack on the back, which, as sophisticated southerners, we all looked down our noses at, which was pathetic now looking back. There were some pretty big crowds though and doing 10,000 copies of Maximum Speed proves it. For a time it was really quite big. It was always music that was the key as far as I was concerned. It was something that, during the early stages, you thought was just a little bit different and when you'd spent a day hunting around Westcliffe-On-Sea, because you'd heard that there was an Army & Navy shop that actually had some Sta-prest originals still in stock and you'd actually found them, with your Hush Puppies and Ben Shermans, it was a bit different at the time.

I've still got punk stuff that I bought from 'Boy' and 'Seditionaries' as it was and you'd been through that and this was something different and new and it gave a justification to the music I'd always liked, like soul music and that. We used to do the discos for some of the events we ran and it tended to be mainly Motown and Northern and not so much of your Small Faces.

More dance music than anything else. So it was music, and for a period it was a little elitist group who were a bit different to everybody else and it was great fun.

The fate that was befalling the London bands, also hit mods' only northern exponents, The Killermeters. As **VIC VESPA** explains:

We did some great gigs and had some great times. Playing the Marquee with Back To Zero, at the Music Machine in Camden when Captain Sensible from The Damned jumped up on stage and dueted with me, the Moonlight Club in Hampstead and Eric's in Liverpool.

But in many respects The Killermetres were our own worst enemies. We were always fighting each other and we used to get drunk a lot. I can't count the amount of times we'd be getting ready to go on stage, I mean actually at the side of the stage and I'd be having a physical fight with the drummer, then we'd get our cue and go on and play! We got signed to GEM Records who, I think signed us simply because they wanted a mod band. They weren't very clued up. They had bands like The UK Subs and Samson on their books. They booked us into CBS studios in London and our manager told us they wanted a mod anthem. We came up with 'SX225' and 'Twisted

Wheel'. The problem was, we really thought we'd made it. Up until then, we had spent all our time in a transit van gigging, then suddenly we were staying in a real hotel for three days and recording in a big studio.

It all fell apart when we went to the GEM Christmas party. We got drunk again and had a massive fight with the UK Subs. Needless to say, we were asked to leave and not long after GEM had a rethink and decided to drop us. They were in financial problems anyway as it turned out and folded, but 'SX225' sold about 18,000 singles, which, by today's standards, would be good enough to get into the top ten!

By the mid eighties our time had gone, our manager was getting tired and he wanted us to go for that psychedelic thing that followed mod, but we couldn't get into it. It felt like we were copying something that had gone before, but we didn't feel that way about mod. For me, 1979 was a great year.

Back in London, **BRIAN BETTERIDGE** remembers an incident that highlights the state of the scene and a hilarious moment in mod terms:

22 September 1979, I was at The Marquee and The Lambrettas were playing that night. We were in the front bar and not bothering to watch them. There had been a lunchtime gig with Long Tall Shorty at The Greyhound in Fulham, and I remember Tony Perfect, Long Tall Shorty and me were in the front bar. The Lambrettas had just finished and all these little mods were in their parkas, even though it was boiling hot in there. Anyway, they were all filing out

singing 'We Are The Mods', and Tony Perfect, who has a stocatto manner of talking, was wringing his hands with worry and he says ' Oh gawd, I wish I'd never started this mod revival!' That was the quote of the year.

By 1980, friction had intensified between mods and skinheads who followed the now dominant Two-Tone stable of ska acts.

The origins of Two-Tone started in 1976 in Midlands Britain. At that time, most of the local musicians who would form the Two-Tone groups were in a host of soul bands. Horace Panter, Jerry Dammers, Lynval Golding, Neol Davis, Charlie Bembridge and Silverton Hutchinson among them. Over time Jerry Dammers' vision formulated as he told Record

Collector in 2009: '*I got the ska idea from hearing a reggae band in Birmingham called Capital Letters. I was already wearing a shiny blue mod suit and suddenly it all clicked. I designed the Two-Tone label*'.

By 1978, Jerry Dammers' band The Automatics was essentially the nucleus and with the addition of Terry Hall from rival band The Squad, they became The Specials.

Pete Waterman has claimed he discovered The Specials, which is disputed by Jerry Dammers, as he said to Horace Panter at the time; *Discovering The Specials in Coventry was a little like discovering an armchair in your front room.*

During '78, The Specials were on a tour with The Clash and as Horace Panter states, the 8th July was a pivotal moment in the history of The Specials when they played Crawley Leisure Centre in Sussex. The behaviour of the racist element of the mainly skinhead audience (not everyone, but a significant number) formed the anti-racism stance that continued throughout their career.

Indeed it is a testament to the courage of not just The Specials, but individual members of the bands like Neville Staples, Pauline Black of The Selecter and Ranking Roger of The Beat, that as black British people, they would face down these racist, right-wing political skins. As Roger said to Neville Staples.

You had to be brave to stand there as a black man in front of a thousand skinheads, have stuff thrown at you and say "fuck off"'.

It was during 1978, that The Specials met a North London band called Madness. Neither band was aware of each other, but a Specials gig at the Hope and Anchor, Highbury was a key moment. Lee Thompson was in the audience along with Suggs who went to see Jerry Dammers and talk about Madness. From there, Madness had their debut single 'The Prince' released on 2-Tone.

By January 1979, The Specials had recorded three tracks, one of which was 'Gangsters' which was chosen as the single. Having signed a deal with Chrysalis to set up and control 2-Tone, Jerry Dammers due to finances (or lack of them) decided to launch one of his label mates on the b-side of the debut single. He chose The Selecter.

Pauline Black had grown up as an adopted child in Romford, Essex. Her experience of

Brighton [courtesy of Graham Very]

being a black person in Britain in the sixties and seventies was sadly commonplace for the times: attitudes, language and behaviour that should be rightly consigned to the dustbin of history.

Pauline had definitely been influenced to a certain extent by watching Ready, Steady, Go in the sixties and being particularly inspired by Diana Ross.

By 1979, she was the lead singer with The Selecter and playing gigs alongside The Specials and Madness or Hazel O'Connor and Secret Affair.

Much like The Specials at Crawley Leisure Centre, for The Selecter, it was Trinity Hall, Bristol in September '79 that became a moment of realisation for Pauline Black. The mixed audience of mods and skinheads had descended into a mass brawl despite The Selecter's efforts to calm the situation. It was at this point that Pauline realised that the band and perhaps Two-Tone itself was in the middle of 'competing tribal factions' as she puts it, even though the core Two-Tone message was one of unity, it was a message lost on many.

The unity message and mixed race bands of Two-Tone were very brave moves to make in the troubling times of late seventies Britain. Those brave decisions continued when, in 1980, The Selecter chose female-led Holly and the Italians and new label stable-mates, all-girl group the Bodysnatchers to join them on a UK tour.

By this time, Madness had long departed after their only single on 2-Tone. Unfortunately for Madness, in the early days they did attract a racist/political element within the skinhead movement. These were people who wanted nothing to do with the unity/mixed race make-up of the Two-Tone bands and targeted them at every opportunity and this was one of the main reasons Madness signed to another label.

Arguably, it was the contemporary sound of ska, the dress sense and imagery of the 2-Tone bands that attracted mods when the mod revival bands were floundering (which was not always their own fault). In time both the revival and 2-Tone would suffer at the hands of various destructive influences, not least a fickle music press, record labels and radio stations. But the over-riding trend towards the warring 'tribal factions' were as much to blame.

By the time the 1980 bank holiday season had begun, mods were the target (sic) for anyone who wanted a fight.

There were other stunts that thrilled the newspapers though, such as the first event promoted by **TONY CLASS** in Brighton at the Drill Hall in 1981, as Tony told Scootering Magazine:
We had about 1,000 people there, and journalists from 'The Sun' newspaper were in there. Someone jumped off the balcony to be caught by his mates, but the bloke from the paper said that they didn't get a photo, and could I arrange for someone else to do it again. I said just wait, and some else will do it. Eventually someone did, but he didn't have many mates. He splattered on the floor and got quite hurt.

Although the real point of mod was lost on many who donned a parka, far more serious scenes were in full swing in other areas of the country like Birmingham. Steve Grey and Mark Sandon were two mods living in the Birmingham area at the time. As **STEVE GREY** said:
Anybody that knows anything about the scene from 1979 to the late 1980s knows full well that it was happening here (in Birmingham).
Grey and Sandon give a clear insight as to why Birmingham became a focal point for mods. First, **STEVE GREY**:
By the time I got to the stage of attending city centre clubs and pubs, the standards had already been set. Tony Reynolds was the leading sixties soul and R&B DJ for mods in the UK, and clothes-wise the early Birmingham crowd had really set the pace. The tailors seemed to know the score, which made life a little easier. I was particularly influenced by the Source Force who had all been attired to a high standard for at least five years by 1984. Strangely enough I think it all stems back to how strict the pubs and clubs were around here and the size of the actual city centre, which is really quite small when compared to Manchester or Leeds. So by comparison, Birmingham had a small number of city centre pubs and clubs and they could pick and choose whom they let in. So as a result, the age of modernists in Birmingham was much higher. A lot of kids I met from the London scene were 15 or 16 years old, yet here there were

very few under 18. As an example, there was the March of the Mods Tour in August 1979. By then the scene was getting pretty big here and it was already club based. I think many of the Londoners that came up couldn't believe how many of us there were. And we were so much smarter, they were really scruffy. They were just a bunch of kids. They were chanting 'We are the mods' and so on. It was a bit embarrassing. I think it shows that there was a need for age restrictions and a smart dress code, which is why the scene here developed so differently to anywhere else.

By August 1979 it was already a big nightclub scene and if you weren't 18 or looked 18 you didn't get in. After all modernism is a club culture. It's not a street culture. The NME and Sounds at the time got it completely wrong, treating it as kids acting out a cliche. They'd killed punk and new wave and they quickly turned their attentions to the mod scene. The live band scene was another problem that London had. Here we had the Dexys, the Beat, The News (who weren't very good) and the Circles, but it wasn't that important here. It was a catalyst for the club scene, which developed very quickly out of it. Where we turned out initially to see the bands, the intermission so to speak became more important. But in London, there were that many bands that the scene was much more focused on the live scene, which is no bad thing but you need the nightclubs and records that you can dance to.

In the end as their scene started to get smaller because of criticism from the press it seemed to go into a cul-de-sac. We went to see The Jam at the Rainbow in March, April 1980 and afterwards we went looking for a club and unbelievably there wasn't one soul and R&B club, as far as I'm aware. And then later in the year I started to hear about the Sols Arms, Euston Road, where Eddie Piller had started a soul and R&B night. Eddie Piller and Ray Margetson had to start more or less from scratch.

The people were a bit older, a lot smarter and a lot more clued up. I even went to see the Purple Hearts at the Moonlight Club in 1981 and really enjoyed it. The audience was more refined; the music in the interval was much better. Once the London club scene had got its act together, I could never fault it for the music. It was good because you would get things played there that wouldn't be played in Birmingham-a lot of ska, bluebeat and rocksteady which disappeared up here from 1980. In 1982,

I went to a few soul and R&B events in London. Even people's clothes had started to improve. However at that time scooter boys had started up and people in London got despondent as the scooter boy scene decimated a large part of the London scene. There were probably more scooter boys in Birmingham than anywhere else, but because our scene was so big it didn't affect us much. It took a few away, but I think in other parts of the country it decimated all the scenes and I think London took a long time to recover. Although the Bush was appalling, the Phoenix club was fantastic, great venue, great music and good standards of dress. The main problem was the people. The girls were alright though.

Next, Steve Grey's long-time friend and co-author of 'From Somewhere Out Of Here', a book about the Birmingham mod scene, **MARK SANDON**:
The only scenes we knew of well and wanted to be involved with were the Coventry and Leamington ones. The Hip Citizens were the major force in Coventry. Leamington Spa had a great scene in the mid eighties with large numbers and also a fascination with a really obscure revival and contemporary music. We found this a refreshing change to the strict sixties direction in Birmingham and thoroughly enjoyed our visits there. As for influence with other cults and movements, there was an element of cross fertilisation with the growing Birmingham Jazz scene of the time, with many mods attending events like the Jazz Tinge and Pen and Wig. Also it was the time of 501s, Penny loafers and Acid Jazz towards the end of the decade which I personally became more interested in as I began to lose interest in a strict sixties music and style direction.

While the '79 mod scene continued in a directionless and confused state, The Jam went from strength to strength with sell-out gigs and rarely being out of the top five in the UK charts with virtually every single and album they released from 1979 to 1982. That year Paul Weller disbanded the group, playing their final, official concert in Brighton on 11 December 1982, although they did make one last appearance at the Polydor Party on 19 December. Just as The Jam had taken their place in music history, so their farewell heralded the demise of mass mod of the seventies. Without The Jam as a focal point and no one quite sure what direction Paul Weller was going to take, the mod scene was fading as fast as it had grown.

The new mod bands were struggling to find the means to survive a fickle music industry. Interestingly, some of the mod bands who formed in the '79 period went on to evolve into new bands outside of mod. Long Tall Shorty's drummer, Mark Reynolds formed mid 1980s underground rock act Rage with ex-Chord Buddy Ascott, ex-Purple Heart Jeff Shadbolt and Steve Moran from Reaction. Tony Perfect left Long Tall Shorty to join early eighties punk band The Angelic Upstarts. The Directions donated a member of Big Sound Authority, and Seventeen from Rhyl re-emerged as The Alarm. Other notable reincarnations included The Crooks who became Blue Zoo, Graduate who became Tears for Fears, Guns For Hire who became Department S and The Q-Tips who were the launch for Paul Young. Of course the mod credentials of these bands were open to question considering their career path after flirting with mod. It is interesting that just as the beat bands in the sixties who began playing R&B for mods went on to other things, so the '79 period gave new bands a useful platform on which to build a career. The trend continued albeit at a more discreet level.

ED BALL was one who had recorded with Dan Treacy and Joe Foster as the TV Personalities and Teenage Filmstars, and was working on another project that was more mod-styled than the previous bands:

The TVPs started in 1977, and I always kept an identity separate for myself as well, so that Dan would write all the stuff for the TVPs. I started The Times in 1980 and we did an album called 'Go With The Times' and 'Red With Purple Flashes' came out in April 1981. I liked the name The Times because it was kind of 'of the moment' and sort of mod sounding.

Others included The Prisoners from the Medway area of Kent and were a real mod favourite and included James Taylor who formed his own quartet and found success with his brand of Hammond grooves. The Boys would contribute Steve Craddock to

Ocean Colour Scene and Makin' Time were to make a massive impact in another guise at the end of the 80s.

Makin' Time were a four-piece blues and R&B outfit that were not happy knocking out 'mod' standards and wanted to be more creative than most of their contemporaries. They were booked to support Fast Eddie at London's 100 Club, but it was another Eddie that had been instrumental in getting them to London.

A chance meeting while on holiday led to Eddie Piller receiving a tape of Makin' Time, and a subsequent visit to Birmingham to see the band confirmed his instincts that they were a 'proper mod band'.

The band were comprised of Martin Blunt, Mark McGounden, Neil Clitheroe and here,

FAY HALLAM:

I started playing the organ aged eight because of my dad, Frank Hallam. He was out five nights a week playing in the 60s and 70s and my mum sang with him. I grew up in a house filled with music.

I met a small group of mods when I was 14 or 15. We formed a band when I was 15. It was pretty terrible, but I enjoyed making music with other people. I met a much larger mod community at 17 when I got together with Martin Blunt who was part of a scooter club in Willenhall. At the time, Martin Blunt was 21 and playing bass in a rhythm and blues band. He asked me to play organ, which I did, but I was bored rigid and lasted only a couple of rehearsals. He wanted me to stay so declared we should get a new drummer, new singer and start writing our own songs. Which we did! I'd already written 'I Know What You're Thinking' a couple of years before, then once I had a band to work with the songs kept coming.

We rehearsed weekly in a closed room at The Longacres, a pub in Willenhall. We'd turn up each week with one, or each of us, having written a song. I wrote about half of them with Martin and Mark writing the other half and sometimes they worked together. I always wrote on my own. I'd play through a song for them, they would moan about the ridiculous amount of chords in it, then we'd be away. That's usually how it went.

When Makin Time started there was a wonderful scene of cool looking people and fantastic soul discos. It was the Northern Soul and 60s music that I loved. I had a scooter for a year and it made me very happy. I got my clothes from second hand shops or I made them. I don't remember seeing Eddie Piller in Birmingham. My memory is rubbish though. Anyway Ed was a fully paid up cockney as far as us Midlanders were concerned and he came in for a lot of ribbing and talk of jellied eels and pie and mash. He was a 21 year old Arthur Daley character with the gift of the gab, but he was enthusiastic, worked hard for the band and was a decent bloke.

Makin Time signed to Countdown with Piller and toured extensively for the next four years until both label and band ran out of steam, but founding member Martin Blunt would return with a new look, a new sound and a new line-up that would take him on to success throughout the nineties. Fay Hallam's music career was far from over and Mark McGounden would return after many years away from music, as we shall see later in this story.

ANTHONY MEYNELL, who had been working to resurrect his career after the demise of Squire, embarked on an altogether different journey, setting up his own label:
With Hi-Lo Records, the world was my oyster. I didn't have to wait for a company to tell me whether they were going to let the American subsidiary release it. I would.
Suddenly, I was getting mail from Germany, America, Spain, Italy, Australia and Ireland especially, and they were all coming at it from the same angle "We thought you'd gone, can you come over, your records are great".
I started selling records, pressing them and distributing them and it became a full-time thing. It was only me doing it and it was a cottage industry thing. My brother played drums and we got a bass player eventually and did a few gigs.
What we realised was that there was a third generation of mods out there in 1982. We did Eddie Piller's all dayer and we went down great.
We went to Northern Ireland and went down a storm. We had a thousand people in the hall, we were on television; it was like being in The Beatles. We had a police escort to the record shop where we signed autographs and all of this was on the back of an independent label. It was phenomenal. It was nothing like before, where we had played second fiddle to somebody else. It was all our own doing and the Northern

Ireland visit is still talked about today. I met David Holmes about three years ago in Tokyo and if anything what he and the others are doing is probably mod now without being revivalist, but he said he remembers that gig in Northern Ireland.

For some, it may come as a surprise that in the midst of the political troubles, somehow a thriving mod scene had grown in the late seventies in Northern Ireland. As Marty McAllister stated, to understand the unifying dimension mod played in Belfast and across the whole of Ireland, you have to understand the country and the times. Belfast mod Paul Williams put it best as told to Marty in 2010:

Back then, Northern Ireland was a hugely divided society. It was horrible. Murder was rife and people never ventured far from their own areas. The only interaction between kids from both (Protestant and Catholic) communities came through rioting. Yet mod changed that for so many young people. All of a sudden you had kids from opposite sides of the community congregating at the City Hall and marching through Belfast city centre wearing boating jackets and parkas.

These kids hailed from some of the most socially deprived and divided areas not just in Europe, but arguably the world. The effect or impact of mod on our society should not be under-estimated.

Three of those young mods were key to the scene on both sides of the border. In Dublin it was **ROB MCDONALD**, while in Belfast it was **GEL JONES** and first up **MARIA MORGAN**: I've always loved Sixties music. My mum was always playing her Dusty Springfield records, but I remember coming home from school one day and my brother Mark and three of his mates were sitting on the wall outside our house. He was 14 at the time and I was just 11 years old.

The school I went to was one where you had to stay there all week and went home at weekend. I was shocked when I saw Mark because he looked totally different from his hair to his clothes and they had a couple of scooters outside too. When I asked him what it was all about, he told me he was a mod. This was in the mid Seventies and Mark became totally immersed in it. Detail was everything to him; he used to sit in the bath to shrink his jeans. He named his scooter 'Herbie' and because we didn't have a garage or driveway, he had to bring it in the house. He even slept beside it!

That was my introduction to mod and I became as obsessed with it as Mark was. The re-runs of 'Ready Steady Go were on TV and I would watch them intently, making notes of the people in audience; what they were wearing, how they were dancing. I was trying to educate myself. Sixties clothes were easy to come by in those days in second-hand shops, so I started putting together what I thought was mod clothes for girls. I went to a disco one night dressed in ski pants, a crinoline crew neck and suede Hush Puppies. Everyone stared at me, but that was when I met Gel Jones. She was dressed in a similar style and we have been friends ever since.

After a few years, Amanda Deards (nee Kavanaugh), Gel and I were getting fed up with never hearing the music we wanted at the clubs in Belfast, so we decided to do it ourselves. We were only 14 or 15 by this time, but we just went to every venue we knew of and asked if we could put a night on. Eventually, the Abercorn said yes and that's how it started, we put on our mod nights. It wasn't long before we decided we needed to go to London. We saved up our lunch money to buy the tickets. We knew a few people already in London, so we stayed with them. The Londoners were a bit wary of us at first, but as we were going over there every other month and meeting people like Andy Orr, Bob Morris and Big Nick, we got accepted.

The first time we went to Sneakers, they wouldn't let us in, but the next time they did and it was just wonderful. Everyone was so smart and sharp. We met the Ugly Buglies who we looked up to. They were mod girl perfection and they confirmed what we always thought about mod style for girls. We became pen pals with them too. It was only when we went to London that we realised we had got it all wrong. To us, in terms of the 'mod style league' it was London followed by Dublin then Belfast.

Although I liked some of the music from the mod revival, I was more into R&B and Soul music and that was what we played at the Abercorn.

The contacts we made in London led to us putting on bands. I know The Scene were worried about coming to Belfast at the time, but here we were, 15-16 year old girls giving them assurances nothing bad was going to happen if they came over!

Of course the political situation was still very tense. The British Army still had a presence in the region and society was divided along religious lines as well as political, but our mod scene really broke new ground. It was the one thing where your background or beliefs didn't matter. We all came together because of our love of the music and the clothes. This was in the days when many people would not even leave their local area; such was the intimidating atmosphere back then. We loved the promoting and putting on the club nights and we wanted to do more. We had the Abercorn; we were doing the fanzine; we put on the first Alldayer in Belfast with 800 kids there and we had the connection with Rob McDonald and the Dublin mods. We decided to organise a coach trip from Belfast to Dublin for a mod night and that was when tragedy struck. We booked a bus to take 100 people to Dublin. We got there okay, but we didn't realise the driver had got drunk while we at the club.

On the way back, the bus crashed into a car. Everyone was shaken up and the crash scene was a mess. It was so bad, it made the newspapers. One of our mod mates called Noddy died in that accident. The mod scene was devastated. Noddy was a Catholic and his funeral procession started on the Falls Road which is a Republican area. The Falls had never seen anything like it; literally hundreds of scooters arrived. It was another important but sad moment when we all came together; Catholics and Protestants to mourn the passing of a mod; one of us. Not long after that, my brother Mark, who had inspired me to become a mod, was killed in a car accident. He was just 18. When I think back, we did so much in a relatively short space of time. We wanted to go somewhere for a May Bank Holiday day trip and Bangor was the closest to us, so that's how Bangor became our 'Brighton' and now they hold a weekender there every year.

ROB MCDONALD:
When Eddie Piller came to Ireland on his own, I met Eddie half way, on the border. We stayed with David Holmes and then went to the Bangor weekender. We had a special connection with Eddie because we brought his bands over, so we would do the Dublin leg and Gel, Maria and Amanda would do the Belfast leg and that's how

we met them through the mod scene. Gel came down to Dublin with The Scene who had played the Ulster Hall, then Gel and Maria nabbed them to play The Abercorn. Gel came with my friends Peter Devlin and Sean Gorman. We were like 14 years old or something. It was Gel, Mandy and Maria Morgan. The Scene played a venue called Wheelans.

Next night it was another gig at Tommy Dorn's Tavern and I was DJ-ing. That was the start of my DJ career. We were the Emerald Society in Dublin and the girls were the Immediate Society in Belfast. We ran a night called Riky Tick which was named after the 60s club in Windsor and it was mod only because the other popular night, Bubbles would let anyone in, so the scooter boys would turn up and these were ex-mods having a go at the mods. Skinheads would come in threatening people, so we had to organise a mod only night. We used to do this kind of formation dance thing, but we got the idea from Bob Morris. We used to go to London: we knew Bob Morris, Andy Orr, Eddie Piller and we copied what they did.

We went to the 1984 Ilford Palais and came back with 60s ska records. There was five of us doing this dance we had learnt from the London guys, but within three weeks the whole club in Dublin was doing the same dance as us.

GEL JONES:
For us, London was the epicentre of the mod scene. The way the guys dressed, they were so sharp. Sneakers 86-87, Eddie Piller turned up at Sneakers and said I couldn't stay with at his house as we had arranged, but the London guys didn't like the looks of us at first because we were sharp looking too, but when they saw we knew Edddie and Bob and Andy, they accepted us. The Irish had a hard time back then.

We caught the last eight months of Sneakers in Shepherds Bush then to Oxford Street, then Great Portland Street.

Mod scene diffused the political tensions for our generation, but there was one occasion when union jack t-shirts were popular for some reason, so me, Mandy and Maria got t-shirts made up with the tri-colour. Myself and David Holmes did Esoteric fanzine, while the Immediate Society put on bands like the Direct Hits, Purple Hearts,

Makin Time, The Prisoners and The Scene at The Abercorn which was on two floors. There is no doubt in my mind that mod brought everybody together in Belfast. We had links in London, friends we knew at the time. When I first came to London, I was about 14 or 15.
We came for the Ilford Alldayer and we were in awe of London. Some were friendly. People like Paul and Vicky Hallam were nice, but most didn't want to know because of being from Belfast. Then people in Belfast thought we were stuck up because we had the London connections.

ROB MCDONALD:
There was so much backstabbing, I left it. I couldn't stand it anymore. The Emerald Society wanted to bring people together, but there was so much jealousy. I think Emerald Society mods were really true to the original ideal of modernism and ditched parkas for macs. Eventually, we became a 'crew' for want of a better term and were known as the Emeralds. One of the Dublin newspapers did a review of a gig by The Blades and mentioned the Emeralds. Our aspiration was to drive sports cars.
Lawrence Moley had a pink Spitfire and the inside was pink fur and he had a pink suit with a pink and black waist coat and pinky, purple suede shoes. I was wearing a madras jackets. I remember one of the lads, Martin, he had a beret, a pink shirt and sunglasses which he wore even indoors. We were almost like 'fundamentalist mods'.
One of my favourite memories was when Makin Time stayed at my house.
My mum says to Martin Blunt 'If you're ever on Top Of The Pops I want you to say 'Hello to Mrs McDonald'. Sometime years later, there was Martin on Top Of The Pops and I said to my mum, "Look there's that guy, you remember? He stayed here that time". And she says, "I knew he'd make it the first time I saw him". (sic)

MARTY MCALLISTER's entry to mod was (as we now know) a well-trodden path:
Punk and New Wave occupied my early teenage years, collecting 7" singles was my hobby. I saw The Clash in the Ulster Hall in 1978, myself and Leo McGuigan went down, terrified 13 year-olds in amongst all the 'real' punks, but it was fun and a great

gig. That same year I bought 'All Mods Cons' by The Jam. I was first aware of mods in the summer of '79. A few scooters started appearing on the roads, mainly on Sunday mornings. I lived in the New Lodge, a small nationalist enclave just north of the city centre. The 'Gardens' as the area was known, was a peace line between nationalist New Lodge and protestant Tigers Bay. I used to watch scooters going by; they were the Tigers Bay Mods, many of whom I would become friendly with. Scooters from all over Belfast were ridden by catholics and protestants; no religious divide; just one thing in common; being mods.

One might surmise that with the political troubles in the region, bands would be somewhat reluctant to travel to Belfast, but this was not the case.
Certainly the work of local legend Terry Hooley (who was instrumental in bringing The Undertones to the world) may have had some influence in convincing bands based in England to tour the Emerald Isle, but a great many did not.
To be fair to those who stayed at home, it must have been a difficult decision in view of the climate of fear that hung over the city at the time.
However, some did decide to go and in tribute, they deserve to be mentioned and given great credit. The most frequent visitors during the mid-eighties were The Scene and Dennis Greaves outfit Nine Below Zero. Other bands included The Jam, Squire, The Prisoners, Makin' Time, The Risk, the Gents, The Rage, Steve Marriott, The Moment, Direct Hits, Purple Hearts and The Threads.

FAY HALLAM recalled her visits with Makin' Time to the region:
When we drove over to Belfast in the mid 80s in our dark blue ex-police van, we were nervous. We were told The Abercorn (where we played) had been bombed a couple of times. All worries were forgotten when we got there because everyone we met was so friendly and lovely and genuinely pleased to see us. We were always well received and had great hospitality.
The Irish were not without their own home-grown bands. The Blades, led by Paul Cleary were from Dublin as were The Vipers and finally, Belfast-based The Moondogs. In Dublin,

> Of course the political situation was still very tense. The British Army still had a presence in the region and society was divided along religious lines as well as political, but our mod scene really broke new ground. It was the one thing where your background or beliefs didn't matter. We all came together because of our love of the music and the clothes.
>
> MARIA MORGAN

one focal point for the mod scene was basement bar in Adair Lane called 'Bubbles'. In Belfast, Barney's and the King Arthur were the other popular clubs, while Bangor was to Northern Ireland what Brighton was to England; the great Bank Holiday destination. But it was one destination and one weekend that will live long in the memory of Irish mods north and south of the border. Tramore is on the south coast of Ireland and it was the weekend of 5th and 6th June 1982 that saw this sleepy seaside town become invaded by an unexpected horde of scooter-riding mods from all over Ireland.

Tramore was exceptional in more ways than one. It was one of the first times mods from across the nation gathered together. There were hundreds in attendance (although no one was counting), but perhaps even more remarkably, there was not one single incident of any kind. The local press were poised, ready to write up exaggerated stories, but they got nothing.

As **ROB MCDONALD** recalls:

At Tramore, a lot of older mods would go, then we came along in suits and they didn't like it. Joe Kinsella was the founder of the Glory Boys in Dublin who were the older mods. Jimmy Mulvaney was the ace face, but he was also the first with a chopper scooter and became king of the scooter boys. Another one would be Aiden Quigly from Cork. The Scene came over and he put on the gig in Cork. He used to have all his suits all around his flat hanging from picture rails !

35 years later, the Tramore Scooter run is still a firm fixture in the Irish calendar and many of the mods from the early Eighties are still running clubs, DJing and ensuring a mod presence north and south of the border.

By June 1981, another interesting development occurred in London. The Face magazine reported on a new club called The London Dungeons. It catered for disaffected mods and punks who wanted something different. This club catered for those who loved psychedelia. It was at the time a fairly small scene, but people came from places as divergent as Birmingham and Southend.

Initially, they were drawn to a clothes stall in Kensington Market called The Regal, founded by Andy Yiannakou and assisted by Graham Pettitt. Andy was a trained tailor and the clothes he made were based on designs of the 18th century Dandys.

He met **ANNE MARIE NEWLAND** around the same time as opening The Regal. Anne-Marie was already selling vintage clothes from her stall called 'Sweet Charity'. Eventually she started designing and making clothes for girls, influenced by Mary Quant, Emma Peel and the classic 'swinging sixties' fashion, as she explained to the Dandy In Aspic website:

My shop was a wow to look at. I used scaffolding for the rails. I had huge pots of paint in the shop to allow people to create graffiti befitting the era. I have some great pictures taken by the famous street fashion photographer Ted Polhemus. I designed the clothes myself and had never had any formal training, but had a good eye for posture so it was easy to judge how the front of a garment was not the same as the back!

I only sourced original fabrics and some of the stuff I found was truly amazing. Needle cord with paisley patterns in yellow and turquoise was one of my best finds, and a roll of textured cotton with super psychedelic designs put me on the map!

Mary Quant was a good inspiration, but I also took a lot from the men's designs which were originally Regency. I was not part of the first Regal as I met Andy Yiannakou after. But as a natural progression I was well established in the Market anyway when I had my vintage shop there. I was next to Jesse Birdsalls and Gaz's Rockin'Blues, a great vinyl record shop. I do remember that my hipster drainpipe jeans cost £17.50 and in the Thatcher years that was expensive. My customers were aged between 12 and 35! I had such customers as Annie Lennox, The Belle Stars, Kim Wilde, Paul Young, and Kid Creole and the Coconuts. I made clothes for bands on photo shoots in a matter of hours that gave us a great reputation. U2 visited the shop when Bono still played the drums and sang. Paul Weller popped in and to be honest the shop was buzzing most of the day.

I advertised in The Face and ID magazines and put out flyers at the Groovy Cellar. Mostly it was word of mouth. Sweet Charity lasted three years until I sold up and passed it on when I went off to India... it was there for another few years.

The Regal moved to a shop in Newburgh Street in 1981 and club nights moved to The Phoenix in Cavendish Square and Planets in the West End.

The psych scene of the early 80s had a few of its own bands too, mainly former mod bands like Southend's The Leapers who became Le Matte, High Tide and The Barracudas. Mood Six were very popular and comprised of former members of punk band, Security Risk, The VIPs and a Merton Parka.

One of the converts to the psych scene was **RICHARD SEARLE**:
I grew up in Eltham in South East London. We didn't have a record player when I was a primary school kid. I grew up during Glam, (Slade, Sweet, T-Rex); but my oldest friend, who lived down my street (Elibank Rd), had a record player and his brother had two Who albums; so The Who were formative, and are still my favourite band.
I bought punk records from 77 onwards, The Stranglers, The Damned, Generation X, Devo, Pistols etc, but I used to follow The Jam, they were 'my life'. I saw them for the first time in 78 (supported by Generation X and Slade). My first parka cost £14 from Paraphernalia in Lewisham). My first bespoke suit, when I was 15, was from a tailor in Lewisham called James Joyce - the jacket still fits.
When the 'mod revival' happened, I'd already started listening to psych stuff (the first Nuggets album, Velvet Underground, Shadows Of The Night, Electric Prunes, Love), so when the 'New Psychedelic' scene reared its head, I was already wearing more 'swinging sixties' gear, my hair was a ridiculous back-combed bouffant. I didn't fit with the British 'mod' look, I was never into Two-Tone. When people ask, I say that I was a 'psychedelic mod'. The 'psych scene' was based around a couple of clothes shops, The Regal and Sweet Charity and a Soho club called The Clinic (in Gossips-Soho); the resident DJ called himself The Doctor- he was my patrol leader in the scouts. The Doctor (Clive) was given the opportunity to record a single on Whaam Records, so he put a band together. We became Doctor and The Medics. It was only supposed to be for the one single, and a couple of gigs, but we had fun and carried on. I left after eight years. We played The Clinic a lot back then. In the 80s it was mostly psych clubs, The Clinic, The Taste Experience, The Pigeon Toed Orange Peel and the Alice

In Wonderland (a club which took over from The Clinic) and I went to The Bat Cave once - once was enough.

This small psych scene would be the portent of things to come and a blurring of the boundaries between the various subcultures with a shared heritage.
Mod went underground in the UK by the early 80s, but it was the very same influences that had sparked the renewed interest in mod in the UK that were doing the same in other places around the world.

In Japan, **MANABU KURODA**, a resident of Tokyo and widely recognised as the founder of the mod scene in both the city and the country, remembers exactly how he got into it: In 1977, I got to know what mod was through The Jam. In 1979, I saw Quadrophenia and it knocked me out. I have been a mod ever since.

In Australia, 1979, the first signs of a new mod scene began. By 1980 and for the next three years the Sussex Hotel became the home of Sydney mods after The Royal Standard Hotel had closed its' doors. It was not long before other venues across the city were opening up to the new mod trend. Places like the Mosman Hotel, The Palisade, Bar Reggio and The Alibi were all hugely popular.
Arguably, the most influential people on the scene were ex-patriots Don and Gary Hosie whose family originated from Middlesborough, North-East England. In his last known interview before his untimely death, **DON HOSIE** spoke about how he and bother Gary became involved in mod and music:
The Sets started off as a three-piece in 1979 with Phil Robinson on guitar, Keith Claringbold on bass and Stuart Hooper on drums. Gary and I used to jump up on stage with them to do 'My Generation', which was usually the last song of the night.
When The Sets broke up all we had were a bunch of bands doing sixties covers that weren't mods, and they didn't have the onstage energy and aggression we wanted. The scene was in danger of losing momentum because we'd also lost our pub The Royal Standard. Gary and I resorted to putting on gigs in our back room to keep the

Tokyo [courtesy of Crazy Numbers Scooter Club]

scene alive and eventually collaborated with Phil Robinson to put together a five piece version of The Sets which was the first band we'd ever been in. To my eternal regret The Sets only recorded one single and one demo session, yet we had so much good material it still annoys me that not more was released. Unlike most mod related bands of the time, we were not content with playing covers. For our first gig, we did ten songs and seven of those were originals. The band were supporting The Introverts, who were good players and the darlings of the inner city press, but at the time even they were still 100 per cent covers.

The Allnighters, who eventually became the most successful of the bands from that scene, still mainly play and record covers to this day. Their main song writer during the early mod period was a guy called Mark Taylor. He was an ex-pat English mod and shared a pad with Gary and myself. By comparison, The Sets were angry young men representing what was at the time a burgeoning movement, so we had a lot to say about the scene. It was always my ambition to release the ultimate mod single using two of our mod anthems "Clean Living, Difficult Circumstances". and "Life On An Li" as the A and B sides. I remember having a scooter in the studio and trying to record a Lambretta Li 150 getting kicked over - the motor that is - as a prelim to "Life On An Li". Unfortunately the magneto generated so much electrical interference that it totally saturated all the equipment and the exercise had to be abandoned. That wasn't the only problem we had. We'd never been in a studio before. We'd gone from rehearsing in a back room to playing the biggest venues in Sydney in a matter of months and we'd never stepped into a studio before.

When we finally got around to recording, we found it hard to play with the sort of discipline required of the studio yet still keep that Sets swagger and rough edge that was so important to the sound. The ultimate mod single I always wanted to record had to be abandoned because we couldn't get the feel right, so we had to opt for a song that sounded good in the studio - "Love Ain't What It Used To Be".

The Sets and The Allnighters were by no means the only bands on the scene. The Introverts, The Reasons Why, Division Four, Fast Cars, Donna and The Daydreams and The Riptides were equally popular on the live circuit. In other major cities across

Australia, mods were making themselves known. Melbourne had a healthy scene and things seemed to be moving along and building nicely until the infamous 'Melbourne Invasion' of 1981. It was the Easter weekend and the Sydney mods led by the Hosie brothers decended on Melbourne. Mods from Adelaide also arrived and according to contemporary accounts, for the most part the weekend went really well, the highlight being a gig featuring Division Four, Little Murders and the Sets at the Crystal Ballroom, St Kilda.

From that point onwards, with the alcohol, drugs and lack of sleep beginning to take its toll, things descended into animosity between the various groupings, although there is no record of any violence occurring.

KELVIN MADDEN from Queensland, who would go on to produce one of the best Australian fanzines "Modern Times" in the late nineties, became interested in mod through music:

My brother can actually claim the responsibility for that. He bought a few Jam albums and I was hooked. I don't think he ever saw those LP's again. I quickly sourced Small Faces, Easybeats, Kinks and Who albums after that. Birthdays and Christmas were great, always got a mod LP. The ex-pats brought quite a lot with them. Most of them brought the music and the right attitude. They also weren't scared to tread where others didn't. Fabulous organisers. For me, it was their musical influences.

The 1981 Easter weekend in Melbourne was probably the biggest event Australia has seen in mod circles. It was fronted by a few bands, Little Murders from Melbourne, The Sets and Division 4 from Sydney. Mods from Sydney, Perth, Adelaide and Brisbane descended on Melbourne for a great weekend of mod mayhem. I don't know any actual figures, but estimates put the numbers at 200 to over 250.

As Kelvin states, mod was fairly wide spread in Australia. Don and **GARY HOSIE** with The Sets, were at that Melbourne weekender, but remarkably, unlike the north - south divide that caused problems back in England, trouble was something of a rarity in Australia, as remembered:

I don't recall any division between the cities. The Sydney scene became divisive after The Sets 1981 Easter tour to Melbourne and I found out later that some of the disgruntled Sydney mods had ambushed a group of Melbournites because they thought the Melbourne mods were wimps. That was an isolated incident committed by deluded individuals. In the main, there was a good rapport between the cities through fanzines and individuals making the pilgrimage to Sydney where it was really happening. The Sets '81 tour was one of the great achievements of Oz mod. Hundreds came from all round the country to be there and everyone got on really well. It was one hell of a wild three or four days and the impact was huge from a mod perspective. Saying that though, petty jealousies emerged from the trip that eventually tore the Sydney scene apart, but that's another long story and bitter memory.

I don't think we will ever see a scene like Sydney 1980 to '81 again. Its forefathers were mainly ex-punks who witnessed the gradual corruption and disintegration of punk, strong individuals determined not to make the same mistakes the punks and most youth cults make - shitting in their own nest. The venues we controlled were cherished and fighting near the places was to be avoided. Speed was never a big part of it. The natural high was the music and meeting new people from diverse backgrounds rolling up every week as the word spread. There was a mixture of talent - the leaders, the fighters, the writers, the musicians, the DJs, the scooter mechanics. All contributed to a self sufficient scene that could organise itself and produce the bands that would take the word to the suburbs. English mods that experienced it thought it was the purist scene in the world. Even Eddie Piller, who was at the centre of the biggest mod scene around, found the Sydney scene fascinating with it's penchant for hard R&B and it's organisational ability. From the point of view of non-stop action, it was the most concentrated period of wild times that I've ever had and ever will have.

Back in mainland Europe, the mod influence was spreading. **HARRY VOGEL** is a native of Munich, Germany:

At the end of the seventies, I got very much into punk and believed in all those ideas about pure, true and above all "independent", non-commercial music. However, the whole music scene changed in about 1982, 1983 and I was looking for something more "honest" - so one day a friend of mine came along with a tape he had recorded in a bar in Berlin, where the juke box only played rare sixties music (today I know it was Freakbeat). Well, we were absolutely enthusiastic about this new sound and started getting into the music.

At around the same time I read an article in a magazine called "Sounds" (the German one, not the English one) about a Psychedelic Revival going on in London. I looked at the pictures of the people and fell in love with that style. Then I saw Quadrophenia, and that was it. I've been into the scene for over 25 years now. The German mod scene started in West Germany, in Hamburg and Berlin around 1980, '81, and in the South of Germany, in Munich in 1982, '83.

FREDRIK EKANDER is from Stockholm, Sweden:
Somehow I was very much into late fifties black American rock 'n' roll and rhythm & blues when I was a kid, 11-12 years old. Then when I found out that bands like Beatles and Kinks did a lot covers of these tracks, I began looking for British, early sixties groups and they all wore suits! I became a lot more aware of my clothes and at the same time the mod boom was happening. It wasn't long until I heard about these other kids who called themselves mods. They listened more or less to the same music as I did, wore suits, but had a green parka too. I got myself one and me and my friends started calling ourselves mods. We found out that there were new bands with the same inspiration and obviously we all got into The Jam, Secret Affair and the Specials fairly quick. Then we were hooked for life and a whole new, and extremely exciting world opened up to us. Mod has been off and on in Sweden since '79-'80.

Back in Britain, the mod population had all but disappeared. Trying to understand what the '79 period was about is perhaps a moot point. If mod is, at base level, about having a good job, money, enjoying yourself and being able to acquire material possessions, then it was in direct opposition to punks' anarchistic pretensions.

MIKE WARBURTON gave this assessment of the whole '79 period:
I have mixed feelings about that time. It certainly kick started the mod scene again in the UK and beyond. The majority of the bands involved however, consisted of ex-punks, with only the slightest links with mod, and in nine out of ten cases, it was definitely a convenient 'band wagon' jump.
1979 mod was very much a media driven event, built up and eventually knocked down by certain elements of the music press.
On a positive note, numerous first rate compilations got released such as, 'Intensified' which was an Island ska album, and 'Allnighters'. These gave mods a taste of the original sounds. The first fanzines appeared in '79 and they were instrumental in taking the scene forward and last, but no means least, the launch of the '6Ts' club in West Hampstead by Ady Croasdell and Randy Couzens gave mods an alternative to commercial pop and '79 revival and they laid the foundations for a club scene that exists to this day. Roger Eagle launched a similar club in Manchester at a venue called Rafters.

In the end the '79 mod scene fragmented. Some turned to the New Romantic scene emerging from London's trendy club land. Others turned skinhead, some just got out altogether, but another significant group of former mods remained, held together by their mutual appreciation of scooters. The scooter clubs that formed during the '79 period carried on regardless, taking at least part of the mod ethos as their base. As John Robb has noted, the scooter clubs were more than just a bunch of like-minded people riding around on their favourite mode of transport.
They became important conduits that sparked long-lasting and important friendships and contacts that would influence music and fashion in the future. Steve Craddock was seen at many a scooter rally, and a certain Ian Brown was spotted on a number of occasions in the north of England riding his cut-down pink chop scooter 'Cranked Up Really High'. Brown's scootering mate John Squire also had a scooter 'Too Chicken To Even Try It' and they were both seen with scooterists around Stockport on many occasions. Although not members of a club, Brown and Squire loved the music and

might meet people like Steve Harrison who became manager of The Charlatans or Clint Mansell of Pop Will Eat Itself.

The scene had numerous people at the fringes, all of who would use the influence of scooterist/mod/northern soul culture in their different ways to carve out careers for themselves in music. The members of the scooter clubs went back to the musical roots of mod and rediscovered northern soul and R&B.

1981 saw the first ever rally at the Isle of Wight, which was organised by the A23 Crusaders scooter club, who included future Radio One and House DJ Danny Rampling among its number. The following year, and for the next five years, DJ Tony Class became involved in organising or part organising successive rallies at the Isle of Wight.

In 1982, Martin Dixon and members of the Lambretta Club began organising rallies for the mod and scootering fraternity. They collated a database of the scooter clubs throughout the country and held national meetings to organise the events.

The annual meetings were known as The Number Ones. The Number Ones were attended by a representative from each of the scooter clubs, although more than one often turned up. In true democratic style, the decision process was by unanimous vote on the day. Before too long the Number Ones became known as the National Runs Committee (NRC). The first season organised by the NRC consisted of trips to Scarborough, Loch Lomond, Great Yarmouth, Morecombe Bay, Brighton, Colwyn Bay, the Isle of Wight, Skegness and Whitley Bay.

In 1985, the August Bank Holiday Rally on the Isle of Wight attracted a crowd of 12,000. The average attendance was a fairly constant 5,000 at most of the other events.

There were at least eight rallies per year from 1982 to 1989, mainly held at coastal resorts. As time went on, the events became better organised with campsites for those who wanted their own accommodation, and the entertainment grew from lunchtime and evening discos to live acts on stage and themed discos at different venues around the chosen resort.

The resorts themselves, although apprehensive at first, saw the benefit of hosting the rallies. The scooters may have made a lot of noise, and the psychological link between scooters and the old mod riots may have played a factor in the locals having doubts about the events, but they soon realised that far from being a nuisance, the rallies were well organised with liaisons forged between the event organisers, the police and the local town councillors.

They had nothing to fear, and the events brought in much needed revenue, that saved businesses when the summer season had been a bad one. The events were not without isolated incidents of trouble though. ·◊·

> By 1982, we had got out of mod. We were more into the scooter boy side of it really. We loved our scooters and we travelled everywhere.
> We just wanted to be different, so we dressed down.
>
> DIZZY HOLMES

CHAPTER 5

By 1981, the mod revival was all but finished. The part-timers moved on and the die-hards reorganised. For **BRIAN BETTERIDGE**, it was a period of readjustment:
My interest in sixties music and the scene itself were two different things really. I continued going to Chords and Hearts gigs through '81. I saw The Chords last gig with Billy Hassett.
There were a lot of mods who latched on to The Q-Tips who were a great live band, I saw them a lot. Also, in '81 there were some psychedelic clubs that opened up and I went for the music. There were a few bands as well and they were dreadful.

Now this is when this awful term 'purist' came in. I hate that term because if someone has integrity and they are pure to themselves, that's okay, but to suggest there is a concept that is 'purist' infers that something is 'impure' and that's when you're on dodgy ground. Then people got into scooters, and there was this schism between the bands that were left and people started getting into northern soul. I like northern soul, but people got obsessed by it and there were the rallies, and there were people involved in the mod scene that I thought were very dodgy and I didn't want to be involved in that. I wasn't in a band, my creative drive had gone, so I continued to collect records and it was easier for me to be on the other side, going to gigs, rather than being a musician.

I've always thought March '81 is important. I've always thought that was kind of the end of that era. On 13 March 1981 I went to see The Jam in Amsterdam and at the end of the gig, a Dutch guy came up to me and said: "You're Brian Betteridge from Back To Zero". He had seen BTZ and remembered me. Another guy came up and said about Bee's By Post and how my brother was a mod in the sixties and that his brother had been in the sixties scene in Holland and that's how he had started collecting records in the same way that I had. That man was Michel Terstegen, who was my friend over 25 years until his untimely passing in 2011. His ambition was to own his own collectors record shop, which he has, Da Capo Records.

He DJ'd at sixties events and was well respected around Europe and America. He was in his own sixties covers band called 'The Other Side' who played all over Europe and have now been put on CD. But this is why I say it was the end of that era, because Michel was someone I met after that era, but met because of that era.

I was still going to see sixties influenced bands who weren't specifically thought of as being on the mod scene. However much they are loved by mods now, and they are, The Prisoners 'Last Forefathers' album was when mods started getting into them. They were thought of as garage, punk with sixties, Small Faces influences.

There was another band called Playn Jayn who were great, I used to see a lot. Some mods went to see them, but they were more sixties influenced than the pervious mod bands. Then there were other bands from America who came from the underground paisley scene on the West Coast, like The Rain Parade and Three O'clock. The one link with that is Anthony Meynell from Squire who went out there and got friendly with those bands. Then through the late eighties, I did loose touch. I was still into the sixties scene, but I was going to see a lot of indie type bands who were friends of mine.

ED BALL remembers Brian Betteridge, but in the early eighties, Ed also met a native of Glasgow who had moved south to the English capital:
Brian had a band called Bees By Post. He was an extraordinary character and I really liked Brian. He could be a bit moody, but he was the closest to me, Dan and Joe, than the rest of the bands, but that's mainly because he got what we were doing. It was a bit more psychedelic inclined than the others.
After '79 with the TVPs and The Times, we did albums as those bands, then by '81 there was a bit of a psychedelic revival with bands like Mood Six and High Tide and Miles Over Matter. There was a compilation called 'A Splash Of Colour' and The Times did 'I Helped Patrick McGoohan Escape' on that, and it kind of reinforced our credentials with the TVPs single called 'I Know Where Sid Barrett Lives' and the more we showed our true colours, the less we sold. It was coming clean about our influences and we developed a hard-core following.
So by the end of '82, The Jam split up and it was wide open. The Truth were being touted to take the lead, and Eddie Piller really got started. I remember a compilation called 'Subteraneans and The Angry Young Men' or something like that. I met Eddie and The Times did a couple of festivals that Eddie organised, happy events and good money. I still had the distribution deal with Rough Trade, and this is a little aside. I always found power in making records. You could consolidate and a group could exist if you made records and did them independently. You made them the way you wanted to and Rough Trade empowered us to do that with both the bands.
Then Alan McGee came down from Glasgow and started the Living Room club and basically put on all his favourite bands. Also around this time, there were bands like The Milkshakes, The Stingrays and that rockabilly, psycho-billy thing going on. The Milkshakes used to remind me of The Beatles 'Hamburg' period. They dressed in

leather jackets and their songs were like very early Beatles. Things were a bit more interesting, but I remember thinking it was a shame those '79 bands hadn't lasted longer and moved onto that sort of thing. You would get some mod characters going to the Living Room. They weren't '79 mods, but they were 'progressive' mods. I think we got in to that psychedelic mod phase of The Who 'Sell Out' period. A bit before that, I used to go to The Groovy Cellar which was a club Dan and I used to deejay at and the Alice In Wonderland we played a couple of times. The moddy clubs were like Samantha's and The Embassy that had modish nights. The Wag did similar stuff.

Back in the mainstream music world, within a three year period, 1979 to 1982, new wave, mod, Two-Tone, disco and new romantic had all had their 'day in the sun'. There was a vacuum where the music industry were struggling to find the 'next big thing'. Independent labels were the only sector of the industry where real innovation could be found. Cherry Red, Kitchenware, Beggars Banquet and Rough Trade were just a few of labels that were prepared to develop new sounds and new ideas.

ED BALL, Dan Treasy and Joe Foster still had a distribution deal at Rough Trade, but things didn't work out quite the way they had hoped, as Ed explains:

Dan and I had a theory and we only talked about it between ourselves, but if you listened to the TVPs and Dan's singing. It was good lyrics and nice melody all wrapped up in this bittersweet voice, and at the time we were the darlings at Rough Trade, but we got dropped in favour of The Smiths and did our own label. Dan maintains more than me, that The Smiths have an element of TVPs in them. I think Johnny Marr is influenced by sixties stuff and in his guitar playing, you can hear a lot of T-Rex. If The Jam set the musical boundaries for mod '79, then The Smiths set the boundaries for the early Creation label stuff of '85.

-

From the embers of the '79 mod scene, scooters again took precedence over style or fashion. The Detour Scooter Club in Midhurst, Sussex was no different in that respect. As **DIZZY HOLMES** explained:

By 1982, we had got out of mod. We were more into the scooter boy side of it really.

We loved our scooters and we travelled everywhere. We just wanted to be different, so we dressed down. We used to wear kilts over our cammies, things like that.
A lot of people started hating mods as well. The scooter boys were really anti-mod, which I couldn't understand because that's where I started from. I think the mod influence had them competing against each other, but it was almost the same thing with the northern and southern lot. It was a shock seeing them fighting, even though they were into the same things.

By 1984, Dizzy and the Detour Club were regularly attending every major rally in the country. That was until the last big event of that year:
We were on our way to Skegness, about 30 of us. There was torrential driving rain that was running freely from a farmer's field next to the motorway causing a flood across the road. Being the first in line on my newly customised Amandos 225, I hit the flood, aquaplaned across it and collided with the crash barrier.
Some of the club came with me to the hospital and stayed the whole weekend. The others carried on. From that moment, the club really disintegrated. Everyone was so shocked, it just fell apart. Over half of them sold their scooters straight away.

TANIA WOODMAN, who married Dizzy some years later, also remembers that fateful day:
I didn't go on that run, but I remember, I couldn't believe they were actually going in that weather. No-one could quite believe it and at the end of the day, a lot of them came home that weekend and couldn't believe it themselves. I think it was just grief.

Having sustained a broken back, Dizzy spent 18 months at Odstock hospital. Although his friends and scooterists did a lot of fundraising for him, with 24 hour sponsored football amongst other things, the happy scene that he was a part of was gone for good and he would be permanently wheelchair bound:
They put me in a home for six months while my parent's house was being renovated. So when I moved back home, I wanted to carry on collecting records. I was on income support at the time, and I couldn't afford the ones I wanted, so I started buying

collections, taking what I wanted and selling the rest. I had a list of 'For Sale' items and every one was hand written. People used to buy stuff and I'd throw their addresses away, then advertise again and say "I recognise that one!" My filing cabinet was the bin. Eventually, I started keeping the addresses and the mailing list has built up nicely since then. Some of those people are still on the list to this day. I also worked for the National Scooter Rally Association (NSRA). I worked for Jeff Smith for about four years. I did all the posting and mailing lists because I had time on my hands. Then about 1986, they went all official and they had to employ someone on a job scheme, so I was made redundant. They gave me a shield and thanked me for my work though.

It would take Dizzy to the end of the eighties and into the nineties, before he could reap the rewards of hard work and determination to make a success of Detour Records.

As Dizzy mentioned, back in 1982, changes were taking place in the mod world. The music remained, but the narcissistic values were gone. Core mod traits remained however, particularly the fierce independent streak that turns its back on the mainstream. These were found among the scooter riders who decided they wanted nothing to do with mod at all. They ceased to use the term and strongly objected to being referred to as mods. Rather, they preferred the term Scooterist. It summed up the central theme of their interest and the tie that bound them together. The clothes and attitude were not necessary, but having a scooter was. The scooter also gave an outlet for creativity and imagination for the owners. Some took the 'less is more' approach and cut down their machines to the bare essentials, the chop-scooter.

Others spent vast sums of money and time rebuilding and restoring scooters. The imagination ran wild and free with bespoke artwork on the scooters panels.

Customising became a lasting trend. 1982 was a turning point for **GARETH BROWN** as well, as he told Scootering Magazine:

The cut-off point is clinical for me. Scarborough 1982. I went there a mod and came back a scooter boy. The scooters were obviously important, but the music was needed to give it an identity, particularly in the early days when we were mostly devotees of northern soul. It was all-important to remove ourselves from the mod image.

Gareth Brown's decision to distance himself from the mod image by becoming a scooterist was one option. Others stuck with the now stereotyped image of mod. The third option was taken by people like **PAUL WELSBY** from Manchester:

Following my brief dalliance with the mod revival, it was pretty much mod by association. I dressed like a mod, acted like a mod, but I wouldn't go anywhere near an organised mod club or event. I suppose I felt a little above that. After all, I thought I knew the secret of mod and fortuitously that was completely reinforced with The Style Council. Possibly the ultimate mod group.

Why go to a Tony Class organised do, mingling with parka clad youth dancing to crap sixties pop music when you could get on a smart suit and dance (on the same dancefloor as The Jazz Defectors) to Flora Purim influenced Latin-jazz of The Swamp Children at Manchester's Tropicana Club? Why play at toy-town mod societies with the Phoenix when you could go to Bar Rhumba and hear Gilles Peterson DJ? Who would want a record by The Moment when Kent were unleashing tons of rare and unreleased classic sixties soul?

Maybe it was an age thing. Maybe it was just natural progression, but the "conventional" mod scene was too retro for my personal tastes at the time.

As for mod rallies, I've never understood their attraction to the mod scene. I've been to them, but have never understood them. Even now, mod for me is a club culture. What pissed weekends away at a dodgy seaside resort have to do with club culture is beyond me. To me mod was (and still is) a living breathing thing. It's timeless. It shouldn't be a recreation of the past. It should use the past as a springboard. I never understand why mods buy second hand sixties clothes. Why do they want to look like something out of a museum? There's so much classic styled contemporary clothes around, Duffer or Paul Smith for example, you can dress in a mod style and still look cool. It's all in the spirit.

In the south-eastern corner of Britain, the next generation of mod influenced youngsters were starting to find their feet in the mod world. Mike Stax from England and Anja Bungert from Germany would eventually find each other through their love of music and the ever

developing and diversifying mod culture. **MIKE STAX:**
I was born in Watford, and grew up in Cheshire, Leicestershire and Yorkshire. I remember first getting hooked on music listening to a reel-to-reel tape my dad had of the Beatles' Rubber Soul and Help! albums. Also, like most kids in England, I watched Top of the Pops every Thursday night and dug stuff like Sweet, Slade, T-Rex, and especially David Bowie. Bowie doing "Starman" and "The Jean Genie" on TV stopped me in my tracks. After that, it was all about rock & roll for me. From Bowie, I found my way to the Rolling Stones (the Brian Jones period), the Pretty Things, the Yardbirds and the Velvet Underground. I was a Brian Jones obsessive, even making a pilgrimage to his grave when I was about 13. That's where the sixties obsession began for me. I was 15 when punk rock hit in 1977, which was also an exciting period, but I lost interest after the initial surge of great bands and shows, while my love for sixties music only increased.

I was influenced by the music and fashion sense of original sixties mods - always loved the Who, the Small Faces, the Action, the Creation, et al - but the Mod revival groups never did anything for me. I never identified myself as a mod; I always identified more strongly with long-haired R&B groups - the Pretty Things, early Stones, Kinks, Yardbirds - the more bohemian side of the coin. Inevitably that led me into the world of psychedelia and American garage bands.

I moved to California in 1980. I heard the Crawdaddys on John Peel's radio show, and was astounded that a new, young band from San Diego could sound so authentically like a British R&B band from 1964. It really blew me away. I tracked down their records and then wrote them a fan letter c/o Bomp Records. In it I mentioned that I was learning to play bass and had formed my own Downliners Sect-style R&B band in Yorkshire, called the Hi Heel Sneakers. A couple of weeks later I got a letter back from the Crawdaddys asking me if I'd like to come over and join the band. I was 18 years-old. I'd just left school and I knew immediately that that was what I wanted to do with my life.

A few months later I boarded a plane for California. In 1983 I started publishing 'Ugly Things' Magazine from my new base in San Diego.

ANJA BUNGERT:
I grew up in Dudweiler, which is a part of Saarbruecken in the southwest corner of Germany. I started being aware of music from a very early age since my parents were both really into music and my dad is (and was at the time) a very heavy record collector. My parents had me young so they were teenagers in the mid-sixties and were into all the good stuff, The Creation, Dave Dee, The Monkees, The Beatles of course mixed in with some 70s Rock at the time, Deep Purple etc.

Once I entered into my teenage years I hated everything my parents listened to and went the polar opposite. In the early 80s I was a full on Goth and my favourite bands were Sisters of Mercy, The Cure, Einstuerzende Neubauten, Joy Division and more. This all changed when a friend of mine came to my house with a VHS copy of Quadrophenia. I think that was in 1984. The very next day we went to our local vintage clothes shop in the search of Sixties clothes, pulled my parents Kinks and Who records, changed my hair style... the rest just developed from there.

The first real band I was in was the Cherylinas from Saarbruecken. Nicole, the singer and then guitar player was already in a 60s Garage band called The Biting Butterflies but she wanted to start a girl band. To start with it was her on guitar and me on bass. We quickly found a singer, Jasmin, and a drummer, Yvonne which were girlfriends of other musicians we knew. A little later Heike joined on organ.

Most of us never really played before and we rehearsed in Nicole's dad's garden shed. I think in about a month we had an opening spot for the Fuzztones in one of the biggest indie venues in town.

The show was crude and not that great to put it politely, but we all were determined. After some changes in personnel we started to actually get good and played a lot of shows in Germany and Belgium at various Sixties and mod clubs as well as a show in England at the infamous St John's Tavern.

We were offered some deal with Virgin and more seemed to be happening. The sixties scene was exploding all over Europe and more people from different countries started to travel and became friends. The Cherylinas kicked me out of the band around 1993.

Back in England, among the new crop of mod converts, was **ROB BAILEY**:
It all started for me at school in Aylesford, near Maidstone in Kent. A good third of the school kids were mod at the time and it was my year plus the two years above us. The older kids probably got into it during the '79 period, but for my year, this would have been around '82, '83, '84. We were about fourteen years of age. It was that, coupled with the strong Medway live music scene with The Prisoners, The Milkshakes and groups like that. So that's where it all started for me with school discos and the like, then we had our own scooter club in Maidstone, the Cool Runnings Scooter Club, which had about 40 to 50 members. We organised our own nights, and that's where the deejaying started around '85-86.
At that point I started venturing back up to London, to clubs like Sneakers and The Biz from the mid to late eighties. The first thing you noticed was the scooters and the clothes, then after that it was the music, and I think that once you get into the music there is no turning back because there is such a wealth of it, you're hooked.
Also at the age of 15, the gang mentality seemed quite appealing and there was lots of that going on at school.

Indeed, The Prisoners were one of the key bands who were not mods, but eventually gained a loyal mod following. Their influences were a combination of punk and sixties beat as **GRAHAM DAY** explained:
I started off playing bass, playing along to Stranglers and Rezillos songs in my bedroom. When me and Allan Crockford started a band in 1978 I found I was too fiddly on the bass and he was a good rhythm guitar player but couldn't play lead, so we swapped. When I heard Syd Barrett playing guitar on The Piper At The Gates Of Dawn it blew my mind. I discovered how you could make a guitar sound so powerful without being 'rock' with loads of unnecessary notes, and it changed the way I viewed the instrument. Similarly with Steve Marriott's guitar sound and playing, it made me question what a typical guitar player is expected to do.
We used to jump on the train to London quite a lot around 1979-80, going up to the Marquee to see the Vapors, The Boys and later The Revillos.

Teramo [photo © Paolo Ceritano]

ALLAN CROCKFORD:

We saw The Jam about 10 times. They were influential on all of us because they were the first big, current band that we liked, rather than dreaming about bands that were long gone.

Taking inspiration from bands like the Pop Rivets who included Billy Childish and Bruce Brand among their number, Graham Day, Allan Crockford and Johnny Symons played their first gig at The Red Lion in Gravesend in early 1980.

By 1981, James Taylor was recruited on keyboards to provide the 'missing element' to the sound they wanted.

Two days of recording in September 1982 resulted in their debut album 'A Taste Of Pink'. Releasing it on their Own-Up label, it was so popular that Rough Trade eventually became the distributor for the album.

It is somewhat surprising that The Prisoners had to wait until January 1983 to play their first London gig at the Moonlight Club, Hampstead supporting the Barracudas, but more gigs followed in the capital supporting The Milkshakes and their own residency at the Hope & Anchor, Islington.

Releasing a new album every year until 1986, The Prisoners amassed a loyal following and arguably 1985's 'The Last Forefathers' is seen as the best of their work by fans.

Perhaps the biggest problem for the band was trying to avoid being pigeon-holed with the various 'scenes', but when Eddie Piller signed them to his label Countdown which was backed by Stiff Records, it was certain that The Prisoners would gain a larger mod following than they already had.

ALLAN CROCKFORD:

I didn't know who he (Eddie Piller) was. He'd been following us around a bit and it turned out he was a figure on the mod scene and had his own label.

We thought 'Maybe this is a bloke of our age who can give us what we want. It seemed like a good opportunity.

GRAHAM DAY:
When Countdown came along with an album offer it put us at a difficult crossroads. We had a choice whether to push on or stay as we were. We had to give it a try. We'd seen our mates The Playn Jayn sign to A&M, but it hadn't done them any favours. The popular music buying public just weren't ready to accept our type of 'retro' music.

The resulting album 'In From The Cold' was a disappointment, not least because producer Troy Tate changed The Prisoners preferred recording process and off the back of that, disagreements with Stiff over the funding came to the fore.

GRAHAM DAY:
I should've seen the writing on the wall, but naively thought we could stick together and do this on our terms. We rebelled against everything they wanted us to do and made life very difficult for everyone, especially poor Eddie Piller, whose heart was in the right place.
Just after we handed the master over, Stiff went bankrupt, so it was all a waste of anger, bitterness, time and money. That was the final nail in the coffin of the band.
We'd started to build a decent fanbase and signing to Countdown brought an onslaught of mods to our gigs who weren't interested in our music and were just there as part of the scene. Gradually, a lot of our original fans stopped coming to see us. We started in vain to wear leather and iron crosses and played Deep Purple songs in an attempt to show we were not mods. The mod scene was more damaging to us.

However, despite The Prisoners break-up, Graham Day, Allan Crockford and James Taylor would go on to new projects and whether they liked it or not, they retained a loyal following that had its roots in mod.
By 1984, the dedicated mods that remained created their own national organisation to set up rallies and events for mods as opposed to scooterists, whose own agendas did not sit well with mod circles and visa versa.
Initially, these events were run by the Phoenix Society and then by Classic Club

International. **TONY CLASS**, who had been involved in mod discos and events for four or five years, was involved in both the Phoenix and Classic Club as he explained in an interview with Scootering Magazine:
The Phoenix Society was a national mod organisation started in late 1983 by Mark Johnson. I was at Weymouth filming the rally when I met him. He had some good ideas about improved communication to let mods know what was going on. The Phoenix List helped keep the mod scene together for three or four years, but it was me that put on all the rallies. Eventually some of his (Johnson's) anti-social activities caused us to ban him from the rallies, and he went on to promote the London Ska Festivals.

The main difference of opinion between the two groups came down to interpretation of style. For the scooterist, having two wheels was enough to satisfy the criteria. Clothes and modernist dogma were not necessary. In order to distinguish themselves from mods, scooterists opted for practical clothing for riding scooters. Parkas were now a mod cliche, and scooterists did not have suits to protect from the elements. The scooterist style came from a number of sources. The classic skinhead footwear, Doc Marten's, were evident. Combat gear was often worn, as were short leather jackets that had more in common with bikers than mods. Full-face crash helmets, jeans, Harrington jackets, trainers, t-shirts, the style was ultimately informal, but effective in its purpose.
To the general public, the scooterist was a puzzlement because the two wheeled transport signified 'mod', but the clothing was not consistent with the perceived image. But what the public thought was of little consequence to the scooterists. They knew who was mod and who was not and that was the point.
For the mods, although they initially mixed with scooterists at the early events and rallies, animosity soon began to grow as the difference of opinion grew. Mods thought the scooterists were scruffy and uncouth and the music at the events was almost exclusively northern soul.
Eventually the two groups had to be kept apart and by 1984 the split was permanent. However, both the scooterists' and mod numbers began to grow significantly. Many mod

societies and mod based scooter clubs formed and by 1986, they joined forces under the banner of The Confederation of Modernist Societies (CMS). The co-ordinator of the CMS was Mark Johnson who had left The Phoenix Society. The various mod societies around the country registered to become an Affiliated Modernist Society (AMS) and the Mod scooter clubs became Affiliated Mod Scooter Clubs (AMSC). The rules laid down by the CMS were:

1. The club must be and remain all-Mod.
2. The club's primary purpose must be the advancement and preservation of the Mod scene.
3. Ownership of a scooter must not be a requirement for the membership in the society or scooter club.

All the members of the societies joining the CMS had to agree with the 'ideals' of the confederation.

A statement of ideals was produced to give those joining absolutely no doubt as to the aims of the organisation:

The Confederation of Modernist Societies is made up of about 100 groups of Modernists all over the world who believe in building a strong and dedicated Mod scene and who also believe that the way to do this is by co-operation and communication within the scene. Although honest differences of opinion exist between people we believe that this is a healthy sign that Mods care about their future. We believe that unity within the Mod scene is more important than any single club, society or person and have dedicated ourselves to ensuring that Mod is a strong and positive culture. And we believe that the basis for this is respect for individuals and their varying tastes and styles and being positive towards other mods.

While we are working with many of the same goals in mind as the Phoenix did when it started up, we also stress something which seemed to be in rather short supply right now within certain quarters of the Mod scene: tolerance!

We believe that there are many styles of Mod music. R'n'B, Ska, Soul, Tamla, Modern Jazz, Sixties Mod Pop, Revival and Modern, and each is equally important to the Modernist scene.

We believe in smart dress and in encouraging those Mods who don't dress quite as well as they might - not shunning them, but helping them. We believe in encouraging the young Mod bands which help to make our culture vigorous and alive - Mod means Modernist. Adopted 19 April 1987.

It was this kind of pseudo-dogmatic approach that alienated as many mods as it attracted. It was perhaps the first time anyone had tried to set the rules and provide a written definition of what mod was. In the fifties and sixties, word of mouth and physical style was how the standards were set. In trying to set the rules, the CMS showed just how authoritarian and dogmatic the concept of mod could be, and as a result, created a reaction against it; most notably in the form of home produced fanzines. Each one had its own definition of what mod meant and how it should progress.

It should be reiterated that Sniffin' Glue from the punk era, and mod's Maximum Speed had set the pace for fanzines, and Ray Margetson's 'Patriotic' had been going for sometime, but **EDDIE PILLER**'s 'Extraordinary Sensations' was still regarded as one of the best. However, Eddie was becoming disenchanted with the scene, until he went on a trip to the other side of the world:

I was probably losing interest by 1984, but I went to Australia and that's when I met Don Hosie and that made me get back into the mod scene. I've never experienced anything like that.

They used to meet before a gig wearing dinner jackets and go to the Regent Hotel in Sydney, which was the best hotel in Sydney, and have cocktails and champagne. Then they'd drive on their scooters to a gig. So they really invigorated me. Don Hosie was the epitome of the 'Face'. He took Pete Meaden's philosophy, created it and made it work. In Britain it all grew around The Jam. Don said "I've got an idea, we're going to be mods". and it worked and he had hundreds of people following him about. Don was always at the front when they rode scooters and your position in the formation as you went down the road, reflected your position in the group. It was amazing. They had paintball guns. They would shoot skinheads with paintball guns. So I would say that through the eighties, while mod was dying in Britain, places like

Australia, Japan and America were on the up. I signed The Untouchables, who were an American mod band signed to Stiff Records and they had a hit with 'Free Yourself'. It was one of the few post 1979 mod hits. I think it got to number 20 in the charts and that was my band. Then off the back of that we had Makin' Time, The Prisoners, The Milkshakes and that whole Medway scene.

Then I had the record labels. The first one was Well Suspect which was named after a shop in Carnaby Street. It had a scooter half in the shop and half out of it, which was a weird and exciting thing. We had Fast Eddie who are the great unsung heroes of the eighties when they were playing black music very well when we were just getting into black music, so they were a band of the moment and they never recorded an album, but their live gigs were always packed out. They had a massive following of proper mods and they played brilliant mod music.

So the first single was Fast Eddie followed by The Merton Parkas single followed by 'The Beat Generation' album which was The Purple Hearts and The Directions and that stuff. Then I did the Countdown label which was the Stiff mod label with The Prisoners, Makin' Time and The Kick and a few compilations. Re-Elect The President was my next venture which was still a mod label with James Taylor Quartet, Jazz Renegades, The Creeps who were a mod band from Sweden and some garage stuff which was quite lively in the eighties and seems to be coming back.

In July 1984, Sounds ran a feature on what was happening on the mod front and spoke to a few of the people who produced the various fanzines on offer. James Blonde of Time for Action fanzine was one contributor *"The people involved with mod now - whether through bands, 'zines, clubs or arranging gigs - are the dedicated few, and not just fashion followers like the majority of '79 era mods. There are some people involved from back then, but not many now there are no big bucks to be made".*

Chris Hunt's Shadows and Reflections was another highly respected publication. He explained what the fanzine was all about *"Shadows and Reflections is an attempt to produce a music magazine that features a variety of alternative music, on a spectrum which ranges from pop and power pop, through new wave, mod, R&B and soul, to*

Leeds [courtesy of Stephen Brazil]

psychedelia and psychedelic pop - all forms of music which are generally ignored by the national music press". He continued "Some people have a fixation with simply imitating the sixties mods, but many others look to the sixties for inspiration and interpret it through their eighties experience. In other ways it (mod) is a sheer rejection of eighties pessimism and an attempt to adopt the forward-looking, optimistic state of mind so obviously present in the sixties. I don't know, choose your own definition of what mod is all about. It means something different to everyone".

Chris's last comment really highlights a fundamental problem that has dogged mod culture ever since the sixties. The interpretation of what it is and what it means. The fanzines of the seventies and eighties certainly catered for all the different strands of mod culture. This is just a small sample of the 50 to 60 publications to be found in the eighties:
'Cool and Collected' based in Chelmsford
'The Modernist Times' and 'E to D' form Suffolk
'Sharp Cuts' from Rotherham
'Empty Hours' from Manchester,
'Fire and Skill' from Cambridge
'Fabulous' from Cardiff
'The In Crowd' from Gurnsey
'007' from London
'Dance With Style' from North Humberside
'Face To Face', 'Motoroller', 'A Taste For Fashion' and 'Immediate Reaction' all from Chesterfield
'Go-Go' from Essex
'Holdin On' and 'Dedicated' from Northern Ireland
'Bewitched' from South Yorkshire
Right Track
Setting Standards.

In late November 1985, 'Timeout' magazine ran a feature on the mod scene. They spent a night out with 'Paul, Jim and Chad' who belonged to a crew known as The Bow Street Runners. The mod allnighter they went to was the 1985 National Mod Meeting at Peterborough. It had been organised by The Phoenix Society.

It turned out to be a disappointing night and many blamed the Phoenix Society. One unnamed source said *"They're out to commercialise mod and rip us off. They're giving a good thing a bad name".*

The Bow Street Runners had been organising their own rival events for a few years. Their motto was 'to adopt, adapt and appreciate'. They were trying to stay faithful to the original modernist ideal of good clothing, good music and good times.

'Chad' explained what it all meant for him: *"I live and breathe mod 24 hours a day, and sometimes I can kick myself for not going further into it. I turned down a chance to get into photography because I knew it would interfere with my social life".*

'Paul' commented on what he saw as the main faults with the scene at the time *"Unfortunately, it's the minority of mods who think like us. Most of them are into live bands, mini skirts and parkas, bouncing around singing 'We Are The Mods' - all very embarrassing. There are good scenes around though. Coventry, Birmingham, Swindon and Liverpool, But too many are just sticking with it through the commercial side, believing what they read in Smash Hits".*

'Chad' also explained the mod attitude to scooterists *"They are a complete bastardisation. All they do is ride scooters, which for me is nothing more than a form of transport. They used to hang around our clubs, which meant a lot of trouble, so we had to enforce a smart dress rule. They have absolutely nothing to do with us".*

The Bow Street Runners were not the only mod 'crew' around London. **DAVE EDWARDS**, now in his late teens, was getting more involved with the mod scene:

The first places I started going to were The George IV on Brixton Hill, just by the prison. Monday nights was a northern soul night, the Marquee on Wardour Street and the 100 Club for gigs plus the Cricketers at the Oval had some great gigs on. Then there were Tony Class' nights at The Bush on Saturdays and live bands on Mondays and Tuesdays.

There were a few Alldayers run by Andy Ruw in the WAG club that I recall. This was

1983, I was 17 and still struggling to get in to some venues such as the Clarendon at Hammersmith and only just managed to blag my way into the Hope and Anchor to see Small World. I loved it all though, it was exciting, there was loads of things going on and we were all still in our teens, had scooters and there were very few people involved who were over 21.

I met Ian Jackson in late 83, early 84. I kind of fell in with The Camden Stylists, Alan Handscombe's crowd. They were dead sharp and Ian was part of the group along with another black mod, Rob Murphy. We used to meet at lunchtimes on weekends, not just clubs or gigs, usually at The Bucks Head in Camden or The Coach and Horses on the corner of Broadwick Street and Poland Street. They were a few black Mods around, Nick Agadinho, Martin Derby from Leicester, Ferdy (never knew his real name!) and Guy who was a football casual who got talking to Alan Handscombe before an all-nighter, went along to the 100 Club and bought into the whole scene. He looked really cool, as did all the black Mods around. Things is we didn't see them as black Mods, just Mods and they looked really sharp. I don't know what happened to Guy but I still see Ian, Rob, Nick and Martin.

The Camden Stylists became important because of the influence some of the individual members have had on mod DJing over the years.

ALAN HANDSCOMBE:

I was born and bought up in the London Borough of Camden. My first introduction to mod was through my pal Rob Murphy. I think he took me to the Phoenix Mod night run by Tony Class after about six months I had ditched my Doc Martens and bought a Vespa. The Camden Stylists were pretty much myself, Rob Murphy, Ian Jackson, Colin Bangs, Tracy Wright, Peter Slade, Jamie Medhurst, Jamie and Bridget Heaven, Adam Taylor, Sue Walker, Shane Cox and others who we knocked around with, (Dave Edwards, for example). It was a name given to us. We never called ourselves that at all. It was a bit embarrassing really .We were the Skinheads and Rudies who infiltrated the Mod Scene.

I was asked to DJ at Le Beat Route down in Soho as Alex Gerry was away. That got me into it around 1983/84. Without a doubt in the 80s the most important club in the country was Sneakers run by Paul Hallam.

IAN JACKSON:
I grew up in Kensal Rise. It was very tough being a black male back in the late 70s and early 80s. I had white friends, but it was difficult because it was considered 'normal' to be racist to people of colour. My introduction to mod came via hearing Motown records and being told about them by my elder sister. Then I saw them on TV and then actually seeing them on scooters in 1979. I went to Sneakers, The Phoenix and a few Northern Soul clubs. I saw a few bands as well.
On the whole, as a black man, I have been well received on the mod scene. There are always going to be a few detractors, but you learn to ignore them.

Indeed, as Alan Handscombe stated, Sneakers (by consensus of opinion) was the most important mod club of the 80s. It was run by **PAUL HALLAM**:
I was born in Staines and grew up in Sunbury-On-Thames. My older sister was a teenager through the Sixties, but I got into music in the early 70s. I told her I liked the Beatles and borrowed her albums. She then introduced me to other Sixties pop music. For my 12 birthday I got 'The Beatles at the Hollywood Bowl' and the Blue and Red albums. My then brother-in-law was into the Stones and Kinks, so he would put stuff my way and I became obsessed with 60s music.
When '79 mod came along, I didn't rate The Jam, but the whole mod revival thing gave me 'Time For Action' by Secret Affair, which I liked a lot. It didn't inspire me to get into mod then. By the summer of 1980, my cousin Barry Hallam came to stay with us and he starts playing me 'London Boys' by Bowie as he was a Bowie obsessive.
Not long after John Lennon died, I decided to go out (almost for the first time really). I borrowed a Fred Perry from one of my mates and a few other bits to try and look the part because I wanted to go to a mod night at Feltham Football Club.
I'm 15 years old, it was a Thursday night and I end up in the back of this van with 30 other mods all wearing those green trench coats everyone seemed to have at the

time and the other thing I remember was the smell of cheap aftershave. So we get to the club which was a pre-fab building and horrible, but I had a great time and by the next day, that was it. I wanted to be a mod.

Everyone at school was a mod and we all used Richard Barnes' book as our reference point. All my mates just looked at the pictures, but I read the text. The mod night at Feltham Football Club shut down, but we heard about a new night at a place called Cheeky Pete's on a Sunday night in Richmond. Cheeky Pete's was a huge venue that was packed with 400 mods. I also heard about a pub where the Twickenham mods used to meet up. The first time I went there, there were 50 scooters outside the pub.

I left school and decided I really needed a job to earn money, but because I had met the Twickenham mods and cousin Barry was still living with us and his diverse record collection got me listening to The Shirelles and Phil Spector among others and by 83 I'm thinking I don't like the music being played at Tony Class's mod nights.

I'm right into Snooks Eaglin and Muddy Waters, and that's what I wanted to hear, so I decided to open a club in March of 83. I went to Margate on my Vespa 100 with a mass of flyers. I started out back at Feltham Football Club and the first night we had 100 people in and they hated it. I was playing Bo Diddley and they thought it was psychobilly music.

Eventually, I got invited to a Pheonix Society meeting. Tony Class was there, he had his Saturday night at The Bush which was phenomenal. I was just 18 and it was the first time I met Eddie Piller and those East London lads. At that meeting, I told Tony I didn't like the music he was playing, and fair play to him, he said, "Alright, think you can do better? I'll get you the Bush on a Sunday night" and he did. Richard Early came up with the name Sneakers and the first night we had about 100 in, then the numbers dropped off just like it had at Feltham, but around the start of '84 something happened and word got around and we were getting people coming from all over the country. We ran Sneakers for just over four years and in '87 when we closed, that last night, we weren't playing any records that we played in '83 when we started. That kind of summed up my philosophy of music progressing. In '83 we were playing stuff like 'Hit The Road Jack' or 'Lets Dance' by Chris Montez. By 87, we're playing obscure Latin Jazz and Boogaloo. At the Bush, it was a back room in a pub. Richard Early did a lot, playing stuff that pushed barriers and what he was playing in the first hour back then are now considered mod club classics. We left the Bush and went to the Clarenden, then the 79 Wine Bar where it was Latin music.

In the summer of '86, I was hanging out with Ady Croasdell and the first time I heard Latin was Andy Orr Drew playing 'El Watusi'. I went out and bought the Ray Barretto album. In '82-'83 people went to the clubs in their area, then the scene contracted and people saw Sneakers as a kind of hub.

I remember the Irish lot that came over. David Holmes' sister lived in Kilburn and he came over to stay with her from time to time. He came to Sneakers and says at age 14 and he saw Paul Hallam DJ and decided that's what he wanted to be which is quite flattering. I've known Tony Shockman for 33 years, but it never occurred to me that he was anything other than a mod. Rob Murphy was known as Black Rob, but only on the basis that so many people had nicknames that distinguished them from other people with the same name, like my wife might be known as Spanish Vicky. It was never an issue. Class, status and that whole bullshit, divisive strata of society simply didn't exist.

Quoting from Paul Hallam's photographic book 'Odds and Sods', Greg (Eddie) Fay was a regular at Sneakers and had this to say:

Admittedly looking back through rose-tinted glasses, I honestly believe that the regular crowd was a harmonious social microcosm; racially mixed, socio-economically representative and no more male-dominated than the rest of contemporary society. In fact the most faboulously fierce stalwarts were Hannah (RIP) and Anita from the Ugly Buglies, an all-female crew of uber-mods, who were resplendently fastidious in their sartorial habits and more wonderfully raucous than any of the men.

STUART CATLING was typical of many a mod who started to feel alienated by the changes taking shape with the emergence of scooterists:

It was around 1984 or '85, I started to move away from it because the whole scooterboys thing was taking over and that wasn't for me. I got more into soul and also became interested in some of those New Romantic bands like the Associates and Heaven 17 because they had a very smart image which was a world away from mod, but it was a very smart look in my opinion. Then I got married and 'grew up' a bit and 'life' took over. I still listened to a lot of mod music, but I didn't really get back into the scene until around 2009.

The scooterists however had far less complications to deal with early on, although the animosity toward mod existed in some quarters. The unrestricted and deregulated dress code meant that others, who until the mid eighties had been enemies of the mods, found the scooterist style much more to their liking. Skinheads and punks were welcomed into the scooterist fold, and with them they brought their own musical influences which found favour at scooter events.

Even rockabillies found their way into scooterist circles for a while, but they did not last too long. The rockabilly / psychobilly flirtation was exactly that; a minor, but fun distraction that soon was out of fashion and unwanted.

TONY CLASS had been involved in the Isle of Wight rallies from 1982, and as he told Scootering Magazine, disputes were non-existent in those days:
I never saw any difference before 1983, that was when you really began to see people on scooters who you couldn't consider as mods. I didn't see the mix being a problem because everyone enjoyed the same music. By 1984 there was conflict between the groups at the Isle of Wight. I hoped it was a one-off but it was worse in 1985, not just between the mods and scooterists, but also between scooter clubs. I couldn't fathom out why scooterists wanted to stab each other. The violence was taking away my enjoyment. My enjoyment of events has always been primary, otherwise I'd give them up.
In early 1986, Chris Burton (Isle of Wight co-promoter in '84 and '85) phoned me up and said: "What about the IoW?" I said I wouldn't do it, but he decided to go ahead on his own. Previously we'd agreed that we wouldn't try it alone because it was such a

big job, but I wished him luck and backed out, because I saw it going horribly wrong. I was proved right with the burning down of the beer tent and all the traders being turned over.

Almost inevitably, with scooter skins came the unpredictable and unwanted skinheads who were more interested in promoting far right-wing political ideas than scootering. By 1985, mistakes had been made by the event organisers by booking Oi bands who attracted the political skinheads.

It should have been obvious that this mixture was likely to become volatile, but the organisers carried on. It all came to a head in 1986. Desmond Dekker had been attacked at the Great Yarmouth Rally, and by the August Bank Holiday at the Isle of Wight, several Oi bands were lined up for the Sunday night. With an estimated 10,000 scooterists in attendance and skinheads arriving on foot on the day, the scooterists were not impressed by the live acts. Vicious Rumours, Condemned '84 and The Business were well known for their right-wing beliefs and following.

As a result, the few hundred who turned up were the Oi followers who had travelled especially to see the gigs. The curious fact is that the trouble had started after the gigs and mainly because the assembled scooterists were fed up with providing their own entertainment and paying sky high prices for on-site food and drink that had risen by 100 per cent in less than twenty four hours.

It all started with a beer tent being raided and moved on to other site caterers. A drinks marquee was set alight and gas canisters inside began to explode. When the fire brigade arrived they were stoned by a group of skinheads. With the authorities refusing to tackle the problem, they merely contained it to the confines of the campsite. That was the green light for pandemonium. Vans were overturned, traders were looted and fights started between various groups. Most scooterists left the site as quickly as possible and those who were still there by morning were obviously not the instigators of the trouble and the authorities, who knew pretty much who they were after, let the remaining hung-over and beleaguered bunch leave peacefully. By the end of the rally season, The Number Ones introduced measures to prevent anything like it happen again.

One other important and influential factor in retaining interest in mods and scooters was the flow of information from the fanzines.

Although they had been around for a good few years, the focus sharpened with the launch of Scootering Magazine in May 1985. In an interview with Scootering Magazine in 2000 **GARETH BROWN** explains how the magazine came into being:

The idea behind it came from a guy called Pete Sherwin from Runcorn in Cheshire. At the time, he bought out a magazine that he wanted to take national, called Scooter World. It was A4 and glossy, and the first issue I saw of that was some time in 1984. By 1985 he'd already talked to people who owned 'Back Street Heroes' - Steven Myatt and Alistair McFarlane - and come up with the idea of a national scootering magazine because of the strength of the scootering movement.

It started as a bi-monthly with Mike Holland as the editor. Steve Myatt penned stuff under the name of Mart. Pete Shewin contributed and several other freelancers. As soon as the first issue came out I did a sample article for them. They wrote back and asked me to cover the forthcoming Great Yarmouth rally. From then on it snowballed and they asked me to be their freelance rally reporter.

Eventually Gareth Brown was offered a full-time job with Scootering Magazine in 1986. A tragic motorbike accident resulting in the death of Mike Holland in March 1987 led to Gareth being promoted to Associate Editor.

Scootering Magazine had not cornered the market though. Scooter Scene Magazine, was also fairly popular as **STUART LANNING** states:

When I launched Scooter Scene, Scootering was selling about 21,000 copies and Scooter Scene 14,000 copies. Within two years, Scooter Scene was selling more copies than Scootering. We were both selling less than 11,000 copies each. That's why we merged into one magazine.

In time, Stuart Lanning would become the editor of Scootering Magazine, maintaining its reputation and purpose which was to cover all aspects of scootering and become a 'must have' for any scooter owner.

Scootering Magazine provided technical knowledge, rally news, new products available by the manufacturers and features on some of the most impressive custom scooters ever seen.

The importance of Scootering Magazine can also be seen in the context of being a conduit for spreading scootering and mod across the world. Scootering Magazine's distribution covers the USA, Australia, Europe and the Far East.

However important Scootering Magazine may be, mods around the world have found music as their main route into the culture.

ANTHONY MEYNELL was one who took his music and mod/sixties inspired image to America:

We got some mail from California that convinced us to go there. They had the Anthony Meynell album, but they didn't know what the difference was between Anthony Meynell and Squire. Mod in California was pop really.

There was a band there who knew everything about Squire and they wanted to back me and it was a huge success. I was in the middle of recording 'Get Smart' which was going to have strings and horns on it and I thought, I'm not going to miss the chance of mixing this in California. This was in 1983. I went to Western Digital, which is Ocean Way where The Beach Boys did all their stuff. What an experience!

I fell in love with the place and they fell in love with me. I did a couple of gigs with this band and although The Jam had been and gone, and I think Secret Affair had played there once, there was a scene, but no focus to it.

Suddenly I was giving it importance by almost being an ambassador and what I was doing was pop. I did cable TV and radio.

Rodney Bingenheimer is an important deejay who broadcasts to 12 million people in the LA area on KROK. He was famous in the sixties for being Davy Jones' double in the Monkees and he is also a complete anglophile who went round San Francisco with George Harrison in the late sixties and he loves English music.

He wanted to interview me and the week before it had been Culture Club who were huge then and the week after was The Bangles who were just coming up, but in the middle was me and I was treated just the same. They thought me and Boy George lived next door to each other over here. They played 22 Squire records back-to-back to 12 million people and you just can't buy that kind of exposure. They just loved the music and when they ran out of records, they gave me an acoustic guitar and I sang live because they wanted to hear more.

That's when I realised that somewhere in the world, someone likes my music. I came back home, 'Get Smart' was finished and it was fairly evident that a normal tour of pubs and clubs would not be any good. Our audience was a lot younger and we had a fan club of 2,000 kids. We did some matinee shows in Greek Street in Soho for kids and when we went on tour we did in-stores and record shops just for kids. They were mods, but they were little kids and we were stars to them, they loved it.

Because of the fan base, 'Get Smart' actually charted, but Gallup took it out of the chart because they thought we had hyped it. We were such a small label, we weren't into hyping it, we were just doing our thing and we had made the album chart and they took it out, the bastards. That was 1983 and we were Squire again and successful internationally. It was at that time that I realised that the mainstream music business would not acknowledge our success. They weren't into Squire anymore and it was obvious that there was no point staying here and struggling when I could be in California and be successful, so after 'Get Smart' I did another album called 'September Girls' and that was different again.

So mod was finding its way around the world. It was still influencing people across Europe. We return to **LAURENT GRUX** and **ALEXANDRE SAILLIDE ULYSSE** to explain how the French scene developed during the mid to late 80s:

Later, during the years 1983-84, after the end of The Jam and the mod revival, those of us who remained faithful to the modernist ideals continued to search for an in-depth knowledge of the various fields of our culture, but our mod life became strongly tainted with violence, which would be described as 'hard mod' However, we need to qualify this term 'hard mod'; for example the OMs of Place Gambetta and their 'capo' Philippe 'Sid' Debarge, or the Smart Boys of Lutèce by Lionel Vélard who

Paris [courtesy of Laurent Grux]

became Chef Vulcain. Hard mod emerged in the mid-1980s in Paris; a kind of 'ultra mod' fringe group, both passionate about mod culture and not hesitating to regularly resort to violence against various opponents. It was around this time that mods would gather at the Place Gambetta and so became known as Mods de Gambetta .

The Mods de Gambetta were already distinguished by the specific nature of their formation and their members. It was made up of several clubs or small structures, such as Les Templiers, the Royal Dandies Scooter Club, the City Gents MS and individual mods, but they united by their membership in the Mods de Gambetta.

Gambetta was for all of us a base of cohesion, recognition and a marker of our determination to continue and develop our involvement and knowledge in Modernism. The selection of members was relatively tight and focused on the personal qualities of the aspirants but also on their ability to commit to the group and their willingness to fully participate in our way of life.

As a result, recruitment was extremely limited and there were little or no errors in retrospect. There were also some scattered mods in Paris, of which two or three were of high quality, but the others in our opinion, did not meet the required standards of mod we advocated.

As we have already pointed out, the Parisian mod scene (mainly Gambetta mods) had a specific characteristic in its practices and uses: the violence, with all its induced behaviours and consequences, was particularly present and recurrent.

A violence that erupted regularly through clashes more or less intense, fortuitous or organized and sometimes bloody with the members of the different bands present in the streets of Paris: BoneHeads, Rockabillies, Psychobillies, Nazis or so-called Leftists, Punks and second-rate shabby mods who were more like scruffy 60s types who disliked the Gambetta mods. We had to simply defend ourselves, and sometimes avoid some specific places, the consequences were clear, we had to fight regularly, but frequently in tailor-made suits!

The causes that led to this violence were various, the most frequent being a hatred of mod by certain groups or others just wanting to fight, ethnic racism against some of our members, and the wrong political pretexts that were attributed to us. Some journeys were made in the streets of the 20th district or in certain places where our enemies were gathered. Outside of Paris, the mods of Avignon, with whom we had quickly developed strong friendships, included similar 'hard' elements in their ranks. In fact Milan was the only other city experiencing violence of a comparable level around the mod scene. It was this violence that led to the band Four By Art to write their song "Who Killed Snoopy" which directly relates the very violent clashes of the Milan Mods against the "Paninari" (local casuals) in the early 1980s. Those fights even included gun fire! The Paris mod scene may have been small, but we got to travel across Europe to attend clubs and events; places like Sneakers at the Bush Hotel, Drummond, The Bizz at the Royal Oak and other mod events in the UK and European nights and gatherings in Spain, Italy, Germany and Sweden.

Perhaps the two best allnighters in Paris were organised by the City Gents MS, then there were the regular evenings of Mod Club 'La Ruche' organised by Alexander SU's 'Obscure Rhythm" N 'Soul Club'.

We also had the 'Mod'WeeKends' organisation in collaboration with the Mods of Rambouillet (Ile de France) with our DJs, some of them highly specialised in a style of music, such as R&B, British R&B, British Beat, Blues,

Across the border between France and Italy, **MARY BOOGALOO** was born in Florence in Tuscany and has since made her home in the UK:

I first started listening to sixties psychedelia and garage, then I slowly discovered the wonders of black American soul and R&B. It was revealing and exciting to realise that mod music didn't just revolve around The Who, The Small Faces or The Jam.

I first came to the UK in 1980 for two years. In those days I didn't follow anything specific, I was into stuff like Iggy Pop, American new wave and early seventies hard rock! It was when I returned to Italy that I got heavily involved with the sixties scene, in particular the mid to late sixties. With a couple of friends we opened a nightclub, devoted exclusively to garage and psychedelia which lasted for well over one year. I didn't consider myself a mod though. As the attraction for London never faded, I moved back at the end of 1985 and I have been here ever since.

For Mary's fellow countryman, **FRANCESCO LISI**, a fascination with The Beatles led this native of Rimini on the Italian east coast, to a mod life:

It all started in the mid eighties for me. I bought all the LPs of the Fab Four, and I began looking for music from the same period. I consider my first mod LP was a Kinks collection, with all the great fuzz classics that make them a great band. I had the "You Really Got Me" guitar riff in my head for weeks and weeks!

But this was not enough for me, so I picked up another LP, and I started to consider myself a mod. That record was "My Generation" by The Who. It was the glossy re-issue on Virgin.

I really didn't know what mod was, but I liked the music so much and my interest in sixties bands grew very quickly.

I grew up with a real sixties musical taste. I was not into Secret Affair or The Jam, and definitely not into the fuzz tones of eighties garage punk bands. I hated the Doors because every young fellow from my school-class liked them, and none of them knew The Kinks, Them or Manfred Mann for example. I didn't follow the crowd.

Then a friend of mine lent me a video of 'Quadrophenia' and it all became clearer. I really needed a parka to let people know what I was in to.

Okay, after more than ten years it all seems a little bit stupid and I'm the first to admit that, but the frustrated mind of a teenager makes him act in that way. At the time, to get an original parka was a mission impossible, but during a spring school vacation in Vienna in 1989, I discovered a second hand shop that had real parkas. I was so excited that to get them, I pretended to my entire school-class that I lost myself for four hours in Vienna, just to have the chance to buy two parkas.

The following winter, I started wearing my parka around Rimini, and I was noticed by the kids of the Smart Drivers and we started a friendship that is still going today.

Indeed, Rimini would provide the European mod scene with another important figure in the shape of **ANDREA MATTIONI**:

I grew up in Rimini. I always loved music from a very young age and when I was around 15 years old I started looking for something different. It's worth remembering that this was Italy in 1981, not the UK. In the UK everything was changing, with the mod revival, punk and New Wave, in Italy everything arrived very watered down and it wasn't as easy to find information on youth scenes, so in the beginning it was just me looking for something new and different. Through this interest I discovered mod bands like The Jam and Secret Affair.

In the beginning of 1982 I met a guy at school who was a year above me, I had seen him around wearing a parka. He noticed that I had mod bands names written with a marker on my school bag and he started talking to me.

He then invited me to go to a club where the Rimini mods used to go, it was called 'Slego'. It was a sort of alternative club, where everything that wasn't commercial would be played; New Wave, punk and amongst it some mod music too. I will never forget when I got there and saw all those cool looking people all standing together, it would have probably been 20 or 30 of them, I was hooked and I have never looked back. The first event that I was involved in organising was a mod rally in Rimini, in September 1983. It attracted around 100 to 150 people.

I suppose it was the first step towards what would become the bigger Easter Rimini Mod Rally which I started organising in 1984, with the help of other Mods from different areas of Italy. Different people have come and gone as part of the organisation throughout the years, but I have done every single one of them, until 2014, when I decided to call it a day on its 30th anniversary.

On the other side of the world in Nagoya, Japan, **NOBUO TANAKA** already had an interest in a British historical figure associated with male style:

Long before becoming a mod, I had been infatuated with the life and the style of an English "dandy" called Beau Brummel who existed in the late 18th century. I thought by becoming a mod, I could in some respect live up to his image. I have been a mod about 17 years and I reckon that the mod look is the ultimate and ideal image for a male. There is no particular or perfect mod icon to imitate, however, I like to embody the essence of this image in my dress and lifestyle the best I can until I die.

I guess the Nagoya mod scene was probably born in 1985. At that time, the main hangouts for the Nagoya mods were live gigs of The Collectors or The Strikes since there was no exclusive mod-type night clubs in Nagoya. We also had more than ten scooters amongst the mods; so, we would often do scooter-runs after the gigs. Sometimes, we'd also make a parade along Sumiyoshi Street that was the Rockers' main hangout then. One of our mates was a DJ at a disco called Dance Hall and when he was working, we would pop into the club and ask him to play The Jam or Specials for us. Those beautiful days lasted only a year and most had left the scene by then. So, Mito, Kuno and me only sustained the scene until Nishio, Takahiro Suzuki, Ozeki (now deceased), Tamoyan and Akira Ota joined us in 1989. That was the quietest period of the Nagoya scene, I recall. Nowadays, I feel time passes quickly and sometimes meaninglessly, but before '89, I felt it passed so slowly. Probably, those quieter times might have been the most substantial period in my growth as a mod, since everything about being mod was exciting and a new discovery for me. Then I felt a bit superior to some of the newcomers, as I was confident that I was already doing what many had never done before.

Across the Pacific Ocean on the American West Coast, a young teenager was formulating musical tastes that would inspire him to begin a music career that would lead to his band becoming a favourite with mods in the UK in the late nineties. **NICK ROSSI** was born in San Diego in 1971, but grew up in La Verne, which is a suburb Los Angeles. He has been living in San Francisco since 1989, when he started going to the university in that famous old city:
I started playing guitar when I was 12 or 13. I had no fashion sense or sense of culture at all. I was just a suburban white kid who liked music. When I was about 14, I started listening to older rock music. It's what they called "oldies radio" over here. Basically, I got into groups like The Beatles, The Jimi Hendrix Experience, The Who and Cream. I was naturally curious and somewhat obsessive so I started investigating who these groups influenced and who and what had influenced them initially.
I remember going on a family holiday trip up the West Coast to San Francisco the summer of 1985 and reading an article in Rolling Stone about LA's "Paisley

Underground". I had something of an epiphany in that it made perfect sense to me all of a sudden that my fashion sense (and lifestyle to a certain extent) should reflect my musical tastes. I desperately searched Haight-Ashbury district for a paisley-button down shirt like the one Donovan wore on the cover of the 'Sunshine Superman' LP, to no avail! Coincidentally, I returned to find that I friend of mine in LA had since "become a mod" and pretty much introduced me to the subculture as it existed then and there. The mod scene in LA at the time was almost entirely influenced by the late seventies UK revival scene.

At times it felt that the only sixties presence was Northern Soul music and Who patches on parkas. Most everything else, it seemed to me at the time, was dismissed as "psychedelic". I was young and fairly wide-eyed, so it seemed no crime to listen to Pink Floyd, Howling Wolf, The Byrds, and John Coltrane.

But my 'freaky' fashion sense ensured my place on the fringes of the scene at the time and nary a step closer. But it was a great time in that I really was open-minded and really tried to expose myself to a lot of different things. It helped me make confident and informed choices later on. Within a few years, I more or less refined my tastes one might say. Certain artists and types of music just stuck with me and resonated much more: mostly late fifties through late sixties jazz, R&B, and soul, funnily enough. My fashion sense refined as well and to a certain degree I tailored it to coincide with my stronger musical interests.

Obviously, when you are a performer, image can be very important, so that certainly was an influence as well. So over the past dozen years or so, I guess my affinity to what most people would consider "mod" has grown much stronger. The musical climate and sense of style in the San Francisco-Bay Area have been influential as well. It's a much more conducive environment to, say, putting on a nice suit and going out to a jazz club here than in a lot of places.

Fellow San Francisco resident **GABRIELA GIACOMAN** was also becoming more interested in mod culture such as it was on the West Coast:

I was born in New York, and lived there in various cities till the age of 10 when I moved to the suburbs of San Francisco (Marin County) and stayed there for seven years until I happily escaped to the city itself. My mother is originally from California and my father from Honduras and are both teachers so they moved around a bit.

My family on the American side had a strong musical tradition, my grandmother taught me lots of Irish-American songs and my mother played guitar and piano and loved singing. We sang lots of Spanish standard songs together with my father when we were little (La Cucaracha!), plus my mom was a big fan of popular 60s folk (Simon and Garfunkel, Joan Baez, etc.) and played that while we all sang along.

At my high school in the 80's a good friend got into the mod scene first and when I asked about her new style she converted me right away. I loved everything about it - the clothes (very easy to pick up beautiful suits at thrift shops in my area at the time), soul music (my first "mod" records were by Sam Cooke and The Miracles), dancing, scooters - I got a Lambretta right away from an ad in a local paper.

My friend got a Vespa shortly thereafter, we didn't realise at the time it was relatively rare for girls to be riding except on the back of their boyfriend's bikes and were pleased to avoid the usual hazing of new people from the older mods in the city. They saw our nice bikes and clothes and assumed we had a super cool secret scene in Marin when in reality there were very few of us and we knew nothing!

I listened to mostly black American and Jamaican music (the usual: r&b, soul, rocksteady). That has been the soundtrack of my life so if nothing else for a musical influence it gives inspiration to strive for excellence. As far as pop goes, I do love The Beach Boys and The Beatles, and most of all The Zombies.

As far as style goes I love the clean and simple looks of early mod girls as well as the usual female 60's style icons (pretty much any French or Italian actress from the era looks fantastic to me, and obviously Twiggy for the hair) but really I have been more influenced by stylish friends for ideas.

Being a female on the scene has been super easy for me. I've found that though there is some initial scepticism, the guys are really happy to have chicks around. For example, the first rally of our female scooter club was boycotted by the big male club in San Francisco as they were sure we would screw it up and embarrass them. When we pulled it off they were so impressed they were trying to organise things with us all the time, and later on decided to break their male only rules and invite females in, not because they were so enlightened but because they were impressed and they wanted help! Once you show that you are serious and can do a good job people tend to be super welcoming. People get tired of going to events where it's all guys!

Back across the Atlantic in late 1986, Tony Class, now in self-imposed exile from the scooterist events, concentrated on purely mod rallies. EDDIE PILLER gives this assessment of Tony Class's contribution to the mod scene:
A lot of people don't talk about Tony Class. Without him there would never have been a mod scene in '79. Tony and his brother ran clubs every night of the week, mostly in south London from 1980 to about 1982 during the dark days when the bands were finding it difficult, Tony Class was doing it every night of the week.

DAVE EDWARDS also has good reason to remember Tony Class with great respect and admiration:
Tony Class gave me one of my first chances to DJ. It was at The Bizz in Tooley Street. Tony has undoubtedly had a large impact on the scene. It's easy for people to say he was in it just to make money, but Tony genuinely loved the scene. He'd drive all over the country to find venues and put events on. I had many great nights out with him. He was funny and lived his life to the full. For me, his nights were an introduction to this great scene of ours, they were fun and yes, we outgrew them but I always had a respect for what Tony gave us. Tony's sons Richard and Jamie asked me to DJ at his funeral which I was honoured to have been asked to do.

In 1986, a national mod meeting in Lowestoft led to the formation of a rival organisation to the Phoenix Society still being run by Mark Johnson. This became a turning point for EDDIE PILLER, as he explains why he began to put distance between himself and the mod scene:
The whole thing got spoilt though when Mark Johnson got involved. He got it organised

and regimented with the Phoenix List, and although it was good to know what was going on, we put up with it for a couple of years until we realised he was involved for all the wrong reasons and it just imploded. That was the end of it for me by 1986.

I tried for years to get away from being a mod. It was things like, I got a phone call from BBC Wales, who said "What's the official mod comment on the death of Steve Marriott?" and I just thought "Fuck off!"

So I grew my hair and grew a beard, but I was still a mod. I wanted to get away from people like Mark Johnson who were just being wankers for that whole period. They were nothing to be proud of in that scene.

Mod is a form of fascism anyway. Not in terms of being racist because its culture is based around black culture, but in terms of its codes and ideas it's very 'fascistic'. It follows set formats and it's very easy to take that one stage further which is, 'Right, now you do what I say'. and when they are all 15 years-old kids, well we could only put up with it for a while.

Johnson coordinated a lot of things and he helped me sell a lot of fanzines, but that was before we knew what he was about. He was in his mid thirties at the time, so he was much older than us. But I'm glad I distanced myself from it.

The thing is, as I get older, I find myself being drawn back to the concept and philosophy of being a mod anyway.

TONY CLASS had a fundamental disagreement with Mark Johnson which resulted in the formation of the Classic Club International (CCI) as Tony told Scootering Magazine, I disagreed with Mark Johnson and the way he perceived things with the Phoenix List. That was his voice, and I wanted my own voice. We employed many people on a committee from around the country so that everyone had a say in what was going on. I've always believed it should be democratic, but eventually having a committee became farcical. The way other organisations see the mod scene is different from the way I see it. I see it as a scene for people that want to go out and have a party.

Musically, mods and scooterists had to rely on rediscovering forgotten tunes and

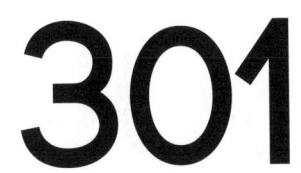

uncovering hidden gems from the past. Northern Soul, R&B and British Beat bands were in the forefront, but those hard-to-find floorfillers began to surface.
Freakbeat was also very popular. Freakbeat represented that period between the end of mod and the start of psychedelia in the sixties. Mark Bolan's rare 'Third Degree', tracks by The Action, The Creation, The Birds and David Bowie's work with the King Bees and The Lower Third were finding a new generation of mods and scooterists.

In America, the psychedelic scene was thriving on the West Coast. **ANTHONY MEYNELL** explains how he came to make connections in America and why he left the UK for a while: My influences have always been power pop and when I was in America, I was very aware of the psychedelia scene there, The Rain Parade, The Bangles, The Three O'clock. I got to meet them all and they had an influence on me. Then there was The Plimpsoles, The DB, The Twenty-Twenty and I found a kinship with those bands because there wasn't another band like Squire in the UK anymore.
The Americans liked 'Girl On A Train' and the 'Get Smart' album because it wasn't overtly mod, but Squire was a pop band and we were well received. Although we looked mod, we were pop as well, but the mod idealism was still there. The idealism that I knew was one of really enthusiastic people, all doing something. They've got a fanzine, they've got a label, they've got an attitude, they want to go somewhere, they want to create something, it's very important and they had a style, which, if it's not dress, it's just self-esteem, or they strive to that anyway.
So that was quite attractive and I wanted to get out of the UK for a while. When 'September Girls' came out it was diss-ed in the press and it was disheartening, so I thought I would go to California, try and form a band and see what happened. I got to meet the right people and started doing gigs and eventually I got a bit lonely, but I had become friends with Ed Ball and Paul Bevoir of The Jetset and I told them they should come over because there was such a scene there. I told them they should come over and do some gigs, they wouldn't even need to get a band together and it was better than struggling back home. They came over and we did some gigs together and some radio and Ed then went back to London and Paul stayed on for a few more months.

We did some gigs as Squire again, but we did our last gig in San Francisco in 1986. Although Squire was great, I always wanted another band and as time moves on, you cease to become relevant anymore. It just seemed to be the right time to stop. I also found that I needed to get back to London, just to put myself back into context really. I continued writing songs and doing gigs and all sorts of interesting things where I was sort of looking for my roots as a writer and being more of a performer instead of dealing with the business side of it. Sometimes you get to a point where you just want to be a fan of music.

By the mid-80s in the UK, the scene seemed into split three distinct camps. The authentic mods that preferred original jazz, R&B and soul club nights; scooterists and a section of mods who were more into live bands. It was something of a barren period, but notable exceptions on the live circuit were Making Time, The Gents, Jetset with Paul Bevoir, The Truth came from the ashes of Nine Below Zero with Dennis Greaves at the helm, The Scene, The Boss whose core support was based in their home county of Essex, Small World, The Onlookers, The E-Types, The Threads and The Moment.

One of the stranger curiosities of that time was Eleanor Rigby. Even her real name is a mystery, but she had generated some interest under the guidance of Russell Brennan; Basically Waterloo Sunset was a mod label predominately set up to put out Eleanor Rigby's releases. After doing well in '82,'83 with live concerts, Eleanor got a lot of major record company interest - but there were always too many sticking points to these deals. She was asked to ditch her mod image in favour of a 'Bananarama' type image, as they claimed it was too restricting.
They were also concerned about the controversial nature of some of her songs like the legendary "I Want To Sleep With You" and "1995" and wanted her to do thee cover versions of sixties songs like a successful group at the time The Belle Stars.
There were two other bands on the label as far as singles went. The Reaction were a mod band from Bristol who originally approached me with a tape with a view to a support slot with Eleanor. We loved the music so much we signed them straight away

and released "Make Up Your Mind" which was an instant mod classic. Record Mirror even called it the mod record of '87. Sadly the group spilt up not long after this and didn't fulfil their promise. The other act was A Beatboy who were the number one mod act in Belgium. Their single "The Honeydripper" sold extremely well for a foreign act.

The Waterloo Sunset label did not last long though, mainly due to a monumental cock-up by the Post Office who, having been paid for a mailout service to 4,000 fans waiting for Eleanor Rigby's new single, forgot to frank the mail and charged the fans postage. Needless to say the backlash crippled the label and it was wound up in 1988.

Despite touring Europe and recording her only album, 'Censorship', Eleanor Rigby suddenly disappeared. To this day, no one has ever been able to explain where she went or what happened to her. Even Russell Brennan has no idea where she is, although it was claimed she had been spotted in the Caribbean some years ago, but it turned out to be a false trail. She has never been found and remains something of a minor pop enigma.

DAVE EDWARDS has good cause to remember Eleanor Rigby though:
I started DJing in 1985, Saturday 28th September to be exact at Caterham Liesure Centre for Eleanor Rigby and The Moment. I'd never intended to start DJing, I was just collecting records when one day my friend Craig Semplis said he bought a set of decks and had been asked to do this gig. Knowing I had a few records, he asked if I'd like to help out and it took off from there.
There were two Eleanor Rigbys, the first one left and her mentor Russell Brennan found a clone. I never knew her real name. The gig I did with her was dreadful. The Moment were on first and they were great, but I found Eleanor Rigby very tacky, thigh length white boots, plastic Mac, too much make up and dreadful songs.
Luckily for us, our last train back to London was quite early so we left halfway through her set. My contact for Eleanor (her drummer no less!) said no one knows who she really was, except Russell Brennan.

Another independent label that would find far greater success through the eighties and

> It's also good seeing a mod lineage going back through BritPop and Acid Jazz to the eighties scene and for people not afraid of declaring their mod roots.
>
> DON HOSIE

nineties was Creation Records. It had found some success with bands like the Jesus and Mary Chain. By the latter stages of the decade **ED BALL** found himself at something of a loose end and accepted an offer from a friend:

I'd known Alan McGee since 1983 and I had my own label called 'Artpop' and put out six albums and a load of singles including the first Small World single. By '86, '87, I was starting to get stretched financially, our sales were dwindling for both my bands, so I joined Creation in 1988, first as an artist, I did an album, then Alan said "Listen you've had your own label, you know how the business works, manufacturing records and how press works, why not work for the label?" So, apart from him and his business partner, Dick Green, I was the next one in. When I did join Creation, it had bands like Jesus and Mary Chain, and Alan had built a reputation with them, but they parted ways and Alan was revamping the label again. He had My Bloody Valentine and House Of Love were just about to break and the Primal Scream were just going into their Stooges, MC5 period. An exciting time, primarily because of My Bloody Valentine and House Of Love.

By this time, Eddie Piller and his Countdown label had run its course, although Eddie had once again broken new ground, particularly on the '54321 Go' compilation which included 'Bend Don't Break' by Stupidity, an Australian band fronted by **DON HOSIE**:

I formed Stupidity for a number of reasons. Firstly to help fill the void left in my life by the breaking up of The Sets. Secondly, to release a decent single to make up for the disappointment I felt over The Sets single and thirdly to prove to myself that I could form a band in my own right. With The Sets, I was basically the dancer, come bodyguard and back-up vocalist. You've got to remember that at that stage, there were only a handful of mods in Sydney surrounded by hundreds of punks that were against us because of the stupid tribal mentality that always tends to infect these scenes. We were all in the same boat for chrissakes, providing an alternative to the bland mainstream, but all the punks had to be stupid about it. A few game punks would try and disrupt the odd mod do, so part of my role in The Sets was to be the free man who could leap off stage and thump punks when required. Having two front men was therefore part survival and part stage act, and when both front men are off stage fighting, what an act! You need to have a few instrumentals up your sleeve though and The Sets covered that too! Stupidity was my way of proving to myself that I could be a front man in my own right.

Back in Britain, and after four years, Makin' Time fell apart under the strain of touring. Things came to a head after a long European tour, playing to the growing mod scene across Europe, but particularly in Germany. By 1986 the band was history. Martin Blunt went back to Birmingham and formed a new band with ex-Prisoners guitarist Graham Day and organist and singer **FAY HALLAM**:
Relations with Mark were not great. At the same time we'd played lots of gigs with The Prisoners. Both bands split at the same time and as I'd started going out with Graham Day it made sense to play in a band together.
Martin had met Jon Brookes and they spent many hours rehearsing just bass and drums. Martin was driven to succeed. We did a tour of Germany and when we got back, because half the band was living in Wolverhampton and half in Kent, logistically it was a nightmare so we decided to call it a day.

Blunt and Brookes went back to the drawing board and started putting a new band together. It would take a couple of years before things came together and they would finally find success as The Charlatans.
The Charlatan's manager Steve Harrison already knew Martin Blunt on nodding terms, as both had been on the scooter scene some years before. Harrison often rode with the Cheshire Midnight Runners, but having been involved with the indie scene and having good contacts made Harrison a sound choice.
In Eddie Piller's opinion though, Makin' Times' demise denied British pop fans access to yet another in a long line of true talent that has never been given proper recognition:
Martin Blunt became very successful with The Charlatans, but Fay Hallam was the driving force behind Makin' Time and she was disappointed when it didn't work out, but she was and still is great. She's like a modern day Julie Driscoll.

Meanwhile, in another part of the Midlands, specifically, the Tamworth/Atherstone area a meeting of minds came about that would last over 30 years. **NEIL SHEASBY** takes up the story:

I first met Phil Ford at infant's school. I was six and he was five. I never knew he could play drums, although at the age of eight he was playing trombone at school. We didn't hang out much outside of school because I was a year older and had friends my own age. So one day my best friend Hammy says "Let's form a band" even though we couldn't play a thing. Our mate Gibby had a drum kit and Hammy was given a guitar. So I went round Hammy's house and the guitar is a wreck. It had three strings, bits were falling off it, but he figured out how to play that riff from The Who's 'I'm Free' on one string and that was all he could play for hours and hours.

So he decided I'm going to play bass. Now I knew a lad from way back called Nick Thomas who came from a post-punk background and he could play guitar. By the end of '82, my dad cottoned onto the fact we had been talking about starting a band. One day he said "So you're starting a band? Are you playing bass then? Because a fella at work is selling one, I'll ask him how much he wants for it". I thought no more of it until I came home from school one day and my dad says "I got something for you. It's in your bedroom". I went up to my room and opened this guitar case and there was a Rickenbacker bass guitar. My dad said "You'd best learn how to play that 'cause it weren't cheap" I've still got that guitar today.

So I got local bass players to give me tips on how to play it and eventually me, Hammy, Gibby and Nick Thomas decided to have a proper rehearsal.

Well Gibby didn't have a drum kit, but Phil Ford did, so he let us go round his house to rehearse and use his kit. Gibby was ok on the drums and by that I mean he could keep time, just about, but Phil would jump on to show Gibby how it should be done and he was amazing for a 12 year old.

We spent a couple of years of doing this, trying to improve and learning songs, but it was obvious Gibby was not going to cut it. He didn't have a drum kit and Phil was so much better, so although it was horrible telling Gibby he was out, we got Phil in.

That's when Mark Mortimer came into the frame because we went to see Dream

Factory and there was Mark with these amazing psychedellic hipster trousers on and he had a brass section and a couple of girls singing, it was just an electric show.

We started following them everywhere. Eventually, Mark told us to get five or six songs together and he would give us a support slot and our first ever gig was at Baddesley Youth Club supporting Dream Factory. We told everyone about it and when we got there on the night it was like The Beatles turning up!

There were girls from school screaming at us, but we did ourselves proud, we didn't embarrass ourselves and that in turn boosted our confidence with each gig after that which really accumulated in the gig at Tamworth Arts Centre.

That night was almost like a happening. It was packed to the rafters, Dream Factory supported by In Crowd.

Sam Halliday did a review in Music Box in the Tamworth Herald and everyone at school was on about it. We got a paragraph, but he really liked us and wanted to do a follow up feature on us. We had a great form tutor at school called Torsten Freedo who allowed us to rehearse at the school hall, so he was very instrumental in encouraging us to keep going with the band.

What both Dream Factory and In Crowd had were people around us who always said "Why not?" instead of "Why?" Both bands were encouraged and supported a lot by parents, teachers, family and friends. It was very important to us.

Over time In Crowd morphed into Dance Stance and at the age of 17 or 18, we found ourselves on the University/College circuit which was great.

MARK MORTIMER gives this account of his own path into mod and music:

My mum was an ex-professional country singer and I was reared on a diet of classical music, country music, the Everly Brothers and the Beatles.

When punk exploded I was 11 and that had a profound effect on my life. From the first discovery of bands like Television, the Stranglers, and the Pistols, everything fell into place for me.

Like most people of my age, my first connection came from the overt mod influences The Jam were espousing and then sneaking in the cinema under age to watch

"Quadrophenia" in '79 further fuelled it. By then my 'mod' experience was widening fast and I'd already started exploring the many branches that led from the main body as I wasn't really much into the 1979 revival bands.

In the very early 80s I managed to sneak into a few events in Birmingham & then played at some with my then group, the Dream Factory, who probably had a 50-50 split of mods and scooterists following us at the time.

Post that era I went to some Untouchables and then New Untouchables events but, to be honest, as I've been a ferociously full-on gigging musician since my mid-teens, I've spent more time on stage than attending clubs.

Dream Factory was the template for pretty much everything I've done since. It was never an out-and-out mod band, it was far more eclectic.

Dream Facorty's problems became apparent because we were not a straight mod revival band. Me and Donald Skinner set out to make it a kind of garage/psych type band and the first recording we did sounded like that. Then Donald joined Julien Cope and Dream Factory drifted into a kind of soul sound. You could never compare us to Makin Time because we were a long way from their type of sound.

I think we just filled a void locally in the Midlands at that time. Remember, The Jam had just finished, but I think we became a local focus for people who wanted another band to follow. And at the gigs, that's pretty much what happened. It really was like being at a Jam gig in the sense that when you got into the venue, everyone else was like your best mate for the next hour and a half. They were extraordinary occasions that I've never seen since. We picked up this dedicated fan base and people really bought into it. The scooterboys started to follow us. We did an interview with Sounds in '84, but they set us up and tried us to steer us into criticising the mod scene. The Sounds article was damning and they really badly misquoted us and we never really recovered from that.

Chris Hunt of Shadows and Reflections fanzine got the original recording of that interview and published it verbatim, which vindicated us somewhat, but I always thought Gary Bushell was behind that whole saga because he was looking to stir it up between scooter skins and mods.

Dream Factory had a single in '85 that got into the lower reaches of the chart and in the Indie Chart, at one point we were above The Jesus and Mary Chain and The Smiths which was amazing. But it didn't quite happen.

We were being looked after by a well-known Northern Soul DJ called Neil Rushton. He was trying to get us to the next level, but by late '86, we were starting to be a bit passé. He did get us into Expresso Bongo Studios to do a session for the Silvertone label who were very interested in us and another band from Manchester. They decided to sign the other band who happened to be The Stone Roses.

After that we fell part due to differences. I wanted a harder sound and others in the band wanted to be more like Sade. So I went to work for Neil Rushton who had set up the Network Record label which was primarily about dance music, soulful house and not long after I joined as head of publicity, we had a number one with KWS 'Please Don't Go'. The follow up was a top 10 hit. It was another cover of 'Rock Your Baby' and they were on Top Of The Pops, but they wanted a brass section for that show, so I got half the Dance Stance brass section and half the Dream Factory brass section on TOTP miming with KWS.

Now Paul Weller was on that show as well and I had met him before. I blagged my way into Solid Bond studios a few years before and got chatting to him. To my amazement, he already knew about Dream Factory because our fans had spoken to him about us at Style Council gigs. He said he liked our music and there was some discussion about doing support slots for Style Council which never came off, but I still have a hand-wriiten letter from Paul saying how much he liked the music. So by the time the 90s came around, I was still working for Network, but the genesis of DC Fontana started then.

Oddly enough, there were two singer/songwriter guitarists in Tamworth, both named Neil Jones. One came in with me with DC Fontana and the other one joined up with Neil Sheasby.

After Paul Weller had ended The Jam, his new venture The Style Council left many Jam fans in confusion and subsequently left them behind. Weller's direction was for a more cosmopolitan sound and look. After the initial singles and mini LP, it was clear he had not surrendered his love of mod, but merely adopted another facet of mod life based in the modern jazz tradition.

Nowhere was this more evident than in the first full album 'Cafe Bleu' released in 1984. The influence of Mick Talbot who joined Weller from The Merton Parkas was clear right from the off and with Steve White, arguably the finest drummer of his generation, providing the dexterity to match Weller's ambitions, The Style Council were far better than people gave them credit for. Not least of which was the technical proficiency of the band to tackle virtually any genre of music.

Although many of Weller's fans had problems with his musical aspirations, it was events outside of music that also led to a distancing of the fan base. Weller's involvement with politics and the 'Red Wedge' venture did not sit well with the a-political mod following. Nevertheless, Weller's influence was to surface in later years. His fascination with modern jazz with The Style Council led to others becoming interested and producing a new breed of mod-based jazz fans that created a scene entirely of their own making and their influence was to be found later in the decade and into the next.

In 1987 sad news arrived from Australia that Ben Sherman, who had sold his shirt company in 1975 and retired 'Down Under', had died aged just 62.

The mid to late eighties were arguably the worst period for banality in the mainstream pop world. There was very little musically for people to get excited about. Tony Wilson's Factory label was still producing interesting music, but bands like Everything But The Girl, Hurrah and Prefab Sprout were finding it hard to break through while The Smiths, New Order, The Cure and Echo and The Bunnymen, were struggling to hold their own. The UK charts were dominated by middle of the road and to put it bluntly, boring bands. The domination of the UK charts and airwaves by The Eurythmics, Michael Jackson, Dire Straits, Queen and the Stock, Aitkin and Waterman stable continued until 1987 when Acid House began to make an impact and at the same time gave others inspiration to provide an alternative to the smiley faced ravers who roamed the country trying to find secret raves that would be shut down as soon as the police discovered their whereabouts. Rave culture became another victim of moral panic by mainstream society. It was not violence so much, but more a concern about a new recreational drug, ecstasy or 'E's as they became known. E's, like purple hearts, black bombers and French blues before them, were designed to keep ravers dancing all night, but as with most drugs, they could prove fatal if misused, and even more so if mixed with alcohol. The tragedy of Leah Betts in the nineties, was perhaps the starkest warning of how dangerous they could be, and to make matters worse, rogue batches of poor quality and more highly dangerous E's were circulating.

Out of rave culture came a curious hybrid, made up of mod, punk and sixties sensibilities with a contemporary twist known as Baggy, not unlike the early work of Primal Scream. JOE FOSTER, now working for Creation Records, explains how Primal Scream interpreted their influences:

Bobby (Gillespie) was an old friend of ours and had this group that did different types of music and basically for the first few records, they chose one style of music they could do at random. It was kind of like The Byrds and then they'd twist it in a different way and then do something different again with it. Then they would find a way of pulling all these eclectic bits together.

At a certain point, there was a reorganisation of the band and Andrew Innes was brought in and Andrew's thing is very cheesy sixties pop and northern soul. He would talk knowledgably about northern soul and then play the Joe 90 theme note perfect. He likes all kinds of odd things that he finds interesting and that's what he did with the band. He would seize on something that sounded oddly interesting, run with it and take it somewhere else. He was a good person to bring into the band to reinforce what they were doing. The big fun is to go to a Primal Scream sound check where they will play all kinds of music just for their own amusement, absolutely spot on. In fact it's quite frightening really, when they play something from a Love album and then play 'The Boy's Are Back In Town' by Thin Lizzy and it sounds better than the original, and that's just testing the system at a sound check. They can do that, and it's very interesting seeing how all these millions of influences shape this eclectic music that's been twisted and developed.

Primal Scream's landmark album 'Screamadelica' found a large scooterist audience as well as indie music fans, and **JOE FOSTER** suggests why the scooterists have taken to Primal Scream:

I think subliminally it would get to people like that because they would hear everything that they were into and somehow they can't quite place how it's fitted in there and that would intrigue them. I think that's the secret of their success among people who are into music. No matter what you're into you would somehow hear it and it's intriguing how they use it and it couldn't have been done better if they had done it absolutely cold and deliberately. Experimentalism is what they like and it certainly works.

The Baggy scene made up of white kids with hedonistic tendencies, created their own sound to suit their time. One city in particular seemed to be fertile ground for the baggy scene. So much so, that it became known as Madchester.

While rave, baggy and America's answer to baggy, grunge, became the focus of attention for the mainstream, the underground mod and scooter scenes were still going and **ROB BAILEY** began attending mod rallies:

The first run I went on, I think it was Lowestoft in 1987 which was a Classic Club International (CCI) do, and we did a couple of others that year. The Isle of Wight, Margate and Folkestone, which were all fairly local to our club. They were within easy driving distance on 50cc scooters. The runs were a real eye-opener, and the trips to London became more frequent and I think after I left school, the local scene died down a bit. There were people like myself who were really into it and others on the periphery who dropped out. The difference between a club in London and a local event were miles apart. Certainly musically and clothes-wise, the attraction to London was stronger.

By 1987, there were less of us. There were still 20 or so who were going to the weekenders, but we were doing less locally and travelling more around the country and going to London more and more.

On a personal level, I had started getting really interested in records and collecting

records. I started playing guest spots at some of the London nights and CCI events and by the late eighties I started doing my own nights with other deejays like Tony Shockman. We did nights at places like The Crown and Sceptre, all-nighters at Herne Bay, The Mojo club, a night at Rails, and Drummonds in Kings Cross.
That was happening from about 1988 onwards when I started doing my own nights and promotions

In the late eighties, **BRIAN BETTRIDGE** came into contact with someone who reminded Brian of a familiar name from the past:
By 1989, I started working at The National Film Theatre (NFT) and at the beginning of 1990, there was a girl who worked at the NFT called Julie who was a bit mod. She came from Romford and she knew people like Eddie Piller, who I knew in the eighties. I think Eddie gets a lot of flack just for being Eddie really. I mean I've got no problem with the Acid Jazz thing, and the times that I see Eddie, he's always really pleased to see me. I know some people can't
stand the sight of him, but I could never say anything against Eddie.
He got people listening to the stuff he was into when he changed from Re-Elect The President to Acid Jazz. He had a huge social scene around him, and I guess people thought there was something in it. At least, that's how I saw it, but I wasn't part of it.
I got to know Eddie in 1980 and I remember him prior to that at the gigs. He says, quite rightly, that Acid Jazz is a label and not a genre. Well, I saw him once and said: "If people think Acid Jazz is a genre and they're listening to stuff on your label, then that can't be a bad thing".
But the fact that we are talking about Acid Jazz as a genre, that it was his label and that it was written as a piss-take on a tape from Gilles Peterson, that shows you that on a musical level, he is influential, whatever you think of him.
He also has a lot of fondness for '79 and he's not snobbish about it. He knows where he's from and he knows where he's at.
Musically, he makes people think when he does things like playing Fela Kuti along with Hammond organ grooves on GLR (Greater London Radio).

It works and doing that is brilliant, but that's my honest view about Eddie's contribution in the overall scheme of things.

When asked about his reputation, **EDDIE PILLER** made this response:
I've always had a lot of stick from people for organising things, but my point was, if I don't do it then someone else will do it and it's going to be rubbish, so that's why I'm doing it. The only things I've heard people say about me is that I'm a flash bastard and I'm tight, but it's rubbish. I do what I do and that's all there is to it.
Someone has to step forward. If I think I can do it I will, and in working class hierarchical situations, I've pissed people off because I was better at organising than they were. I never told anyone to not go to this club or that club, I just said, come to mine, so then you get enemies.

Eddie Piller was still into mod, but not quite as involved as he once was. When he met Gilles Peterson in '87 they formed Acid Jazz Records.
Peterson had been a DJ for quite a while and had experimented with mixing elements of Northern Soul, Jazz Funk, Reggae and Hip Hop. The first release on Acid Jazz was 'Frederic Lies Still' by Rob Galliano. It was a spoken poem laid over Curtis Mayfield's 'Freddie's Dead'. The track set the tone for the label.
Eddie explains how he came to form the label, what he was trying to achieve:
There are loads of versions of where Acid Jazz came from. I think the name was probably invented by a DJ called Chris Bangs, who was not a mod but was part of the soul scene. In fact, Rob Galliano once described Acid Jazz as the coming together of mods and soul boys.
Soul boys through Gilles Peterson and the mods through me and if you mixed the two up, you got Galliano, The Young Disciples and The Brand New Heavies.
I know why I started Acid Jazz. I deejayed at a mod weekender in Lowestoft in 1985 and played Archie Bell and The Drells' 'Tighten Up' which not a particularly radical tune, it's 1966, it's a mod tune. But because it's got a funk beat to it, everyone walked off the dance floor. I thought this was the end for me, because if those people couldn't

understand that it was a mod tune, then they weren't mods in my opinion. They can dance to Freakbeat all night if they want to, but if they can't get 'Tighten Up', one of the greatest dance tunes of all time, then forget it.

I met Gilles Peterson about the same time and it was very easy to step across from the mod scene to his scene, because he was playing 'Wack Wack' by Young Holt Trio and Jimmy Smith and Jack McDuff and the organists, which is what we really liked, so you could hear better mod music on the jazz scene and there was none of that dress code stuff that was in the mod scene at the time.

The jazz scene was ready made for us and it was much more open and they had girls in it as well. There were hardly any girls at all in the mod scene.

We already had James Taylor a few years before Acid Jazz came about. It seemed the next logical step.

We were dancing to modern soul, northern soul, two-step soul and jazz funk, then overnight, everyone went on a 'Special Branch' tour to Ibiza and they all started taking ecstasy and people like Andy Weatherall and Judge Jules, who were basically rare groove DJs, they got into house. For six months Acid House was really exciting.

It had nothing to do with mod, but after a while, we wanted to go back to our soul, jazz and R&B, but no one was interested, so we had to come up with an angle to promote it. There were a couple of clubs. Cock Happy at the Cock Tavern in Smithfields and Voice Your Choice in Cork's Wine Bar in Mayfair which me, Dean Rudland and John Cook used to do.

John was the graphic designer for Countdown. These were the early Acid Jazz nights, added to Ronnie Scott's and Gilles Peterson at The Wag club. So it was a brilliant scene, it was better and easily replaced the mod scene, but you could still be a mod and be in it.

Also in 1987, a young 14 year-old was making a few quid with an after-school job. His name is **PETER CHALLIS**:

I'm originally from Northamptonshire but moved around the Midlands as my mother was a district nurse, and she had to go where the job took her. We settled in the mid

70's in a small village called Earl Shilton, just a few miles outside Leicester. I went to school in Earl Shilton and then onto high school & college in the neighbouring village of Barwell.

Growing up around two older brothers and a sister you could say I was born listening to music; plus my mother always had her radio on - from the minute she got up it was on and filled the house with tunes and banter.

Also my parents had an old upright piano and they played regularly, so did my sister and one brother played guitar. I used to go to sleep in a crowded bedroom to the sound of an old Dansette playing various tunes of the 60' and 70's - David Bowie, The Beatles, Wings, and The Jam amongst other groups.

You could say that Mod found me; having such a wide baptism in music I've been interested in many genres to be honest - and the journey to mod has been an interesting one; with many incarnations along the way. However the 60's have a magical hold over me and that's where it all started I guess.

The Small Faces really do it for me - the soulful swagger and the cool clothes are what finally turned my head.

Living in a Midlands outpost it's not been easy to find or get to mod gigs or clubs growing up - however we did have a couple of local bars - called Karns and The Greyhound, which regularly put on a variety of bands and quite often they would come up trumps.

Scooter rallies have of course been a venue of choice over the years and one in particular that became a regular spot on the calendar was Mersey Island - end of the season and usually decent weather - I always enjoyed the Ska and Northern soul room.

I've been in the shoe trade since the tender age of 14 - sweeping up after school in a shoe mould-making factory and then worked full time there when I was 16. The two local villages (Shilton & Barwell) boasted around 15 shoe factories in the late 1980's and it was a vibrant hardworking area.

British Shoe Corporation was down the road in Leicester and was home to some of the country's famous retail chains of the day - Dolcis, Saxone, Freeman Hardy & Willis

& Trueform - to name a few. I soon joined there and became a post boy - the place was vast and you needed to ride a bicycle to get around the place. They opened up many opportunities, sent me on footwear college courses, factory visits, store visits and eventually around the world in making and buying shoes.

Another young man who would come from the mod scene to create a highly successful career is **DEAN RUDLAND**:

The first record I really remember making an impression was a Drifters Greatest Hits which my mum bought in the mid Seventies and played a lot. After that I got into the Beatles, The Jam and then 60s soul through the mod scene.

In the mid 80s, when I was 15 or 16 years-old, the mod scene had moved on from the revival period and into 60s soul and R&B. the records had to be looked for, but were available, so I started pestering DJs for titles and artists and got a collection together via charity shops, car boot fairs and second-hand record shops.

Everyone on the mod scene back then was young; hardly anyone was over 20 and it was very much about doing your own thing, so along with a couple of other guys (one of them being Dave Edwards), we put on a night at a wine bar in Victoria that my dad found for us. We started DJing and got the bug.

Eventually, after the mod scene, I started hanging around the jazz scene just as it evolved into Acid Jazz. I did the club at Cork's with Eddie Piller and I was at university not far from the Acid Jazz offices. One day I popped in to see him and he offered me a job. I was there for five years where we signed some of the biggest artists of the 90s, plus we had our highly successful Totally Wired compilation series which was a few old tracks, some of our favourite current releases and some of the Acid Jazz new bands. That's where I got a reputation as a compiler.

Then I met Tony Harlow who was in charge of Blue Note Europe and we started doing the 'Blue Series' which included the hugely successful 'Blue Beat Breaks' and 'Blue Juice' compilations. From there, I went into the world of back catalogue; relaunching EMI's Stateside label, working with Fania Records and eventually being A&R consultant for Ace Records, running their BGP subsidiary.

Brighton [courtesy of Mary Boogaloo]

Having got Acid Jazz up and running, **EDDIE PILLER** attempted to secure a deal with one of Britain's mod and music icons:

What I'm good at is picking up on something early and building it to the point where it goes commercial and selling it on.

I had The Brand New Heavies on Acid Jazz through London Records for years, and with Jamiroquai, well Jay Kay is a superstar and we couldn't cope with it. Just three of us in a little office in Hackney. So he needs to be on Sony. What pissed me off was Sony rewrote the press release and said they gave Jamiroquai to Acid Jazz to develop, which is bollocks. I tried to sell the band to Sony many months before and they didn't want to know, so I took it to America where success counts. Over here, it's all very snobby. I've always been on the outside of the industry. Anyway, Jamiroquai were just coming through. I had Mother Earth coming through, so I thought I had a lot of good stuff and wanted something big and Paul Weller was doing his first solo album on his own, but he had a deal in Japan. So I went to see Roger Aimes, who is now Head of Warners Worldwide, and I told him I wanted to sign Paul and they would pay for it, it was all in the business plan. They would sign Paul, Jamiroquai and all the other bands and he turned it down.

I was a bit despondent because I couldn't sign Paul without getting someone to pay for it, but he did a couple tracks for us and some backing vocals and hung around the studio working with Marco Nelson, Matt Deighton and Ocean Colour Scene and he was a massive inspiration.

Inspite of it being fashionable to slag Weller off at the time, especially when he said casuals were the logical extension of mod, he just wanted to get away from it. I mean every gig he did he was surrounded by kids in parkas going "We are the mods", I mean, come on. It must have driven him mad.

So I think Acid Jazz was perfect for Paul because it was mod, but not mod, if you see what I mean? You didn't have to be a mod to be in it and I also think it gave him the room to express the elements of funk that he tried to express in the late Jam with 'Beat Surrender', 'Move On Up' and 'Stoned Out Of My Mind', but didn't quite work because I don't think the musicians were flexible enough to do it.

I think he was always into the Acid Jazz concept, but it wasn't until we came along that he could see a lot of people he knew anyway, who were into the same kind of thing. He was at the offices after work and going to the clubs and he deejayed at the Magic Bus once for us, but he is my total hero. Without him, there would have been none of this. There would never have been Acid Jazz, because without him, I would never have got into music.

By 1989, Gilles Peterson took a job with Polygram to set up Talkin' Loud Records and left Eddie Piller to carry on alone with Acid Jazz. It was not easy for Piller, particularly his relationship with the established music business.
Just as Paul Weller was becoming frustrated by the staid and 'balance sheet' mentality of the power brokers in the industry, so Eddie Piller found himself in the same predicament. An article in Soul CD magazine highlights the problems Eddie was facing:
Having signed The Brand New Heavies to Acid Jazz, Eddie poured his life savings into recording their first album. On its completion, a tape was played to the head of A&R at a major record company. The man (who Eddie refuses to name) listened to the tape for about two minutes. Then he reached over, took out the cassette from his machine and threw it into the wastepaper basket.
"Now," he said, "have you got any proper music to play me?"
"I think it just sums up the attitude of the music industry, which is run by 45 year-old, well-off, badly-dressed men who have money and power but don't have a fucking clue. That's why we just see bollocks in the charts. You don't see music in there, and that upsets me".
Even though Acid Jazz had a hard time getting their music released, it is testament to Eddie Piller's resolve and determination that bands like Jamiroquai and Brand New Heavies have become household names, even though his contribution to the early days of their careers seems to have been overlooked. Not that it particularly bothers Eddie.

By this time, **RICHARD SEARLE** had left Doctor and The Medics and briefly joined a new band that had a loyal following:
Boys Wonder were friends, they were truly great. They sacked the bassist Chris

Tate and I filled in for a hand-full of gigs (a couple of head-lines at the Marquee and supporting The Hoodoo Gurus at the Town & Country, now The Forum).Tony Barber then joined.Despite being 'in vogue' they were dropped by their record label, Sire, and then sacked Tony Barber. The Medics had stopped being fun by this point, so when they asked me to join permanently, I did so. The band then started a long downhill spiral of musical styles, band wagon jumping and failed attempts to get re-signed. By the time Boys Wonder finished, we were truly shit.

DAVE EDWARDS was a massive Boys Wonder fan at the time and was going to see many bands:
I always checked out new bands and had seen The Charlatans early on as a four piece when they played with a The Dilemmas at the LSE. I'd followed Boys Wonder who mutated into Corduroy, Boys Wonder was possibly the best band I've ever seen and basically invented Britpop eight years too early.
I loved Corduroy and Mother Earth, I knew keyboardist Bryn from meeting him in a record shop.
Acid Jazz put some great stuff out, they still do, they had another band called Subjagger who were brilliant. I've always felt that if there's a strong live scene, there'll be a healthy club scene. I know some people don't like live bands but for me it goes hand in hand.

RICHARD SEARLE takes up the story of Corduroy's emergence:
Acid Jazz were one of three record labels that the newly formed Corduroy went to see. Ed Piller booked us into his studio two days later. His first words to me were "Are you a mod?".
Acid Jazz became a refuge for displaced survivors of the mod revival, mainly because it was owned by one, but musically it was all over the place.
The Sandals came from the 'beat scene'; Emperor's New Clothes were proper jazzers, and Mother Earth just wanted to be Traffic. Some bands initially did appeal to mods (JTQ and then Corduroy) but I think musical tastes changed with the labels

output, which became quite 'fusion' orientated. Fifteen minute hip hop, jazz funk, jam sessions by stone-heads with pubic beards wearing socks on their heads - just isn't very mod.

We each had very different musical tastes, but we all shared a love of film music; this was the inspiration for the Corduroy sound at its best (the first two albums). By the third album, that uniting force had vanished (lost through ego and endless Steely Dan records). I will always regret not leaving Corduroy after the second album.

I guess the second album, 'High Havoc' was my proudest moment along with supporting Blur at Alexandra Palace (with Pulp and Supergrass). That was cool.

The Acid Jazz 'scene' meant that people would listen to you, who normally wouldn't, simply because they were into 'the scene'. At its best this meant that there was a family atmosphere between the bands, and a sense of belonging, plus lots of work. At its worst, by the time Acid Jazz stopped being known as the record label and became regarded as a music genre, the bands couldn't develop. When Brit-pop over shadowed and became more fashionable than the Acid Jazz scene, bands identified with 'the genre' were ultimately finished. The 'scene' itself moved back into the clubs eventually with Acid Jazz Records buying The Blue-Note Club.

The combination of Gilles Peterson and Eddie Piller in the first instance, and then individually when they took their own paths, laid the platform for bands to gain exposure to a wider audience.

When people talk of Acid Jazz as a genre, it inevitably includes the work of Peterson at Talkin' Loud. Between them they helped to bring a resurgent Incognito back to a wider audience as well as promoting the work of Galliano, Corduroy, The James Taylor Quartet, New Jersey Kings, Max Beesley, Terry Callier and Mother Earth, who were led by Matt Deighton who went on to work with Paul Weller before embarking on a solo career. That same platform opened the door for non-Acid Jazz acts like Omar, Misty Oldland and Mica Paris to be included in the genre. The final 'seal of approval' for the genre came when London's Jazz FM Radio gave airtime to most, if not all of the above mentioned musicians.

Mods of a certain age recognised the influences behind Acid Jazz, especially with ex-Prisoners James Taylor included, and that in itself is quite mod. To take an influence and give it a contemporary twist.

Away from the Acid Jazz scene, long-time mod scene favourites Fay Hallam and Graham Day started another band that included Allan Crockford and Wolf Howard. The Prime Movers was a marked departure from previous bands, as **FAY HALLAM** explained the main influence behind the band's songs:
Misery! I don't listen to old stuff very often, but I did listen to the Prime Movers albums one night a couple of years ago. It struck me how negative my songs were then. I was influenced by the underlying Medway melancholy. Medwaycholy.
Wolf hit the drums with huge force. Allan could play anything you threw at him. Graham played guitar like some sort of angry ear-splitting maniac. I had to up my game technically and also compete in volume. My songs became more powerful and a whole lot darker. You can't play Deep Purple type stuff and sing about puppy dogs.

GRAHAM DAY gave this assessment of the band:
I love the first album. It's totally raw and full of energy. We recorded it as a three-piece but never gigged as a three-piece. Fay used to join us on stage for half the set and then started writing songs and was soon with us full time.
The band changed pretty quickly due to Fay's influence. I have no idea what really happened to the sound, it turned into Deep Purple during the next two albums, and live I thought it was great, although pretty self-indulgent and very strange. I was quite happy to go along with it at the time because it was something different, but looking back on it I don't understand it at all.

On the European continent, a new club had started in Stureplan in Stockholm, Sweden at a venue called Bo's Bar in 1987. Uppers has always had a wide music policy ranging from sixties music, northern soul, jazz, R&B, ska, latin, acid jazz and easy listening. It has also introduced new bands and deejays to the public and provided an alternative to the mainstream. Within ten years, Uppers would become much more than just a club night for people interested in a particular style of music and clothes.

On the British mod rally scene, things were developing that would fracture the wafer-thin bond between the various groups. Most notably, it was Classic Club International that saw the first move on the scene.

TONY CLASS remembers when he first noticed a split forming, as he recalls in an interview with Scootering Magazine:

The people that started the Untouchables were the people that used to DJ for me. The reason they broke away - I think - is about money, and I want you to print that. The significant time was Great Yarmouth 1989 when I played the Charlatans 'The Only One I Know'. The dance floor was jam packed with people dancing, but around the edges were all the smartest people who don't usually dance anyway, because they're too busy looking good for themselves with their heads up their own arses. These are the ones that complained to me about playing that record.

However, becoming increasingly bored with the way that the CCI had gone about organising their events and with CCI's apparent lack of interest in developing beyond what had already become a standard set, a small group of South-East mods decided to break away and try to do something for other like-minded mods. The aim was to take a different approach to events and introduce a greater element of choice and to hopefully improve the mod scene overall.

Although pirate rallies had been run in the past through Paul Hallam and The Rhythm and Soul Set, no-one had breached the seemingly invincible position of the CCI.

By the spring of 1990 and the CCI Bridlington rally, it seemed to many that the CCI had reached a low point. There was an air of despondency among some of the older faces. Paul Anderson (Smiler), (Putney) Sean Tracey and Phil Otto got together to discuss the possibility of organising their own rallies. After resigning from the CCI committee later in the year, Anderson attended a meeting with fellow dissidents, Putney Sean, Phil Otto, Rob Bailey, Andy Hyde, Dave Edwards, Dom Strickland and Don Bassett at The Pontefract Castle in London's West End. It was decided that the group should form a network of clubs and rallies. The choice of two names were proposed, 'Knights of the Round Table' or 'The Untouchables'. They chose the latter.

It was not an easy decision to make for those concerned, as **DAVE EDWARDS** explained:
It was a difficult time as I said I wouldn't leave Tony, I genuinely liked him and he had given me a bigger stage to play on. I owed him that at the very least and am still indebted to him, rest his soul. But I was friends with all of those involved and understood the reasons they wanted to split from the CCI. I said I'd help them with flyers and DJ at their clubs but I made it clear that I would stay loyal to Tony alongside Ian Jackson.
It got to the point though where Tony's rallies became less populated by mods and more scooterist. It wasn't for me and hardly any of my mates were going and eventually I told him I was leaving. I think he understood and we stayed friends, Tony would DJ in my local pub and we did a couple of nights together at The Electric Ballroon in Camden.

ROB BAILEY explains his reasons for the formation of The Untouchables:
By the mid eighties Tony Class had decided to have less involvement with the National Scooter runs. From 1978 to about 1984, I believe, there was just one set of mod runs and as the eighties wore on, those people became less interested in mod and more interested in scooters, so the dressing up fell by the wayside and I think mods had a pretty hard time of it. This is why Tony Class and Mark Johnson started The Phoenix runs in 1984 for mods.
It was a bit before my time when it was just one organisation, then when there was one for mods, that's the one I went to. I've never had the pleasure of experiencing a National Scooter Run.
I think the problem was, and I also think it was echoed by a lot of other mods at the time, that Tony had been involved in it from the early days of the late seventies and hadn't really been able to move along with it and grow with it. Myself and others were trying to encourage him to do that with great difficulty. But by the very late eighties,

London [courtesy of Michael Merchant and Rob Murphy]

I think Tony was caught between two camps. People from the early to mid eighties wanted something a bit different than what Tony was offering. There were less of those people by then. The indie thing had kicked off and Tony was thinking about where he was going to find a new audience for what he was doing.

He ended up staying in the middle, trying to please both crowds and doing neither one thing nor the other.

On a personal level, it was very difficult for me because I got on very well with Tony and I thought he was a thoroughly good bloke and a great laugh and somebody I did have a lot of respect for.

With my mates, we had been doing our own nights for a while, which had become quite popular and I don't think Tony at that time was doing any regular club nights anymore. I don't think the London crowd were that interested at that point and there was a lot of pressure on myself and other people like Phil Otto, who was very active in The Clique.

Sean had been around a long time and was a well-known face and they were people I was hanging out with and we took responsibility for providing what our mates wanted but were not getting. To me it's all about going away with your mates and having a laugh, but at that point quite a few of my mates were still mods and were well into it, but they weren't interested in going away to CCI runs, so it was like 'where do you go from here?', you want to go away with your mates, but they don't want to go, so I think it was also a case of our age group being mature enough to hold our own dos.

As I said, personally, it was very difficult for me because I had been treated very well by Tony and given an opportunity to do something that I love. Tony was a fantastic deejay and a party deejay and he's definitely suited to the scootering crowd, you know? They like that wet-T shirt, dropping your draws, screaming, shouting and swearing over the microphone type of thing, the Irish jig and 'Up With The Cock' at the end of the night, they love it and it was a laugh to us at first, but when you take it seriously, which is what we were doing at the time, and certainly more seriously than Tony was, we just grew out of it. That's how I read the situation.

Some people might use the Charlatans thing as an excuse, but then there is another

argument to it, and this relates to Phil Otto, who won't mind me naming him, who was in a band at the time and playing good music. They wanted a break and needed a break and people who were mods and in bands and making good music, they weren't getting played. Now alright, the Charlatans had one person who was in a previous mod band, but they weren't pro-mod by any
means, and they were getting played, whereas people who were into the scene and in bands weren't getting pushed to the extent that would like to have done. So I think that's where a lot of those arguments came from.

There was a bit of confusion early on because some people couldn't make up their mind which direction to go, but I felt the London scene had out-grown what Tony was doing. I wouldn't say all the mods had out-grown it, but I would say about 60 per cent had. There were still a lot of mods who were still mods but weren't going anywhere, but the 60 per cent I'm talking about were the significant shift. The 30 per cent that were left had a particular loyalty to Tony. It was a period of people trying to decide what they wanted to do. Some were
doing both, but we were trying to do the more authentic thing and go back to the roots a bit more. Tony was trying to do that, but also the more modern things, '79 and the current thing. I don't think it really recovered from that. I think if he had played a lot more indie, he might have picked up more of that indie audience, but he didn't and he went back to entertaining the scooterist audience. They are the people that love him anyway and he was great at what he did,
but it's only funny for some people for a certain amount of time.

I was doing my own club nights which was separate from The Untouchables, but we decided to do a club night in London, which was the Mildmay Tavern. It was to fund the forthcoming runs for that year, so everything we made from those gigs went into a kitty which, from that, we managed to create a database and a newsletter every two or three months, telling people about events and telling them there was an alternative to what was going on.

The first run we did was Easter 1991 at Hastings in The Pier Ballroom which went very well. It was a period where, no one knew what was going to happen, but we were very pleased with the outcome. I think we had about 400 people at that one, which wasn't a bad start, especially as mod was going through a difficult period. The media hated it.

Saturday November 10, 1990 at the Mildmay Tavern became The Untouchables first event under the promise of "500 % Mod - A do with style but no Class" in reference to Tony Class who ran the CCI.
After a short period of unrest, where some of those who joined The Untouchables, had second thoughts and returned to the CCI, the first settled line-up was Anderson, Otto, Tracey, Strickland and Bailey, being quickly joined by another former CCI committee member Maz Weller. The Untouchables never set out to be an organisation along the same lines as others before them.
It was set up as an information service without hierarchy, without rules and without memberships. There was no such thing as an Untouchable, but merely an organisation free from the restrictions of a written constitution, membership cards or any other rigid criteria that plagued previous groups.
What it did do, and very effectively, was to provide a free newsletter mailed to anyone who asked for it, that listed events, rallies and a new and improved DJ policy for the events they staged that paid for the production of the newsletter. Producing 2,000 newsletters and individually mailing 600 of them while the rest went to clubs and shops in Britain and all over the world was not a cheap service.

By the early nineties, **BRIAN BETTERIDGE** found himself getting drawn to a scene that he recognised as being very definitely influenced by mod. Although he had not completely lost touch with what was going on, a chance meeting led to an unlikely, but welcome opportunity:
I met this girl Julie and we talked about the mod thing and of course this is 1990 and the time of The Stone Roses and The Charlatans. Now the first time I heard The Charlatans, I knew they were influenced by The Prisoners.
I was going to see The Prime Movers. I'd been seeing Graham Day's bands since the eighties, and also I realised that bands, particularly in London, were made up of

members who had been in mod bands of the eighties. They had to endure playing rallies where they weren't being listened to because the audience was waiting for the records and started doing the gig circuit because at least people would come and listen to the music.

A lot of them never made it, but there was a bit of a mod influence going on in London clubs. At Prime Movers gigs you could tell the influence of some of the audience and I realised that some of the people going to Prime Movers gigs were the same people Julie knew. What I hadn't realised was that the scene had moved on from the sixties-based thing that I knew and there were some new and decent people about.

I started going to a few Untouchables dos. I know Rob Bailey and although I have a few issues with him about the concept of the Untouchables, I get on well with him on a personal level. Through the Untouchables dos I met a guy called Dave Edwards and we've been friends for ten years. He comes from the Waterloo area and his earliest memories are of him and his mates at the age of 13, riding round the Wellington on their bikes and trying to look through the window until the landlord told them to piss off. He has deejayed for the Untouchables and is a massive soul collector and he loves the revival period, although revival is not the right word.

For some people revival is a dirty word, even today. It was an aberration, not a part of it and that just pisses me off so much because, to me everything is all relative, and everything they're into wouldn't have happened if it weren't for '79.

If they had been me, or Bob Manton or Tony Perfect or Eddie Piller in '79, are they saying they would have said 'I don't like what's going on I'll wait ten years'? No way, they would have been involved. Sixties music and '79 is important to a lot of people. It's all relative.

Also in the early nineties there was a band called The Direction. Not 'Directions', but The Direction and Detour records put them out. I kind of knew them through other people and Dave Edwards suggested that a lot of people had the Back To Zero single and that The Direction should have me on to do 'Your Side Of Heaven' in the encore. This was '91-'92, so he arranged it and I rehearsed with them and I sang 'Your Side Of Heaven' two or three times and there were people who knew all the words. So from the early nineties, I was going to a lot of mod clubs and sixties influenced clubs like Quintessence when that started in London. I remember a mate of mine, Lawrence, said 'You know The Stone Roses are the biggest thing in Britain at the moment and their second album sounds like Squire!'.

To get a summary of how mod developed during the eighties, who better than mod stalwart **MIKE WARBURTON**, who attended most of the major mod events during the decade, but was distanced enough from the London scene to give this very blunt assessment:
There were some excellent clubs and a first rate dress standard. The delight of discovering shops such as John Simons, Johnson's of Kings Road, and Kendal's of Shepherds Bush for the first time can not be surpassed. The downside, which eventually ruined the scene, was the Phoenix List and mod rally set up, which was a pathetic attempt at 'over organising' by a clueless 'non-mod' who attempted to use mod as a means of lining his own pocket. Thankfully, the Phoenix List is long gone - never to return. The Acid Jazz 'neo-mod' scene was in some respects mod's salvation. Musically, the Acid Jazz scene was a little too 'late' for my taste, although I do like quite a few hammond organ sounds such as Brother Jack McDuff and Lou Donaldson. Dress-wise, I consider shops like Duffer of St. Georges to be 100 per cent mod. After all, taking a classic style and updating it very slightly is the very essence of mod.

Mod culture, after all the trials and tribulations of the ten years between 1979 and 1989, still refused to lay down and die. As Britain moved into the final decade of the millennium, mod was to find yet another lease of life, and this time, it was not to be seen as a destructive youth cult that could be viewed as some sort of freak show. Mod became recognised as the influential factor, even though the media, the fashion industry and the music business did it's utmost to deny post-war modernism it's rightful place in British cultural history. ◊·◊

> I think what it comes down to is charismatic people fronting it. These are people who are brave in starting a clothes shop or a record label or a band or a club, these are great people.
>
> ED BALL

CHAPTER 6

The Untouchables had established regular crowds of 500 plus at their events which included rallies and all-nighters like Night Train at the Russell Arms in Euston, London. What was becoming clear, was the fact that the mod scene was diversifying its outlook in the nineties. At clubs and events, the music policy had loosened to the point where it was now acceptable to have different DJs playing soul, Latin, jazz, beat and ska, all on the same night. Another major shift in nineties mod, was the relatively low priority placed on scooter ownership. Classic sixties cars and in particular minis were much in evidence at events. But one thing never changes no matter how much time passes and how many trends come and go. The strict smart dress code was still in force among the mods. The nineties would see renewed interest in mod style and it was still finding new converts around the world. Most notably in Japan. **DAISUKE USUI** from Nagoya, became interested in The Beatles following the tragic death of John Lennon in 1980, even though he was only nine years-old at the time:

After that, I gradually got to know more about the artists who influenced The Beatles, and other British bands. I was wholly impressed by the gear my idols owned. Only afterwards, I discovered the style I was into was called mod. Finally, I got interested in mod itself and became one. I have been a mod about 20 years.

In 1995 I lived in Stoke Newington, London for about a year and a half. I thought it was really cool since England is the birthplace of mod, and some mods were still about. The nineties mods looked exactly same as the people in the pictures I'd copied from sixties magazines or books. I was envious of these Brit mods because they had longer legs, those hipsters fit them so well and most of them were much taller than me!

There seemed to be less unwritten rules about mod taste or sensibilities and they seemed to know how to relax and enjoy themselves as mods.

I preferred dancing to good music and talking with my mates about cool gear than discussing what a mod should be. In a way, it was a lot fun for me to be with the English mods who took themselves less seriously.

TAKU YAMADA, also from Nagoya, found mod via the print media:

When I was a high school student in 1991, I saw a special mod edition in a fashion magazine. I was captured by it and afterwards I just followed the trends I had seen there. I've been a mod for 20 years.

In arguably Japan's most famous city, Tokyo, **HANNA HASHIMOTO** was inspired more by fashion than music:

I was deeply impressed by sixties hairstyles and make-up, and also, I felt the hairstyles of mod girls were even more sensational and attractive than some of the top models in the sixties.

Fellow resident of Tokyo, **FUMIO NAWA**, discovered mod after watching a certain cult British film:

The biggest reason I became a mod was after watching Quadrophenia. I first saw this film when I was in high school. Afterwards, I fell head over heels in love with mod. Also, because Japan is usually deeply influenced by American culture, I felt this British thing was so fresh and attractive. Eventually, I got a M-51 shell parka and a Lambretta, and started going to nightclubs. I joined a scooter group, The High Numbers and formed a band called The Marquee. I went to the Whisky A Go-Go club in Tokyo every weekend and would lose myself, I would go mad every time.

In Italy, **FRANCESCO LISI** began his deejay career in somewhat inauspicious circumstances:

I became a mod DJ officially in 1991. In those days, white music was not popular like today. Parties and rallies in Italy had the dance floor totally ruled by northern soul that came from the Kent Compilations, so I really had no chance to play my records in this "stompers" mod world, before a DJ contest in Torino. At the time I was not so popular in the mod scene, because my haircut was too long (I had an early Keith Moon cut), and my clothes were a little bit too mod/pop art, so the organiser of the contest, really tried hard to boycott me just saying that he made a mistake and booked too many DJs, and he did not have enough space for everyone. I was the one to lose out, but Italo Adriani, a well known and respected Italian DJ, took my side over the organiser, and after a tough but firm face to face discussion with the organiser, I had my set fixed again and I had the best time slot. At 1:00 am I started playing some "obscure" songs like 'Bring It To Jerome' by David John & The Mood or 'Don't Look Back' by the Remains and many others that are regarded today as classics. The dance floor was totally empty for the entire time of my 30-minute set. I'll never forget it!

After more than 20 years, I like to think that I started a new course for the mod scene. In fact, six months later someone organised a 'scandalous' British R&B Party with only white R&B music from 1963-1966, and the whole Italian scene was shocked that a mod party could exist without northern soul.

The same year that Francesco made his debut at a premier Italian mod event, also became something of a watershed year for British music.

In 1991, rumours were rife that Paul Weller was in the process of launching a solo career and there were some other interesting bands on the fringes of making the big time. The other key event in terms of mod history was the untimely death of one mod's great icons: Steve Marriott.

On the 20th April 1991, Steve Marriott died in a house fire at his cottage in Arkensden, Essex. He was 44 years-old. Fittingly, although unsurprisingly too late, the mainstream music business via the Ivor Novello Awards, recognised Steve Marriott for his outstanding contribution to British music.

Long-time mod and Small Faces fan **JOHN HELLIER** was devastated at the news of Marriott's passing, but by a strange turn of fate, an opportunity to keep Marriott's memory alive came about:

Around the time of Steve's death somebody sent me a copy of this new Small Faces fanzine and, possibly because there was so little on the band at that time, I really enjoyed it and contacted the editor in the Liverpool area. He wrote back to me and asked if I'd like to contribute an article or two, which I did.

After four issues the guy told me that he wasn't going to do anymore as he couldn't afford the cost of putting it together. I decided to take it on and took it over from issue five. We went glossy and took it upmarket.

Previously it had been a very basic cut and paste job albeit an attractive one. In the 20 years or so since then, I've taken the print run from 100 to 5,000 and it's now read worldwide. The internet and social networking have obviously helped considerably to obtain this.

The first annual Small Faces Convention was at the Ruskin Arms in Manor Park in 1997. On the bill that day were six bands plus special guests PP Arnold, Steve Cradock and Love Affair's Steve Ellis. As with the magazine these events have come on in leaps and bounds and the Convention now regularly attracts fans from as far afield as Australia, USA and all over Europe.

Meanwhile, Creation Records was going from strength to strength, building on the successes of the late eighties. Former scooter club member turned house DJ Danny Rampling worked with Ed Ball on one of his projects. However, Danny was not the only person with scooter/mod connections from the past who got involved with the label, as **ED BALL** explains:

Danny did a remix on one of my Love Corporation things, but if you go back to '89, all the people that were into Acid House were remembered for being in the mod scene ten years previously.

You had people like Grant Flemming, who I met in '89 running the dance thing at Creation and getting the Primal Scream remixed by Andy Weatherall who flirted with the mod thing.

We were like acid mods. We were doing lots of it then, but I did an interview as Love Corporation in NME or Melody Maker and I'm wearing a hooded top with a target on it. It was like taking mod in another direction. Progressive mod again. I suppose it's an age thing, growing up through these things.

It's a combination of people really. You've got Eddie Pillar, who's kind of in the middle and a mod at heart, then there's a band of musicians. Then you've got someone like Morrissey, who always comes out with choice quotes and so damn English and we all understand that. Then you get Bobby Gillespie in 1990, 1991 doing interviews and he was dressing like a mod and had great mod clothes and said he had mod sensibility, but the music was house remix stuff. So you end up with spokespeople and whatever is going on in music and they make some sort of connection with it and they connect with the public.

Aside from Creation, those other interesting bands began to make themselves known to the wider public.

On December 31, 1991, John Power finally quit The LA's. After 'There She Goes' had finally risen from cult status in 1990 when it made Top 20, The LA's front man Lee Mavers had a row with Go! Discs over the constant re-recording of their one and only album, which failed to sell. John Power wanted an outlet for his own compositions and formed Cast in 1992. A couple of years of line-up changes and relentless gigging led to Cast releasing 'Finetime' as their first single and 'All Change' their debut album. As with so many of the bands emerging in the wake of the baggie and grunge scenes, Cast's influence was based on what can now be described as British pop's best traditions. Three-minute, guitar-based tunes with sound lyrical content and attitude that can be found in many a track by The Jam, The Kinks, The Clash et al.

It did not take long for the scooterist and post-modern mod fraternity (as author William Austin likes to call them) to latch on to Cast. This new audience for John Power's band was not purely for the music, although that was a major reason, but because Cast had adopted a semiotic of the mod / pop art scene. Namely the durable roundel motif. Add to this, the band's presentation and image of itself as a mixture of baggy, mod and casual, it was obvious that the scooterists and post-modern mods would take to Cast.

Ocean Colour Scene were formed in 1989. All four members originated from the Birmingham area. Simon Fowler and Damon Michella had previously been in The Fanatics, while Oscar Harrison and Steve Cradock had been in Echo Base and The Boys respectively. After a stuttering start that saw OCS re-record their debut album in part at Paul Weller's Solid Bond Studios, it took five years of hard work and knock-backs before OCS finally received recognition.

Their determination not to give up, and with a helping hand from Paul Weller who saw their potential, reaped just reward in the unlikely shape of DJ and TV host Chris Evans who gave the band a chance to air 'The Riverboat Song' live on his new TV show TFI Friday and subsequently adopted the catchy guitar riff as one of its main themes. That was 1996 and with the exposure OCS had on the show, the single performed well in the charts as did the album 'Moseley Shoals'. OCS have never denied their mod influence stemming mainly from the British beat bands of the sixties and the likes of The Jam, Buzzcocks and more recently the Stone Roses. Unlike some bands who could be described as post-modern mods, OCS, and particularly Steve Cradock were in the thick of it during the eighties on both the mod and scooter scene. On that basis, their mod credentials are more substantial than their contemporaries, but in line with the post-modern mod scene of the nineties, they did not refer to themselves as mods.

London [courtesy of Tomás McGrath; photo © Simon Fane]

They did not wear parkas or go on and on about 'Quadrophenia'. Ocean Colour Scene merely reflected the changing times of the modernist culture which had finally shed the stereotype and was being placed alongside mainstream culture. No doubt their detractors will argue that they are not a real mod band, but the question of what defines a mod band remains unresolved.

Menswear were another band that had a torrid eighteen months in the spotlight, but were arguably the closest band to mod that Britpop ever produced, not least because of Johnny Dean. As he told The Chap magazine in 2015:

I used to spend hours trawling around charity shops to look for these particular kinds of clothes. I used to dress in a very 60s way.

Fellow band member Chris Gentry tells of meeting Johnny Dean in their hometown of Southend:

I'd never met anyone like Johnny. It was like someone had taken a person from a 60s film and put him in the modern day. I had long hair, but within 24 hours of meeting him I'd turned into a mod.

However, Johnny Dean tempered his mod affiliations by claiming:

I wasn't a mod. I was interested in the look, the 60s as a decade, it celebrated being British. At that point grunge was king, so by dressing smart I was rebelling. Then when Blur's 'Modern Life Is Rubbish' was released, it was like a call to arms.

It was becoming clear that the Britpop era was not a mod revival by any means, but it did have an influence.

Blur's Graham Coxon and Damon Albarn are products of a time when youth cults still had impact. Both of them as schoolboys were heavily into the rude boy look that bridged the style gap between mod and skinhead in the early eighties, and both were influenced by the 2-Tone stable of Specials, Madness and all. As the eighties wore on, The Smiths also had a marked influence on the pair, and after an almost cliched rollercoaster ride of ups and downs with their fledgling band, Blur finally came together in 1989. Coinciding with the surge of the 'Madchester' and baggy scene, it took a year for the Blur's debut single 'She's So High' to see release. The music press liked it, but it struggled on sales. Their second single 'There's No Other Way' made Top 10 and Blur made their first appearance on Top of the Pops. It was not until the release of 'Modern Life Is Rubbish' in 1993, that Blur adopted the modernist imagery. The publicity shots revealed how easy it was to 'pick-and mix' the modernist influenced styles.

Harrington jackets, desert boots, Fred Perrys, Ben Shermans, three-buttoned suits, Lonsdale t-shirts, Doc Martens; Blur used the myriad of mod imagery without allowing themselves to be labelled. The reason for using the style, was to oppose the dominant American Grunge bands like Nirvana whose style was 'lost generation' depressive. They went for shapeless, uncoordinated pseudo-punk imagery.

As Alex James noted in his biography 'Bit Of A Blur', the imagery used in the publicity shots had a surprising consequence:

We were always a kick-arse live band. A curious thing happened as we toured 'Modern Life'. The audience changed. Throughout the first record the crowd had been mainly girls, but now the front row was mostly men. Suited and scootered, like a lost cavalry, came the mods.

The follow-up to 'Modern Life Is Rubbish', 'Parklife' and the singles from that LP propelled Blur into the forefront of what was now becoming tentatively known as BritPop and as serious rivals to a much heralded band from Manchester. 'Quadrophenia' star, Phil Daniels had been a guest on the title track 'Parklife', and again, Alex James explained how that came about:

We'd been watching Quadrophenia on the tour bus and we sent the track to Phil Daniels, the lead actor, and asked if he wanted to sing the verses. He said yes, simple as that.

Phil Daniels takes up his side of the story from his own biography:

One day Steve (Sutherland) told me there was some young band with a song they wanted to talk to me about. Steve put me in touch with Damon, so I had a chat with Mr Albarn, and he told me that he and Graham Coxon were fans of my work. They arranged for me to come down to the studio they were using at the time. When I turned up I was treated like royalty. I had long hair then, which I'd grown for (the stage production) Carousel. I think they thought I'd be a short-haired nineteen-year-old, wearing a parka.

'Parklife' was a huge hit and reminiscent of The Small Faces / Kinks 'music hall' Britishness and gave all the indications of having mod sensibilities.

Like wise, and to a lesser extent, can the same be said of Oasis. Their mod affiliations are far less obvious, if non existent. As with their contemporaries, Oasis were influenced by punk bands, as well as The Smiths and The Stone Roses. It was a chance meeting between Noel Gallagher and Clint Boon of the Inspiral Carpets at a Stone Roses gig that Noel got his first taste of 'band' life as a roadie and guitar technician with the Inspirals. While Noel was in the USA, his brother Liam had joined a band back home in Manchester. Liam's new band The Rain, decided to change its name, and the three members plus Liam became Oasis. Before too long Noel had joined the band as well. In 1993, Oasis played support to all-girl group Sister Lovers in Glasgow, and from that gig came their introduction to Alan McGee.

Oasis signed to Creation and joined an illustrious line-up of contemporaries like Primal Scream, Ride, Teenage Fanclub and Sugar. On the live front they played support to Dodgy and The Verve among others, and their reputation grew rapidly until the release of their debut single 'Supersonic' in 1994. In the same year they played the Glastonbury Festival where Noel declared that Oasis and Paul Weller were the only real class on the bill. In August of '94 Oasis released their first album 'Definitely Maybe' to massive advanced orders and entered at no.1.

The accusations of being a retro band came flying from every quarter as Oasis's thinly disguised influences were apparent to everyone, but their supreme confidence, musical ability and 'punk' attitude cast off much of the criticism. Their second album, '(What's the Story) Morning Glory ' released in 1995 saw Oasis become one of the most successful bands of the decade, occasionally going head-to-head with Blur for chart supremacy. Guesting on the last track of the album, 'Champagne Supernova', was Paul Weller. The Oasis image was not one of modernism by any definition, but more a baggy/casual hybrid. It was enough for Oasis to acknowledge their musical influences without adopting any complete aesthetic. Indeed, Noel Gallagher freely admitted that his bedroom wall was covered with posters of The Jam. They led the field in the BritPop phenomena of the mid nineties. Their third album cover did exactly that. 'Be Here Now' displayed scooters, the now familiar union flag and other 'mod' semiotics, but no-one has ever tried to pin a label to them.

With all the influences that shaped Oasis and Creation Records on display, even Noel Gallagher and Alan McGee could not agree on which influence was the stronger, as **ED BALL** states:

Alan McGee saw Creation as a punk label because punk informed Alan as a teenager, more so than the band, The Creation who he named the label after. He was a fan of The Who and The Creation, but it was more the punk influence, The Clash and The Pistols. Noel always insisted it was a mod label, because Oasis were on it, which is an interesting opposition of influences. Mod has had a massive influence though. I would say it influenced the Primals more than me, they are best exponents of that influence. They have everything from Miles Davis to The Who in there, so the Primals definitely. I suppose Oasis did, but it was much more obvious. Another thing is that Britain and arguably England is a brilliant world catalyst. It's almost like an A&R satellite for things that originate from America, but are too dangerous and too hot to handle. They come to England, get kicked around a bit by the English, then taken to Europe, where it gets hammered out and honed down, brought back to England, sorted out a bit more and then flogged back to the Americans.

The same happened with Acid House with the Chicago beats thing. It was too hot to handle. It was not only black, but had a slightly gay connotation. It came to England, to The Hacienda in Manchester and in London and took on an English stance. It went to Europe, to the clubs in Ibiza and worked itself out, then came back again, became a hit and we sold it back to the Americans as Depeche Mode. I think this is what England does best. It's small entrepreneurs with big hearts who know how to organise small dingy clubs and get things going. I think what it comes down to is charismatic people fronting it. These are people who are brave in starting a clothes shop or a record label or a band or a club, these are great people. I think Alan was great, especially in his early career. When I think of Creation, I think of him. He gave really good quotes in interviews and was bigger than the label and anyone on the label and when he was in Biff Bang Pow, he was a better songwriter than most of the bands as well.

As with others like The Charlatans, Shed Seven, Suede, Supergrass, Dodgy and The

Verve, Oasis became synonymous with BritPop, a media-friendly tag to corale the guitar-based bands. As with most cultural trends, there are differing opinions.

Like Ed Ball, **JOE FOSTER** was close enough to Oasis and the so-called BritPop era to give this analysis:

Creation Records was a song driven thing and it was people in sixties style bands without being retro. I think it worked to a certain degree, because if you look at the way people form bands now, you look at Oasis, they are recognisably like the TV Personalities or the Jasmine Minks, they're not like Duran Duran, you know? It doesn't mean they are like the TVPs, they're not, but you can recognise the same genre. It's the same genre as The Creation (the band). It's not like they wear teddy boys clothes. As for the rest of that Britpop thing, for some it was basically an affectation where by they were influenced by Oasis, and with other people, probably Supergrass and people like that, they were too out of the loop to have been influenced by that, so theirs might have come from their record collection or something.

The more out of the loop they were, the more genuine their reaction to something would be. But with Oasis, one of their self-perceived coups was making it as a national band and having a celebration gig at The Hacienda. They had The Creation as support and that's when they felt they had really made it with a legend supporting them. It was after that, they went to all the triumphs that most people would be impressed with. I think that's the point where they knew they really were big.

For someone as dedicated to mod ideals as **PAUL WELSBY**, the BritPop era only served one purpose:

The only thing of any relevance to me was the fact that by association, BritPop brought Paul Weller back to a wider audience. Nothing more nothing less.

Alternatively, **EDDIE PILLER** recognises the influences within the bands, but sees it as a form of progression:

Just look at Oasis, they're so mod it's unbelievable. Then Ocean Colour Scene who were mods anyway, so they have to be. So it will continue, but it will get further and further away from the Pete Meaden thing and look how much mod philosophy has changed in three generations by word of mouth. It's always going to be there, but you can't pin it down and each generation sees it differently, but we're onto the sixth definition of mod now.

In 2009, Mojo published one of their early 'Ultimate Collectors' magazines known as 'Mojo Classic'. In the 'Britpop' edition, Paul Gorman identified the mod influences on the period:
Liam, Noel and Damon were wearing button-down cotton-mixed shirts which made a defiant statement of Britishness, plugging into Britpop's roots in mod, skinhead and casual street style. Fred Perrys were worn as a suedehead salute by Blur, Menswear, Echobelly and Elastica, and the ubiquitous parka made reference not to original Goldhawk Road mods of the 60s, but the revivalists depicted in Franc Roddam's 1979 film Quadrophenia. The visual identity of Britpop relied on a set of stylistic options, all of which appeared to stem from a single template: Paul Weller.

In fact, Mr Weller drafted in fashion design team Burro to create his 'look' for his comeback UK tour. One of the Burro team was Olaf Parker who had this to say about the ideas behind what Burro were doing: *It was contemporary mod, late mod. Not The Jam. We didn't go about it by saying, 'Lets's look at a picture of The Small Faces and copy the clothes'. It was just a move in that direction.*

Regardless of the relevance of Britpop to mod culture, one thing cannot be denied; it had an influence on a new generation of young people that led them into the realms of mod. Among those impressionable young people was **DARRON CONNETT**:
I was born and bred in Shepherds Bush, West London. It's a place that has a strong historical mod heritage. I guess anyone from there was touched by the mod shadow we all live in. As a kid I heard many drunken stories about it from various gents in the local pubs; everyone knew different members of The Who etc. West London has changed so much in the last 20 years, but mod can still be seen everywhere you go;

whether it's famous settings from the Quadrophenia film, (Cookes Pie & Mash to name one), to the back drop of 'Absolute Beginners' in Ladbroke Grove.
According to my mum, since day one I was always singing and performing for the family. I just loved to sing and write songs. Music was always around me; soul, 60s, R&B, reggae, rock, plus the pop stuff on the radio and I loved it all. Looking back, I was always known as a singer, even at school I never stopped and immersed myself in the art. My older cousin Billy was the one in the mod revival scene and I really thought he looked so cool in his Sta-Prest and Fred Perry's, but in truth I was too young, so the 90s Britpop scene got me into mod. A lot of people of my age group did the same, but some deny it now. I don't know why they do because it was such a great time and just as relevant as the '79 revival, but without the cheap suits and fancy dress boating blazers. I love Oasis, Blur, Pulp and all the other bands of that time, and as soon as I allowed myself to find my own individual take on it, I was off.
To me, that's what it's all about. A lot get it wrong and a lot get it so right, I'm still in awe when I see someone as sharp as a tack, because it means their clothes have been thought out and not thrown on.
Not long after I left school I got signed with a band I was in called 'Contagious'. We were a sort of funk, soul, pop outfit and Talking Loud looked at us before we signed to Savage Records. They didn't get us, they wanted us to sound like U2. Acid Jazz should of snapped us up we were much more suited to that genre. I thought I would never do a 9-5 job again, but things don't go that way do they. The label folded as did we, but it was a good learning curve and it's never put me off.

In the Midlands, **MARK MORTIMER** had put a new band together after the demise of Dream Factory:
DC Fontana first started in the mid-90s as a casual hang out for a group of close mates in Tamworth. There were no delusions of grandeur or egos - it was a vehicle for our songs, but was mostly about having a laugh and playing for smiles.
Back then we didn't expect any success as we were already at an age where we'd been playing in groups for a while so there was no naïve expectation or visions of 'stardom...'.

It wasn't really a serious project for years, so our story is unusual as most bands get that early passion and frenzy at the start and then it fizzles out but with DC Fontana it went the other way and we were more passionate & frenetic as time went on.

The original line up was myself and drummer Nigel Horton (we are the only two surviving originals today) along with Neil Jones on rhythm guitar, ex Dream Factory man Lloyd Barnett on lead guitar and singer Frazer Douglas.

I am proud that we were the least clichéd band followed by people from the mod scene. There's no doubt our musical horizons were very wide and we enjoyed being unpredictable, experimental and never conforming to any perceived expectation.

For every mod-friendly influence in our sound there was an equal amount of something else. Some say they can hear psych influences and some soul because of the brass section and some jazz vibes.

On the other side of the world, in California, **NICK ROSSI** was gaining good experience as a young musician inspired by mod and sixties music:

I led a group called the Monarchs from 1993 through 1995. We backed R&B vocalist Ron Silva, who most people know from a band called the Crawdaddys from Southern California. With Ron we released an EP on the Get Hip label (US), which is actually quite good. I still stand by it and I am proud of it.

I briefly had my own group just before the Monarchs, which attempted a lot of the same type of material The Nick Rossi Set had taken on. I just didn't have my act together yet, so to speak.

My first proper group was the Loved Ones. Bart Davenport and I put that group together in Berkeley back in late 1990 and early 1991. I appeared on their debut EP also on the Get Hip label. So it's been more or less and R&B and jazz agenda for me for the past 20 years now.

I would rate Ray Charles, Brother Jack McDuff, Mose Allison, Booker T. & the MGs, Oscar Brown Jr., and Big John Patton all near the top of my list of favourites. Lee Dorsey, Garnet Mimms, and Willie Mitchell are also up there. There's also the English influence as well: Brian Auger is one of my absolute favourite organists and Georgie

Munich [courtesy of Harry Vogel]

Fame has turned me onto some of my absolute favourite music. A lot of those UK club acts: Zoot Money's Big Roll Band, Dave Davani, people like that. Mick Eve, who played tenor sax with the Blue Flames, the Night-Timers, and Gonzales, has also become a latter-day inspiration just for being such a great person and good friend.
Style-wise, I would say musicians influence me most as well. See the above list! Also the obvious things like Blue Note LP sleeves. Actually pretty much whatever American jazzers were wearing in the late fifties and sixties.
Certain film stars have their place as well: Marcello Mastroianni definitely, Michael Caine to some extent, Oliver Reed, Paul Newman and Jean-Paul Belmondo.
The line-up for The Nick Rossi Set in 2001 was myself on the Hammond organ & vocals; Fil Lorenz, tenor sax; Joel Ryan, trumpet; Sebastien Lanson, guitar; Lukas Vesely, electric bass guitar; Brian Fischler, drums.
The band got together in the autumn of 1997 and played its first gig in December of that year at the In 'n' Out Club in San Francisco with a completely different line-up. It really began in fairly casual jam sessions with John Kent (drums), Alec Palao (bass) and myself. I eventually took the helm and started giving it more shape and something of a direction.

Alan Palao would play a major role in the renewed interest in a 'forgotten' 60s West Coast band, Powder in due course.
Also on the West Coast, ex-pat Mike Stax's Ugly Things magazine was going from strength to strength and had set up his own psych/garage band The Loons.
Meanwhile, **ANJA BUNGERT** had left The Cherylinas and decided to make a move that would eventually take her half way around the world:
Shortly after The Cherylinas, I moved to London. I was approached by Babz who was involved with Toe-Rag studios. She wanted to do a 60s Garage Girl band and they did not have a bass player yet.
The new band named The Diaboliks played all over Europe and the Western USA, we made a lot of different records and were the purveyors of the no-fi Garage sound which Toe-Rag studios is now so famous for. That is pretty much the only place we

ever recorded other than one session at the now defunct Pathway Studios (The Damned). I also worked for Babz at Babzotica, which was a great clothes boutique with her creations. It was 1993. London was pretty much the most exciting place to be at the time. I ended up living in Streatham which at the time was cheap and my best friend Jayne Pountain lived there. Within a couple of years everyone lived in Streatham which was great, we had a neat little community of friends within walking distance. The sixties thing just really took off with tons of clubs, bands and people. Everything was still a little strict mod, but a few of us were more into the swinging London 1966 and Garage thing so we blended the two and it seemed to work and take off. Britpop also stared at the time which brought a lot of new people, some of which stuck and became serious, but overall the whole Britpop thing was a pretty big joke to me. There were so many better bands in our scene already.

MIKE STAX recounts how he first heard about The Diaboliks:
I first came into contact with Anja when she wrote a letter to Ugly Things magazine telling me about the Diaboliks. We struck up a pen pal friendship, and when the Diaboliks came to America I set up a show for them in San Diego with the Loons. I saw her in London after that, and again in Germany when the Loons and the Diaboliks played together. That friendship eventually blossomed into a romance. We did about a half a year of back and forth between continents with massive phone bills, letters and faxes to tide us over, but it was clear that we wanted to be together. I eventually Anja moved to California and she really liked it here so we stayed. By 1998, the Loons bass player left and Anja was the obvious, natural choice as a replacement.

Back in Britain in August 1994, Melody Maker published an eight page pull out claiming to be an 'everything you ever needed to know' feature about mod. What it actually achieved was very little, except to add to the confusion and perpetuate the myth and misinformation about the subject. It is a recurring problem. People who know nothing about mod, and are not really interested in it, are usually the ones who end up writing about it in the music press.

The feature 'Touched By The Hand Of Mod' showed just why mod has become a loose generic term for people who are fascinated with the sixties. They cite Satre, Ginsburg and Kerouac as authors of 'mod' books. Graham Coxon, Kevin Rowland, Townshend, Marriott and David Hemmings as 'mod' icons. 'Get Carter', 'Blow Up' and 'Performance' as 'mod' films. The up-coming 'mod' bands featured were, by their own admission, not really mods. Mantaray and Thurman were simply sixties influenced, just as all the other BritPop bands had been.

In its defence, at least one part of the feature tried to explain Blur's role in the renewed interest in mod. The first thing journalist Taylor Parkes points out is that Blur are not mods, just new mod icons. Graham Coxon would be mobbed by post-modern mods at the London club Blow Up. Unfortunately for Mr Coxon, being mobbed does not constitute icon status in mod terms.

However, those frequenting Blow Up were redefining what mod meant in the nineties. Paul Tunkin opened Blow Up on October 16th 1993. It was meant to be a reaction to Grunge. Blow Up's first flyer utilised the roundel and arrow synonymous with Pop Art and by association - mod.

Just one week before Blow Up opened, Paul Tunkin deejayed for Blur at The Forum in London while the band were promoting 'Modern Life Is Rubbish'. It is widely accepted that Tunkin's set that night was the blueprint for the music policy at Blow Up.

The club quickly became very popular and Andy Lewis joined as an additional DJ. Originating from Watford, Andy Lewis's parents both had musical inclinations. By the age of 11, Andy had decided to swap the cello for a bass guitar. Among his fellow pupils at Watford Boys Grammar School were future members of the bands Gene and James. While at university in Wales, Andy played in a mod revival-styled band called Dim Disco Heno (No Disco Tonight) and was collecting records with a zeal common among his mod-influenced peers.

On his return to London, Andy Lewis was often found at Wendy May's Locomotion night. His friendship with Wendy led to being offered the chance to DJ the first hour of the club, and eventually stand-in for Wendy if she was unavailable. In an interview with Scootering Magazine in 2012, Andy Lewis explained what happened next:

I was hanging out in Camden, buying records, and I met a guy called Paul Tunkin at Out On The Floor Records in Inverness Street. He was putting a night on and invited me to play because he knew I had some interesting records and could bring a few people along. That was where it started and we had a vote to decide what the club should be called and Blow Up got the biggest cheer.

According to Lewis, mod purists hated the concept of Blow Up to begin with, but he noticed that over time, those same mod purists returned week after week and their influence in terms of sartorial style was having an impact on those who were not naturally drawn to mod culture.

It was Andy Lewis who brought in former 'Camden Stylist' Ian Jackson to DJ at Blow Up: **I wasn't into Britpop, but what happened with Blow Up in Camden, it was the last time that area really took off in terms of pure energy, music and bands. There was an element of excitement that made people want to be there.**

Although the club was not a mod venue by any stretch of the imagination, it did play a very key role in reviving interest in classic British pop culture and in particular the sixties. Again, by association, mod became acceptable, fashionable and influential.

It could be argued that Paul Tunkin, Andy Lewis and their guest DJs had a massive influence on their customers at Blow Up. It is fair to assume that a great number of people may well have got into a whole lifetime of music because of the club.

But it did blur the boundaries between mod and sixties pop culture.

BRIAN BETTERIDGE, almost 15 years after Back To Zero had folded, was keeping in touch with what was going on:

I was going to Blow Up from the word go. Blow Up started in Camden and I liked the fact it was playing sixties stuff, but they were playing other stuff as well and it wasn't a mod club. Ian Jackson is a veteran mod deejay anyway and Andy Lewis, a terrific deejay, has been with it from day one. It started in late 1993 at The Laurel Tree in Camden, and I started going not long after that.

It's still going of course and it's probably best known for the band Menswear starting there, but Menswear was something different and I don't count them as part of it. People were going there and listening to a whole range of Sixties music and the fact that it had an influence on Britpop is fantastic and it's going to be remembered.

Paul Tunkin, who runs Blow Up heard that I had a huge record collection and he asked me if I would deejay at Blow Up, which I did a few times, and I was even doing a 'lounge' session because I had that stuff in my collection.

I was being asked to deejay quite a bit during the mid Nineties before groups came on. I remember when Weller's 'Changing Man' came out, I played '10538 Overture' by ELO and I had loads of people coming up and saying 'That sounds just like 'Changing Man,' but that's why I was playing it.

I really enjoyed deejaying and eventually got a residency at places like the Super Elastic Plastic Bubble, which was more psychedelic and the Lava Lounge where I did a Sixties set. I'm glad to have seen that whole Britpop thing happen in London.

I still went to a lot of mod dos and the elitist mods really hated the fact that other people were getting into their music. I remember Christmas '94 there was a mod bash, and a lot of people who went to Blow Up got a flyer and thought, 'I'll go along to that'. Well, my friend Jane was complaining bitterly and saying 'I feel like something this close to me has been contaminated by all these new people'. and I thought what is your problem? I thought it was terrific.

The other thing about the Britpop bands was that they brought in other influences and made things interesting, so I was all for it.

But in my personal life, I went back to College and took a degree in History and as a student, you either had time and not the money or vice-versa for going to clubs and gigs. Then while at college I was introduced to the Internet and learnt how it worked and kept in touch with people and kept up-to-date with what was going on through that. Thanks to technology, it came full circle because through the website, it led to Sam getting back in touch and Back To Zero got back together again albeit briefly to record the album that should have happened back in '79. The title 'It's All Relative', pretty well sums up my opinion of mod across the board.

While Blow Up was holding sway in London, its Northern equivalent was no less important. DJ **MARK ELLIS** tells how Brighton Beach came into being:
I briefly had a mod dalliance in 79/80, but got well into it in the Autumn of 1984. It all just felt right. I fell in with some very sharp Leeds mods in '85 and by the end of that year I was collecting records and deejaying. 1986 was the real head turner for me. A scooter, tailored suits, getting hipped to a huge variety of mod related styles and music. I came out of a rocky relationship breakup in 1994 and had just returned from a jaunt to London to look for work and escape. Old Indie music loving friends had given my contact details to their mate Richard who was setting up a club in the same vein as London's new night Blow Up. Richard came to visit me at my parents' house in my humble mill town. First record I played him was '98 Cents Plus Tax' by Detroit City Limits and his eyes lit up, shook my hand and gave me the second room DJ job at his soon-to-start Brighton Beach Club. The following week, the club launched at the Cockpit in Leeds. I was to start on the second week, so turned up to check the vibe.
I was absolutely knocked out by the atmosphere. The venue was rammed to standing room only with all manner of very cool people. Edwyn Collins and Paul Cook were there and it was a very dynamic, fully charged evening.
I DJed for a full five hours in an upstairs section of the second room the following week. There was no dancefloor to speak of near my decks and I saw folk nodding heads, sticking their thumbs up and sipping drinks around me. Quite a few young well-dressed mods coming upstairs to introduce themselves. Someone said I should go downstairs to see the dancefloor. "Dancefloor?!" I replied. I went down and pow - the floor was packed.
It never stopped. That club ran every Friday for the next decade (and the rest) to crazily busy nights. 700+ souls in there, both rooms playing great tunes. Some fabulous bands played there too. Shed Seven, Verve, Bluetones, Supergrass and Corduroy to name just a few.
In 1996, Richard and the other organiser Colin decided to hold monthly Brighton Beach nights at the cavernous and cool Sheffield City Hall. The same two room set up only bigger. That was immensely successfully. So many friends made it to this

and the Leeds nights. Shortly after, we started another night at Leicester University. More DJs were put on the roster. The university thing came about mostly through necessity, but we had a strong student following. In the early 2000's, Sheffield City Hall had to close for building improvements, so we moved to Sheffield Uni. By this time I had moved to London and was less involved with the club. I knew the Kaiser Chiefs on nodding terms before they became that band, and they most certainly were regulars there as were Shed Seven members. The main room was massively Britpop, Indie and 60s pop and soul. The 'mod' room played a heady mix of funk, soundtracks, hammond grooves, Mod Jazz, Soul, Freakbeat, Garage Rock, Library, Rhythm 'n' Blues, Rocksteady, Ska, latterday mod choons and psychy type stuff. I never went to Blow Up, but our music policies were similar from all accounts. Guest DJs included Gav Needham,, Lee Miller, Jo Sadler(Leeds), Wayne Dearman (Rotherham), Tony Pass(Stockton on Tees), Janine (Skipton/Liverpool), Joe Dutton, Gav Arno and Mik Parry (Sheffield), Simon Tipper (Brum) Ian Grinham,(Nottingham), Rob Bailey (London)... to name just a few.

PETER CHALLIS, who would make his name in mod-styled footwear in the new millennium was one of the regulars at the Leicester Polytechnic nights:
One great night that was a regular haunt for a few years was a night called Brighton Beach - held at the Leicester Poly (before it became a Uni) - this was a fantastic evening with a variety of rooms and more often than not a 60's film was projected onto one of the large walls. We thought we'd found mecca - great tunes, nice birds and beer - fab times indeed.
Despite this new post-modern mod/generic sixties trend, there was still a market for the music of the mod revival period as one man was soon to find out.

In 1992, **DIZZY HOLMES** and his successful Detour Records mail order business was still going strong. But a new phase of the companies development was about to start when the postman dropped a demo tape through Dizzy's letter box from a band called The Persuaders:

I was still buying and selling, but mod records were becoming harder to get. There were a lot of bands out there who were not necessarily mod, but they couldn't get a deal anywhere. Mod in the industry was a dirty word, but I liked The Persuaders record and thought I would give it a go. We put it out on limited edition. Just 300 copies with wrap around sleeves.

From that moment on, Detour became more than just a one-man operation. Although Dizzy had help from other people from time to time, including his mum, a long time friend from the days of the Detour Scooter Club was using her secretarial and business skills to lend a hand. **TANIA HOLMES** eventually became a business partner:
I used to do the odd letters and bits and pieces for him, and after a while I just thought 'This is ridiculous, we might as well join the two together'. It just went from there.

That first single by Margate based band, The Persuaders, 'Finished Forever b/w In The Night' was released in January 1993. It sold so well, it was obvious to Dizzy and Tania that the market for mod-influenced music was definitely there.
Detour continued to flourish to the point where, in 1995, it became a limited company. 1995 also saw the creation of Tandiz Music Publishing. This was something of a necessity for Dizzy and Tania, especially when they started getting hefty bills for copyright payments from industry body MCPS. With Tandiz securing copyright deals, Detour Records was ready and capable of handling their most successful release and band to date. As **DIZZY** explains:
We knew this guy called John-Paul. He had a single and asked us if we could put it on our mailing list. We bought ten copies, they sold well, so we bought another ten. When the label really got going, we asked him for another single. So he gave us four tracks that had been recorded, but unreleased for Eddie Piller. There was a bit of a dispute with Eddie about the single, but it got resolved and we are still good friends with him.
Again, 1995 was to be something of a watershed year for Detour. The same band that had given Dizzy those four tracks, released on Detour their one and only album. 'The Self Preservation Society' by The Clique, which included the famous 'Italian Job' chant used

on Channel Four's Big Breakfast, sold over 5,000 copies. Originating from Tooting, South London, The Clique were on the brink of making the big time despite going through more than their fair share of personnel changes. Detour Records began negotiations with One Little Indian Records, owned by Icelandic singer Bjork, to release the album and take The Clique on to stardom. However, One Little Indian ran into financial trouble and the deal collapsed. The effect on Detour was crushing disappointment. For The Clique, it was terminal. By the end of 1998, the band folded, but to get a sense of just how close they came, **TANIA** recalls interest from some unlikely sources:

Mark Lamarr was a huge fan. His house got burgled, and he had a copy of the album. It got stolen, so he phoned us up and asked for a new one. It was Mark who got them on Radio One, but The Clique were going through a break up and their performance didn't really come across as good as The Clique really were. Trevor had gone and he was replaced by a female vocalist and she had only been in the band about a week and suddenly she's playing on Radio One. It's a shame because they were brilliant and when they got the chance to show what they could do it didn't work. They didn't get the recognition they deserved. Melody Maker did a big mod front cover and we didn't even get a mention and yet The Clique were pulling in huge crowds. We always said, if the deal with One Little Indian hadn't gone belly up, The Clique would have been bigger than Kula Shaker. Although they didn't last long, they deserved it more than Kula Shaker.

As **DIZZY** states:

The Clique should have been bigger than Kula Shaker. When they did that album 'K', they were the support band for The Clique. Kula Shaker did 'Hush'. A great song, but The Prisoners were doing that ten years before and they were another band that should've made it big.

ROB BAILEY, now running the successful Untouchables organisation, also felt disappointed about the demise of The Clique, especially as his friend Phil Otto was the bass player in the band:

There have been hundreds of groups who, had it been down to pure talent, would have got a lot further. I've seen some cracking modern sixties influenced bands over the years. Not all of them sound authentic, but bands like The Acrylictones for example, they draw influences from the past, but not overtly so and again they were on Detour and they were far more fashionable to that period than The Clique, who were a fantastic band, but had a more authentic sound which in today's way of things, they were not a group that would sell a lot of records.

The Clique were using all vintage gear and they looked fantastic on stage as well. They really dressed the part and in hindsight, perhaps too much. But again, they were from the scene and still on the scene today.

It's the same story as The Prisoners and Graham Day, they stuck two fingers up to the music industry because they felt their image and music was being compromised. Ultimately, that was more important to them than pawning themselves to the industry. I respect those people.

Aside from The Untouchables connections with The Clique, they were about to embark on their most ambitious event to date, as **ROB BAILEY** explains:

In 1994 we started doing European events and this was the rather odd thing. The British scene had always had enough people and was very self-contained and there were a few Europeans who came over to English events, but not the numbers that we have now, and certainly we were not going out there like we do now, organising events. Again, Phil Otto, who was playing in The Clique at the time and playing across Europe, was making contacts out there. They were on tour with another Detour band called The Apemen in Saarbruken in Germany, which is where Modstock came about. That was the first Untouchables European event and the idea of that was to get all the different organisations across Europe and the deejays and bands from each country playing at this festival and that principle has been with us ever since, so much so that we now do two events a year, one in Spain and one in Italy. That's where the whole thing became more integrated. It's so much cheaper to travel around Europe now, and with the Internet, it's easier to communicate.

Gothenburg [photo © Mary Boogaloo]

We had European mods coming over to our events and there were European mods living in London who came as well, so it wasn't as if we were complete strangers.
I think they would be the first to admit that mod was created in Britain and it would have drawn influences from Europe, but what is unique about it is that it takes those influences and makes it British, giving it a British twist. I would go around Europe deejaying at nights and weekenders and very often stay at people's houses and they would have union flags on the wall or on the back of their parkas, so they clearly like the British mod thing.
Over the last seven or eight years, I think we have picked up on some good European music which I can't remember being played before we started doing these events. Now there's French Beat, Dutch Beat, Spanish and German stuff, and it's being played here as well as in their own back yard. The mod scene was playing European stuff before Blow Up had even been born.

But The Untouchables were not the only people to have an international dimension. **ANTHONY MEYNELL** found interest in his music from even further a field.
Although Anthony had found success in America during the eighties, it was the Far East that beckoned in the nineties. As CDs supplanted vinyl, back catalogue reissues were gaining momentum. Anthony's long-time friend Paul Bevoir had released CDs of Jetset material on the Tangerine label. Paul convinced Anthony to do the same with Squire back catalogue. From the interest generated by the reissues of Squire albums, Anthony began to find inspiration again: I started thinking about making another album, but a solo album and by 1993-94, I had so many songs, I was going to do it myself.
Then someone in Japan imported a lot of the Squire records and I was doing the solo album. They wanted to put that out, so I went to Japan to gig as a solo. This is quite scary because when you're in a band, you go mob handed, but when your solo, it's just you on stage and it's something else. So I did my solo stuff and some Squire songs like 'B.A.B.Y. My Baby Love' as acoustics in Tokyo.

Meanwhile, Paul Weller had found a new lease of life after the disappointments of the late eighties and the demise of The Style Council. Weller returned to his first love, the guitar and with it, he discovered a vein of writing consistency that had been dormant for some time. His first solo release in 1992, 'Paul Weller' was a far better album than some critics would concede. With new producer Brendan Lynch at the helm, the album had variety, depth and texture that combined the old Weller influences with the newer ones, particularly the emergence of the Acid Jazz scene.

The following year Weller released 'Wildwood' to great critical acclaim. Suddenly Weller was 'cool' again. He was appearing on TV shows like Later with Jools Holland and TFI Friday. His band has been a loose pool of top draw musicians including the ever-reliable Steve White, Steve Cradock, Damon Minchella and Mother Earth's Matt Deighton. By 1995, Paul Weller was back on top and being cited as inspiration by many new bands on the 'Britpop' wave. 'Stanley Road' came to be seen as the pinnacle of Weller's phoenix-like rise from the perceived ashes of rock has-beens. However, in the fickle, media and image driven nineties, Weller's success became a focus of envious destruction. When 'Heavy Soul' was released in 1997, the media decided that they had given Weller quite enough praise and had bestowed due homage, but it was time to take the gloves off. Quite what they expected from Heavy Soul is unclear, but a new derisory term had been invented for Weller and before too long, the Brit-popers were now to be known as 'Dad Rockers'.

Like most musicians, Paul Weller's career has had its ups and downs. From a mod/rock perspective and for many people, The Jam, along with The Small Faces are the greatest mod bands of all time. **EDDIE PILLER** gives his assessment of how Paul Weller has dealt with mod over the years:

The Small Faces were of a time where they didn't have to stand and say "We're mods". It was their life and that was it. Whereas Weller looked around him and saw punk and all kinds of shit going on and said we're going to be mods and we're going to be different, and they did change the consciousness.

I don't think Paul Weller really knew what it was going to turn into in 1978, but once it got going it was unstoppable and it followed him around like a millstone for ten years and I don't think he managed to get rid of it in The Style Council either. So it wasn't really until he got to his solo career that he could look back on mod and be a bit more comfortable with it. I think up to the third Jam album he was totally into it. The last three albums, he was doubting it and The Style Council was his way of trying to distance himself from it all, but even that was still mod.

In the wake of a Tony Blair-led New Labour election victory, and indeed a victory for media spin and imagery, 'Dad Rock' was totally uncool. Weller had found a new audience though. They may have been dads and mums, but these were people who had a grown-up with Paul Weller supplying the soundtrack to their lives, not to mention bands like The Smiths, Stone Roses and many others besides. All of whom represented a genre that, for want of a better term, could be called British adult orientated pop.
Needless to say, Weller took the media coverage in his stride. He had been down that road before and was far better placed to deal with it. In some respects, his new contemporaries, Oasis, OCS, Blur have taken a leaf out of his book. Weller once told Jonathan Ross on TV that he would always be a mod and he would be buried a mod. His style was still very mod-influenced and his attitude to the media was pure mod. Get what you want from them,(publicity for your work) but choose carefully those who are worth talking to. With a fan base as loyal as Paul Weller's, a poor review makes very little difference to album or concert ticket sales, and so it has proved to be.
Away from Paul Weller and the BritPop frenzy, Dizzy and Tania Holmes had got back into the mod/scooter scene in 1994 after finally getting Detour Records established, as **DIZZY** recalls:
We always did one rally a year. We always did Margate, but then we started doing The Untouchables rallies because of the stall. It was great until The Untouchables split. That was a big falling out.

For **TANIA**, the scenes shift to the late sixties period brought with it, its own complications:
It got too much for me; all that psychedelic dressing. You know, the 'Austin Powers' look. I felt like I had to put on all the black eyeliner and white lipstick. I felt false, and the music we wanted to hear wasn't being played. It wasn't even like the classic

modern soul stuff, it was so obscure you didn't know what it was, let alone whether you could dance to it.

The divisions that had plagued the mod/scooterist scene down the years were about to resurface. The Untouchables organisation suffered a major split as **ROB BAILEY** explains: There were two different agendas going on. Up until 1995, I was doing my day job and my club nights and it was getting too much and as the mod scene was becoming more fashionable with the Brit Pop thing, I decided to try and spend more of my day in a more constructive manner and try to do a better job of it than what we were doing. For the others that were involved, it was still a part-time thing for them and that's where clashes came. I wanted to spend more time on it and I was hassling people like Dominic who was doing the artwork for the newsletter to get it out on time. To them it was still a hobby. I wanted it to go up another level, but it was never anything personal. That was really why The New Untouchables started. But again, it was a period of uncertainty, as some people were trying to decide which way to go. I think with some of them and the deejays I was working with, they all decided to continue with me. At the end of the day, it's those guys that make the night, coupled with the fact that I'd gone out and established the venues and business relationships, plus I think there is really only enough people to sustain one group of events. So eight or nine months later The Untouchables called it a day. It really goes back to what I was saying about taking The Untouchables on to do something more and different, taking more risks and putting older groups on. I don't think the others were particularly against it, but they weren't particularly for it either.

When we started the New Untouchables, it was like having the shackles off. Whilst myself, Jason and Paul had a sort of democratic outlook where we sat and talked about it all, I had far more independence to try new things. The Untouchables would have a meeting and everyone would have to agree to things, whereas Jason and Paul were happy for me to be a bit more experimental. That's why we've had The Action, The Yardbirds, Herbie Goins and Brian Auger playing live.

The Untouchables split in 1997. Although the organisation continued for a while with

> I grew disdainful of authority and The Who represented a voice for me. The band was a refuge away from society. The mod culture provided a place of belonging and gave me an identity that was different to everybody else. We never tried to mask ourselves as a British band, but there weren't many of us playing that style.
>
> RICHARD MARTIN FROST

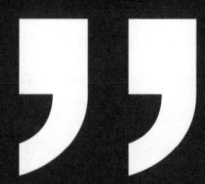

Maz Weller at the helm, it soon folded. As with previous splits that were all too frequent in the eighties, the problem of consensus could not be resolved. With the old organisation gone, the way was clear for Bailey to set up his new organisation his way. It was not long before The Mousetrap Mod Allnighters were being staged in north London, and Bailey's considerable contacts were being used to the full with the pick of top mod DJs and top live acts regularly appearing at New Untouchable events.

Arguably Bailey's greatest coup was reforming The Action for eighteen months or so, during which they played some memorable shows both in Britain, Spain and the USA: The Action came about simply because people kept saying to me 'We can't see The Small Faces anymore, we can't see The Who, not in the way we would like to see them'. The Action were one of the biggest mod bands of the sixties and one of the most respected and certainly one of the most talked about. I think it's because they managed to capture the American soul thing in their own way, coupled with the fact that they had George Martin producing them at Abbey Road studios.
So people were asking me a lot and it was humanly possible because they were all still alive. It was just a case of putting the jigsaw together and finding the people. Certain people had a number here or a number there, and a guy called Doug Bannon had a couple of numbers. One or two were elusive, but eventually I found them all and the first attempt was a total no, no. They weren't interested. A few months later I had another go and at least managed to get everyone round a table and have a beer. To my surprise everyone got on well and they started to think it might be fun and I put a sensible package together for them. I had a lot of involvement finding rehearsal studios and funding the whole project to make it feasible to happen. It started early in 1998, about March, with a view to playing the Isle Of Wight in August, but Alan King, who had never stopped playing, was really the only one who was 'match-fit' so to speak. It took a considerable amount of rehearsing, which they did, and it worked out well in the end. At the Isle Of Wight, they got a football-crowd reception that night and it was one of the best things we've ever done, as well as the subsequent gigs. They went to Spain, Germany, Italy and the first London show, which was their first in thirty-

odd years, at Tufnell Park, we had 750 in that night. Liam Gallagher, Robbie Williams and various other Brit Pop people were there. So that gave it more profile.

We wanted to contact people who really liked the band or were good mates with people in the group, with a view to getting them to see the show and let them know The Action were out there doing it again. I did my homework and contacted Paul Weller, Robert Plant, Rod Stewart and Phil Collins, who has been well documented about his admiration for the group. He was certainly the first one to respond, but I was out in Spain at the time. When I came back, he left three different messages for me because at the time, my answer machine only lasted a minute, so if you wanted to leave a longer message, you had to phone back, but I wasn't anticipating Phil Collins phoning me. His enthusiasm was so clear that we used it for the opening of the video and much to my surprise, he left his home telephone number in Zurich. So I rang him back and talked for about ten minutes. He wanted recordings of the shows, photos, just anything we had as well as drummer, Roger Powell's home number. Phil had openly said he based his whole drumming style around Roger's, so about an hour and a half later Roger rang me saying: "You'll never guess who's been on the phone to me!". Phil came over and took them out to dinner, they went out to Zurich to tidy up the recordings we made and when we launched the video, Phil came over to compare the launch and it's developed into a very good friendship. He played with them at the 100 Club that night, so there were two drum kits.

Now Roger is left-handed and Phil is right-handed and they're both bald, so it was like a mirror between them. He is a fantastic drummer and an all-round nice guy.

ROGER POWELL had this to say after the shows:

It was exciting and it felt like there was unfinished business, that somehow we hadn't really closed the circle. We knew it wasn't going to be the same as we weren't twenty anymore, so we knew it was going to be different but it was still worth doing as it was nice for people to see us again. It was awesome.

I'm really pleased we did it as we got to meet people like Jane Shepherd, Ian Hebditch and Rob Bailey.

It is fair to say **ROB BAILEY**'s ambitions and vision for, not just the fledgling New Untouchables, but for his 'internationalist' approach has paid dividends over the last 20 years or so. Certainly his early involvement with the Euro Ye Ye rally in Gijon, Spain has helped that event become one of the majors of the year:

Felix and Juan started Euro YeYe as national event back in 1995. I attended as a DJ in 1997 and fell in love with the place, the event and the people. The Untouchables had been holding our annual Modstock event in different cities Saarbrucken (94), Barcelona (95) (where I first met Felix) and La Rochelle (96) which were fantastic events. So, in 1998 Trouble & Tea & New Untouchables presented our first joint adventure with a truly international mind set at the stunning Oasis venue, which would be our home for the next seventeen years. Euro Ye Ye is still my favourite event after twenty years.

Because of the more generalised music policy and relaxing of the sometimes uncompromising attitudes that had been around in the mod/scooterist scene, the Isle Of Wight had resolved it's former problems, such as they were, and the two disparate groups began to forge a fairly comfortable coexistence. Although neither had compromised on their styles, mods and scooterists seemed to find it easier to respect each other on the basis that both shared a common heritage of music, transport and style, albeit in differing interpretations. Dedicated club nights began to spring up all over the country. It was now possible to gain ready access to a night of pure Northern Soul, or pure R&B, or pure freakbeat, garage, psych, beat, revival, or a mixed bag of the lot.

As examples, in London, Art Gallery ran Lordy Lord at The Clinic in Gerrard Street, however, Art Gallery became much more than a club night as **ALEX BANKS** explained:

Art Gallery began life in 1996 as a DJ collective. We wanted to put on a night that was more contemporary than was on offer at the time. We wanted to play 60's Soul, Funk, Jazz and Psych, but wanted the night to recognise that it was the 90s not the 60s! There we're too many nights at time that looked more like a fancy dress night. We likened them to the people who go to the country at the weekends and dress up to re-enact famous battles. We took our name from The Artwoods Album 'Art Gallery'.

It made perfect sense to myself and co-founder Chris Brookes as we were really into 60s Pop Art as well as the 60s music. This also influenced our logo. Our first night was the one off 'The Beat Bubble Ball' on the 22 of Decemebr 1996 at the Clinic in Chinatown. In 1997 we started a residency at Paul Hallam's Popcorn night at the 100 Club. Our aim was to build up a following, then start our own night. In July 1997 that happened, we went back to The Clinic Speakeasy and started the infamous Lordy Lord. This ran until 2002. Starting on Thursday night we quickly moved to a Friday night and finally a Saturday, albeit what turned out to be the last Lordy Lord as The Clinic closed down. During the Lordy Lord years we launched the clothing line in 1999. We began with a run of t-shirts expanding slowly with sweatshirts, accessories and casual jackets. We sold in independent boutiques around London. The collections were always very small and in very limited runs. In 2010 I decided to re-launch AGC with the intention of growing into a bigger brand. Our aim is to stay a specialist brand and it's very important we keep a soul and don't sell out like so many of the bigger boys!

The New Untouchables ran The Mousetrap Allnighter at Jaqui's on the Seven Sisters Road and The Purple Pussycat at Zazoom in New Burlington Square, then there was Hipshaker in Portsmouth and Smarties and Modesty in Brighton organised by Backstreet Boogaloo. In 1995 **MARY BOOGALOO** became a DJ and a key figure in the organisation as she explains:

At the beginning of Backstreet Boogaloo, I started buying 7" singles exclusively, which appeared to be the only acceptable support for DJing. Apart from the fact that the majority of soul and r&b was only ever released as singles, the other motive was that nobody would have taken you seriously if you only had LPs. Stupid and absurd, I know, but that's the way it was. It's a hobby I enjoy very much and the reason why people like me as a DJ, is because I'm very much in touch with the crowd. I dance a lot myself, so I automatically understand the dance floor.

My boyfriend at the time, David Nimmo, founded the organisation in 1994. There were four people involved then, but no one wanted to do anything apart from turning up for DJing and getting paid, so it was inevitable that I took over the way I did. I took care of membership, publicity and even PR. I even managed to persuade the others that we should invest the club takings into producing a quarterly magazine, which later on added some prestige to our clubs and created some kind of an impact in the nineties mod scene.

The venue we were using increased its capacity from 120 to 200 and we were under tremendous pressure from the management to sell out every time. So we had to let more general public in, but this caused the mods to stop enjoying the exclusiveness of our nights and at the end there was only about a five per-cent mod attendance. It was time to stop.

One club though, that really put itself on the map, to the extent that Record Collector Magazine ran a small feature on them, was The Hideaway in Manchester. Originally situated at The Mitre Hotel, its success meant moving to The Waldorf within a year.

The Hideaway was founded by **PAUL WELSBY**, Neil Henderson and Mike Warburton. Paul explains why the club was formed:

We'd been going to mod clubs for years, but the amount of soul and R&B they played gradually decreased. We weren't hearing what we wanted to hear. All we wanted was an original mod club, where we could hear real one-hundred per-cent mod music.

I think it's fair to say The Hideaway Club had turned into a club for the disenfranchised. The membership included mods disillusioned with hearing mod-sixties white approximations of the real thing. Soulies from the northern soul scene who can't afford £300 to get a half decent record and were looking for something new and different and hepcats from the fifties scene who wanted to hear just a little more passion in their music. All these disparate groups get together once a month in a room over a pub in Manchester and pay homage to black dance music of the late fifties and early sixties from America - the roots of today's rare soul scene.

Much of the inspiration for The Hideaway, stemmed from Manchester's long tradition of R&B based clubs like The Twisted Wheel. Because The Hideaway's influences were plain for all to see, they had no problems filling the club. Neither did they have problems booking some of the legendary DJs from the north. People like original mod and Pendulum Club DJ Barry Tasker, who came out of retirement for The Hideaway, Brian Rae, Carl Willingham and Roger Banks as well as nineties contemporaries Mark Ellis and Lee Miller. The only live bands to play The Hideaway were The Nick Rossi Set and the Gene Drayton Unit.

The Hideaways appeal was never exclusively to people from Manchester and the surrounding area though, as **PAUL WELSBY** explains:
The Hideaway boasted a card carrying membership that extended from Edinburgh to Brighton and Cardiff to Grimsby. The atmosphere on a packed night was incredible. At the top of the stairs leading to the club, groups of young mods stood chatting and laughing. Inside as the beat filled the air, the friendliest and most knowledgeable crowd around did what they do best, sliding across a talc strewn dancefloor, wheeling and dealing with rare 45s, and shooting the breeze. The only two criteria on the playlist are that it's got to be passionate and it's got to have a dance-friendly beat. We were certainly not the first group of DJs to play this music. You may very well have heard several of the tracks played elsewhere, but you would not hear this kind of playlist in one night anywhere else in Britain, guaranteed.

Not content with just the club, Welsby, Henderson and Warburton started publishing New Breed Magazine which focused its attentions on soul and R&B music, as well as 'traditional' mod issues like clothes. Paul explains how New Breed came into being:
Neil was writing 'A Sixties Direction' (ASD) at exactly the same time that I was writing 'The Modernist Review' (TMR) and we found we were covering very similar ground, had similar reasons for doing them and had similar aspirations for our fanzines.
TMR was just something to do. It also coincided with me moving job but not home. So at the time, 1995-96, I was staying during the week at my mum's in Manchester while my wife Chris and the kids were still in Woking. So I had a bit of time on my hands during the week. It was also something of a reaction to the number of people openly

referencing mod incorrectly. It was the legacy of Britpop I guess. I suppose it was my arrogant attempt to take mod back underground. To inform those that were looking to be informed. It seemed a natural progression for Neil and I to pool our efforts to produce something that would take what we were doing onto the next level. Something that allowed us to tackle subjects in a bit more depth and with a bit more style.

The scooterists, however, were not to be left out. Many of the clubs organised events of their own, many of which included a live act and this was another underground string to the not inconsiderable bow of the mod/scooterist scene.

The nineties had seen a trend for live music, but live music that suited a more diverse taste than whichever bunch of wet-nosed pre-pubescent teens were flavour of the month on Top Of The Pops. The original pop generation wanted to hear their favourite songs and bands, but most of them were now defunct, unless you counted the Rolling Stones and Status Quo among your favourites. Arguably, the first 'act' to take advantage of an untapped market was the Bootleg Beatles. These were four men who looked, played and sounded like the genuine article.

From then on, a mass of 'bootleg bands' began hitting the road. The so-called tribute bands ranged from The Illegal Eagles to numerous Queen, Stones and Abba acts.

The mod fraternity were not left out though. The Who and The Jam were summarily revived in a couple of very popular line ups and they were kept busy on the club circuit. The same went for bands that reformed, or acts that never went away. Ska bands like Selecter, the Specials and Madness reformed. Bad Manners had always been faithful and stuck with the rallies and events through the lean times.

People became more interested in seeing what was left of the originators. Mose Allison and Georgie Fame could be found at least once a year at London's The Jazz Cafe or Pizza Express in Dean Street.

Others came out of retirement or found themselves in more demand than they had been previously. Chris Farlowe, Alan Price, Colin Blunstone, Long John Baldry Manfred Mann and The Action all found themselves playing to packed audiences. The faithful were still being rewarded.

The indefatigable Edwin Starr was still in great demand, and many a soul singer had been shocked, to put it mildly, that they have a genuine cult following in Britain. However, not everyone was able to enjoy a revived interest in their music. On 4 June 1997, Ronnie Lane past away at his home in Trinidad, Colorado. He had been suffering from progressive multiple sclerosis for some time. His care was funded by Jimmy Page, Rod Stewart and Ronnie Wood among others, as royalties from the Small Faces catalogue were tied up in legal wrangling until Kenney Jones and Ian McLagen eventually won their legal battle which came too late to help Lane financially.

While the worlds of mod and music mourned Lane's passing, on 2 May 1999, Glory Boys Music, sponsored by Scootering ran the Mods Mayday 1999 show at The Forum in London's Kentish Town. It was a 20 year anniversary of the original Mods Mayday of 1979 and featured some reformed bands especially for the occasion. The line up included Purple Hearts, Ian Page from Secret Affair, Killermeters, Small World, The Circles, Long Tall Shorty and one other band as **ANTHONY MEYNELL** explains how Squire came to be on the bill:
I was intrigued that they had the balls to do it. I met Paul Robinson, who was the first one and his enthusiasm was enormous. We immediately connected because this wasn't some opportunist, he was really into the idea and it meant something to him and his past. I don't know if I was the first to be asked, but I was the first to say yes and I got the headline. I never lost touch with mod, even though I've never been a member of a scooter club or anything like that. I'm always in Carnaby Street in Soho, so I get to know what's happening in London and now my son works at the clothes shop Merc.
I knew the gig wasn't relevant to anyone today, but people would come out of the woodwork for it, so with the end of the millennium, and all sorts of little revivals going on, it seemed like a good time to celebrate. The organisers went away and came back to say that if I was doing it, then The Purple Hearts wanted to do it. They went off to find some more bands and slowly but surely word got out. A lot of them were Detour bands, but I was really pleased that The Purple Hearts had joined in because I was such a fan of them and we had never really met. It was fun, sixties and pop and we had been rehearsing for six months, but when the horn players came they really kicked in and

it peaked at the right time. We did a few gigs just to see what would work and to get rid of stage nerves. I said Mods Mayday '99 would be the last gig for Squire because you couldn't keep it going with a band that big and dropping to a four piece would be pointless. Fortunately, by the time the gig came round, a lot of bands wanted to be on it and instead of being last on at nine or 10 at night we were last on really, really late. It was a long day, but I think we had the right show to close it with though. Some might think it was a shambolic affair, but what else was it going to be. It didn't have anything to do with mod really, and the mod websites I subscribe to either ignored it or dissed it or didn't really care. Well, that's okay, but there were a thousand people there who really enjoyed it. I say well done to the organisers for having the balls to put it on and thank God it went off successfully and the record (on Detour) was okay and it was well documented. Immediately there was talk of doing another one the following year, but it fell apart straight away. We did one last gig where my two sons joined the line up and the whole lot of us packed off to Spain. I didn't want to do it at first, but just couldn't resist the chance to play those songs with my sons. We were on with The Pretty Things and a band from California called The Tell-Tale Hearts.

For **VIC VESPA** and The Killermeters, it was Dizzy Holmes determination that got them back together after a long lay-off:
After the band split, I went to Leeds University and got an Art degree. Not long after, I got a letter from Dizzy who told me he'd been trying to find The Killermeters for two years. I think it came via our publisher. Anyway, we spoke on the telephone and Dizzy and Tania came up from Sussex to see me. Now, I didn't know anything about Dizzy, but once you meet him and see what he's achieved with his life, you can't help but have utter admiration for the guy. He told me he wanted to put out all this Killermeters stuff and showed me what Detour had done up to that point in time. So the band got together and we did a few publicity shots for a record shop in Huddersfield and the local paper, The Huddersfield Examiner did an article on us. It wasn't long before we decided to do a gig and it took three months of hard work rehearsing. We decided to have our gig at the Polish Club in Huddersfield and we were amazed with it. We had about 300

in and turned away at least 100 on the door and that was without any advertising! Our problem was the limited amount of people we could let in because of fire regulations, but we had all sorts of people there. Some were curious because they'd never seen us before, some were fans from the '79 period and what surprised us the most was they came from all over the country. Then Dizzy told us about the Mods Mayday '99 gig and we met Paul Robinson. That day was just fantastic. It was great meeting up with The Chords, The Purple Hearts and all the others again. The most amazing thing was I was standing at the bar chatting to people and having photos taken, when this guy came up to me and he could hardly control himself "Vic, Vic please sign this cd! Oh this is wonderful to meet you". It turns out he was from Austria of all places, but he was like the biggest Killermeters fan ever! But that whole day is something I shall never forget. After that, Paul Robinson sorted out some gigs for us. We did the Isle Of Wight, other events and club nights. Then Detour put out the 'Charge' EP and that brings us up to the present day.

As if to emphasise the growing international following, mods from right across Europe and from as far as Japan attended the Mods Mayday '99 event, and as with the original, a follow up album was duly released on Detour Records later in the year.

The resurgence of mod in the nineties meant that there had to be a down side, and that down side was the very fact that mod influences were deemed trendy by the image-conscious fashion opinion formers. It ranged from the sublime to the ridiculous. People in the fashion industry like Oswald Boateng suddenly decided that the classic mod suit was very definitely the invention of Jamaican rude boys and sold a variation of the suit at ridiculous prices. Even sadder was the decision of the high street stores to go as far mod as they dared by making a variety of not-quite-mod suits that had three buttons and all looked very much the same.

On the plus side, Clarke's Shoes found a renewed interest in their original Desert Boots. Mod stalwarts like Lonsdale, Ben Sherman, Levi's and faithful retailers like Sherry's, Jump The Gun, Merc and John Simons (who can count Paul Weller among his regulars) found new customers on the back of the trend, and rightly so. It also gave other well known brands a chance to diversify. Lambretta and Vespa went into production of their own designer clothing.

Other establishments also flourished as those searching for genuine articles could now satisfy their desires by visiting dedicated second-hand stores like What The Butler Wore, Yesterday's Bread, and Too Much Boutique.

ROB BAILEY believes the renewed mainstream interest in 'mod' and sixties culture is a turning of the tables:

Mods are great 'thieves'. They take a bit of this and a bit of that and they make it unique in their own way. That's what mods are good at and I guess it was inevitable that people would thieve off of us eventually, which is exactly what they've done. The high street and clubs like Blow Up have done it with the music and the clothes.

JOHN SIMONS, who has lived through every stage of modernist development for sixty years, still had his shop in Russell Street, but later moved to Charlotte Street. He is still one of the few, if not the only clothes retailer selling authentic Ivy League and modernist apparel. If ever there is a clear case of blurred boundaries in this new millennial post-modern mod age, then John is more qualified than most to comment on where mod is today:

John Simons has been open since '78-'79. Our shop has never really survived on just mod customers anyway. We still don't get that many. We get a lot of people who were mods in the 60s and still shop with us, but we don't get many mods, the 21-22 year-olds shopping with us. I think they're uncertain about what we do. It's a bit too subtle. A lot of them feel more comfortable with a slightly more enlarged look. The odd one might come in and buy a Harrington or something. In the last ten years, there have been guys in the 35 plus age range coming to us who were interested in it when they were in their 20s, and they are still interested in it, rather than young people. We might sell the odd pair of Bass Weejuns, and very occasionally, we get a group of them who come in and are very familiar with it and very comfortable with what we do. I think a lot of it is blurred today, because the pop groups sort of infer an interest in mod. So the thing is kind of blurred together. That form of mod is mass isn't it. There's millions of them. You have to decide for yourself whether they're mods. I mean they have that Oasis type haircut, the walk and that sort of thing. It's post-modern mod. I mean (the post-modern mod) is definitely out there, and each group is informing the other.

But, would and could modernist clothing, the Ivy League look, survive in this post-modern mod era? JOHN SIMONS gives an honest answer:
No, not the way we do it. It'll die with us. You might have to go here, there and everywhere to find stuff, but not condensed into one store like we do, and people's heads are so full of myth and disinformation. Even when you get it exactly right as we do, people don't always have the money to channel into that part of their lives. The Jermyn Streets and Saville Rows will always be there, but not us. It just seems to get harder and harder. To be honest, the shop may not last much longer. The thing is, the designers are the influence now, and no-one has the knowledge based in reality to know what to do. It's all based in myth, art school myth. You'll probably find a few people who will be determined to learn and find the things that we sell, but it won't be easy. This is the designer syndrome at work. But a lot of the mods and other people have been very good to us over the years and they think that what we've done is very important.

John's assertion that myth and disinformation surrounds the post-modern mod world is one of the main reasons why this book was written. There have been some notable improvements in recent years to clear away the myth and redefine the boundaries between the sub-cultures inspired by mod.
The record companies were a little slow on the up-take as usual, but better late than never, by 1997 most of those who had back catalogues were now reissuing long forgotten gems, and some utter rubbish. Northern Soul got a much needed boost from the originators like Ian Levine who went on to make a documentary video of the scene and the music. Richard Serling, Russ Winstanley and Kev Roberts all contributed compilations of classic Northern.
Indeed, Goldmine had been producing CDs for the market. The Detour label concentrated on the revival bands with an impressive array of back catalogue. Decca

Tokyo [courtesy of Crazy Numbers Scooter Club]

also released their 'Scene' series, which could be erratic in pure mod quality but well worth a listen, if only to figure out was 'on the money' or not.

One label that has been consistently 'on the money' has been the Kent label. A subsidiary of Ace Records, Kent's success is mainly due to deejay Ady Croasdell's expertise and dedication to compiling high quality albums with excellently researched sleeve notes. The reissue market had become a thriving one by the end of the nineties, but this mainly reflected the buying power of the adult music buying public, plus the fact that the music industry had decided to focus on the teen and pre-teen pound and lost a great many customers who simply were not interested in the industry's latest 'three minute wonder'. They would rather spend their cash on long lost or previously-owned albums remastered on CD.

The up-turn in mod/scooterist fortunes also had an impact on the scooter trade. Many a former mod or scooterist was reminded of 'the good old days'. Some had families that had finally grown up and flown the coup, others just could not resist the temptation and scooter sales shot up as a consequence giving rise to more scooter shops for sales and service, not to mention the roaring trade in customising. Certainly Scootering Magazine have never been short of features on custom jobs.

Perhaps the most significant development of the mod/scooterist scene in the nineties has been the growth of interest internationally. Mods and scooterists could be found in Australia, Austria, Spain, Ireland, Italy, New Zealand, France, Philippines, Belgium, Germany, USA and Canada.

The growth of the internet helped to improve the communication between the mod and scooterist nations. Web Sites like The Boiler, Modculture, Jimmy Cooper's '79 band sites and Mod Links were important for people to establish contacts.

Certainly, Uppers.net was a useful resource for mod worldwide. The original club nights were still going, but by the mid nineties, Uppers became a record company as well. The ethos of the record label was a reflection of the club; independent, eclectic, but always with mod sensibilities. It was at about the same time that the internet site came into being. Quickly realising the demand and potential of the internet, Uppers joined forces with fanzine publishers and club organisers Snap! Mod Society and within a relatively short

space of time, Uppers.net was bringing together people of all colours, races, creeds and ages from around the world, all with one common interest, modernist culture.
To highlight the extent to which the international mod community has come together, you only have to take a look at the Vulcans Scooter Club Annual Custom Show and Party in Paris, The All Saints Mod Holiday in Italy, The Euro Ye Ye Weekend in Gijon, Spain, The Secret Scooter Society's Scooter Rage Weekend in San Francisco or The 6699 Weekender in San Diego.

For **ROB BAILEY** and the New Untouchables, their visit to San Diego gave them a good idea of how mod has developed American style, even though Rob knew of mods existence in the US long before 1999:
I knew about American bands through the Countdown compilations and they had Australian bands as well, but that was the only experience I had of the American bands through the eighties.
I think Squire was quite successful out there, but my only experience was the 6699 thing. Then we got American groups like the Nick Rossi Set coming over to play for us. I think there are pockets of areas like California that has little hotbeds of mod scenes, but the place is so vast, people can't do what they do here, like come down from Manchester for the night or go up there. They've got the music, but not the history.
They might have heard about mods in the sixties and they might have looked like mods, but I don't think they had any concept of it. My mate Paul Owers, who was involved with The Untouchables, he lived in Washington DC for two or three years and there was a mod scene there. Perhaps it was more of an 80s thing for them.
I think around San Francisco and that area, they were fairly hip to it and there were American mods who came here in the eighties and I met quite a few of them.
I think the garage, punk thing was a lot bigger at the time. But they were pretty switched on.
Jason Ringgold is an American who I started The New Untouchables with; he went back to the States. He ran the website for us and our email discussion group for mods worldwide. Then there was Nick Rossi and a guy called Dan Geddes.

The New Untouchables co-organised the 6699 San Diego event with Mike and Anja Stax whom **ROB BAILEY** had known for a few years:
Anja and I have been friends since the Untouchables days when she lived around the corner from me in Streatham in the nineties.
I met Mike through Anja when they got together and then married. Apart from both being wonderful people. Ugly Things magazine has been at the forefront of underground Rock n Roll music from the 50's/60's/70's for thirty-five years and a constant source of information and a fantastic way to escape the twenty first century for a while. Both have played in bands before and after they met, they formed the fabulous Loons who played Le Beat Bespoke twice.

ANJA STAX explains how the event came to be:
The weekender was initially our idea and we co-organised it with the New Untouchables. The idea came about since I just moved over to San Diego and there was not that much Sixties stuff going on (after being spoiled living in London for all those years with clubs, weekenders bands etc.).
So we started a monthly club called Hipsters, which at the time was still referring to a pair of trousers, unlike these days. We were thinking how much fun it would be to do a weekender. Mike had just got in contact with Dave Aguilar of the Chocolate Watchband so it seemed like the perfect opportunity to get the band back together. We wanted to incorporate some English bands so that's how Rob got involved. The whole weekend was amazing.
The line up included The Chocolate Watch Band and John's Children as the main headlining bands. We also had The Loons, The Conquerors, The Chasers, Quant, the Nick Rossi Set, and all of the Hipsters DJs - Mike and Anja Stax, Tony The Tyger, Josh Entreken (RIP) as well as the NU gang with Rob Bailey, Speed and Mark Ellis. There was a lunchtime event as well as a Scooter run and competition so the format was a lot like the NU UK rallies at the time. Unfortunately we did lose money with it but I still call it a major success. We had a good turnout (pre- social media) and amazing atmosphere to see all these bands.

MIKE STAX gave this assessment of the event:

The 6699 weekend was a landmark event in San Diego. Nobody had attempted a sixties weekender on that scale before and we went all out, including bringing over bands and DJs from London to give a suitably international flavour.

In retrospect there are many things we could've done different or better, but we were in largely uncharted waters so we just found our way as best we could.

Being responsible for John's Children playing their first ever show in America made us particularly proud. They were especially pleasant to deal with, easy going about all the arrangements and really getting into the spirit of the weekend, hanging out with fans and so on. We took a financial hit with this one, but the memories were more than worth it.

As Rob Bailey correctly stated earlier, Squire and **ANTHONY MEYNELL** did have success in California, but Anthony sees the future of mod developing into something else again, and highlights a possible pitfall, if mod gets too bogged down in what has gone before:

Where there's a mod, there's a fanzine, there'll be clubs, music, something happening, silly arguments about what you wear or listen to. For me it's about someone discovering music and maybe going back in time to discover where it came from, getting into it, forming your own ideas and taking it on, but it's not a bad starting point, and it's such a wealth of music. I discovered fifties and forties music, blues and everything.

That odd section called 'mod' is quite funny and endearing to me because I'm part of it in some respects, but I'm pleased it has a longevity. It has tried to reinvent itself and I think some people do get confused by the sixties imagery of mod and mods in the seventies who were really soul boys.

Mods in the eighties were probably, not Blur, but someone else, and mod now is... well who cares? They're are possibly the French bands like Air, who are much more stylish. If you're looking for style and attitude, they are there. It's not the garage band that want to sound like the Yardbirds because it's irrelevant. But if they are having fun, then more power to them because they will evolve into something else, but as soon as you say 'I can't go there because mod didn't' your dead in the water.

Music is certainly a cornerstone of the mod foundation. Like-wise, the deejays that play the music in clubs or on radio have been just as influential in inspiring people to become interested or get involved. That deejay tradition has continued down through the decades to the deejays of the new millennium. **ROB BAILEY** names a few of his favourite deejays from the last two decades:
There's been a lot of good ones. Going back to the eighties, Paul Hallam definitely. Don Bassett, Ian Jackson and Tony Shockman. Then in the nineties including European deejays, there's Pid from Birmingham, Speed whose real name is Pete Wild, Gavin Evans, Nick Hudson, Lee Miller. European-wise, Michael Wink, Philip Golbert from Belgium. From Italy, Andrea Mattioni and Francesco Lisi.

One of Rob Bailey's fore-mentioned deejays, **FRANCESCO LISI** believes Italy set the standard for events across the continent:
I think the best mod rally in Europe is at the moment the Eastern Mod Rally in Rimini, the biggest and the funniest. I have played there since 1983, and for me, year after year is the chance to see a lot of friends from all over Europe. I think Italian mod is quite spread out across the country, but there are two sides into the Italian mod scene, one more sixties-oriented, and the other one more '79 and Northern Soul-oriented. I'm a proud fan of the first.

DAVE EDWARDS was another scene stalwart who was attending many European events including Rimini:
I started going to Rimini in the mid 90s, it was a real eye opener. Andrea Mattoni had lived in London for a little while and used to come to The Lucas Arms ska do I ran in Kings Cross with Chris Dale. He invited us out there one year and it was fantastic, I think I did about 15 Riminis overall, I'd go as punter if I wasn't DJing, it was probably the top Euro event in my eyes. I've got to DJ in Barcelona, Valencia, Rome, Ravenna, Turin, Antwerp, La Rochelle, Munich and visited other cities to attend mod nights.
I think the Euro mod nights have been brilliant, I've made many great friends all over Europe, there's a more relaxed attitude but dress wise, they are so sharp and

passionate about mod. Undoubtedly they've had a big influence on the UK scene, especially at Rob Bailey's Nuts events where he regularly puts in Euro DJs. Fair play to Rob, he latched onto it pretty quickly and took it on board.

By the late 90s and into the noughties, Rimini organiser **ANDREA MATTIONI** had built a solid reputation as an organiser and DJ:

Between 1987 and 1991 Rimini had a thriving mod scene and in these years we run many regular clubs under the Smart Drivers banner, but the bigger events were definitely The Italian Job in Rimini and The Autumn Stone in Cattolica.

Throughout the 90's I was DJing at nearly every main event around Italy and many across Europe, Including representing Italy at every Modstock weekender organised by the Untouchables. The list of events where I DJed around Italy and Europe would just be too long to mention. I was also organising the Cattolica Rally. The first one was in 1997 (I think) with the Untouchables; it was part of the Modstock concept, which was basically a European Mod rally organised by the Untouchables, with the help of local people, in different countries. It started in Germany in 1994, then Spain, France and finally in Cattolica. After The Untouchables split, the weekender carried on with a Smart Drivers/New Untouchables collaboration until 2004, when we realised that the views of the two organisations were heading in two opposite directions and we decided to call it a day. I've never been directly involved with the All Saints Weekender, which started in Riva del Garda and then moved to Lavarone, but I took part to every single one up until 2005 and I used to DJ at most of them. Once again the people involved in organising this event have changed throughout the years, although I think that Alessandro Detassis is the only one who has been involved from the beginning and still is. All three events attracted many people from all over Europe. In Rimini in the beginning, it was mainly mods from the continent, Germany, Austria and France in major part, then in the 90's we started inviting DJs and bands from the UK and started to attract quite a big crowd from there too. The same was for Cattolica, with the New Untouchables being directly involved it meant that a big crowd also travelled from the UK and also from Germany and Austria. For both events we always invited guest DJs and bands from different

European countries, to try and attract as much of an international crowd as we could. The same thing can be said for the All Saints weekender in Lavarone, which is also located quite close to the Austrian/German border.

In Sweden, the scene there was bolstered by the Uppers organisation, but **FREDRIK EKANDER** explained the health of the scene in greater detail:
It's mainly the three big cities: Stockholm, Göteborg and Malmö/Lund. Then you have small pockets around the country - and for some strange reason certain small cities - like Örebro and Borlänge - keep seeing the birth of new mod kids every now and then. The term 'mod band' is a really difficult one if you ask me.
The one Swedish band that most clearly label themselves as a mod band, is the Moving Sounds with my old friend and ex-band pal Fredrik Forsmans, whose one of Sweden's coolest organists. Three other bands worth mentioning and that I would put on at any mod event are; The Roadrunners, The Spyders and The Hives. The Men is a raving R & B band from south of Sweden, with ex-Girls member Ola Främby. We also released a great power pop group called The Gwen Stacy's on Uppers Records a few years ago, but I'm not sure if they're still together. Sad to say, but it's the clubs that I'm involved in myself, Soul and Uppers, that are the best. The Freeloader is good for blues and hard, black R &B. If I go to any other Swedish clubs it's usually only to party, but they're usually quite uninspiring when it comes to the music and how people dress. Also I go to the occasional northern all-nighter to dance. Over the years (since I started in 1982) it has been all of this. Today, I don't really know. I guess, due to the (relatively) large amount of soul clubs and northern all-nighters being held until quite recently, a lot of the kids are very much into northern (too much into northern in my opinion.) That's why we started the Freeloader to bring the original mod music to the forefront. Also, a lot of the kids who are into indie music are flirting very much with mod, and a lot of times I think they are more my idea of mod, than the northern kids. There is a small group of really, really sharp kids who are very dedicated and cool. And that is true on a general level for Sweden I think; there is not a huge amount of people - not even a scene per se, more small groups of individualists who are very particular in regards to music, clothes

and attitude, which I think is a very mod in itself. It is a quite an exclusive culture today.

From Sweden, we head south to Munich, where **HARRY VOGEL** gives his assessment of the German scene:
There are more people in the west, but here in the south it's quite a nice little scene which is changing and has changed ever since I entered, which is a good thing. You can see that there is a development, although certain trends keep coming again every ten years or so. When I started, most people were into US sixties punk and psych and dressed like that, then soul became big and a more sober, sharp style was predominante, then people became more interested in UK freakbeat and the swinging London style. At the moment the west is rather into swinging London/psyche style, here in the south a lot of people are more mixing up scooterist and mod styles, not me though - I sold my old Lambretta because I was fed up with having to repair it every weekend - I'm not a mechanic, I'm a grammar school teacher, man. Basically I think there's a healthy mixture of any possible style, and the scene keeps moving on.

Next we head across the Atlantic, to America and California to be precise. **NICK ROSSI** gives us a fascinating insight as to why mod has survived in the US, but first, he reflects on his experiences in Europe:
I have only performed in England and Spain. I really consider the mod scene to be a viable and vibrant thing in both England and on the Continent, at least much more so than over here. A lot of people are tremendously enthusiastic, have a great sense of style, and know quite a lot about music. Some of the hippest people I have met are from abroad. Most of the larger cities in the US seem to have some sort of mod scene, whether it's traditional mod-types or indie-kids that have taken on some of the fashion aspects. The Internet has turned up quite a few pockets all over the country in some of the most unlikely places. But the simple fact remains that the United States is a huge country, plain and simple. It's seems to be very difficult to get any real sizable amount of these types together in the same place in the same way that some European rallies do. At the end of the day, I think mod means so much to so many different people and

perhaps this is even more so the case here in the States. America has a long history of anglophilia. After all there never really was a "Cultural Declaration of Independence" in the US until maybe the emergence of jazz. I would venture to say that even more obscure aspects of English culture and subculture than mod have found favour in the Americas. So it's no shocker to me that it has found so many American devotees. Plus it's an English subculture that has an integral American component; namely music, which is still my excuse for being interested in it! Mod was appropriated fairly early-on over here in both its commercial and more esoteric aspects by a number of people in the mid-sixties, so I don't think it was really that difficult to revive. The San Francisco Bay Area seems to be on the ebb at the moment and I am not sure if the rest of California and the West Coast are any better off. Fragmented, disparate and disjointed. Frankly there are just not enough people into similar things. Rather it's a handful of people into vaguely related fashion and music that occasionally hang out together. It seems very difficult to have an R&B club or a psychedelic club here at the moment, so most dos are more "catch-all sixties" which have varying amounts of interest. Personally, they don't interest me. Add to that, that it is daunting for DJs to push the boundaries of what is acceptable to play at the few clubs there are and it makes it hard to say that things are swinging. I love R&B but it's damn difficult to go out and hear it anywhere these days!

One American who got a taste for European mod and liked it so much, she decided to cross the Atlantic permanently was **GABRIELA GIACOMAN**:
I went to the New Untouchables August Bank holiday at the Isle of Wight in the late 90s, accompanying the Nick Rossi Set from San Francisco. It was a bit of a dream voyage, we all went to Ronnie Scott's to see Georgie Fame which was a really good show, and then Rob Bailey found me a Lambretta to rent for the weekend, so I rode that from London with my friend from New York on the back. It didn't start out too well, another friend had rented a P Series Vespa, and, for the first time in history, the new-ish Vespa breaks down while the Lambretta (SX150, same as I had at home), was fine! We were in the rain in Brixton when it happened, and quite nervous, a

couple of punk types hanging out across the street were eyeing us up and we had to escape to a gay bar to await assistance. But eventually I made it to the Isle Of Wight accompanied by two mods that turned out to be police officers. Everyone warned us about the terrible scooterists but we found them really friendly and more than 2,000 bikes on the island was really a good buzz. The show went well although the band was somewhat mystified by the crowd. They stood with their arms folded to quite danceable music. This had never happened in the US so we all assumed they hated it but then everyone came up after the show to say how great it was. This proved to be a good lesson for me, when French Boutik played the UK the first times, the same exact thing happened and I had to convince the guys that this was just the English way and that people actually liked the band. Other than that, the DJs were quite varied and the weekend was great. I ended up with a flat tyre and no spare tube or patch kit the last day so got a lift back up to London where the guys went on to play up north while we visited friends in Ireland. The whole trip almost ended in tragedy, we were due to meet the band at the airport the morning of the flight back, but found out on the last night that the hotel bar stayed open as late as guests wanted. We took full advantage of this so were running late and also not anticipating the long Heathrow security line. I was a bit freaking out when realized we would miss the flight and that our friends would worry. But then we spotted the band, in back of us in the queue! They eventually put us all on substitute flights and we made it back and slept for a few days.

From the West Coast of the USA, we head south east, across the Pacific Ocean to Queensland, Australia, where we find **KELVIN MADDEN**, who wrote and produced the Modern Times fanzine:

I wouldn't call myself a mod these days, and I wouldn't say I have always stayed mod over the years, but I certainly still hold on to the ideals that exposed me to some of the best music, clothes and of course the scooters which I am more into these days. I think after seeing "fads" or "phases" in music and fashion, I've definitely become disillusioned with a lot of so called mods. Especially ones that call themselves a 'mod' as they are only in it because they found the word in the NME or the dictionary. The scene in Australia isn't huge compared to some countries, but it has always been very healthy. It's had a few ups and downs, but it's always there. In the last few years there has been a lot happening; nightclubs, scooter clubs, northern soul 'do's', all sorts of things.

Remaining in Australia, this is what **DON HOSIE** had to say in an interview shortly before he sadly passed away:
I find myself using the phrase "I used to be a mod". a fair bit, so I suppose I don't consider myself one. My idea of what a mod should look like and act like has been tainted by several generations of un-hip pill poppers in ill-fitting loud clobber, or dressed like 'Dave the mod Yob' in Quadrophenia, warming scooter seats outside clubs rather than getting down to action. So it's hard for me to align myself with what unfortunately has become the public face of mod, even though it's left an indelible impression on me.
Saying that, I still love seeing stylish mods out and about. A scooter always turns my head and I'm always glad to see mod references in advertising, band clips or the news media. I still get all my clothes tailor made. I learnt a lot about fabrics and the rag trade lingo being a mod, so I draw up my own designs and fax the drawings over to my tailor in Hong Kong. I get exactly what I want and it's actually cheaper than getting crap off the rack here. It's also good seeing a mod lineage going back through BritPop and Acid Jazz to the eighties scene and for people not afraid of declaring their mod roots. This was nicely in evidence at the Mother Earth end of tour party in 1994 at The Basement. We were invited to play so we appeared as The Perennials, a sort of Stupidity/Mustard Club composite. We got up and ripped through our originals and some R&B covers, bringing real rock & roll to the Sydney jazz mecca for the first time. the trendies and funksters didn't know what hit them and must have been wondering what the hell are these geezers doing at this party? Meanwhile, there's ex-mods up the front removing all the furniture and groovin' away. they must have been even more confused when they saw the Mother Earth guys and Eddie Piller's Acid Jazz crew digging it too. We reminded the ex English mods of The Jam and Nine Below Zero, so there were a few misty eyes out there. Basically it was like an ex-mod convention with all the Oxford Street trendy clubbing set on the outside not knowing what was going on because they weren't aware of the history behind it all. It was great

seeing all these ex-mods remaining true to their roots. They could be into Acid Jazz and still dig us because of the mod connection.

Moving north across the South China Seas, we come to Japan, where **DAISUKE USUI** gave the low down on the mod scene in Nagoya:
Usually, we only have a monthly club event called Dance Craze at Club Buddha, in Shinsakae, Nagoya. This club event has been held there for more than 10 years, and it's still going strong. We also hold Mods Mayday once a year. This is the biggest and most favourite mod festival amongst Nagoya mods. At this time, we all come together along with loads of DJs and bands that are also invited from other cities, and the audience also comes from everywhere.
We seldom do scooter runs or all-nighters as we did before. The scooter runs are always daytrips to the countryside or parks. They're more or less like a picnic and I quite enjoy them. We've not only got the above mentioned monthly club, but recently, a very cool mod couple, Kensuke & Minori, have opened a sixties style café called Trinity downtown in Nagoya. It's become the most popular hangout among Nagoya mods.
I reckon there still are five or six fairly lively scenes in Japan. The biggest ones would be in Tokyo, Kyoto, Osaka, Kobe (Kansai region) and Nagoya as far as I'm aware. As for the Nagoya scene, there seems to be around a hundred mods. In the mid nineties, there used to be more than twice as many as now. On the other hand, the scene now is more friendly and down-to-earth than during the mid nineties hype period, as everyone now seems to really enjoy being a mod or hanging about with mods.
There is also a big Japanese sixties and seventies crossover scene that branched off in the mid nineties. More people especially ex-mods became interested in a Japanese cult sixties movement called G.S (Group Sounds). This scene has been steadily growing and it has become bigger than the mod scene especially in Nagoya. There is a clothing shop called The Other (Osu, Nagoya) run by ex-faces of the Nagoya mod scene, Hata and Takahiro Suzuki. They also have a small indie record label called The Other label. Their charismatic drive has made the Japanese sixties and seventies scene bigger and they are also highly respected by mods here too.

Still in Japan, we move on to Tokyo and an in depth description of mod from **FUMIO NAWA**: The most famous club would be 'shinjuku JAM' where a great mod event called March Of The Mods, organised by the founder of Numbers (a scooter squad) called Manabu Kuroda, was regularly held. It has been the biggest status symbol for any mods band to play at this event. 'El Sonola' (Roppongi, Tokyo) where 'Whisky A Go-Go' organized by Blue Dress, is regularly held. I was raised up to be a proper mod by this event as were other Tokyo mods. I would pop into there regularly to learn new steps, and of course, to chat the chicks up! If you find yourself checking out the scene here in Tokyo, I strongly recommend UFO Club (Koenji, Tokyo) where my band called The Marquee holds a club event called Better Days. The How (Nagoya) regularly makes an appearance here too. I guess UFO Club is the best underground club in Japan now. However, as far as I'm aware, the best mod club is probably Club Chitta (Kawasaki, Japan) that is regarded as the Mecca of mods since Tokyo Mods Mayday has been held here every May. Actually, the Tokyo Mayday once hosted hundreds of scooters and over a thousand mods from all over Japan. I personally believe that the current mod scene in Tokyo can roughly be divided into three groups: The revival mod scene is lead by Manabu Kuroda. The original mod scene lead by Blue Dress who are an exclusive mod group who organise clubs, run mod shops and issue free print material called Sir-Face. They once invited Mr. Rob Bailey from The New Untouchables as a guest DJ at their club, and they also brought northern soul into the Japanese mod scene earlier than anybody else. The British Beat and Freakbeat scene is lead by The Marquee. I can confidently say that the level of scooter decoration among the Japanese mods is impressive. I really want to show off our scooters to those British mods and scooter boys. The best scooter shop I would strongly recommend is Jungle Scooters run by Mr Furuta who's got surprisingly a lot of knowledge about mods, and his sense of restoration and decoration of scooters is just amazing. His choice of scooter accessories and other gear such as clothes is really cool since this shops original T-shirts have become must-have items among the Tokyo mods. They even sell replica overalls for Innocenti factory workers! We (The Marquee) are often invited to Mods Maydays held in other regions of Japan. It always surprises me that each mod scene in this tiny country is really different from the other. I appreciate this difference.

MARY BOOGALOO, an Italian resident in the UK gave her assessment of the differences between the British and Italian mod scenes in 2001:
The biggest difference between the Italian and the English mod scenes is a full and correct understanding of the movement. I think in Italy modernism is either misunderstood or taken very superficially.In Italy, things are quite static and they are unwilling to see beyond certain self imposed boundaries. People seem to be submerged into this erroneous idea that mod is either about northern soul or freakbeat. There's a worrying degree of ignorance in that. How can they call themselves mods and being so uninterested in exploring the real origins of modernism?

MIKE WARBURTON, who has remained involved in the mod scene in one form or another for the best part of 40 years gave this assessment of the scene in the early Noughties:
In 2002, the mod scene seemed to be returning to its roots after the 'Swinging London' trivia of the mid-nineties. Clothes-wise, it was good to see more mods wearing suits and younger mods paying attention to detail in both music and clothes. Having two rooms at the major rallies such as Clacton and Margate was a definite step in the right direction. The atmosphere at clubs was more relaxed than in the past, with everybody getting on, which is all to the good. Likewise, it was good to see rockabillies and northern soul fans accepted in the mod clubs. As far as the Hideaway Club was concerned, special thanks has to go to Manchester's 'fifties' crowd for all their support and encouragement. Hopefully more small clubs will spring up, as in my opinion, they are the lifeblood of the scene. Clothes-wise, fashion seems to be going in more of a mod direction by the season. If people are making their first purchase from Duffer or Hope and Glory or John Simons, mod has something to look forward to.

As the 20th Century came to a close, we lost one of the great DJs and a legend in his lifetime. On 4 May 1999, Roger Eagle of the Twisted Wheel passed away. ◊·

> We ran Sneakers for just over four years and in '87, when we closed, that last night, we weren't playing any records that we played in '83 when we started. That kind of summed up my philosophy of music progressing.
> PAUL J HALLAM

CHAPTER 7

As the new millennium began, the mainstream media's interest in mod dissipated in the aftermath of Britpop. Mod went back to its underground roots once again, but things were still happening. It was still finding new converts and expanding its cultural remit while retaining much of the original ethos of great clothes, great music and great clubs. Also, the harsh realities of life and the passing of time would come to haunt mod culture over the coming years as heroes and icons left us.

In 2003 one of the people who had been seen as 'one of our own' was Edwin Starr who passed away in April of that year and two years later, Long John Baldry died in September 2005.

But at the very start of the Noughties, four new books arrived on the scene; the original edition of 'The Influential Factor', Terry Rawlings' 'Mod - A Very British Phenomenon' and Paolo Hewitt's 'Soul Stylists' and 'The Sharper Word.' They were long overdue as very little had been available since 1979 and Richard Barnes' book 'Mods.' Other books of note that appeared over the first five years of the 2000s included Mike Ritson and Stuart Russell's 'The In Crowd - The Story Of Northern Soul' and Keith Rylett's 'Central 1179' which documented the Twisted Wheel in Manchester.

Bar Italia, that enduring café that first opened its doors in 1949, acquired its own scooter club in 2002. Led by Nick Robins, the group met every Sunday night and the membership was modernists who were regulars at the café. Over the next 15 years, the Bar Italia Scooter Club was to lead many prestigious ride-outs and became one the first ports of call when movie or brand photoshoots required a modernist slant.

Musically, new bands were arriving on the scene; Big Boss Man, Little Barrie, The Embrooks and Gene Drayton Unit among them. And those bands were supported by the promoters like Rob Bailey at New Untouchables, even the Hideaway Club in Manchester entertained a few bands, especially for their annual weekender event.

With the advent of the internet and emails, making connections across Europe and the World became easier and the flow of information about events was more accessible and more cost-effective. Others were returning after a hiatus. **FAY HALLAM** was among them:

I took a break from music for about seven years. I went to Christchurch College, Canterbury for four years and had just had my two boys. I had no time for being in a band. I started playing again around 2000.

Although relatively short-lived, Fay got the band Phaze together, which eventually became the Fay Hallam Trinity. As one of very few female musicians favoured by the mod scene, her longevity is a testament to her craft:

First and foremost I'm a songwriter. Without a good song you've got nothing. I try and look ok, I can play keys a bit, sing a bit, but it's songwriting that I've improved on the most over the years. Writing and recording music is like having a child... to conceive the idea, then other people get involved and add their brilliance to the sound of it...

never knowing quite how it will turn out. I love the process and it brings me a lot of happiness. I don't think I'll ever tire of it. To know there are people who love my music like I do is a wonderful thing indeed. We probably like a lot of the same music too. We are connected by a love of good music. Everything I've ever heard has influenced my song writing. I listen to all kinds of music from soul and disco to Queens of the Stoneage. Elvis Costello said recently that he nicked the start of Crossroads for something. It could be anything that catches your ear. I heard 'Begging' for the first time in ages and was inspired to write 'Dancing'. Other times I will play the piano until I find something I like. The words always come at the same time as the music.

There is definitely a strand that runs through everything that inclines towards soul beats and all the great 60s/70s music I like and, I hope, integrity. I write music that I hope sounds good and is pleasurable to listen to. I want to make each album better than the one before and I know I'm doing that.

But how does Fay feel about retaining a loyal mod following, irrespective of her personal music journey?

I think it is because my music is good and the people who like it have good taste. I am incredibly appreciative of their support. It's a two-way thing.

2001 was the last time the New Untouchables hosted at the Isle Of Wight. **ROB BAILEY** explains why they departed to set up elsewhere:

The reason we left the Isle of Wight after the 2001 edition was the atmosphere had changed. It was no longer a mod weekender with the Scooterist invasion. I had a gentlemen's agreement with Jeff Smith from the NSRA which he honoured. I would plan our events around NSRA so we would be the opposite ends of the county. However, the more mod end of the scooter scene was already starting to attend our weekender at IOW. Jeff was coming under increasing pressure from his members to switch to Isle of Wight August Bank Holiday. I believed if thousands of scooterists came, the atmosphere would change and that Ryde simply was not big enough. Jeff kept his word until the sad demise of NSRA. VFM filled the void and set up at the Ice

Rink and the rest is history. On a personal level I didn't enjoy the final edition either and the time was right to start something new. First Margate in 2002 and 2003 and then Brighton 2004. Just like the Isle of Wight a decade earlier we started Brighton with 250 dedicated modernists.

The major European events at the time included Cattolica in Italy, the Bubblegum Weekender at La Rochelle, France, and in 2004, the Stateside Satisfaction Weekender in San Francisco which was co-organised by former New Untouchable, Jason Ringgold and Rob Bailey. Ringgold had not long returned to his native land after a prolonged residency in London.

2004 was an especially busy year for the New Untouchables. Aside from the trip to San Francisco, Rob Bailey embarked on his most ambitious project at the time; Modstock 2. It was designed as three days celebrating mod and sixties culture and the line-up of bands and DJs did not disappoint.

What made the event so unique was the international dimension. Supporting The Action were Les Cappacino from Japan. The Apemen arrived from Germany and DJs came from Belgium, Spain, Italy, Sweden, USA and Japan. UK DJs were represented by some of the greatest ever: Ady Croasdell, Paul Hallam, Roger Banks, Jo Wallace, Chris Dale, Lee Miller and Alan Hanscombe.

The UK bands were also an unbeatable line up: The Aardvarks, Solarflares, Yardbirds, Prisoners, The Creation and Gene Drayton Unit.

In the world of the mainstream, the influence of mod culture was still being found. The stereotype was being neatly formed in the wake of Britpop; a three or four piece guitar-based band with a touch of aggression (but not too much); any item of clothing bearing the Fred Perry, Lonsdale, Ben Sherman brand. Footwear by Doc Marten or Clarks. The Ordinary Boys from Worthing, fronted by Sam Preston certainly looked and sounded the part. Indeed, some thought they may be the next 'big thing', but after a few brief years of modest chart success, the death knell of the band was sealed when Preston took part in Celebrity Big Brother. Neither his, nor the fortunes of The Ordinary Boys were to be quite the same again.

Similarly, The Rifles acquired a mod culture following. Formed at Redbridge College in 2003, their first gig was at the Bull and Gate in Kentish Town a year later. Their first release came out on Blow Up Records (formed by Paul Tunkin off the back of the success of the club night).

Over the next 15 years, The Rifles released a number of albums and singles. While their fortunes would fluctuate with appearances on Sky TV's 'Soccer Am' or supporting Paul Weller at The Forum in 2007, they have managed to consolidate their fan base and keep going.

2003 also saw the release of "the album we should have made in 1979" according to Brian Kotz. Back To Zero, which consisted of Brian and original guitarist Sam Burnett, recorded all the material they had written in the revival period, but had never been committed to vinyl. 'It's All Relative' was a title that resonated with the opinions of both musicians; whatever your take on mod culture might be, all of it is relative and relevant to someone. Brian decided that the album would be the closing chapter for that part of his life, so the pair never played live, although Sam did put a version of Back To Zero together for a short period as interest in mod culture gathered pace around 2013.

Back in the Midlands, Mark Mortimer had a fluid line-up of musicians in his newest incarnation: DC Fontana. At the same time, fellow Atherstone resident **NEIL SHEASBY** was having a tough time of things:

Neil Jones had a band called Walrus Gumboot based in Tamworth, not far from where I lived, but we first met in London bizarrely enough. I was in a band called Mandrake Root by this time and we played at The Laurel Tree where Blow Up used to be held. Walrus Gumboot was supporting us.

At that time, my best mate Hammy was in a very bad way with his cancer and by the time we got to that night at the Laurel Tree, my heart wasn't really in it. Mandrake Root was coming to an end, but I remember watching Walrus Gumboot that night and thinking Neil could really sing. He excited me and reminded me of all the good things like Winwood, Marriott and those sort of people. So Mandrake Root imploded and life was at a low ebb for me and I really thought about packing up for good, but my girlfirend (now my wife of 20 odd years) Claire encouraged me not to give it up. She was the one who suggested going to see Neil Jones's band and have a chat with him. I didn't want to split the band up, but I thought we might write a few songs on the side just to keep my hand in. I was turning 30 years old and didn't really have the enthusiasm to start all over again putting a band together. So I went to see him, this would have been the start of 1997, and just told him where I was at and what I wanted to do and would he be interested in doing some song writing as a side project.

Two weeks later he split Walrus Gumboot and that was when Stone Foundation came to be. It took us five or six years to find the right musicians for what we wanted to do and it was the same for DC Fontana. Ian Arnold was playing in six or seven bands at that time, but we managed to nab him. There was some crossover of musicians from both camps. Trombonist Spencer Hague, Ian Arnold and Trumpet player Lynn Thompson all played in DC Fontana or Stone Foundation at one time or another.

MARK MORTIMER takes up the story:

Steve Trigg was another one. He phoned me and asked if there was an opening for him as a trumpet player in DC Fontana. At the time, there wasn't, but I kept his number and asked around to find out more about him. He'd done stuff with Steve Winwood and others, so his reputation was top notch. When Trigg joined us, he really helped to knock the band into shape because they were a bit inexperienced but good musicians. I had also spotted Karla Milton on myspace.com and thought she looked cool, so she joined us as a backing singer and things were going really well for a while until half the band left with Karla to form the Karla Milton Collective. Of course, now Steve Trigg has become an intergral part of the Stone Foundation brass section.

By 2005 Neil Sheasby and Neil Jones were finally ready to release Stone Foundation's debut album 'In Our Time'. This was followed in 2008 by 'Small Town Soul' and 'Away From The Grain' in 2010. And this album became the real launch pad for the band to progress. They had started making new connections, not least of which was
MARK BAXTER:

I was the right age in 1979/80 - ie 17/18 - to hit The Jam and the film Quadrophenia just at the right time, with the both of them making a massive impact on me. But, recently I have thought of a couple of uncles who liked their clothes and music and I think they also influenced me as a younger kid to get into a mod mind set. I have always liked clothes and picked up on the style element of the scene very early on. Paul Weller, for me, was and still is a massive influence. Almost like the older brother I didn't have. He tipped me off in his interviews to good music, books, films and imagery too, that have all fed into my 'mod' machinery.

Mono Media was a club night which was started by me and a fella I got to know, known as Northern Andy. He was from the North, but also had a fine knowledge of Northern Soul, so the name stuck. Anyway, we started a one night a week night in a local pub on the Walworth Road in 1996 and that ran until 2000, by then it was me running it alone and bringing in new pals to DJ a mixture of 60s pop, soul, ska, soundtracks, jazz and all the stops in between. When it finished, the name sort of attached itself to me and the various projects I was then undertaking, like the books, PR for companies and now films.

Baxter had also begun an association with Darron Connett in the mid 2000's to work with him on his new project. After a false start to his career with the ill-fated 'Contagious' **DARRON CONNETT** was not prepared to let his aspirations melt away:

I hung around the Music Box studio with Steve Roberts from Bass-o-matic and learnt my craft; recording, singing ,writing etc. Fast forward a few years and my solo thing came about. By this time I was more alternative and had strong mod leanings but refusing to try and sound like Paul Weller and Oasis like everyone else.

I hooked up with Mono Media and Mark Baxter and set about another chapter. We were like Arthur & Terry from the TV show 'Minder'; ducking and diving to get noticed and we did alright, releasing the 'Onwards & Upwards' EP which had 'Just A Boy' on it that still seems to be a favourite.

We also released a vinyl single 'Soul Clean' backed with 'Ego Ascending' as a double A-side and that went great. We had a great time and both learned how the industry of media worked, we even sold out the 100 Club which is an achievement on its own.

We remain great pals and always support each other's projects. Connett was formed by me and Glen Fuller. We wrote some songs, recruited other members on the scene which was a conveyer belt type situation as we had many members coming in and out, but all top fellas and outstanding musicians. I'm very proud that I've had the opportunity to play with them all.

We had a great little run and were received well. Paul Weller invited us personally to come to Black Barn and record after hearing our first album 'Waging War On The Obvious' which was amazing as he's a big hero of mine.

Charles Rees who produced Weller's album '22 Dreams' was behind our recordings, so much was learnt and I'm very pleased we got the chance.

We then got asked to record in America, so we flew to Chicago and recorded our 2nd album 'Love & Curses' which was again a great experience. We also got the opportunity to play at some big venues to packed houses.

After a while, I wanted to pursue other things as an artist. I was getting cabin fever and itchy feet as I felt the fun was dwindling and we needed a break to do other things.

It was around this time, that a former founding member of the Immediate Society in Belfast was re-establishing herself on the mod scene again. **MARIA MORGAN** had been living her life away from mod for a number of years until she got an invitation to go out with an old friend:

As we got to the late 80s thing changed. Gel Jones and I went to London to live permanently, but I didn't last too long. I missed my family too much, but Gel stayed and people like David Holmes and Amanda Deards were more interested in the Style Council and the 90s scene. I became a bit of a recluse and life took over. I got married, had kids, but then around the late 90s a mod revival night started.

One night I went along with Amanda and it was lovely to see so many old friends from the early days. It was after that, I said to Amanda, "Let's do it again, like the old days". So we set up our club night 'Snap'.

We decided to do one or two a year and whatever money we made from the night would go to a charity nominated by the audience. New people came along as well as old friends. It was a total R&B night. By this time I was involved with the Solid Bond Scooter Club and playing records at different places. I don't class myself as a DJ. We were putting on bands at the Empire in Belfast and trying different things at Snap like an all-female DJ line up or 'Snap, Crackle, Psych' which people didn't really understand at the time. The psych scene has taken a long time to even get off the ground. That's why I have so much admiration for Sarge Sargent and Paddy Johnston. They started the Dr Crippen's night and never gave up. They kept it going when nobody was really into it, but as we were getting older, it seemed like the logical progression. I do Snap every year and the mod scene both North and South of the border is in good shape now.

In 2008 **GRAHAM DAY** retired from music. His most recent incarnation, Graham Day and The Gaolers recorded two great albums and then disappeared as he explained:
For me the Gaolers were amazing. I'd sort of retired and had been playing bass with the Buff Medways. Billy [Childish] decided that had run its course and that was that, but my mate Dan from a band called the Woggles was over in England visiting some friends and we met up in London for a beer. He told me I should start a new band with him and the Woggles bass player. Sounded like a great idea so they flew back over a couple of months later and we made the first Gaolers album, 'Soundtrack To The Daily Grind'.
There were no real plans to tour as it was a bit of a logistical nightmare with them both being in the USA, but it was so good we just had to. It sort of carried on from there. I thought our second album, 'Triple Distilled', was the best thing I've ever done and we did some great tours, but touring takes so much energy and time, and we could never do single gigs as it was too expensive to bring Dan over, so we ended up not playing again. I've never said it was finished but it sort of fizzled out. After that, I sort of retired.

Also in 2008, the mod revival period lost one of its favourite sons as Jez Bird, lead singer with The Lambrettas died on 27 August 2008.
In 2009 second edition of Paolo Hewitt's 'A Sharper Word - A Mod Anthology' was published

Jakarta [courtesy of Dimust Utomo]

and included the original first chapter of 'The Influential Factor' alongside revered authors like Nik Cohen, Tony Parsons, Tom Wolfe, Colin McInnes and Dick Hebdige.

That same year, two contrasting developments took place at polar opposite ends of the 'mod spectrum'. Oasis frontman, Liam Gallagher launched his own clothing range and store Pretty Green. The name of the brand was inspired by a Jam album track and the clothing was undeniably influenced by mod culture. Mr Gallagher said he was inspired by his love of clothes and the apparent lack of availability of clothing that matched his personal style. Among the mod community, the emergence of Pretty Green caused a certain amount of controversy with disputes about its relevance, quality and pricing structure in relation to modernism. It could be argued that the debates around Pretty Green were a portent of things to come in mod culture. It represented a marked split in opinion. Those who supported the brand were regarded as 'part-timers' by those who took modernism more seriously.

Also in 2009, **ANDREA MATTIONI** finally got everything in place to start a new annual event in Lowestoft, Suffolk:

I have actually moved to the UK twice, the first time was in 1989, with four friends from Rimini and the reason was purely the mod scene. Unfortunately 1989 was also probably the worse period for the scene, so after a few months we decided to move back to Italy. The second time was in 2007 and this time the reason was my then girlfriend (now wife) Maggie. Obviously my involvement with the mod scene and the fact that I had already many friends and knew lots of people in the UK helped us taking this decision. I had been having conversations about organising an event for years with Kurt Fricker, Matt Hudson and Lee Miller on separate occasions. We all agreed that, even though there where many good events around the UK, at the time there wasn't any event that was specifically for a modernist crowd, with a strict smart mod dress policy on the door. One night Matt, Kurt and myself were at the same mod do in Northampton and we started to seriously talk about it (as serious as a conversation fuelled mainly by alcohol can be). The following day Kurt phoned back with two options of venues that we could use and that was it. We had a first meeting and decided to involve Lee Miller in the organisation, because I knew he was of the same idea. So four like-minded people decided to put on a 100% mod weekender, with no compromise and no interest in making any financial profit. The first Dreamsville took place in 2009 and although it is now a big success, it has not always been easy. In the third year we had about 120 people through the door and we nearly considered giving up, then we decided to give it another go for the following year and good job we did. The weekender has slowly begun to grow again until it became the sell out that it has been for the last few years. The secret to our success I suppose is being true to ourselves and being coherent with what we advertise, all we ever wanted to do was to organise a mod rally on a UK coast town, strictly for Mods, with a smart dress code and a 'no drink on the dance floor' policy, with current DJs spinning only original vinyl. The fact that we don't have any interest in making any money obviously helps, we don't really care if we have 600 or 200 people, as long as we can cover the expenses, therefore we don't really have to come to any compromise, we clearly advertise Dreamsville for what it is, if you like it you go, if you don't like it you don't, as simple as that. Luckily it looks like a lot of people do like it.

In the Autumn of 2010, **PETER CHALLIS** had decided to leave Ikon Footwear and start his own shoe company:
I spent 12 years of my life building the brand from nothing to a credible middle market footwear brand. Previous to that I re-started the Frank Wright label after the factory had closed in the mid 90's. At Ikon I managed a small team of people and along with my wife and brother; we took immense pride in our endeavours there. Delicious Junction came about because a number of previous clients asked me to help them out and I suppose it's the best way I can express myself - I can't play an instrument and I don't sing too good - what I feel I do best is create shoes to make people happy and put a smile on their feet. I love the process and hopefully the result is a cracking pair of shoes at the end of a great suit or outfit. The inspiration is from spending over 26 years working in the footwear trade and being intensely interested in what makes a great product and why it appeals or doesn't. The grass roots starts in the

late 50's and 60's and the genres and subcultures that sprang out of those decades and continue to flourish. I also listen a lot to what people have to say and I meet a number of interesting people along the way who just love to talk about shoes; and I also collaborate with people and hopefully bring out the best of their ideas too.

Delicious Junction also did things a little differently to other 'brand' businesses. Their catalogue was more of a magazine featuring interviews with recognised names from the mod culture scene who worked with the company to design shoes: Terry Rawlings, Gary Crowley, Paolo Hewitt, Neville Staples, John Hellier, Steve Cradock, Jonny Owen, Steve White and upcoming bands Stone Foundation, Darron Connett and Joel Rogers from The Last Of The Troubadors, Terry Shaughnessy with his band The Universal and Billy Sullivan who fronts The Spitfires. These new bands also received sponsorship from Delicious Junction to assist with recording and release costs for their music and of course, footwear.

Over on the West Coast of America, a new single appeared during the winter of 2010. Nick Waterhouse released 'Some Place'.

Born in Santa Ana, but raised in Huntingdon Beach, California, Nick Waterhouse started playing guitar at the age of 12. Unlike most of his contemporaries, Waterhouse's musical influences included Mose Allison, John Lee Hooker and Van Morrison. While at High School, he began his musical career with Intelligista who became a well-respected band on the Orange County underground music scene. That band split when High School finished and Waterhouse set off for San Francisco State University.

Whilst there, he became a DJ, took a job at Rooky Ricardo's Records in the Lower Haight District and became friends with Matthew Correia of the Allah-Las.

Despite several attempts to find a suitable band to play in, nothing materialised, so Nick Waterhouse decided to go abroad to study and his destination was London.

After a year away, Waterhouse returned to the West Coast and in 2011, he recorded his first single 'Some Place' which became a massive collectable among DJs. The following year he released his debut LP 'Time's All Gone' and embarked on a series of gruelling tours to support it. His 'stock' was riding high with the UK mod audience, as his brand of traditional Rhythm & Blues resonated with them. 2014's album 'Holly' pushed Nick Waterhouse to a wider audience across Europe. With 2016's 'Never Twice' he has become a much-sought-after artist.

At the same time another new artist had a hit with a track called 'Inhaler'. Miles Kane had already made a name for himself with bands like Little Flames, The Rascals and Last Shadow Puppets and was another musician influenced by the wider definition of mod culture.

If nothing else, mod culture has inspired an entrepreneurial spirit which has manifested itself more than ever in the last 15 years. These are small relatively successful businesses supplying a demand to an eager market.

As we have seen, Art Gallery Clothing and Delicious Junction Footwear came from people already into mod. But they are not the only ones. Several shops have opened around the UK selling all things mod-related and with the rise of the internet, online shopping has become a 'norm'. From brands like Nicholson & Walcot handmade scarves to Teri England Attire, Hipster UK in Luton or The In Crowd in Fareham, these businesses continue to thrive. And new clothing labels have emerged: DNA Groove from Italy, Charles Caine Shirts or Scott Fraser Collection have all established themselves recently.

One particular success story from an online perspective is modshoes.co.uk. Founded by **ANDREW LINDSAY** in 2011, Andrew gave this opinion as to why that entrepreneurial spirit thrives in mod culture:

Mods are do-ers. They are not passive in any way and can almost be OCD (obsessive, compulsive disorder) about things. They're driven to find that 'holy grail', whether it's a rare record, information or the slightest minute detail, they always strive for perfection (in whatever form that may be). But it is that drive to do things and create something new that sets it apart. It was that 'can do' attitude that led to me forming modshoes.co.uk. I grew up in a village called Cottenham in Cambridgeshire and like many of my contemporaries; music was my entry into mod. As a kid, The Specials and Dexy's Midnight Runners got me interested, but my seminal moment was seeing The Milkshakes and The Prisoners on Channel 4's The Tube in 1984. Fast forward a few decades and I found myself in a covers band playing mostly mod-related tunes and my attire was pretty much a Fred Perry and white jeans which were ok, but I felt the need to look sharper and smarter.

One item I was particularly keen to find was a really good quality brogue. I did some investigating online and found some nice ones, but the prices were frankly ridiculous. Now my professional background was in web designing, so I knew all about how search engines and the internet worked, so I set up a blog page and started writing about this quest to find a pair of good quality, affordable brogues. This was in early 2011 and the first month I had 500 hits. By the April of that year I had 4,000. I started doing little videos about shoes and they were getting 20,000 views.

Eventually, I decided to start selling shoes online. The name Modshoes was deliberate because I knew that when people typed into their search engines, 'mod shoes' would be one of the most used terms and so it proved to be. People type it in and there is my site, top of the list. The business has grown from there really. We have stalls at a number of mod and scooterist rallies throughout the year and we have expanded our range to the point where we source our own stock from across Europe. We know our market and try to be ahead of trends, but we always aim for designs that are classy, well-made and not available on the High Street. And we never compromise on the soles either. They have to be leather. I would say our tasselled loafer; the 'Duke' has been our most popular so far and we are really pleased with the ladies range that we introduced.

Of course, advertising has been a real plus for us by linking up with internet radio shows like Alan May's 'Glory Boy Mod Radio Show' and 'We Are The Mods with Warren Peace'. Those shows gave us access to the chat rooms where we could connect to their audience who were also our potential customers.

Also that year, another new development in mod culture began in an unexpected part of the world. **IQBAL DJOHA** began his clothing label 'Wondersoul' in his hometown of Jakarta, Indonesia:

I remember being fascinated the mod scene through Ska music when I was 13. It was 1998 when Ska was very popular in Jakarta. The Specials was one of my favourite bands. One day my friend brought me a SLC Punks dvd and that was when I saw a gentlemen, dressed fine in suits and posing with his scooter. Thought it was Ska 2 Tone style at first. The internet wasn't big in Indonesia back then, so we had limited access to that media. It was not easy to find the information of everything mod.

Around the year 2000, the internet started to become available for everyone and the definition of mod was growing among us. First it was the music; then the fashion and scooters. More and more people in Jakarta wanted to become a mod.

Social media let us connect and share the information to each other. 'Quadrophenia' was also influencing us to dress up and ride our scooters together.

I don't know exactly how many there are, but I think there are hundreds of them. That's what I see at mod events in Jakarta. Actually you can also find the mod scene in several cities in Indonesia. Such as Bandung, Malang, Surabaya, etc.

I created Wondersoul in 2011 because... to be honest it's hard to get UK mod clothing in Indonesia. I used to hunt for Fred Perry's, Ben Sherman's and Harrington jackets at the flea market. I learnt about the style from the book Spirit of 69 - Skinhead Bible by George Marshall. I borrowed it from my friend and it was photo-copied!

I did lots of hunting back then. But then I realised, it's about time for Indonesia to have local mod brand. It can be more affordable and I hope we got something to be proud of. And I also want to contribute something to the scene through Wondersoul.

My personal favourite event so far is the Jakarta Mods Mayday 2010. This was my first time being part of the organising team for the event and we got 300 scooters that joined the first Scooter Runs.

As time went by, I focused on throwing a more intimate party called Jakarta Soul where the DJs spin some late 50s to early 70s music. It has been running for five or six years and sometimes we have guest DJ appearance from other countries. I can tell the crowd is always dress to impress. And more people are dressed in local products from 'Wondersoul' to other brands; from vintage clothing to tailor-made. Some say that Jakarta Soul throws the best proper mod party in Indonesia.

The scene in Jakarta might not be as big as in the UK. But it's a solid community. Mods and skinheads usually come together and fill the dance floor, while lots and lots scooter boys will join the crowd in the big event such as Jakarta Mods Mayday.

In January of 2011, personal invites went out to a number of people asking if they would like to be extras for a day of filming at Sandown Racecourse. The film would eventually be known as 'Outside Bet' based on the novel 'The Mumper' by Mark Baxter and Paolo Hewitt. Stars of the film included the late Bob Hoskins, Dudley Sutton, Jenny Agutter, Rita Tushingham, Phil Davis, Linda Robson and Calum McNab.

However, the extras on set that day were mostly unknown to each other, but had Baxter and Hewitt as the common link. Among those who froze on that chilly day were Neil Sheasby and Neil Jones (Stone Foundation), Darron Connett and Jeff Shadbolt (Purple Hearts) to name a few. The film became something of a comedy cult classic.

MARK BAXTER takes up the story:

I left my 9-5 to make the most of the situation I found myself in when 'The Mumper' took off and the deal to make it into a film was done. I needed to make a few bob as that project got underway. I have always been a buyer and seller. I come from a rag and bone man (not the singer) tradition, so I'm used to picking things up cheap and moving them on at a profit.

I applied that same business sense to my clients. I worked with them when they were quite small and began to help to grow them into bigger and better known brands. I always say selling is selling no matter what the item is; a book, film, a pork chop or a tin of beans. You create a buzz and a demand for that item. I've just got a knack of doing that I guess.

My first real PR job was when I ended up working with Sir Paul Smith on a book launch at his Floral Street shop in 2005. I arranged for a few scooters to turn up on the night and that went very well. The best day would be the Bar Italia 65th anniversary celebrations. We had Suggs and Adam Ant and many others play live in Frith Street on a glorious sunny Sunday, with approx 15,000 people turning up and we raised £10,000 for Great Ormond St. on the day. It was just wonderful.

Two very sad personal events led me to becoming an author; the death of my dad suddenly from cancer and losing our baby in the same year, the year being 2000.

I don't mind admitting it, I was floored that year. I was completely lost. I was very close to my old man and to see him die so quickly was horrible and losing a baby a few weeks later, well I have no need to say anymore on that.

Anyway, once I got to the end of that year, I just seemed to seriously 'wake up' and realise that life is very precious and very short and all these things we say we are going to do, in reality, we do very few of them.

I just knew I had to stop talking and have a go at the things I wanted to do. One was to write, so I wrote. I had a limited education and my grammar was shocking (it still is) but I wasn't going to let anything stop me. With the support of my wife Lou, I was given time to explore and refine ideas. Two very important mentors popped up at that time, Paolo Hewitt and Dean Powell. Both had a very large part in my development to what I am doing now and that will never be forgotten. In truth, once we had signed the deal to sell 'The Mumper' to the producers, myself and Paolo had very little input on the film. We were paid and that was that. We still tried to suggest clothes, music, etc, but they had a team on board to deal with that. At the end of the day, it was a massive learning curve and one I wouldn't have missed for the world. We were well treated on-set, so no complaints at all. I'm very proud of 'Outside Bet' and to have Bob Hoskins in it, well, don't come much better than that for me.

Not long after the 'Outside Bet' had gone into post-production, a new club started in London as **DAVE EDWARDS** explained:

Giles Plumpton and I had talked about doing a night for a little while. We wanted something with more Jazz and R&B as opposed to a "northern soul" night. We purposely don't use the term "northern" on our fliers. We'd done a few nights called 'Steppin Out' previously and talked about doing a night called 'Hot Barbeque'.

I was coming back from football with Reuben Bellingham and he said his neighbour Joe was DJing at this new venue in Islington and we should pop along. We called Giles up and met him there and Joe suggested we take a look at the back room. Our jaws dropped when we walked in. "Why don't you do a night? It's free to hire and you're the first people to see it, today's the first day it's been open" said Joe. He'd actually fitted the venue out and had set us up. So started Sidewinder in March 2011, thinking we'll get a couple of months out of it. We're into our 7th year now!

New bands which had a mod/sixties inclination and attracted a mod culture fan base were appearing on the live scene. The Electric Stars from Manchester began in 2011. By February 2012, they signed to Dizzy Holmes' Detour Records and released their debut 'Sonic Candy Soul' to great approval by the ever-growing mod culture ranks. They would become regulars on the live circuit and like many of the new bands, their profile would be raised by their involvement in a charity event that would show a different side to the generic, stereotyped image of mod culture, but they also used a form of social media that began in 2004 and by 2006 became available to anyone with an email address. The explosion of Facebook, then Twitter, Instagram and the other platforms of social media meant the old print media and music press were no longer of use. Bands could build their own fan base by direct contact through their computers. With other technological advances in digital formats and platforms to release new material, being signed to a major label in search of success was no longer a 'must'. Studio costs were becoming affordable and with the advent of crowd funding, paying for the entire recording process became easier.

A band did not need a recording contract with a major label to become a success. They could record and release what they wanted, when they wanted and sell directly to their fan base. It really all depended on your levels of ambition, expectations and commitment. By this time, the mainstream music business (which includes radio, television, major festivals and print media) were wallowing in a 'bunker' mentality of zero-risk, low investment, high return 'safe' product.
In fact, it could be argued that the music industry was more interested in the 'brand' potential of a performer than they were in their ability to actually sing without the aid of 'auto correct'; the software that could make anyone sound pitch perfect in a studio.
But the majors could always rely on their back catalogue to boost profits and when (according to the UK Official Charts website) an artist need sell a mere 7,500 copies to

make the Top 40 singles chart and a miserly 4,000 to make number 40 in the album chart, the cash-cow was no longer a million-selling single, it was the old material, repackaged, remastered, reinvented in every available format that made money. This is why a sudden renewed interest in vinyl exploded with so many reissues of back catalogue, even supermarkets began stocking product, but given that the industry had presided over the decimation of the independent music retailer sector and even HMV were struggling to survive, this was hardly a surprise.

DJ and club promoter **PAUL HALLAM** gave this analogy of the situation as he saw it:
Many years ago, I saw Bo Diddley at Lyceum with Meteors on a Sunday night. 300 people were in there and 250 of them were there to see the Meteors. Roddy Radiation and The Tearjerkers were on first. I think he organised the gig and because more people had come to see the Meteors, they put Bo Diddley on at 9pm and as a 16 year-old mod I was really excited to see him.
Nowadays, you get what I call the 'Mojo Generation' who see a list of the top 500 albums of all time in Mojo magazine and think, 'Oh we need to go and see them'. Well I remember seeing the MC5 at the 100 Club in the early 90s and there was 200 people in there, then all of a sudden they come back 15 or 20 years later with the drummer from the Libertines in their ranks and they're selling out the Royal Festival Hall.

One band was quietly going about its business, building its fan base, self-financing and releasing its music. In 2010, a booking for a gig began an incredible chain of events that was to continue over the next seven years and beyond. **NEIL SHEASBY** takes up the story:
It started with a promoter who was doing things at northern soul events. He was bringing people over to sing live, but with backing tracks. One of the first guys that we came into contact with was Steve Calloway.
The promoter said he wanted a band to work with him and he thought Stone Foundation would fit the bill, so he asked us and we thought, well here is a chance to work with some proper, bona fide soul artists, so we jumped at the chance.
Then Nolan Porter came over and we just hit it off right away. Since then we have

London [courtesy of Rob Bailey]

brought Nolan back ourselves and then we got Joe 'Pep' Harris from Undisputed Truth. It's been a privilege and an honour to work with these people. Then the arena tour with The Specials in 2011 happened and was more by luck than judgment.

John Bradbury (RIP) happened to be at Fiddler's Elbow in Camden on the same night we were playing there. I think The Specials were looking for a certain kind of soul band rather than another ska outfit and we fitted the bill. We got on really well with everyone and it has been one of the highlights of our career.

Since then we've supported The Blow Monkeys, The Selecter, The Beat and The Truth. By the time we started work on the album 'To Find The Spirit', things got more surreal. Carleen Anderson formerly of Young Disciples and Paul Weller's band sang on 'When You're In My World'. Pete Williams from Dexy's is a great songwriter and played on 'Wonderous Place' and 'Stronger Than Us'.

Denis Bovell did a remix of 'Don't Let The Rain' and Andy Fairweather Low was just great. His nephew, Lee, is a fan of the band and he kept on to Andy about doing something with us, and he agreed to do backing vocals, so we had a day trip to Cardiff and he sang on 'Hold On'. It was great just to sit and chat with Andy and hear a few stories of those early days of modernism and the whole Sixties era.

Interest in Nolan Porter's career received a welcome boost. This, in part, had been aided by Paul Weller covering Porter's Northern Soul classic 'If I Could Only Be Sure' on his 2004 album 'Studio 150', but Porter's appearances with Stone Foundation culminated in an extraordinary show at London's 100 Club on 7 July which turned out to be one of the events of 2012. **NOLAN PORTER** explained the chemistry between himself and the band: There is a real musical camaraderie between SF and myself. We both really love soul music and SF's sound really shows that these guys have been raised on soul music and have a deep understanding of its cadence and meaning.

Also we have the same warped sense of humor! I enjoyed recording a new version of 'Crazy Love' more with SF than when I recorded it all those years ago. I've become such good friends with them. I owe them so much and we find it mutually gratifying to help each other's careers.

2012 saw the launch of the book 'The A To Z Of Mod' by Mark Baxter and Paolo Hewitt. Held at the Fred Perry store, Seven Dials in Covent Garden, London.
It was attended by a who's who of mod past and present; Billy Sullivan of The Spitfires, Phil Daniels, Daphne Sherman (widow of Ben), Neil Sheasby and Neil Jones of Stone Foundation, Cass Pennent, Dave Edwards and **DARRON CONNETT**'s new band Last Of The Troubadors (TLOTT):
Joel Rogers was a promoter and sometime acoustic songsmith that I met through doing gigs on his nights. We became mates and talked about doing something as I'd told him I was looking to do something else after Connett. We set about writing songs then got Luke Jeffries on Drums and Rob Pyne (ex The Rifles) on bass and set about recording our debut 'Sooner The Better' and gigging around Britain.
The sound of TLOTT was very different from CONNETT. The influences were wide and varied from pop, grunge, soul, rock, but we had crafted a sound very much our own. The Connett/Rogers song writing team was proving a winning one and we were having fun doing it.
Our second EP 'Don't Stand On Shadows' came out on Delicious Junction Records and had the legendary 'Buzzcock' Steve Diggle guest on guitar for a couple of tracks.

Despite a decent following, the recruiting of Tony Marshall to the band and supporting The Rifles on a UK tour, TLOTT sadly came to an end in early 2015, but Darren Connett had already left the band to pursue a new direction.
Spitfire's frontman Billy Sullivan had been playing guitar since the age of eight, inspired by the likes of Paul Weller and Noel Gallagher. Initially in school bands and rehearsing locally in his home town of Watford, he began writing his own material. One of the Spitfires early gigs outside of Watford was supporting The Last Of The Troubadors in South Wimbledon.
Just prior to recording their debut single 'Spark To Start b/w Sirens' at Black Barn Studios, the band went through a major line up change with Sullivan joined by Matt Johnson and Sam Long. With Stuart Deabill taking up the management duties and sponsorship from Delicious Junction, their career gathered momentum and continues to this day.

Arguably, the one event 2012 that confirmed mods influence on popular culture in Britain was the opening and closing ceremonies of the London Olympic Games. Conceived and directed by Danny Boyle, the overall theme was celebrating the best of British heritage and the nation's contribution to popular culture. The 'bookend' events to this sporting extravaganza included a hefty dose of music and mod culture was part of it. From tracks by The Jam, The Who, Specials and Blur, to live appearances by Liam Gallagher with Beady Eye, Ray Davis of The Kinks, Madness and the Kaiser Chiefs performing a rendition of 'Pinball Wizard' accompanied by fifty or so mods on scooters entering the Olympic Stadium, the watching global audience could be left in no doubt that mod (by any definition) was firmly a part of British popular culture.

And mod had its own competitor, self-confessed mod culture cyclist Bradley Wiggins. He had already made a guest appearance on Eddie Piller's Modcast radio show prior to becoming the first Briton to win the Tour De France and gain further success at the Olympics, becoming one of the most decorated Olympians in British sporting history. It could also be argued that Sir Bradley (knighted in 2013 to add to his CBE in 2009) was one of the first 'celebrity' mods. Another in that category was actor Martin Freeman.

In August 2012, another new band from Paris released its' first EP. 'Les Chats de Goutttiere'. French Boutik announced themselves to the world of mod culture. Here is guitarist and songwriter **SERGE HOFFMAN**:
I was in a bit of a retirement from playing in public for a few years after my last group (Chatterton) split up in 1991. I still played and composed and got together with other musicians for one-off sessions, but didn't find any kindred spirits to form a group with. Also, I got really into graphic design and was concentrating on that.
I was DJing at a friend's bar in Paris when I met Zelda in 2007, we hit it off immediately talking about music and the song ideas I had, and she offered to try to write lyrics to the music I had written. Then I discovered that she also was a drummer and we started to try to put together a group. I met Elian, our bassist, at another nearby bar shortly thereafter and Zelda's friend Flora started to sing with us.

Before long, **GABRIELA GIACOMAN** joined the band as the lead singer:
Serge, Zelda and I all met each other at various soul nights in Paris in 2010. Serge was DJing at a place called 'Ne Nous Fachons Pas' in the 9th district (named after the goofy 60s French film, a really cool place which is sadly now closed) and Zelda came with some skinhead friends and they got to talking about music. He had some compositions but no lyrics and she liked to write so they got together to do the first French Boutik demo, 'Kinky Allumette'.

I met Serge around the same time at a soul all nighter in the 18th district. Actually, it is funny now that I think about it, I went there with Olivier Popincourt and friends from his former band and not only did I eventually end up singing for Serge's band but Olivier now guests with us on keyboard. And myself and Zelda guested on his record recently. We all saw each other again a few weeks later when DC Fontana came to play at 'La Flèche d'Or' (which sadly just closed). Myself and Scott the organist ended up first at 'Ne Nous Fachons Pas' and then at Serge's place drinking and listening to music. Ironically, none of the resulting combos are soul bands, but we all love that music and it is nice to have a little community. Serge does not DJ these days as he is so busy with band things, but lots of friends do so there is always good music after the show if we can get someone booked with us.

It was more recently that we met our current bassist Jean-Marc Johannes. He used to come to all our shows and take fantastic photos, and had a great memory of seeing one of Serge's first bands years ago. Apparently a few alternative student types were there and sat on the floor, and Serge yelled "Stand up you hippies" at them from the stage.

French Boutik was one of many new bands that benefitted from the explosion of podcasts; the phenomena of Internet based radio.
One of the early and most popular mod-related internet radio shows was Eddie Piller's Modcast. Primarily, it was a chat show with invited guests and two regular co-hosts. The mainstay was Dean Rudland and, for a relatively short time, Jonathan Owen.
Broadcast on a monthly basis, Eddie Piller drew on his immense contacts within music and mod to get guests that included Rick Buckler, Geno Washington, Gary

Shail and Mark Wingett of Quadrophenia, Ian Page and Paolo Hewitt among others. Due to a serious health scare, Eddie Piller had to suspend his activities until he recovered in 2013. Having been restored to full health, Eddie and his long-time producer Sarah Bolshi were involved with the establishment of a new dedicated internet station based in the West End; Soho Radio. The station recruited some high quality DJ/presenters who included Andy Lewis, Gary Crowley and former frontman of 80s band Blue Rondo A La Turk and a legend of The Wag Club, Chris Sullivan.

On the 23 November 2012, internet radio saw the first ever episode of 'We Are The Mods with Warren Peace'. Having been expelled from USA-based radio station Thumbin', the show moved over to Wake The Nation Radio.

In his typically spikey manner, **WARREN PEACE** gives some background to his rise as a podcast radio host:

I grew up in Newport Pagnell, Bucks which most people know thanks to the infamous M1 service station made famous by Frank Spencer in the 70's. I discovered mod in the 80's thanks to family members who lived it and because in my school, it was the cool thing to do. It was either that or Spandau f**ing Ballet. Frilly pirate shirts or parkas. Steve Strange or Steve Marriott. No one back then swore an oath to the 'mod gods' or claimed 'mod for life'... that's a myth. We just had fun.

We preached the gospel according the Jam-era Weller and discovered Gino Washington through Dexy's. We learned as we went along. We got better at it and discovered a passion for soul music and the irrefutable benefits of knowing a good tailor as we developed. I did a late-night show at a US radio station back in the mid 00's, playing 50's/60's jazz mainly. Because it was 'graveyard shift, not quite ready for a prime time' show, I could be a little more outspoken which was really to amuse myself and pass the time in between Coltrane tracks and shots of scotch. This is how the trademarked 'Warren Peace rant' came to be. I was moved to an afternoon spot, assuming this might curb the scotch intake and because I was gaining a ground swell of fervent listeners, most of whom hated me but couldn't tear themselves away from the radio. I had learned a valuable lesson early on in my career that people love to be offended. My most loyal listeners, even up to the day I retired, were the ones who'd piss on the flames if I were on fire.

Finally, after one rant too many, the station manager suggested that I'd be better 'suited' for internet radio. They shut down my show on air, live. A fist fight ensued which was actually broadcast as it happened. Someone out there probably has a copy of that... it's hilarious by all accounts. I just remember it being painful and thinking, 'what the f*** do I do now?". It was about this time that I started to hear about these small mod scenes cropping up in remote postal codes (Indonesia, Thailand, Colombia etc.)

Mods tucked away in regions most of us can't even find on a map, creating a mod scene that, for the first time in history, was on their terms, not England's; basically thumbing their nose at the mod 'elitism' in the UK/Europe dictating to them what mod should be, how to dress, what scooter to ride.

They were just getting on with it rather than talking about it, which I found inspiring. Shortly after, I started 'We are the Mods!'

The name itself was a blatant reference to Quadrophenia which I knew would piss off the elitists. Dallas was an unlikely location - not exact a bastion of mod culture -but in many ways it was perfectly removed from the UK scene to where I could remain uninfluenced by what was going on there as well as putting 5,000 miles between me and the mods issuing death threats. It's also close to Austin, Texas which was home to the late Ronnie Lane and Ian McLagan (the latter of whom I was lucky enough to interview live on the show). 'We Are The Mods' became the most syndicated global mod show at the time with two major sponsors footing the bill.

I had become really irritated at older mid-life mods not wanting 'the little herberts' to jump on the bandwagon'. It was these sad aging bastards with their ill-fitting Fred Perrys on carnival float-type bikes - the antithesis of mod swank and swagger - turning off the kids who are discovering mod for the first time and sending them running back to Radio 1 and into the arms of Lady GaGa or Katy Perry.

The show's genesis was a reaction to this and a lot of other bullshit and hypocrisy happening in the mod scene that no one was openly discussing at the time. One

example being the 'look sharp, always' ethos of mod, and there's these guys with their beer bellies pouring over the belts of their unhemmed trousers telling a slim-line 17-year-old how he or she is not doing mod right. It was a joke.
Irish listeners were the first to pick up on it at the time. I remember reading a lot from them online. "Warren is a gobshite, BUT... He's got a f***ing point and he's saying what we're all thinking". They hated me and my proverbial bullshit but were relieved someone was out there with a loud voice and a radio show of some significance - calling it as they saw it. It all snowballed from there. I was rattling a lot of prominent cages in the mod scene. Nothing and no-one was off-limits and some prominent 'Faces' blacklisted me from early on. I called out the writers of the fictional 'mod rule book'. Here's Warren Peace's rule book," I said. "Rule 1... there are no f*** rules". That's when it really kicked off.
Prominent mods, writing style blogs and getting their suits tailored in Thailand... preaching "attention to detail" and the importance of a three-button suit while forgetting quality is as much the thread count as the button count. I joked about it on the show, but a box of poo balls disguised as chocolate really DID find its way to my address in Dallas.
You'll remember when we three hosts of the show did an appearance at March of the Mods in 2013, I had to hire a minder due to death threats! That's was a little disconcerting, but I was on a mission and nothing was going to stop me at the time, least of all a few internet trolls spewing their hate and vitriol. The only thing I somewhat regret is publically burning the book 'Mods' by Richard Barnes.
A lot of people thought it was a cheap publicity stunt, but it had a deeper meaning to me personally. The book's cover advertises '150 pages of photographs from the original mods'. It was like a bible when I first discovered mod. It was our only real reference book back then, but to many, if it didn't appear in those pages, it didn't happen. It wasn't 'real' mod.
Interviewing Gill Evans (now Catling) an original early mod was eye-opening to me. She was involved in the scene in the very early 60's when mod was in the jazz and coffee shop stage. They didn't even have a word for it, so they called themselves

'Continentalists' due to the Italian and French fashion that inspired their early look. In her part of the country, Birmingham, mods carried walking canes and actually danced with them! That's something you've never read in Richard Barnes' book, but its undeniable mod history. Like the boys, or some of them, wearing girl's make-up as a pre-cursor to glam a decade later. That's something else neatly swept under the rug and ignored. I burned the book in protest. There was something more... a lot more to the subculture than 150 black and white pictures and a fictitious mod rule book. I didn't care who I offended. It had to be said. Loudly. With 1,000 kHtz of power behind me, a microphone in my left hand and a bottle of scotch in my right.

Having hosted the show single-handedly for a number of episodes, **WARREN PEACE** decided to bring in some additional help:
Alan 'Hacker' Hudson was an ace face from my schooldays with a deft knowledge of mod's revival era and scooters with often differing opinion from my own. I like a good debate and it made for good radio.
Penny Lane had hosted a mod radio show (Punks In Parkas) based in Winnipeg Canada. She was a young mod, new to the scene and learning as she went along. I thought the combination of the two would give the show a good balance, which ultimately, it did. The listening figures went through the roof.
The tipping point was when Graham Lentz came on board to replace Hacker, who needed a break from the rollercoaster ride that had become 'We Are The Mods!' Graham was a mod historian and published author; an authority, prominent on the UK scene and a great radio presence who offered a different perspective from my own. It was also about this time I started booking celebrity guests. Geno Washington, The Kink's Dave Davis, Ian McLagan, Mark Wingett, P.P Arnold, Carl Barat, Phil Davis, Vicky McClure, Alan McGee etc. The listening numbers were mental. The Mod Generation website ran a 'Best of' poll. 2012 I think it was. 'We are the Mods' won 57% of the popular vote for best Mod Radio show. To put that in perspective, Eddie Pillar's Modcast was runner up at 7%! As you can imagine, the mod elitists were up in arms and accused The Mod Gen of rigging the poll. They never did another poll after

> Acid Jazz were one of three record labels that the newly formed Corduroy went to see. Ed Piller booked us into his studio two days later. His first words to me were "Are you a mod?". Acid Jazz became a refuge for displaced survivors of the mod revival, mainly because it was owned by one, but musically it was all over the place.
> RICHARD SEARLE

that and I suspect our success may have had something to do with that. It was just unfathomable to these people that this upstart from the UK-based in Texas and his two cohorts were taking the mod scene by storm. I'd look at other Podcasts as see the listening/streaming data. Big shows were doing 500-800 downloads. We were north of 95,000. We were ranked the #3 podcast on iTunes... iTunes! Other than the poll results that year, the highlights have to be the guests. My interview with Geno Washington has to be up there because he was off his tits... high as a kite! He still says it was his best radio interview ever and I cry with laughter when I listen back.

My interview with Ian McLagan was his last before his untimely passing and he was in great spirits. It was a very candid, honest half hour and we became friends afterwards, exchanging numbers and staying in touch. My on-air duets with Judy Street singing her northern soul classic 'What' and Rhoda Dakar with me being a terrible Kenny Rogers to her Dolly Parton singing 'Islands in the Stream'. I always felt that, love me or hate me, my interviews were my strong suit. I always had a knack for putting interviewees at ease and getting them to do things they wouldn't normally do on-air. Breaking bands like French Boutik, The Riots, RAF, The Most etc. I'm still very proud of that. Reading my hate mail made for some of the funniest radio moments.

Another high point is a Christmas special we did called 'O, Come Keep the Faith All' Radio gold. People still talk to me about that one and every Christmas, it racks up another 5k streams and downloads on Podomatic.com.

Two bands that did benefit from featuring on 'We Are The Mods' were The Travellers, later to become Gemma and The Travellers and The Riots from Moscow.

Here, **ROBERT P** from Gemma and The Travellers explains how they formed and the impact that mod culture had on their career:

We met 2008. We always had a love for the 60's music, sound, culture and clothes; that's maybe why the mods appreciate us. It's been great to find many mods who appreciate our music and vibe, even though we have not tried to win over the mod scene as such.

The Travellers were a duo from 2008 with support from a couple of musicians from

2011 to 2014. That project was ended and we formed a soul band called Gemma & The Travellers in 2014 until the present. It is easy to confuse them but the influences are very different. For The Travellers, the first release was 'Blue' EP in 2008, 'For the Waves' EP on 12" vinyl in 2010, 'Summer With No Sun' single in 2012, 'Stay' in 2013. The first single for Gemma & The Travellers was 'I'll Do My Way' in 2014 and we came out with our first full length album in 2016, 'Too Many Rules & Games'.

Warren Peace picked up on our previous project The Travellers, and gave us some great exposure to the mod scene. Then we did some shows and a live session for New Untouchables which really boosted us in the UK. Soul DJ Craig Charles got into our work and played us on BBC6 Music.

Our musical influences range from Aretha Franklin, Julie Driscoll, James Brown, Sharon Jones & the Dap-Kings and Marva Whitney to Sonny Knight & the Lakers, Lee Fields & the Expressions and Dyke & the Blazers.

We sent our single, 'Too Many Rules & Games' to Helmut at Legere Records. He liked it and asked to hear demos of the rest of the album and we signed for the release late 2016 for the album in 2017.

For The Riots, however, things did not go according to plan. Such was their popularity following the release of their debut album 'Time For Truth', that an expectant UK fan base were buzzing with the news that the band were to go on a five date tour of the country.

A UK promoter had booked venues and included French Boutik and other popular new bands to join The Riots tour, but an oversight put paid to whole thing and what followed can only be described as a debacle. At the last minute and due to complications with the relevant UK authorities, lead singer Sasha Balatov was refused entry into the UK. His two band mates had no problems and actually made the flight to London. There have been several allegations about what happened next, especially with the two who did make it to the UK. The only certainty is that once in London, they could not fly home until their allocated flight date.

The tour actually went ahead and again, allegations were made about the circumstances surrounding the tour. The only other certainty was that a lot of Riots fans were less than impressed; some were angry that The Riots did not get to play and blamed the promoter for the whole mess. Irrespective of the allegations and who was at fault, the episode did little to further The Riots career.

They did play on numerous occasions across Europe during this time and gained even more fans, but the ill-fated (non) UK tour cast a shadow over the band who struggled to regain the early momentum. New record releases were few and far between and not even the unwavering support of radio shows like Alan May's 'Glory Boys' on 6Towns Radio nor 'We Are The Mods' with Warren Peace could help put The Riots back to where they were.

As Warren Peace mentioned, his interviews with various people had a massive impact on his listeners. **GILL EVANS** explains how she came to be on 'We Are The Mods':
It was only when I came across Thiery Stueve's website 'Jack That Cat Was Clean' that I thought 'Well here's someone who is into it and understands mod', so I contacted him and wrote my first article for him with a couple of photos in 2012. He said we were just the kind of people he was looking for; orginal mods with photos.
I've been pushing the mod look even when nobody would listen, so when Thiery published my interview on his site, I had more interest and Lloyd Johnson was one of the first to get in touch off the back of that and we had a lovely chat about the old days. Somebody saw the photo of me sitting on the Morris Minor and Warren posted it on the 'We Are The Mods' site. So I saw it and messaged Warren about the car. Then Warren contacted me about doing an interview in 2012 which went online later in the year. It was like I was ticking off my 'bucket list'. I was on a mod website, I was interviewed for a radio show and then after that, the BBC contacted me to be in their TV programme 'Mods, Rockers and Bank Holiday Mayhem'. Then Del and I opened Mod Togs because we thought the original mod look was being diluted too much and it is a way of bringing back many of my original designs from the early days.

Another significant development on the mod scene began as an idea in 2011 as **EDDIE PENNY** explains:

I grew up in Netherley, a district of Liverpool. In 1979 I bought The Jams 'Setting Sons' album with my pocket money. The album came with a lyrics cover and I was drawn to the line on the 'Private Hell' track that said: "The morning slips away in a valium haze and catalogues - and numerous cups of coffee".

I found that line really personal to myself and basically everything that I know about the mod movement before and after 1979 I can trace back to that album and the line that got me hooked.

I staged an event in Liverpool called Project 11, it took place on the 11th day of the 11th month on the 11th year with 11 bands playing for 11 charities for an £11 entry fee. March Of The Mods came about with me coming up with a better idea than the Project 11 idea. If we took over a day in this way, could we now top that by taking over a whole month?

I actually set March Of The Mods up a year before I told anyone. I purchased intellectual property rights, .com domains and set up Twitter and Facebook accounts without adding people in order to have the March Of The Mods name in place on everything and to be ready for the following year. We then put the idea out-there for people who then bought into it by asking if could they stage an event and be a part of it. If I am honest I had high expectations for our first year in 2013 because I knew we had a strong idea and feedback was good from people who wanted to come on board which just confirmed my gut feelings.

The biggest surprise we had in that first year was through a lady called Lesley Ackers who was a Barclays Bank employee. Lesley offered to double the money raised by all the events up to a combined maximum of £25,000, so on that first year March Of The Mods handed £50,000 over to charity and Lesley helped make all that possible. Lesley now runs the Liverpool leg of March of the Mods.

That year also saw the welcome return of an Acid Jazz favourite as **RICHARD SEARLE** explained:

We reformed in 2013 to promote a Corduroy CD box-set released by Cherry Red Records, featuring three of our five studio albums plus a Japanese live album, plus a previously unreleased live album via Acid Jazz Records.
It was a very positive response; getting lots of international invitations for shows as well as UK interest. We are currently writing new material with every intention of recording a new album of our groovy, spy themed, organ-fueled, raw garage, punk-jazz, dirty mod, fun.

But Corduroy were not the only ones to return to the music scene in 2013.
GRAHAM DAY's five year hiatus also came to an end:
The Prime Movers did our first album, 'Sins Of The Fourfathers' on a German label, Unique Records. 2012 was their 25th anniversary and they asked us to play a one-off show playing that album at their party near Dusseldorf. It sounded like a fun plan, but too much effort to just play one gig, so we added three gigs and made it a mini-tour.
It also wasn't interesting or long enough just to play songs off that album, so we added a few Solarflares and Prisoners songs to the set. It was so much fun and went down really well, so we decided to carry on doing it. But by the end of the mini-tour we'd dropped most of the Prime Movers songs and were playing more Solarflares, Prisoners and a couple of Gaolers songs, so it seemed ridiculous to call it the Prime Movers any more.
We came up with the Forefathers because of the Prisoners reference and stuck my name on the beginning just to tie up the fact we were playing songs I'd written in all the bands over the years.

Such was the popularity of Graham Day and The Forefathers, the band decided to record an album, revisiting some of Graham's vast catalogue of songs covering his entire career dating back to The Prisoners. 2014 saw the release of 'Good Things' which gave Graham, Allan Crockford and Wolf Howard a new lease of life. Crockford also had his own side project Galileo 7 underway.
The influence of the internet and social media was firmly establishing itself in the public

domain. A prime example of this is Levanna McClean from Bristol who would become a 'poster girl' for Northern Soul.

In 2013, while in her late-teens, Levanna's musical taste was influenced by her mother who had been a Northern Soul fan back in the 80s. While forming her own contemporary musical taste with artists like Amy Winehouse, Levanna soon learnt how to dance to Northern Soul. She started making videos of her dancing to Northern classics and posting them onto Youtube.

One video in particular mixed Pharrell Williams' massive hit 'Happy' with a song with the same title by Velvet Hammer which is regarded as a Northern classic.

Filmed on the streets of Bristol in one 'tracking' shot, this video received 2.5 million views on Youtube and directly led to Levanna joining a troupe of Northern dancers accompanying Pharrell Williams with a live performance of 'Happy' at the Brit Awards in 2014. Since that time, Levanna McClean has become a DJ and released a Northern Soul compilation cd on Universal.

Back in Birmingham meanwhile, 2014 was a very difficult time for **GILL EVANS**, as she explained:

Del had been very ill for three years, but no one knew about it. We used to follow a band called the Quikbeats from Birmingham and go to other dos on the mod scene. I had to give up my last shop to look after him. He had cancer and had to go to hospital three days a week, so I set up a studio at home so I could look after him. Del past away in February 2014 and I was totally lost at the time.

Now I have a lot of friends on Facebook and the Brighton weekender was coming up in August of that year. Del and I had been there many times and my Facebook friends were asking if I was going to go. I wasn't planning to go until three weeks beforehand because I would have to go on my own, but so many people I knew from Birmingham were going, I changed my mind and decided to do it. I got a coach from Birmingham to Brighton with one change in London.

When I got there, I made lots of new friends and loads of people were asking to have their photo taken with me, but one of the people I met was Stuart Catling. He couldn't remember my name, but I told him to look me up via Modtogs and then we kept in touch and the rest is history. I'll never forget Del, but life has to go on.

STUART CATLING also recalled first meeting Gill Evans:
We met at Brighton at one of the New Untouchables August Bank Holiday weekenders. I was sitting at a table outside the Volks Tavern as everyone does, chatting to a few people. I looked up and saw Gill and thought, 'I recognise her' because I'd seen her on TV. We got chatting and I told her I thought she looked great on TV and even better in person and that was it. We kept in touch, dated a few times, got on so well and eventually, that was it, I was in love with her by then.

We have this great connection with the music and the fascination with clothes and smartness. We despair sometimes at the current trend for being scruffy and not bothering with your appearance, but it's nice when we're out in Birmingham or somewhere and a total stranger compliments you on your clothes. When you look good, you feel good.

A lot of people just don't understand mod at all. People like Gill and Del, Lloyd Johnson, Robert Allbatch, they were driving the fashion of mod pre-1964 and people who saw them followed what they were doing. Then from '64 onwards, people were copying what the bands were wearing which I don't think was what mod was about really.

Gill Evans and Stuart Catling were married on 6th June 2016.

Indeed, 2014 was a difficult year all-round. Not only had Del Evans gone, but on the 14 May, Jeffrey Kruger, owner of The Flamingo Club passed away at his Miami home. Just 11 days later on the 25 May, Tony Class also died and by the end of the year, on 3 December Ian McLagan left us. It was a devastating time for those who knew them and for mod culture community.

However, the year saw even more interest in mod and the cinema release of Jonny Owen's film 'Svengali' was just one of the high points and much like 'Outside Bet', it was not a film about mods per se, but the reference points of mod culture were there. The central character has obvious mod culture leanings, but he is of a more contemporary type; a melting pot of mod traits.

Jonathan Owen had been a relatively new name for many mod culture devotees. He had been a co-host on Eddie Piller's Modcast early on and DJed at the first Modcast Party. He then filmed some short excerpts from his original script for 'Svengali' and became a Youtube hit. Off the back of that venture, the film finally got the backing it needed to become a reality.

For a so-called 'low-budget' film, the cast was impressive; most notably Martin Freemen, Alan McGee, Maxine Peake, Matt Berry, Roger Evans and Vicky McClure who had already made a name for herself as one of the lead characters in Shane Meadows' award-winning 'This Is England' trilogy.

In terms of mod culture and British pop culture, 'Svengali' ticked all the boxes. The soundtrack included everything from mod club classics like Jacques Dutronc's 'Le Responsible' to 'Weedbus' by The Stairs; an important band who bridged the gap between the fading 'baggy' scene and Britpop.

Apart from being a well-scripted, well-made comedy, it was the subtlety with which Owen addressed some of the issues that hung over the mod scene itself that proved to be particularly interesting and funny. Nowhere was this more evident than the exchanges between Owen's character of 'Dixie' and that of Martin Freeman as 'Don' the record shop-owning veteran 'purist' mod.

Having secured a distribution deal for the film with Universal, Jonny Owen had a genuine British success on his hands, but despite his rising star and that of his new partner Vicky McClure (a romance that began on the set of the 'Svengali'), they still made time to make a personal appearance at a March Of The Mods in event in Reading the same weekend as the premiere of the film.

March Of The Mods itself, was now advertising itself as being 'in aid of Teenage Cancer Trust', a charity that had Roger Daltrey as its honorary patron. **EDDIE PENNY** puts the relationship between the two organisations into perspective:

On the whole it was well received originally by Teenage Cancer Trust. We had the odd few questioning our motives, but like everything respect has to be earned and I think that grows with every passing year that we stage these events.

In 2014, things really took off for us, but if I had to single one thing out that made a massive difference that second year, I would say it was Kate Ross-Kellam for the massive commitment she brings to the group, but really the biggest factor in any event is the paying public. They came in their numbers and they continue to buy into the event each year. Without doubt my proudest moment is that Liverpool put March Of The Mods on the map and it's not really a city you would associate with the mod movement, but it has it's little place on that map now I think, so for me personally that was and still is my proudest moment. For the event, the proudest moment must be giving everything we earn away to charity. It shows a passion from the band, DJs, venues, the people who stage the events and the public who pay to attend these events, it's a great commitment from everyone involved.

It is a testament to just how well things had gone for the organisation, that it was not only new bands who got involved. Some more familiar names lent their support and played MOTM events. These included Geno Washington, Squire, and Chords UK.

Shortly after March Of The Mods fundraising campaign had ended for 2014, at Easter the New Untouchables hosted Modstock 4 at 229 The Venue. It was another landmark line up featuring the original members of The Velvelettes, Brenda Holloway, Kenney Jones, Eddie Phillips, Les Cappuccinos from Japan, The Mergers from Germany, The Apemen, Stone Foundation, The Misunderstood, Kaleidoscope, The Loons, Squire and Secret Affair. For Dave Cairns and Ian Page, the 50 year celebration of all things mod was also a time of reflection for the band. **DAVE CAIRNS:**
I'm proud of what we achieved and what we continue to contribute to the mod scene with our new album and our live shows, which was never just about music but a lifestyle choice for so many people, but it is also about reaching others with our music who have never been into mod culture. Mod culture has always been with us since the sixties and as I said, it's more about a lifestyle, where fashion and music come together and is a continuing influence with new acts I've seen and of course Britpop. Just look back at any of the Oasis stage shows for instance. Take a walk round Tate

Modern and you'll see its influence in modern art too. It's a unique part of our heritage which I hope will always flourish.

Back in 2009 we accepted an invitation to play the ice rink at the Isle of Wight Scooter Rally and we packed in 2500 and haven't stopped taking bookings since. Secret Affair has always been about presenting a great band and entertaining people to the best of our ability and the fact that we have managed to write, record and release a new album (Soho Dreams) over thirty years later should tell you what we have always been about.

IAN PAGE:
Well, I don't really dwell on the past very much. I don't keep souvenirs, keepsakes or newspaper cuttings. I don't think I even own a complete set of our albums. I do think we made a valuable and sometimes under-rated contribution to the on-going continuation of mod-influenced culture.

Mod culture, style and music permeates contemporary fashion and culture everywhere and all the time, to the extent that there are many young people out there wearing clothes and listening to music that draws heavily from a mod culture they may not have even heard of.

Our Modstock show was just that... a show, not a bunch of guys standing stock still on a stage playing for an audience they do not care about. Every show is our own blend of soul, dance, a little dash of hammond groove and hard R&B. We come to entertain.

MIKE and **ANJA STAX** brought their band The Loons over from San Diego and had this to say about their experience. First, Anja:

That was an amazing experience. To me it felt like a home coming. The Loons played a really good show that night (one of our guitar players had just stepped off the airplane a few hours earlier so we were all nervous if he would make it in time). It was so great to see all my old friends and have them come out and support the band. Very special. Even more so as after we played we were met by most of The Pretty Things backstage who were praising our version of Alexander and giving us all their attention. We love them so much!! No better people around. Of course playing as "The Misunderstood" was also major. I remember at one point I was sandwiched between Glenn Campbell, Ray Owen and Tony Hill and I could only laugh and shake my head to myself, how lucky was I to share a stage with these legends and prove myself to be good enough to do so. It was quite emotional in a very good way.

MIKE STAX: We'd played a few shows with Glenn Campbell in the States, and they were really magical, but bringing it to a bigger stage in London really felt special. Being up onstage performing those songs is a surreal, almost transcendent feeling sometimes. Nobody plays like he does - those sounds are absolutely unique to him - so being a part of those songs feels just incredible. During the 'Misunderstood' set I stepped back and left the spotlight to him and I could feel the whole room hold its breath while he was playing those riffs and solos. To look out over that sea of faces and see all their jaws hanging open in awe, gazing at Glenn, was wonderful. Also, I could see how happy Glenn was to be playing those songs again and being appreciated as a truly visionary musician. Bringing Tony Hill onstage to join us, along with Ray Owen of Juicy Lucy just added to the surreal feeling.
Like Anja said, the Loons played a great show that night. We knew we had to do well and everybody stepped up and played really well. Knowing that the Pretty Things were out there cheering us on really helped too. They're such a huge inspiration for us. A few days later we played a small gig in Bournemouth and Dick Taylor joined us onstage to play "Rosalyn" and "Alexander"- another highlight!

Mike and Anja Stax were not the only ones to cross the Atlantic to be at Modstock. JORDAN CINCO from Chicago was also in attendance:
My older brother is the one responsible for getting me in to mod-scooter culture after seeing his collection of records, sharp-looking clothes, and I fell in love with his two scooters (Vespa Super 150 & Lambretta Special 150). This was in the late 1980s (around '88-'89). I was hooked and got recruited to join my first scooter club, Chicago's finest, Allez Cats S.C. formed in 1986.

There were mods before 1986 though. It was a short-lived scene that started in the early 80s for the first generation of mods in Chicago. Some of the guys who started it were part of the punk/new wave scenes and converted to mod during the 80s revival. Allez Cats S.C. was a mod/ska, scooter vintage club. I was one of the youngest members back then at the age of 15. A couple of us from ACSC are still active through to this day with a new club, Chicago Mayday S.C. formed in 2006 with new generation of vintage scooter enthusiasts that keep the tradition alive in the windy city.

We knew about events like San Diego in 1999 and San Francisco in 2004. A few of us went to one of the events that was earlier than 1999, but we had our own scene going on also during that time. We had good enough events already to keep us busy all year around in our city back then. Chicago used to host one of the biggest events and scooter rallies in the 90s run by my good friend John Manion, who started 'Mod Chicago' in the early 2000s.

In the early years of 'Mod Chicago', we attracted crowds from east to west coast and handful from Europe. Chicago is the home of the ska record label - Jump Up Records', established in the early 90s and is still going strong. Mod and ska alike are all under one roof, supporting one another in the Midwest of America.

We don't have a big mod scene here in Chicago compared to our counterparts from California, but there's a good united alliance of mods from our city and neighboring states. Especially with our club (ACSC) which consists of 20 members. We spearheaded rides and events with other scooter clubs around the Midwest region attracting friends from all over. We are a combination of mods, skinheads, scooter boys and girls. The music at our club nights varies from Motown to R&B, soul, traditional ska and reggae.

'The Crowd' are the key players on the scene, but good thing about our scene is we don't have to identify who's who. Everyone supports one another when they can. We're a very small group in a big city, so we need everyone's contribution to keep the scene alive. It's all about respect. Besides, we don't pay attention when it comes to some negative stuff or people who like to stir up the scene. No drama or politics, period! I have visited the UK a few times and had some amazing and very interesting experiences, and Modstock 4 was just great. Lucky enough for me, I met a lot of wonderful, good people and attended top notch events every time I'm in London town. London and the UK are pretty much the 'mecca' of mod culture that mods around the world look up to. But there's also politics and drama on the scene that you can't avoid when you have so many events going on. There's still handful of us keeping the tradition alive after all these years in Chicago. We may be small in numbers, from the past, present and to the future, but Chicago is the place to be for a mod. Like Willie Dixon said about the blues "The Blues are the true facts of life expressed in words and song, inspiration, feeling, and understanding". That is how we feel about mod culture here.

Another person who had travelled half way across the world to be at Modstock in 2014 was **LUISA GEE** from Mexico:
It was incredible! One of the best experiences of my life. I travelled to England because I needed to be there; it was like going to Mecca. I had to see the places where everything mod came from. I had to walk through the streets where several heroes walked and be part of the celebration of the 50th anniversary of mod life. I call it "my graduation in the underground". When I saw the advert for Modstock 2014, the bands, DJs and everything going on, I knew I had to be there. I saved for months and months to pay for the flight. I didn't go out, buy clothes or records. When stepping onto British soil I was still anxious, dying to be among all the mods in the books and videos I had seen for years, but I also feared the experience. I idolised the British mod scene so much, that I thought I would 'freeze' in front of them. The first show I attended was Nick Waterhouse in Hackney, but I didn't find any groups of mods, only one girl and her boyfriend with whom we did not interact at all. We were soon at one of Rob Bailey's Nutsmag nights at Blues Kitchen in Camden. It was a great fortune to meet Rob and Graham Lentz who kindly accompanied us to the hostel where we were staying and they made us feel very welcome. By the time Modstock arrived, I had already toured London and Manchester. I had been at the home of Carlos Vargas and Chris Morgan, two great friends who opened their doors to us and they

filled the evenings and nights of music, beers and walks. Their kindness was greatly appreciated. When the first day of Modstock came, I could not be more nervous and I found lots of Italian scooters and mods that arrived at the site. Taking a step inside 229 The Venue, I observed what I wanted, lots of mods and all styles. From there, nerves, emotion and anxiety turned into fun and happiness. I went to England to live my mod dream. I had this image of British mods being immaculate and impeccable at all times, but at Modstock I realised they were human, just like us. They enjoy dancing, laughing, drinking and socialising. That is when I realised Mexican mod had potential to survive. Mod does not belong to us, but that we adopt and even adapt to our lifestyle. Traveling around England going to parties, allnighters, shows and visiting mythical places made me realise mod in Mexico was as good as any scene anywhere; that we have what it takes to be ourselves, we are effusive, emotional, demanding and mods. We had such a great time. We went to West Ham's Boleyn Ground, attended a soul night in Rugby, we met Paul 'Smiler'Anderson in Reading. We chased Les Cappuccino to a coffee shop in Brighton; chasing the Strypes. We spent a couple of days in the amazing house of Thierry Steuve (RIP) with his family and friends in Brussels, Belgium.

LUISA gives us an insight into the history and current state of mod in Mexico:
I was born in the western area of Mexico City. I discovered the mod world through music. Approximately 15 years ago I was a fan of Jamaican music; the sound of the Skatalites, Prince Buster, Derrick Morgan, Alton Ellis, Jackie Mitto and Laurel Aitken. It was ska and rocksteady that led me to know more rhythms. Obviously, as a passionate music fan, I was constantly in search of old and current singers, so I got into soul music, I got into the Motown sound, then southern soul and from there I jumped into English music. I discovered The Jam, Kinks, The Who, Small Faces, in short, it was in a new beginning. During those years I was into the Rude Boys/Skinhead scene that was really very small in comparison to today where there are many more in Mexico City. I maintained a relationship of exchange with them. I sent and received fanzines, records, videos, patches, etc, therefore the first time I read

Mexico City [courtesy of Luisa Gee]

the word mod was in the old local fanzines where they told the story of the rude boys and the skinheads. It was around this time, two videos were very popular on the scene: 'The Harder They Come' and 'Quadrophenia'. By then, I already knew the mod icons (music, scooters, parkas) but it was 'Quadrophenia' that characterised all my references; that is to say the film put a face and a supposed personality to that world that I knew, above all, musically, rather than by way of living life. By amalgamating all those images that I saw in the film with the music that at the time I knew, I felt in front of a new challenge, in front of a new universe to discover. I looked for fashion, I got more music. I discovered Graham Bond, Georgie Fame and I went back to the blues: Muddy Waters, Howlin' Wolf, Bo Diddley and some of the compilations of Decca Originals. They were my musical guide and I was discovering a new world with its details and secrets. In Mexico City the mods were counted on the fingers of one hand. Until then I had entertained some Jamaican parties in homes of close friends, but it was in May 2005 that I officially started to DJ at a party with a set of 'Revival Mod'. From there I took it for granted, I liked mod music, I was attracted to the mod philosophy and I was inside. The attraction to mod is the 'obsession' of it. That which breaks boundaries and leads you to a taste as particular as mod, cannot be more than obsession. It is like an unseen badge, showing a taste, showing a choice of 'being' without explaining anything to anyone. They just know. The Mexican mod scene cannot be characterised by quantity. The numbers have been variable. There have been mod parties, club nights and weekenders. There have been mod bands, several fanzines have circulated, but there is not a big scene. There are mods in various states: Tijuana, León, Monterrey, Puebla and Mexico City, but there are not that many in number. The Mexican mod scene is great because although there are not many of us, we are dedicated to it.

During the last five years or so in Mexico City, the 'Clan, Mod & Soul Society' club night that my former partner and I had, was a benchmark in terms of music and parties.

The Chewing Gum Weekend has been the largest mod event that exists in Mexico with three or four days of celebration, live shows, flea markets, rallies, etc. That has been going for 10 years. During the years 2008 to 2013, we had a healthy scene;

really young guys with their girls arrived. We had a house bar, 'Hooligans Café' which were the best mod nights in Mexico City and the mods were noticed. The 'Hooligans Café' defined that period, but there were other parties and club nights like 'Time For Action', 'In & Out' and 'Cool Cats'. The DJs and their records were improving. It was more R&B and Ska. One of the Mexico mod anthems was 'At Full Speed' by Los Flechazos from Spain. We met in various places to talk about music, clothes; we shared tailors and fabric stores. We walked through the streets when there were no parties, we shared fanzines and European books and every time some of us received new articles we shared them. There was the 'Underground Modzine'; the best mod guide in Mexico that contained reviews, original interviews, research and interesting sections like 'My favorite 45 rpm' in which old collectors and music fans presented their favourite albums. The content was always original. The first fanzine was accompanied by a cassette and then compiled CDs, which also showed the quality and knowledge that was developed during all those years in Mexico.

Throughout Mexico there have been mod exponents, bands like Los Padrinos, Hide Times, Los Ramparts, Bridge House with Beat sound. Soul and R & B, parties like 'Tijuana A Go Go' in Tijuana, 'Living For the Weekend' in Leon Guanajuato, 'Revival Times' in Puebla, 'Oh! Yeah' in Mexico City among other projects that have come and gone. At the moment in Mexico, mod has been very particular, it exists and it is a fact, but it is still more underground and even more exclusive than other scenes like skinhead. I have set up an organisation with an old friend, Luis Martinez. We call ourselves 'Move On Up!' And we have held parties that have fortunately returned to give encouragement to the mod scene in Mexico City. We started in October of 2017 with a party that included a fashion catwalk. We gathered the best exponents of clothing made in Mexico related to the mod scene and we invited old and new DJs. We presented our own club beer, in short a whole festival in one night. At the moment we have three parties and fortunately they have been a success. At the last one we presented Gaz Mayall from the Gaz 'Rockin Blues in a private club in the centre of the city. Currently in Mexico there are mods that have been on the scene for many years, like Guy from Tijuana, but we have not increased the amount with new members. We have our record stores, clothing brands such as Buzz & Fuzz, parties and DJs. Today people know when there is a Mod party and who is behind it. Hopefully new elements will emerge and it will continue. Despite its difficulties, despite not being my culture, despite what you might think of a Mexican mod, we exist and from here we have adopted the mod lifestyle to suit us. To live the life is the maximum. This is my world today and I could not have it any other way...

Another mod who had made annual visits to London from 2010 onwards is **GABRIEL RODRIGUEZ CRIADO**. The only year he and his wife did not make it to the UK was 2014. However, Gabriel gives us an insight into the emergence of mod in Argentina, a nation that has had close ties to Britain for centuries, but that relationship was severely damaged in the early 80s when the two nations went to war.

I was born in a small city called Longchamps in the south, which is about 30 km from Buenos Aires. There are other cities in Argentina with names in English like Glew, Bandield, Temperley, that is because the landlords of these fields in the middle of 1800s belonged to English people. The British tradition in Buenos Aires and the Patagonia was very strong up to 1950 and for this reason British culture was and is still very strong in the music, the clothing, etc. The first riff I heard was 'My Generation' by The Who at the age of 14 in 1981. In my home the only music that you would hear was The Beatles, Gerry and the Pacemakers, Hollies, etc. On the FM Radio you could hear only the bands of the time like ELO, Supertramp, Bee Gees, Eric Clapton, and there were some specialist Prog Rock shows with bands like ELP, King Crimson and Yes. In May of 1982 the British music was banned for all radio and TV stations across the country. The Malvinas (Falklands) War had started. In the sixties and seventies music in Argentina was dominated by British bands, and any bands in Argentina at the time who covered British songs sang phonetic 'English'. The majority of people could not afford the very expensive schools and colleges where you could learn English or French to a high standard. That was exclusively for the wealthy in society. The only band that sang in English correctly was Los IN (The IN). They recorded very good versions of 'Happy Jack', 'Tin Soldier' and others stuff of The Who and The Small Faces between 1966/1969. The other problem was that vinyl was very expensive. Most people could only afford to buy singles. This has been a recurring problem in Argentina; for example in 1992 the value of the Compact Disc was $18 US. The weekly salary in those times was $14 US! Even Taiwan had a higher weekly wage than Argentina in the 90s at $17 US. So that was why music and the instruments like guitars, bass and amplifiers always were expensive. Everything about mod appealed to me. The music from The Who, Small Faces, The Creation, The Action, and all the Northern Soul, Jazz, etc to the revival and the second wave with The Jam, The Chords, Secret Affair right up to today with Paul Weller (who is an icon) and the new generation like Miles Kane. The great classic clothes brands like Fred Perry, Merc, Ben Sherman, Lambretta; It is about the scarfs, shoes, harringtons, parkas... and the new level like Pretty Green... and of course... the scooters... my first and only one was a Siambretta (a scooter made in Argentina in the Lambretta style). It was a gift from my father when I was 15. The scene in Argentina is very small, just a few pubs and clubs in Buenos Aires city where people meet in public venues. But on the other hand, there are lots of private parties all the time in houses or saloons with DJs playing 45s . We have many covers bands, one is called The Brightones, playing The Who, Small Faces, Kinks, Beatles and other sixties songs. The Brightones have their own sixties-influenced original material also, but there are not many others with a mod influence in their music. In the sixties we had bands like Los In, Los Walkers (from Uruguay), The Combo´s, Los Shakers (from Uruguay too and one of the best). These bands sang in English, but it was not really mod. They did covers of British bands as well as their own material which was more like the Rolling Stones style.

We have gained our knowledge of mod through the internet, searching through all the websites we can find. While we share the same passions as the UK mods in terms of style, music, clothes and scooters, it is not exactly the same. We are in Argentina after all. It is a historical idiosyncrasy between Argentina and Britain that dates back to the 1880s when wealthy society invested in new enterprises here.

For example the first and only Harrods store outside of London was here. It closed I think in 1996. The first official Polo Match in the World was in Hurlingham City in the Buenos Aries province, and all the railway stations in Buenos Aires were built by English architects and engineers. The relationship between Argentina and England was strong and closer at that time. One of our favourite visits to the UK was 2015 when we went to the Hyde Park concert to see The Who and Paul Weller. That was a real mod event to me. I also remember going to a club in Bloomsbury Lanes off Bedford Way, London in 2010. There were scooters parked outside, 'Zoot Suit' by The High Numbers was playing and everyone was in mod clothes.

Both New Untouchables and March Of The Mods were among the many avenues by which new bands could gain more exposure. In addition to podcasts like Eddie Piller's Modcast, 'Glory Boys' with Alan May, 'We Are The Mods' with Warren Peace and the Nutscast Sessions from the New Untouchables among the mass of mod-related shows, the opportunities to play live were better than ever.

Bands like Electric Stars, The Universal, Lemontops, Heavy Sol, Sha La Las, French Boutik, Mockingbirds, Spitfires, Trambeat, The Sound Of Pop Art, Magnetic Mind, Hypnotic Eye, New Street Adventure, Gemma and The Travellers, Samuel S Parkes, The Most from Sweden, Past Tense, Marta Ren from Portugal and Men Of North Country from Israel (to name a few), all found willing promoters and appreciative audiences. Arguably, the most electrifying and most talked-about gigs were by a French band called Les Grys Grys. Their octane-fuelled R&B covers were likened to the great beat/garage bands of the sixties like the Pretty Things, Yardbirds or The Sorrows.

These live shows were complimented by small independent record labels that seemed to spring up from nowhere. Copase Disques, State Records, Crocodile, Legere, Soundflat, Chez Nobody and many others helped to keep the momentum going. Detour Records was still going strong, signing up the Electric Stars, Sha La Las and Past Tense as well as maintaining their impressive rare punk/mod revival/powerpop back catalogue.

ROB BAILEY recounts how New Untouchables played a part in helping one young band make it to the next level:

It's extremely important to me to give young bands and DJs opportunities, some have gone on to do brilliant things. The most memorable is probably The Strypes as it's such a remarkable story. Four young lads from Cavan (a small town in Ireland) playing authentic R&B with such style, energy and craftmanship at the tender age of fifteen and making those songs their own. We did three gigs in one year with less than one hundred people at the first show. The band got signed at their second performance at Crossfire with Sony, Mercury and Universal chasing their signatures. The final show at 229 for Le Beat Bespoke was a sell out in the main room with London Rock n Roll royalty in the audience. Others that also stand out are The Horrors and Les Grys Grys.

2014 was a busy year for mod culture and literature was not to be left out. 'Mods - The New Religion' was written by **PAUL SMILER ANDERSON**. Paul had been an ever-present on the mod scene dating back to the early to mid-80s as a DJ and contemporary of Dave Edwards, Rob Bailey, Ian Jackson and Eddie Piller. He explains how 'New Religion' came into being:

I'd always been interested in writing, and started writing mod fanzines back in 1985. I first thought about writing a book back in 2002. I had a couple of ideas that never progressed, then I made it really hard on myself and decided to write a book on 60's original mods and started that back in 2005. Getting a publishing deal is hard work. You must understand only one percent of books actually make it to publication. Self-publication was not an option as my vision of it would cost far too much and I didn't want to compromise. I knew it had limited appeal for many publishers because of the subject matter, so I needed either a music book publisher or one that dealt in fashion or youth cultures. Obviously that limits the publishers who deal in those genres. I finally finished the book in February 2011, so I approached a few publishers and got my list down to who I thought were really interested. Lloyd Johnson put me in touch with Adelita Publishing, but after a bit of interest they said 'not at the moment'. Paolo Hewitt tried to help me get Prestel interested but they didn't think the book would suit their output. Eddie Piller at Acid Jazz was obviously really interested as he had published my previous book on the band The Fleur De Lys and I was helping write sleevenotes for his Rare Mod series of LP's, but he realised that my book was going to be very expensive to initially fund. My big hope was Omnibus as they are the biggest music book publisher in the world so I approached them, but in June 2011 they declined citing that they thought my book would 'cannibalise sales' of their own 'Mod - A Very British Phenomenon' by Terry Rawlings. I explained that the book was over a decade old by then and that mine was different. I asked if they would let me show them exactly what I had written and the photos I had. They agreed and I went to London in August that year to meet managing editor David Barraclough who I'd dealt with all along via email. I was in there for three and a half hours! David loved it and said it was my passion for the subject that finally convinced him. There then followed four months of various emails and phone calls, waiting to see if he could convince the other staff members plus the MD to believe in the book. I finally received the news that it was to be commissioned on December 20th 2011. That was one happy Christmas! The publishing deal was completed in February 2012 and it took over three years to actually come out due to them changing publication dates. That said I am really happy with the results and glad I went with them and they have been very supportive ever since. I decided very early on that I wanted to research the project in the old school way, I tried to avoid social media sites and I decided to track down people to be in the book by getting the odd phone number written on a piece of paper. Then each time I did an interview I would ask the other person if they knew anybody I should speak to and it just kind of escalated. I must also stress that my good friend Damian Jones was really helpful. We had written the Fleur De Lys book together, and he didn't have the time to co-write the mod book but he was really helpful and often helped in getting contacts or driving me to interviews and I will always be eternally grateful to him. One mad thing that did happen via social media was that I got a message from a Michael Tenner. He'd seen my profile picture on Facebook, and at the time I was using a picture of me in a suit taken in 1988. The photo was black and white and yet Michael had assumed it was from the sixties and asked me if I was a mod he'd known back in the day. I looked at his profile and saw an old bloke, who was living in Tasmania, holding a big fish, and so I was a bit confused, but I sent him a message asking if he was Mickey Tenner from the Scene Club days. He responded and from there we built up a friendship via Skype. So we did all our interviews that way. It was almost fate that he'd found me. I got to meet and interview lots of my musical heroes during the course of the research including Eddie Floyd, Martha Reeves, Herbie Goins, Jimmy James, Derrick Morgan, Owen Gray, Chris Farlowe, Terry Nolder of The Eyes, Ian McLagan of The Small Faces, Ali MacKenzie of The Birds... the list goes on. What is nice, is that I have remained friends with quite a few of them and we stay in touch. Two people I never got that I really wanted was Georgie Fame, who I got hold of but was not interested, and the legendary Prince Buster. My good friend David Edwards had set up a meeting with Buster after he had agreed, but sadly he had a stroke and went back to Jamaica and later passed away. I wanted 'New Religion' to be a social history document on the original mod movement of the 1960's; to show it was so much more than the clichéd 'Mods and Rockers fighting on a beach element'. More importantly it was for the original mods that paved the way and created the culture. The most important critics of my book are those from the original early days and the fact that people such as Mickey Tenner, Jeff Dexter and Mickey Modern have praised it, is good enough for me. Luckily all the reviews that various magazines gave the book were very good. The book actually made the Sunday Times Top Ten hardbacks in the month it was released. Later on I found Paul Weller had been given a copy of the book, and through this we have built up a good friendship with Paul naming the book as an essential thing to take on tour in a NME interview. The greatest part for me though was being able to dedicate the book to my young son Joe. That really meant a lot to me. I'd like to thank everybody who supported and bought the book and showing faith in me. God bless 'em.

By 2015, Darren Connett resurfaced with his latest incarnation, Black Noire. This was far removed from anything he had done previously and again had support from Delicious Junction. With lush production values that was influenced by Scott Walker's solo work, ultimately, it was not easy to reproduce those same values in a live setting, so the band only had one EP release during its short life span, but 'God loves a trier' as the saying goes and Darren Connett is definitely a trier. Two years later he would resurface once again. **MARK BAXTER** and Mono Media Films released their next production straight to DVD in 2015. The documentary was about one of the great British Modern Jazz legends of the 50s and 60s: **Well, it was a film I wanted to make for a few years. I had become a massive Tubby**

Hayes fan from first hearing him in 1984/5 on a Paul Murphy compilation. I was fascinated by him and so tried to get funding from the BBC and Sky to make the documentary, but I got nowhere. I had sounded out a couple of guys who I had met on my travels to see if they would help me make it, but drew a blank. They thought I was mad as it was so expensive to make documentaries. But nothing was going to deter me from what I wanted to do, I just kept ploughing on. Then I met camera man/ director/ editor Lee Cogswell on a video he was making for the band Stone Foundation. I liked Lee's unfussy way of working and he did that expertly. So I sounded him out and he said he wanted to work with me, so we formed Mono Media Films and set about creating 'A Man in a Hurry'. We would have never had made it without fantastic support from our wives, families and ultimately our investors who backed the idea whilst the non-believers just laughed at the idea.

Then people like Simon Spillett, Sam Pattinson, the guys at Proper Jazz and Martin Freeman among a few others, sprinkled magic on it in their various roles. I went out and found the money to make it and then set up the interviews, locations etc. Lee did an absolutely amazing job on the edit. Once finished, I started the promotion and went off selling it and it worked. It picked up a life of its own really. People were talking about and discovering Tubby, which was the intention in the first place. The DVD sold really well from the off in 2015, we had some great screenings and that continues three years later. I just knew it was a great tale with great music and it is ultimately a modernist story. All I can say is Viva La Tubbs!

DAVE EDWARDS was still running the monthly Sidewinder nights with Giles Plumpton, but he also got involved with an event that would be regarded as one of the majors of the year: I'm very proud of Dreamsville, the vision that Kurt Fricker, Lee Miller, Andrea Mattoni and Matt Hudson had to start it has grown into one of the most anticipated events of the year. I was asked to step into the breech when Matt went to Australia. We struggled at one point when we had to change the date late on but now it's firmly established. The hotels and bed & breakfast houses in Lowestoft are booked up a year in advance. We throw a lot of ideas at each other to try and make the next one better but the demand is phenomenal. The planning starts straight after the event, looking at what we can improve, looking at any problems etc and sorting out the best guest DJs we can get.

In January 2016, French Boutik were back supporting the latest vehicle for Graham Day's creative output; Senior Service, at the legendary Half Moon, Putney. The event was promoted by Steve Worrall under the name of Retroman Blog. Senior Service was an instrumental band, playing mostly original material with a few covers of classic late 60s and 70s TV and Film themes with the core of Day and Wolf Howard were complemented by Jon Barker and Darryl Hartley. The gig was arguably the one that took French Boutik to a new level in front of a packed house and enhanced their growing popularity in the UK .A few months later saw the first ever UK and European shows by original 60s outfit Powder. They started in London with the New Untouchables promoting at Blues Kitchen, Camden.

RICHARD FROST:
I must say that we were very much looking forward to playing the UK. Ecstatic is a better word. To have the opportunity to play to a European audience was certainly a dream come true for me personally. It's the culmination of a lot of years. Primarily, we played our original 1968 songs from the 'Ka-Pow' CD 'Gladly' and 'Turn Another Page'. We also showcased a couple of our new songs that we're very excited about and hope that everyone enjoyed hearing them too!
Indeed the retrospective collection 'Ka-Pow' was very well received:
Of the 1967 -1968 recordings, the only media that exists are studio acetates. Ace's marvellous technical staff; using state of the art technology, were able to remove the distortion inherent in the old media. The response has been excellent and much appreciated. Bang up job on the booklet artwork and liner notes thanks to Alec Palao and photos by the late Frank Zinn. We play the same way we did back then really. We're old school minimalists. Pretty much plug-in and play. I play my guitar parts as I did then. It's the same with the drums and bass. We owe it to our audience to be as original sounding as possible. As far as music is concerned I've journeyed through

a lot of different musical genres over the decades but the mod influence has always been there in one way or another. Thomas and Richard Frost wrote and played some country numbers but we wore crushed velvet trousers and looked more like members of Marmalade. I think over the years I've gained a keener awareness of art and fashion overall. I'm happy to see so many young people picking up the flag.

2016 will be remembered for an unprecedented amount of celebrity deaths, many of them unexpected, such as Prince, David Bowie and Lemmy of Motorhead.
Mod culture did not escape the angel of death in 2016. On 15 November, Mose Allsion, a man who had inspired the likes of Van Morrison and Georgie Fame among others, died at his home in South Carolina, just four days after his 89th birthday.
But it was in October of that year that the mod scene across Europe was in mourning at the sudden passing of one of its legendary names.

Thierry Steuve was just 55 years-old. His involvement on the mod scene went back over 35 years. He was the first European DJ to play a mod event in Britain. He played DJ support on tour with Paul Weller, Amy Winehouse, Sharon Jones, Charles Bradley and Beady Eye to name a few. Known by his DJ moniker 'Thierry Steady Go', he was a record collector 'par excellence' and once told the story of how his mother gave him 3,000 Belgian francs to pay for dental treatment, but on his way to the dentist, he stopped at a local record store, Top Trente, and spent all the money on records instead.
To understand Thierry's importance to European mod, **ALEXANDRE SAILLIDE ULYSSE** and **LAURENT GRUX** explain the impact he had in Paris:
Our obsession with mod culture was clearly evolving after 1984, with the changes taking place on the British scene. We were definitely moving away from the stereotypes that came after the revival period. We wanted more authentic music and clubs, but mainly it was the clothing with an obsession for trousers, jackets and suits tailored by a master tailor. But our research and our deepening of the true modernist culture took place in a radical and exponential way when we met Thierry Steuve. It began with an exchange of fanzines between the City Gents 'Agent OO Soul' and the Brussels-based

'Six Exciting Reasons' which was a very high quality publication. Thierry Steuve was our true 'Continental Face'. Our friendship began when we made our first two visits to Brussels which continued with his numerous trips to Paris. Indeed, this contact and then the ties of friendship quickly woven with Thierry Steuve in the mid-1980s, undoubtedly allowed the "Mods de Gambetta" to deepen their knowledge of the real Modernist culture. Thierry instilled a new enthusiasm and a sort of cultural revolution in the mod Parisian scene which regularly frequented the National Mod Rallies (CCI), the weekenders of the Untouchables and the 'pirate mod' runs at Hayling Island in the late 1980s and early 1990s. We were always more modernists, in style, music, clothing, readings, etc... It is mainly for this reason, and purposefully, that the 75 M.N.S, and its official information and dissemination body 'The Modernist Circle', absolutely want to make known and preserve the true modernist culture.

The assertion that Thierry Steuve was a 'Continental Face' is no exaggeration. The multitude of tributes across social media at the announcement of his passing is testament enough and he will live long in the memories of the hundreds of people who knew him across Europe.

Meanwhile, podcaster, **WARREN PEACE** was very much alive (to the dismay of some) (sic) and had changed the name and format of his 'We Are The Mods' podcast and by 2016, he decided to bow out of broadcasting:

Honestly, I felt I had said all I could say about mod without it being repetitive and redundant. My good friend, the actor Jonny Owen had joined the show and we found ourselves debating whether mods should wear trainers. I took one step back and said... "this is a bridge too far". Enough was enough because, who cares? Jonny, Penny and I had started broadening the discussion to include politics, pop-culture etc. and the expanded discussion points deserved a new identity. Hence, Max R&B was born. We expected to lose a huge portion of our mod audience but the listening numbers (downloads and streaming) kept growing. I decided to wrap the show in late 2016 after the 'artistic apocalypse' that happened that year. Bowie, Lemmy, Carrie Fisher... an endless list of celebs who passed that year. I thought the timing was appropriate.

451

In September 2017, the mod and psych worlds were rocked by the sudden death of Virgil Howe, drummer with scene favourites Little Barrie.

After crowd-funding campaigns, which were becoming an ever more popular means of financing recording and production of unsigned bands, French Boutik released their debut album 'Front Pop' to great acclaim among the scene and Darron J Connett returned once more under his own name, ably supported by Paul Hancock, Phil and Izzy Sorrell and Manuel Perazzoli to release an equally acclaimed album titled 'Loyalty Lies'.
This story began with John Simon, Gill Evans-Catling and Bar Italia. Thankfully, all three are still going strong. John Simons has a major documentary made about his life and times by Mark Baxter's Mono Media Films. He now has his shop located on Charlotte Street, London, but **MARK BAXTER** explains how the new documentary about John came about: Well John was interviewed by us for our Tubby Hayes film and he enjoyed that, so I was delighted to be asked by him to take a look at finishing a previous documentary that had been started on him by stylist and writer Jason Jules. It is a great idea and it was only the lack of funding that prevented it happening before. Lee Cogswell and I took in the previous knowledge we had learned on our Tubby film and we made it a larger story really. It says a lot about the man himself, that the likes of Sir Paul Smith, Dylan Jones of GQ, Kevin Rowland, Paul Weller and Suggs all agreed instantly to talk about John Simons. We've also got some shop punters in the film all talking about the love of the various shops John has had over the years. Once again, we are investigating the history of the movement we all love so much, namely modernism. I'm very happy with the film. There is a lot of interest in it and it is a story that hasn't really been told properly. Once again, we are going back to the source and letting that speak for itself.

Gill Evens-Catling and husband Stuart are happily settled in the Midlands area and are still great supporters of mod events up and down the country.
Bar Italia is still going, almost 70 years after it first opened and seems to be surviving the gentrification and cultural/historical vandalism of property developers in central London. Amazingly, the Gaggia coffee machine that was installed in 1949 is still making coffee

to this day and its neighbour across the road on Frith Street, Ronnie Scott's Jazz Club is also still going strong. On Wardour Street, a blue plaque was erected to commemorate Jeffrey Kruger MBE and the entrance of the Flamingo Club.

New Untouchables are showing no sign of slowing down, even after more than two decades. Here **ROB BAILEY** gave this summary of what New Untouchables has achieved over the years:

I'm very proud of what NUTs have achieved over a lengthy period and at times when interest in what we are passionate about was not always a given. Working with artists I have loved, let alone meet and in some cases become good friends with them, has been a real honour. The Sonics first ever show outside the USA for Le Beat Bespoke in 2008 was special and the biggest gig we have promoted so far with two sell out nights at the Forum. Stax Revue with Steve Cropper, Eddie Floyd and Duck Dunn plus special guest Bill Murray on tambourine was amazing. Same goes for the Tamla Motown Revue with The Velvelettes & Brenda Holloway. The final show with Arthur Lee & Johnny Echols of Love at the first Le Beat Bespoke was incredible. Modstock is once a decade and both the 2004 and 2014 events surpassed all expectations with as global audience which included all aspects of the scene including Music, Art, Fashion, Film and Scooters. Crossfire Allnighters and Le Beat Bespoke festival have been running for well over a decade. Despite the huge gamble moving away from the IOW in 2002 Brighton has continued to grow and become the biggest event in the mod calendar in the world. On a personal level, DJing at Glastonbury in 2013 after the Rolling Stones, was a wonderful experience. The seven compilation albums featuring selections from my DJ sets also entitled Le Beat Bespoke which started back in 2004. And of course, the Mousetrap Allnighter which has been running twenty-eight years at the same venue with the same owner.

2017 saw Stone Foundation become the success story of the year, if not of the decade. With the release of 'Street Rituals' which had major involvement by Paul Weller who also produced the album, the record and resulting singles had official chart success with no major label involvement, as **NEIL SHEASBY** explains:

By the time Stone Foundation had settled into things, we tried to get as many support slots as possible, especially in London with the likes of Geno Washington, Nine Below Zero, Wilko Johnson and then we would follow those up with our own gigs at the Borderline for example, and we found we were picking up fans off the back of those support slots who were coming to our own shows which culminated in playing the 100 Club. But the thing with those fans, whether they were mods or not, they were the people who would go on social media or talk to their mates and tell them about us, then other people would get on board and the fanbase just grew and grew until we end up playing places like the Royal Albert Hall for Teenage Cancer Trust or the Sheperds Bush Empire. We don't kid ourselves about it, we know our core support is of a certain age, although we are noticing more young people coming along, but I think our appeal is that we remind the older generation of all the great bands from the past, but at the same time, not wallowing in nostalgia. It's re-engaging with people and DC Fontana did that too. Nothing that has happened since would have come about without Mark Mortimer and Dream Factory.

JOHN HELLIER still regards himself a mod after best part of 50 years and gives this assessment of the scene today:
I'm very old school and not easily impressed, but it warms the cockles of the heart to see so many young guys and gals still into the scene and hopefully carrying it forward for many generations to come. The most obvious difference is the fact that we always looked forward. Clothes and music changed almost on a weekly basis. Mod today is all about retro even though a lot of them wouldn't admit it. The scene is very healthy and that's all that matters. For somebody like me that was born in 1949 the sight, sound and experience of mod is summed up by a smoky, crowded Saturday night club where Junior Walker and the All Stars records are playing full volume.

RICHARD SEARLE now runs the 'Well Suspect' subsidiary label of Acid Jazz. Here is his take on the mod scene:
It's easier to be a mod now, clothes look right. We mostly had to sort through charity shops and jumble sales to get authentic styled gear. The kids these days look sharp.

Musically, if The Strypes are anything to go by, it's gonna be great. My favourite band on Acid Jazz Records at the moment is Men Of North Country.

Here is **DAVE EDWARDS** take on mod of the 21st century:
I still love that basic look of a white Fred Perry, 501s, desert boots/loafers and a crop. Classic street mod look. I love the classic three button suit. My ears still prick up when I hear a scooter go by, it's those things that first attracted you to it. The images from Richard Barnes' Mods book are burnt into my mind and recently Smilers book was amazing. I'm totally obsessed by it still, I'm 51 (as I write!) the music, the clothes everything. Seeing the smart young kids around at the moment, it's still inspiring. And I'm still learning. I think being involved with the 100 Club still tops anything I've done. I still get butterflies when I go in there, it's the history of the place, it's dripping from the walls. I've done a few great gigs with Fred Perry such as the Sir Peter Blake polo shirt launch in Spitalfields and a five hour set in Selfridges for a new season collection launch. I did the Rhythm Festival for a couple years which was great, watching bands such as Nine Below Zero, Pretty Things, Eddie and The Hot Rods and Prince Buster, then DJing a two hour after party set. At the moment I really enjoy the Acid Jazz Modcast Boat parties, a great day of music on the Thames with the sights of London as a backdrop.

The last word on this thing we call mod culture is left to someone who is the future of mod along with his own generation. **LUCAS GOMERSALL** and Katie Town are one of the most recognisable young couples on the current modernist scene. 22 year-old Lucas explains how he became a modernist and how he came to start up his own successful club night:
I know exactly why I got into the mod scene. I remember when I was a kid I used to watch episodes of 'The Saint' with Roger Moore in it and thought, I want to dress like that! I thought he looked really elegant dressed in chisel-toe lace up shoes with stunning three button, three piece wool suits with slim lapels and breast pocket flaps, you get my point? I started trying to dress like that when I was 14 and made a right hash job of it, but then I didn't have the money to look like an actor with his personal tailor on Regent Street. A year down the line a friend of mine turned around and said

> "Mod will always innovate for the future, have a rich heritage in the past, but most importantly live the present day like there's no tomorrow.
> LUCAS GOMERSALL"

"you look like a mod". Hey presto, I'd found it! My family members were never into mod and as a result I had to do a lot of research and made sure I got myself out there to clubs. I used to approach people who were very much a part of what I considered to be the elite mod groups at the time to understand what they had and what I didn't. Most of the time I felt like I they wanted me to f**k off because I wasn't particularly well dressed, but in fact, a lot of them were pretty nice and had gone through the same thing themselves beforehand. They were cool and they knew it. What appealed to me and still gives me inspiration is when I looked at the original 60's photos and films. I saw a group of young people who aspired to have the best things and made their peers (and parents) jealous of material possessions and societal positions they created for themselves by being top dogs when walking into a club. I identified with that as I came from a working-class background where I didn't have a lot. My main problem was that I was 50 years late, so had to make do with what I could create and who I could find who was also nuts enough to be into this. Safe to the say that the people I have met through the scene, old and young alike, still manage to keep my sanity in check. My long-suffering girlfriend Katie Town is a great example of the type of person I identify with as she is a real sharp dresser and knows her onions about the early-mid 60's mod scene and dresses appropriately to suit. I couldn't go out with a 'normal' girl as it would bore the pants off of me. Most of the older generations have been pretty good with welcoming us into their venues and introducing us to other people as contacts for clothing, records etc. To be honest we don't really expect anything and we look to integrate with what exists and better it. I really don't see the people I hang around with, of any age, any different from myself as they still have the same mind set.

I appreciate the diversity of the scene and I believe that's what it's all about. I don't see the need to mention the names of anyone who is supportive as there are literally way, way too many, but without them we wouldn't have anything as close to what we do today. I started Fast Way of Living out of necessity. For ages I had Bob Morris and Dave Edwards nagging me and Ryan Brown into putting on an event to cater for the younger crowd that was going to be more accessible. The story of it goes that one thing I thought was odd about the scene then (2014 - 2015) was that the music was almost unrecognisable from what I deemed to be a mod club. I went to literally hundreds of nights out and I never heard a single Sue Record or Rufus Thomas track. Ryan and Guy Joseph had stopped putting on the infamous Ham Yard events, and after that I think everyone started to lose track and miss the point. It all changed when I started to go to Sidewinder.

One summer afternoon a few years ago, Bob organised a venue for an after party for a London scooter rideout in Hoxton. This was where I met most of the great DJs who I now regularly ask to help me run Fast Way of Living. They restored my faith instantly. I think that I was both a bit shocked and emotional when Richard Early (of Sneakers fame) played "Sally, Go Round The Roses" which is one of my favourite tracks and was featured on Ready Steady Go which was one of the first I'd heard that day. I stayed all day and made sure I spoke to everybody to learn what they played and listen to the music. Ian Bryden stayed a bit later with me and we had a great conversation. I'll always remember him spinning Arthur Alexander's "A Shot of Rhythm and Blues".

After this restoration of faith, Bob found us a small venue in the Elephant and Castle called the Long Wave Bar which was literally an old shipping container converted into a bar. We used to stick a set of decks on the table and run it once every couple of months as a free venue. Initially we had about 15 people turn up and they seemed pretty impressed with the music as we took it back to basics and had some great DJs. Thanks to word of mouth, this started to grow and grow until we felt the need to search for a larger venue where we could really get the feeling right and when I went to one of Ian Jackson's clubs in the Hanway Social, I decided to ask the boss, Jason, whether he'd be happy for us to run a one-off night there. When we had our first night, Jason catered for us very well and we felt that the atmosphere was perfect for what we do. From then on we decided to run the club three times a year and will hopefully be expanding in future to do day events etc. We ensure there is a smart dress policy as we want it to strictly be for mods. Even our main door men, Dave Rhys Lewis and Mark Strange are mods/ex-mods and ensure that we keep it strictly for our crowd.

The most flattering thing in my opinion is that the young crowd are so excited to get involved and get there literally from opening and stay till it closes every time. Mixed with the older faces it gives us an edge that can't easily be replicated. The people who enjoy our club come to experience best of the new breed and I like to think that we are the premium event in London by being the most authentic club out there, but with a dedication to ensuring that it is very affordable by keeping entry costs as low as possible. Interestingly, I have a lot of original mods come to Fast Way of Living and they swear that the club is the closest to the basement sweat pits of Soho in the 60's than anything they've been to since. I find that original mods have fantastic senses of humour and still to this day really wear their clothing and look like they were born looking great. One thing I can't stand is when people are condescending with how I should dress etc. The people who do this tend to be the less smart people on the scene who aren't into it as much as I am and frankly haven't done their research.

I appreciate they feel like they have to get a bit nostalgic, but it's insulting when I've worked so hard to do what I do. However, the people in the know give some great advice and give great insight on things that I haven't seen before. This is taken by me as constructive and a compliment. But then I have had this quote from Mark Strange which makes me very proud and happy: "I was absolutely gobsmacked at the end of the one of the Fast Way Of Living nights, astonishingly the younger generation blew me away by staying behind to help tidy up the venue and support closing down. They are so excited to be a part of the club, they are determined to keep it running smoothly for all to enjoy, get stuck in and be a big part of the future of the London Mod Scene" Defining mod is a really difficult thing to put your finger on, but I'm going to give you my opinion. The definition of mod to me is getting out there and enjoying every part of life that you possibly can with friends who are the most diverse set around, but all have mutual aspiration to feel great about themselves. I listen to the best music ever made, dance silly things like the Hitchhike which makes me giggle and everyone joins in and wears beautiful clothing all together in a cool underground venue. Mod will always innovate for the future, have a rich heritage in the past, but most importantly live the present day like there's no tomorrow. ·◊·

POST SCRIP

The following exchange is Neil Sheasby and Mark Mortimer in conversation about the way things have changed and their opinions on the state of music and popular culture today. I found it to be a fascinating and interesting exchange and felt duty bound to include it somewhere in this book:

NEIL SHEASBY:
The big difference now is I think the art of music is gone. It's become totally disposable. Years ago you would buy an album, listen right through it and appreciate it as a 'whole' piece of work. That doesn't really happen anymore.

MARK MORTIMER:
But then when we were growing up, you'd hear a band you liked, but you'd get drawn in to find out more about them; what their politics might be, how they dressed, what their influences were; it was like a complete package. When The Jam released Sound Affects, I remember the interviews Weller did and there was one where they asked him to list his current top five tunes. It was people like Jimmy Witherspoon, a Small Faces B side and other stuff from the sixties and I just thought that was just as important as their album, finding out what the influences were.

NEIL:
And those interviews in the music press were where I got into a lot of stuff. Again, taking Weller as an example, he might mention Curtis Mayfield and then the Five Stairsteps. I'd never heard of the Five Stairsteps, so I would go and check them out. And it was titles of books and all sorts of cultural influences that led me onto other things. You don't get that anymore with popular music. But that passion that drove us back then is still with us.

MARK:
From 76 onwards, was the start of the building blocks that formed who we are now.

NEIL:
2017 has been unbelievable for SF, but I've said this often before, if the opportunity arises, are you prepared for it? And that's what has happened this year, we've been in the right place at the right time and we've been lucky, but we have always been prepared for this.

MARK:
When you consider the way things are in the industry is now and the way things are stacked against the likes of us, it's nothing short a of a miracle what SF have achieved. You've worked tirelessly for decades for this moment and it's paid off.

NEIL:
It's not forced really. We made records for ourselves really, but everything has just fallen into line. We found out Mark was sending those records to Weller. I don't know if he listened to them or not, but things have happened nicely for us. I always thought we were on that trajectory with or without people like Weller being involved. Obviously, that has been a massive help to us. We've always tried to take the best music experiences that we've had in the past and transfer them onto SF with the way we do our gigs, the record sleeve designs, all that kind of stuff.

MARK:
I think in 1984, both Neil and myself, we knew that this was not going to be some kind of two year stint like a lot of people did back then. You know, you do your couple of years mucking about in bands, but eventually, you move on to other things. With us, we knew we would still be doing music in 30 or 40 years time. It was never going to leave us. The sad part about it is that Neil and I play the same instrument so we can never be in the same band. ·◊·

London [photo © Derek D'Souza at www.blinkandyoumissit.com]

BIBLIOGRAPHY

The following were invaluable to my research:

BOOKS

Austin, William
Cast: Tell It Like It Is
Chameleon 1997

Barnes, Richard
Mods
Eel Pie 1979

Black, Pauline
Black By Design
Serpent's Tail 2012

Blake, Mark
Pretend You're In A War:
The Who & The Sixties
Aurum 2014

Brown, Gareth
Scooterboys
Omnibus 1996

Carr, R. Case, B. & Deller, F.
The Hip
Faber & Faber 1986

Clayson, Adam
Beat Merchants
Blandford 1995

Cohn, Nic
Today There Are No Gentlemen
Weidenfeld 1971

Connikie, Yvonne
Fashions of a Decade: The 1960s
B T Batsford 1990

Constantino, Maria
Mens Fashion in the 20th Century
BT Batsford 1997

Daniels, Phil
Class Actor
Simon & Schuster 2010

Fordham, John
The Sound of Jazz
Hamlyn 1989

Frith, Simon
Sound Effects
Constable 1983

Frith, Simon & Horne, Howard
Art into Pop
Routledge 1989

ed. Frith, Simon & Goodwin, Andrew
On Record
Routledge 1990

Gillman, Peter
Alais David Bowie
Hodder & Stoughton 1986

Gray, Steve & Sandon, Mark
From Somewhere Out Of Here
Walsall Local Hist. Cen 1997

Grey, Edward
Decade - The Sixties
Wayland-Hove 1989

Hawthorne, Nigel
Sixties Source Book
Virgin 1989

Hebdige, Dick
Subculture & the Meaning of Style
Methuen 1979

Hewitt, Paolo
The Jam: A Beat Concerto (revised)
Boxtree Ltd 1996

Hewitt, Paolo
The Small Faces
Acid Jazz 1995

Hewitt, Paolo
The Sharper Word
Helter Skelter 1999

Honeyford, Paul
The Modern World by Numbers
Eel Pie 1981

Hutchinson, Roger
High Sixties
Mainstream 1992

James, Alex
Bit Of A Blur
Abacus 2008

Jones, Dylan
Haircults
Thames & Hudson 1990

Knowles, Eric (Cons)
Art Deco Antiques Checklist
Miller 1991

Lester, Paul
Oasis-The Illustrated Story
Hamlyn 1995

Loog Oldham, Andrew
Stoned
Secker & Warburg 2000

Marshall, George
Spirit Of '69
STP 1994

McAleer, Dave
Hit Parade Heroes
Hamlyn 1993

McAllister, Marty & Adam Cooper
To Be Someone: Mods in Ireland
Heavy Soul 2011

McDowell, Colin
The Men of Fashion
Thames & Hudson 1997

McLagan, Ian
All The Rage
Pan Books 2000

Melly, George
Revolt into Style (Rev.)
Oxford Uni. Press 1989

Morgan, Johnny
Ocean Colour Scene: Belief Is All
Chameleon 1997

Neill, Andrew
Faces: Before, During and After
Omnibus 2000

Pantere, Horace
Ska'd For Life
Pan Books 2008

Paytress, Mark
20th Century Boy: Mark Bolan Story
Sidgwick & Jackson 1992

Polhemus, Ted
Street Style
Thames & Hudson 1994

Rawlings,Terry & Badman,Keith
Empire Made
Complete Music 1997

Reed, John
My Ever Changing Moods
Omnibus 1996

Ritson, Mike & Russell, Stuart
The In Crowd
Bee Cool 1999

Roach, Martin
Blur
Omnibus Press 1996

Robb, John
The Stone Roses
Ebury Press 1997

Robb, John
The Charlatans
Ebury Press 1998

Roetzal, Bernhard
Gentlemen
Konemann 1999

Rylett, Keith & Scott, Phil
Central 1179
Bee Cool 2001

Savage, John
England's Dreaming
Faber & Faber 1991

Slater, Tom
Carnaby Street
Hobbs 1970

Staple, Neville
Original Rude Boy:
From Borstal To The Specials
Aurum 2010

Stern, Jane & Michael
Sixties People
MacMillen 1990

Stringfellow, Peter
King of Clubs
Little, Brown & Co 1996

Swenson, John
The Who
W H Allen & Co Ltd 1981

Talyor, Tadhg
Top Fellas
Surefire Productions 2013

Thorne, Tony
Fads, Fashions & Cults
Bloomsbury 1993

Whiteley, Nigel
Pop Design: Modernism to Mod
Design Council 1987

Winstanley, Russ & Nowell, David
Soul Survivors
Robson Books 1996

COPYRIGHT NOTICE

Despite our best efforts, the publishers were unable to locate the copyright holder for the following book:
Cohen, Stanley · Folk Devils & Moral Panics · MacGibbon & Kee 1972
The publishers would welcome contact from the copyright holder.

MAGAZINES

Record Collector editions: 363 (June 2009), 366 (September 2009), 399 (March 2012), 401 (May 2012), 412 (March 2013), 413 (April 2013), 417 (August 2013).
Shindig Magazine editions: 39, 43, 45, 64, 65.
Scootering Magazine editions: 160 (June 1999), 369 (March 2017).
The Chap editions: 80 (April-May 2015), 81 (June-July 2015), 91 (Spring 2017).
The Face: 14 (June 1981).
Uncut: January 2011
Mojo Classic: volume 2 issue 7 Britpop
All In Good Time: Issue 1 (Spring-Summer 2012), Issue 2 (Spring-Summer 2013)

INTERVIEW SOURCES

The following interviews were conducted in person by Graham Lentz:

John Simons
20.08.1998 and
10.02.2001

Jeffrey Kruger
03.06.2000 and
06.10.2001

John Waters
21.04.2001

Pauline Waters
21.04.2001

Dizzy Holmes
17.01.2001

Tania Holmes
17.01.2001

Brian Betteridge
02.08.2001

Ian Harris
04.08.2001

Goffa Gladding
26.07.2001

Ed Ball
01.10.2001

Rob Bailey
11.10.2001

Joe Foster
29.10.2001

Anthony Meynell
17.11.2001

Vic Vespa
20.03.2002

Eddie Piller
03.05.2002

The following interviews were conducted by email by Graham Lentz:

Paul Welsby March 2002	William Hassett 2017	Mark Mortimer 2017
Mike Warburton April 2002	Mike Hassett 2017	Paul Hallam 2017
Harry Vogel November 2001	Gel Jones 2017	Eddie Penney 2017
Kelvin Madden November 2001	Rob McDonald 2017	Alan Handscombe 2017
Mary Boogaloo November 2001	Darron Connett 2014	Rob Bailey (update interview) 2017
Daisuke Usui November 2001	Gill Evans Catling 2017	Warren Peace 2017
Francesco Lisi December 2001	Stuart Catling 2017	Andrea Mattioni 2017
Nobuo Tanaka January 2002	Fay Hallam 2017	Andrew Lindsay 2017
Hanna Hashimoto January 2002	Peter Challis 2013	Mark Ellis 2017
Fredrik Ekander December 2001	Gabriela Giacoman 2017	Ian Jackson 2017
Nick Rossi January 2002	Dave Edwards 2017	Gabriel Rodruigez Craido 2017
Taku Yamada January 2002	Richard Searle 2017	Luisa Gee 2017
Fumio Nawa January 2002	John Hellier 2017	Robert Peterson 2017
Kazuo Nemoto January 2002	Jo Wallace 2017	Maria Morgan 2018
Satoshi Terakubo January 2002	Iqbal Djoha 2017	Mark Baxter 2018
Manabu Kuroda January 2002	Alex Banks 2012	Paul Anderson 2018
Kensuke Ota January 2002	Mike Stax 2017	Laurent Grux 2017
Serge Hoffman 2017	Anja Stax 2017	Alexandre Saillide Ulysse 2017
Gary Crowley 2017	Neil Sheasby 2017	

Specific interviews from other publications:

John Simons, The Modernist Review (20.08.98)
Long John Baldry, The New Breed, Issue 5 (Summer 2001)
Chris Farlowe, The New Breed Issue 4 (Summer 2000)
Roger Eagle, The New Breed Issue 2 (Autumn 1999)
Alan Fletcher, The Modernist Review Issue 3 (Autumn 1997)
Keith Rylett for The Influential Factor (1999)
Russell Brennan, The Modernist Review Issue 5 (Spring 1998)
Steve Grey & Mark Sandon, The Modernist Review Issue 6 (Summer 1998)
The Killermetres, The Modernist Review Issue 4 (Winter 1997)

The following interviews were first published and are reproduced by kind permission of Stuart Lanning, editor of Scootering Magazine:

Russ Winstanley, Scootering Magazine Issue 154 (November 1998)
Tony Class, Scootering Magazine Issue 151 (August 1998)
Gareth Brown, Scootering Magazine Issue 179 (March 2001)
Rob "Yob' Williams, Scootering Magazine Issue 178 (January 2001)
Kevin Roberts, Scootering Magazine Issue 162 (August 1999)
Eddie Piller, Scootering Magazine Issue 162 (August 1999)
Pauline Corcoran, Wapping Wharf Magazine, by John Hellier (2011)
Graham Day, newuntouchables.com/nutsmag (2016)
Richard Frost, newuntouchables.com/nutsmag (2016)
Ann-Marie Newland, dandyinaspic.co.uk (2012)
Dave Cairns & Ian Page, newuntouchables.com/nutsmag (2014)
Roger Powell, newuntouchables.com/nutsmag (2012)

The following interview was first published and is reproduced by kind permission of Kelvin Madden, publisher of Modern Times Magazine:

Don Hosie, Modern Times, part 1 issue 4
Don Hosie, Modern Times, part 2 issue 5

ONLINE RESOURCES

Bar Italia website
Nick Waterhouse website
Zani.co.uk
Ben Sherman website

OUR SPONSORS

21ST CENTURY MODERNIST MUSIC & CULTURE

Gigs, Clubs, Weekenders, Festivals, Shop & Magazine

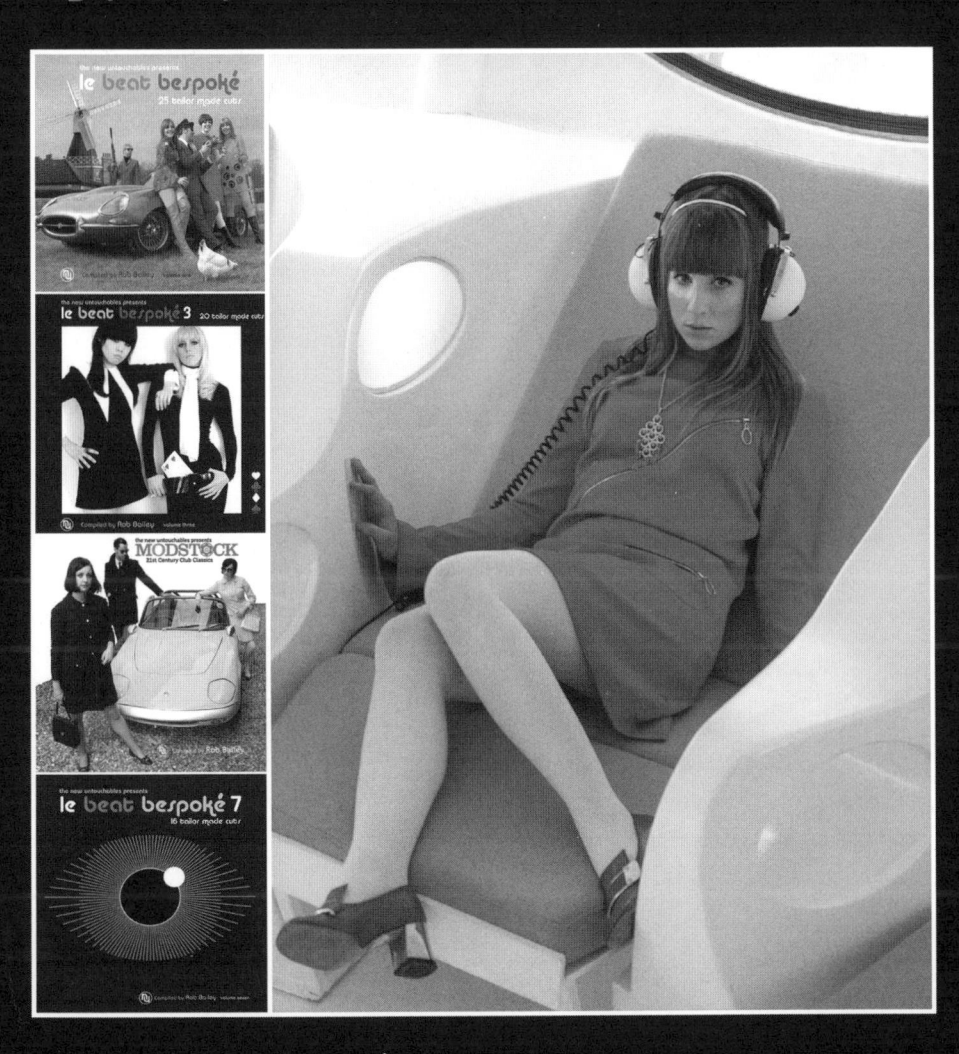

»NEWUNTOUCHABLES.COM

SANT AGNELLO

DESIGN BY:
MARK BAXTER AND DELICIOUS JUNCTION

FIND OUT MORE ON
WWW.DELICIOUSJUNCTION.CO.UK

MAKING THE WORLD
A BETTER PLACE
TO LIVE IN

DESIGN WITH A MODERNIST TWIST

WWW.BOOGALOOJAM.CO.UK

MOD SHOES
Smart Shoes For Smart People

Above The Harrison & Marianne
Part Of Our Small Run Exclusive Shoe Collection

5 Star Review
"What a treat to find this company –
such great style and wonderful service!"

www.modshoes.co.uk

ARTGALLERYCLOTHING.CO.UK

ART GALLERY

SINCE 1996

© GRAHAM LENTZ

All rights reserved.
The moral rights of the author have been asserted.

First edition published in Great Britain by GEL Publishing 2002
This edition published in Great Britain by
RKL Publishing 2018
35 Black Swan Close · Pease Pottage
Crawley RH11 9BB

Hardback: ISBN 978-09542552-3-7
Paperback: ISBN 978-09542552-2-0

No part of this book may be reproduced, stored in or reproduced into a retrieval system, or transmitted, in any form or by any means (electronic, mechanical, photocopying, recording or otherwise) without the prior written permission of both the copyright owner and the publisher of this book.

DESIGNED BY:
Mary Boogaloo · www.boogaloojam.co.uk

COVER PHOTOS BY:
Derek D'Souza · www.blinkandyoumissit.com

Printed and bound in Great Britain by:
Biddles Books Ltd.
East Winch Road · Kings Lynn · Norfolk PE32 1SF

A CIP catalogue record for this book is available from the British Library.